Peter McLeod

Kim Plunkett

Edmund T. Rolls

Introduction to Connectionist Modelling of Cognitive Processes

Introduction to Connectionist Modelling of Cognitive Processes

Introduction to Connectionist Modelling of Cognitive Processes

Peter McLeod,
Kim Plunkett
and
Edmund T. Rolls

Department of Experimental Psychology,
Oxford University

OXFORD NEW YORK TOKYO
OXFORD UNIVERSITY PRESS
1998

Oxford University Press, Great Clarendon Street, Oxford OX2 6DP

Oxford New York
Athens Auckland Bangkok Bogota Bombay
Buenos Aires Calcutta Cape Town Dar es Salaam
Delhi Florence Hong Kong Istanbul Karachi
Kuala Lumpur Madras Madrid Melbourne
Mexico City Nairobi Paris Singapore
Taipei Tokyo Toronto Warsaw

and associated companies in
Berlin Ibadan

Oxford is a trade mark of Oxford University Press

Published in the United States
by Oxford University Press, Inc., New York

© Peter McLeod, Kim Plunkett and Edmund T. Rolls, 1998

The `mac_tlearn` Installer was created using
Stuffit InstallerMaker. © 1990–96 Aladdin Systems, Inc.

Reprinted 2002

A catalogue record for this book is available from the British Library

Library of Congress Cataloging in Publication Data
McLeod, Peter.
Introduction to connectionist modelling of cognitive processes
Peter McLeod, Kim Plunkett, Edmund T. Rolls.
Includes bibliographical references and index.
1. Brain—Computer simulation.   2. Connectionism.   3. Cognition—
Computer simulation.   I. Plunkett, Kim.   II. Rolls, Edmund T.
III. Title.
QP363.3.M395   612.8′2′0113—dc21   97–41671

ISBN 0 19 852426 9 (Pbk)

Typeset by Footnote Graphics, Warminster, Wilts.

Printed in Great Britain by The Bath Press, Avon

Acknowledgements

No textbook could be written without a background literature. This one is no exception and we wish to acknowledge the debt we owe to all the researchers whose work we have used to illustrate the connectionist approach to modelling cognitive processes. There are two sources to which we owe a special debt. The first is to David Rumelhart, Jay McClelland and the PDP Research Group who produced the two volume book *Parallel distributed processing* in 1986 and the simulator handbook *Explorations in parallel distributed processing* in 1988. These were the stimulus for much of the enthusiasm for connectionism which has swept Cognitive Science in the last decade and our debt will be obvious to any reader of this book who is familiar with the earlier volumes. Our second is to those who developed the `tlearn` simulator which is used in this book, and helped with the development of the exercises. In particular we wish to thank Jeff Elman and Steven Young. Without their contribution this would be a much less useful book for the reader who wishes to get to grips with practical connectionist modelling. A complete introduction to the `tlearn` simulator is provided by Plunkett and Elman (1997). We have reproduced the user manual from that book (adapted for Windows95) and the exercises in Chapters 5, 7, 9 and 10 are based on exercises in chapters 4, 8, 11 and 10 of that book.

We are grateful to the Cognitive Science Society, the American Psychological Association, and the following authors and publishers for permission to use published material as the basis for our figures:

Figure 2.2 and table 2.1 are based on: McClelland, J. (1981). Retrieving general and specific information from stored knowledge of specifics. *Proceedings of the Third Annual Meeting of the Cognitive Science Society*, pp. 170–172. (© Cognitive Science Society and Lawrence Erlbaum Associates.) Figures 4.1, 4.2, 4.3 and 4.6 are based on: figures 1, 3 and 4, and tables 1, 2 and 3 of McClelland, J. and Rumelhart, D. (1985). Distributed memory and the representation of general and specific information. *Journal of Experimental Psychology: General*, **114**, 159–188. (© American Psychological Association.) Figure 4.5 is based on: figure 2.1 of Hertz, J., Krogh, A. and Palmer, R. (1991). *Introduction to the theory of neural computation*. Addison-Wesley, Redwood, CA. Figures 5.9, 5.10, 5.11 and 5.12 are based on: Hinton, G. (1986). Learning distributed representations of concepts. In *Proceedings of the 8th*

Annual Conference of the Cognitive Science Society. Erlbaum, Hillsdale, NJ. (©
Cognitive Science Society and Lawrence Erlbaum Associates.) Figures 6.6 to 6.9 are
based on: figures 9, 11 and 12 of Rumelhart, D. and Zipser, D. (1985). Feature
discovery by competitive learning. *Cognitive Science,* **9,** 75–112. (© Cognitive
Science Society; published by Ablex Publishing Corporation.) Figure 7.7 is based on:
Elman, J. (1990). Finding structure in time. *Cognitive Science,* **14,** 179–212. (©
Cognitive Science Society; published by Ablex Publishing Corporation.) Figures 8.3,
8.4 and 8.5 are based on: figures 5, 10 and 11 from Seidenberg, M. and McClelland,
J. (1989). A distributed model of word recognition and naming. *Psychological
Review,* **96,** 523–568. (© American Psychological Association.) Figure 8.6 is based
on: figure 12 from Plaut, D., McClelland, J., Seidenberg, M. and Patterson, K.
(1996). Understanding normal and impaired reading: Computational principles in
quasi-regular domains. *Psychological Review,* (in press). (© American Psychological
Association.) Figure 9.10 is based on: Elmann, J. L. (1993). Learning and development in neural networks: The importance of starting small. *Cognition,* **48,** 71–99.
Published by Elsevier Science—NL Sara Burgerhartstraat 25, 1055 KV Amsterdam,
The Netherlands. Figure 9.11 is based on: Elman, J. (1990). Finding structure in
time. *Cognitive Science,* **14,** 179–212. (© Cognitive Science Society; published by
Ablex Publishing Corporation.) Figure 10.1 is based on: figure 1 from Baillargeon. R.
(1986). Representing the existence and the location of hidden objects : Object perma-
nence in 6- and 8- month-old infants. *Cognition,* **23,** 21–41. Published by Elsevier
Science—NL Sara Burgerhartstraat 25, 1055 KV Amsterdam, The Netherlands.
Figures 10.6 and 10.7 are based on: figures 7 and 10 of McClelland, J. L. (1989).
Parallel distributed processing: implications for cognition and development. In
Parallel distributed processing: implications for psychology and neurobiology (ed. R.
Morris). Clarendon Press, Oxford. (© Oxford University Press.) Figure 11.1 is based
on: figure 4.3 from Morton, J. and Patterson, K. (1980), A new attempt at an inter-
pretation, or, an attempt at a new interpretation. In M. Coltheart, K. Patterson and J.
Marshall (eds). *Deep dyslexia.* London, Routledge, Kegan Paul. Figures 11.2 and
11.5 are based on: figures 10 and 11 of Plaut, D. and Shallice, T. (1993). Deep
dyslexia: A case study of connectionist neuropsychology. *Cognitive Neuropsychology,*
10, 377–500. (© Lawrence Erlbaum Associates.) Figures 11.3 and 11.4 are based on:
Hinton, G. and Shallice, T. (1991). Lesioning an attractor network: Investigations of
acquired dyslexia. *Psychological Review,* **98,** 74–95. (© American Psychological
Association.) Figures 11.6, 11.7 and 11.8 are based on: figures 1, 2 and 6 of Farah
M. and McClelland, J. (1991). A computational model of semantic memory impairment: modality specificity and emergent category specificity. *Journal of Experimental
Psychology: General,* **120,** 339–357. (© American Psychological Association.) Figure
11.9 is based on: figure 6 from Cohen, J. and Servan-Schreiber, D. (1992). Context,
cortex, and dopamine: A connectionist approach to behaviour and biology in

Schizophrenia. *Pscychological Review*, **99**, 45–77. (© American Psychological Association.) Figure 11.10 is based on: figure 1 of Cohen, J., Dunbar, K. and McClelland, J. (1990). On the control of automatic processes: A parallel distributed processing model of the Stroop effect. *Psychological Review*, **97**, 332–361. (© American Psychological Association.) Figure 13.2 is based on : figure 7 from Van Hoesen, G. (1982). The parahippocampal gyrus. New observations regarding its cortical connections in the monkey. *Trends in Neurosciences*, 5, 345–350. © Elsevier Science Ltd, The Boulevard, Langford Lane, Kidlington OX5 1GB, UK.

Although every effort has been made to trace and contact copyright holders, in a few instances this has not been possible. If notified the publishers will be pleased to rectify any omission in future editions.

Contents

Prologue   1

What is the problem?   1

What connectionist models can do   2

Part I   Principles

1   The basics of connectionist information processing   8

Neurally inspired information processing   8

Five assumptions about computation in the brain on which connectionist

models are based   11

Symbols and elementary equations   15

Connectionism in a nutshell   20

Exercises with **tlearn**   21

2   The attraction of parallel distributed processing for
modelling cognition   30

The representation of knowledge in connectionist networks is distributed   31

Distributed representations are damage resistant and fault tolerant   32

Connectionist networks allow memory access by content   34

Retrieving information from a distributed database   35

Constraint satisfaction in connectionist networks   45

There is no distinction between 'memory' and 'processing' in

connectionist models   48

Problems for distributed representations   49

3   Pattern association   51

The architecture and operation of a pattern associator   51

A pattern association network   52

The Hebb rule   54

Learning with the Hebb rule   54

Recall from a Hebb trained matrix   56
Learning different associations on the same weight matrix   56
Recall reflects the similarity of retrieval pattern and stored patterns   59
Properties of pattern associators   61
Generalisation   61
Fault tolerance   61
The importance of distributed representations for pattern associators   62
Prototype extraction and noise removal   63
Speed   63
Interference is not necessarily a bad thing   64
Further reading   65
Training a pattern associator with **tlearn**   65

4   Autoassociation   72
The architecture and operation of an autoassociator   72
Architecture   72
Learning with the Delta rule   74
Properties of autoassociator memories   75
What an autoassociator learns   76
Storage of different memories on the same connections   78
Pattern completion   80
Noise resistance   81
Forming categories and prototypes from individual experiences   83
Discovering a prototype from exemplars with an autoassociator   84
Learning different prototypes on the same matrix   87
Further reading   88
Autoassociation exercises with **tlearn**   88

**5   Training a multi-layer network with an error signal:
hidden units and backpropagation**   96
The perceptron convergence rule   97
Gradient descent   99
Gradient descent with a sigmoid activation function   103
Linear separability   105
Solving the XOR problem with hidden units   107
Hidden units and internal representation   108
Hinton's family tree problem   108
What the hidden units represent in the family tree task   110
Backpropagation   112
The problem   113

An informal account 114

Local minima 114

Backpropagation and biological plausibility 116

Exercises: learning Exclusive OR with **tlearn** 117

6 Competitive networks 127

The architecture and operation of a competitive network 128

Excitation 128

Competition 129

Weight adjustment 129

Limiting weight growth 132

Competitive learning in the brain 133

Pattern classification 136

Correlated teaching 137

Further reading 138

7 Recurrent networks 139

Controlling sequences with an associative chain 139

Controlling sequences with a recurrent net 140

State units and plan units 141

Simple recurrent networks (SRNs) 142

Learning to predict the next sound in a sequence 144

Attractors 145

Learning sequences with **tlearn** 148

Part II   Applications

8 Reading aloud 155

The traditional '2-route' model of reading aloud 156

The connectionist approach 157

The Seidenberg and McClelland model of reading aloud 158

Replicating the results of word naming experiments 161

What has the model learnt? 165

Limitations of the model 166

The Plaut, McClelland, Seidenberg and Patterson model 167

Input coding 167

Pronunciation 168

Reading with an attractor network   169
Componential attractors   171
What have these models achieved?   171
Further reading   172
Reading aloud with **tlearn**   172

9   Language acquisition   178
Learning the English past tense   179
A symbolic account of past tense learning   180
A connectionist account of past tense learning   183
Early lexical development   187
A connectionist model of early lexical development   188
Evaluation of the model   192
The acquisition of syntax   194
Further reading   202
Learning the English past tense with **tlearn**   202

10   Connectionism and cognitive development   210
Stages in development—a challenge for connectionism?   210
The development of object permanence   212
Modelling the development of representations which could produce
object permanence   212
Evaluating the model   218
The balance beam problem   219
Modelling the balance beam problem   222
Running the model   224
Evaluating the model   231
Stage-like behaviour from continuous change   234
Variability in learning   234
Individual differences   235
Critical periods   238
Further reading   240
Modelling the balance beam problem with **tlearn**   240

**11   Connectionist neuropsychology—lesioning
networks**   243
The simulation of deep dyslexia   245
Hinton and Shallice (1991)   246

Attractors 248
Attractor basins 249
Lesioning an attractor 250
Is the result dependent on fine details of the model? 251
The interpretation of double dissociation 254
Modelling a deficit in semantic memory 255
Modality and category specificity in semantic memory 255
Modelling an asymmetrical double dissociation 258
Modelling an information processing deficit in schizophrenia 260
Selective attention 260
Modelling the Stroop task 262
Lesioning the model 263
Further reading 265
Exercises with `tlearn` 265

12 **Mental representation: rules, symbols and**
connectionist networks 268
Learning minority default rules 268
Default mapping 269
Minority defaults 270
Symbols and distributed representations 273
Representing mental types 274
Symbolic attractors 275
Levels of explanation 276
Further reading 277

13 **Network models of brain function** 278
Memory formation in the hippocampus 278
The role of the hippocampus in memory formation 279
Information flow to and from the hippocampus 280
The internal structure of the hippocampus 281
A computational theory of hippocampal operation 283
A neural network simulation of hippocampal operation 286
The performance measure 287
Running the model 288
Performance of the network 288
Invariant visual pattern recognition in the inferior temporal cortex 292
How not to achieve position invariant object recognition 292
The flow of visual information from retina to temporal lobe 294

VisNet—an approach to biologically plausible visual object
identification   294
Testing the network   297
The importance of the trace rule for forming invariant representations 299
Brains, networks and biological plausibility   300
Further reading   302

14 Evolutionary connectionism   303
The evolution of goal directed behaviour   304
The evolutionary advantage of the capacity to learn   306
Innately guided learning in speech perception   308
The Nakisa and Plunkett model   309
Network training and evolution   310
Speed   311
Cross-linguistic performance   311
Categorical perception   312
Nativism or constructivism?   313

15 A selective history of connectionism before 1986   314
McCulloch and Pitts (1943)   314
Logical operations with neuron-like computational units   314
Computing AND, OR and NOT   315
Producing the sensations of hot and cold   316
Hebb (1949)   318
Neuronal inspiration in psychological modelling   318
The Hebb synapse   319
Rosenblatt (1958)—the perceptron   320
Minsky and Papert (1969)—a critique of perceptrons   323
The XOR problem and the perception of connectedness   323
Hinton and Anderson (1981)   325
Hopfield (1982)   326
Content-addressable memory in networks with attractor states   326
Input patterns and energy   327
Novel inputs produce higher values of E than memories   329
Changes in state lead to a reduction in E 329

Appendix 1 Installation procedures for `tlearn`   331

**Appendix 2 An introduction to linear algebra for neural
networks**   333

Appendix 3   User manual for `tlearn`   340

Bibliography   376

Index   383

Prologue

The brain of the newborn child contains billions of neurons but the child can perform virtually no cognitive functions. After a few years, receiving continuous streams of signals from the outside world via its sensory surfaces, it can see, understand language, and control the movements of its body. The brain has discovered, without being taught, how to make sense of the signals arriving from the eyes and ears. 300 years ago Thomas Traherne realised the extraordinary nature of this untutored transformation from chaos to comprehension. The aim of cognitive science is to answer his question: How is it brought to pass?

What is the problem?

As adults we can see, walk and understand speech without conscious effort, and we have no memory of a time when we could not. Nor can we remember the process by which we learnt to do these tasks. So perhaps it is difficult to imagine that there is any problem in learning to see or to understand speech. To see how extraordinary this achievement is, consider what the infant must do to recognise words in continuous speech. If spoken words were presented in isolation and each example of a word was the same, as it is in print, it might not be too difficult for a child to discover that these units were significant. But this is far from the case. Words in speech do not come with gaps around them. You hear isolated words because you recognise the words which the speaker used. But in the original signal the sound patterns for most words run into each other without breaks. The separation of the speech stream into successive words is a construction of your speech recognition system. It is not there in the original signal. So how did you ever discover that the input should be broken up in this particular way?

If words were always the same it might seem possible for the child to recognise these regular units even if they came in a continuous stream. But the signals arriving at the ear corresponding to a given word are quite different when produced by different speakers, or by the same speaker in a different context. Even when a word comes from the same speaker in the same context it will seldom be the same signal at the ear because speech is superimposed on all the other random background noises in the environment. If the child had been given the concept of 'word', and a specification of its likely duration and properties, one could imagine it starting to extract some regularities from the speech stream. But nobody would start to teach a child to understand speech by telling it what a word was. Without any idea of what to look for, or even that there is something worth looking for, how could the regularities which are hidden in speech be discovered? There is such infinite variety in the input that it seems impossible for the infant to get started. Why should the brain ever discover that the word was a unit when the pattern of nerve firings arriving from the ear could be grouped in so many different ways? Yet every child does discover how to extract words from the endless variety of speech in the first few years of life.

Such problems in understanding speech, and ones of similar difficulty in learning to see or to control movement, have, for years, seemed quite intractable. But in the last decade there has been a revolution in our understanding of how a system like the brain, given streams of input from a structured world by its sensory receptors, could come to discover that structure. Part of this revolution has been the discovery of how cognitive functions could be performed by a system which computes with simple neuron-like elements, acting in parallel, on distributed representations. The investigation of what can be achieved by models which perform parallel distributed processing is called connectionism. As a taste of what connectionist models have achieved we will outline three examples which will be described in detail later in the book.

What connectionist models can do

Connectionist models have given a precise match to data obtained in experiments with human subjects. For example, in experiments which measure the speed at which adult readers can read individual words aloud it is found that the time taken depends on both the frequency of the word and the regularity of its pronunciation pattern. Regular words are those like GAVE which follow the common pronunciation for their spelling pattern. Exception words are those like HAVE which have an unusual pronunciation for their spelling pattern. Overall, people can name common words more quickly than uncommon words but this effect interacts with the regularity of the word's pronunciation—it is more marked for words with an irregular

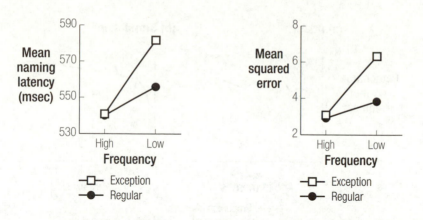

Figure P.1 A comparison of data from experiments measuring the speed at which human subjects pronounce English words (left) or the error produced by a connectionist model pronouncing the same words (right). See chapter 8 for further details.

pronunciation. Typical data, demonstrating the interaction, are shown in the left of figure P.1. The filled circles show the average speed at which subjects name regular words of high frequency (e.g. MUST) or low frequency (e.g. MODE). There is a small effect of frequency. The open squares show equivalent data for exception words. Here there is a large effect, with low frequency words (e.g. LOSE) pronounced considerably more slowly than high frequency words (e.g. HAVE). The right of the figure shows what happens when the same set of words used in the experiment with normal subjects was presented to a connectionist model which had been taught how to pronounce all the monosyllabic words in the English language. The output of the model is error rather than reaction time but it can be seen that the interaction between frequency and regularity is reproduced.

Connectionist simulations do not just mimic results which are already known. Their predictions have suggested fruitful areas for experimentalists to investigate. For example, when children start producing the past tense of verbs they initially get them correct, and then they begin to make errors. A child who correctly uses the irregular form 'went' to express the past tense of 'go' might say 'goed' a few months later. Eventually she will revert to using 'went' correctly. (Adding -ed to the verb stem is the way that regular past tenses are formed in English, so 'goed' is called an over-regularisation error.) This paradoxical behaviour has been cited as evidence for the theory that linguistic development proceeds in stages. In this case, the argument goes, the stages are: (i) the child learns individual words (such as 'went'); (ii) she acquires rules such as 'add -ed to form the past tense'; (iii) she discovers that rules have exceptions. A connectionist simulation of children acquiring the past tense by Plunkett and Marchman produced over-regularisation errors, like children, but it did not produce stage-like behaviour. Irregular verbs were not all regularised once

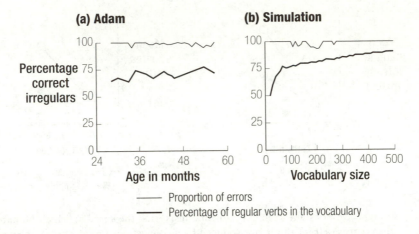

Figure P.2   Left: The production of over-regularisation errors during a period of 30 months by a child called Adam. Right: The production of over-regularisation errors by a connectionist simulation of a child learning to produce the past tense. The thin lines shows the proportion of errors as a function of age (Adam) or vocabulary size (simulation). The thick line indicates the percentage of regular verbs in the child's/network's vocabulary at various points in learning. See chapter 9 for further details.

over-regularisation appeared, as the stage theory would predict. The model produced a mixture of correct and erroneous past tenses, with the rate of production of over-regularisation errors generally less than 5%. The discrepancy between the model's predictions and the standard theory sent experimentalists out to discover the fine detail of the pattern of production of over-regularisation errors in children. Figure P.2 shows data from one of these children, Adam. It can be seen that although he continues to make occasional mistakes on irregulars for a long time, they are always rare. At no time are more than about 5% of his irregulars incorrect. It can be seen that the model predicts behaviour, which at a general level, is similar to Adam's. It is quite unlike the prediction of the stage model which would expect no errors in stage 1, a high error rate in stage 2, with performance gradually recovering to no errors in stage 3.

Connectionist simulations have suggested solutions to some of the oldest problems in cognitive science. For example, if you know somebody, you will recognise them from whatever angle you see them. This is such a commonplace of our everyday experience that it may be hard to realise that the achievement is in any way remarkable. In fact, how to form a representation of an object which will permit recognition from any viewing position is a notoriously difficult problem. The image produced by someone seen in profile has little in common with that produced when they are seen full face. Indeed, as figure P.3 shows, it may have more in common with someone else in profile than with itself from another view. How can you form a representation of someone which will allow you to recognise them in the future when they present a different image?

Connectionist models have shown ways that this can be done. The stimuli in figure P.3, three faces in seven different orientations, were presented to a connectionist face recognition model described in chapter 13. The test for view invariance is whether units in the output layer of the model respond to one particular face independent of the view which it is shown. If so, then the net has built up representations which have discovered what is in common between different images of the same person even though the images themselves have little in common. Figure P.4 shows the response of one particular output unit. It responds to any view of the third face, and little to any view of the others. The model has achieved view invariance.

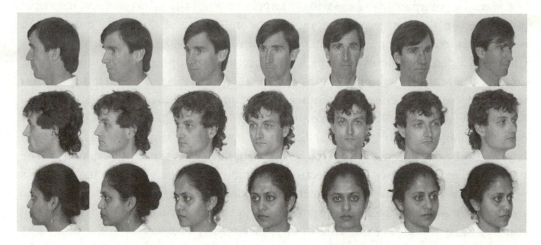

Figure P.3   Seven views of three different faces shown to a connectionist face recognition model.

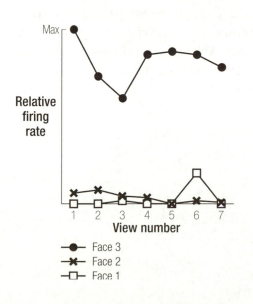

Figure P.4   Response of an output unit to the seven views of the three faces shown in figure P.3. See chapter 13 for further details.

The rest of the book divides in two—principles and applications. The first seven chapters describe the basic principles of connectionist modelling, and common network architectures and learning rules. Chapter 1 describes the aspects of the organisation and interaction of neurons in the brain on which all connectionist models are based. Chapter 2 describes a number of general properties which all connectionist models display—fault tolerance, content addressability and computation by constraint satisfaction. Chapters 3–7 introduce four common architectures —single layer feedforward, multi-layer feedforward, competitive, and recurrent— with simple examples of the sort of computations they can perform. These chapters also introduce four learning rules—Hebbian, Delta, backpropagation and competitive learning. Chapters 8–12 describe the application of the principles and networks introduced in the first seven chapters to the modelling of cognitive processes in normal adults, their development in children and their breakdown in patients. Chapter 13 describes networks which mimic information processing in two specific areas of the brain—the hippocampus and the temporal lobe—and their application to the processes of episodic memory formation and the development of view invariant visual representations respectively. Chapter 14 describes connectionist models which evolve by natural selection rather than by learning. This process is applied to the development of speech recognition devices in the new-born infant. The final chapter is a history of connectionist modelling, from McCulloch and Pitts's proposal in 1943 that logical operations could be performed by neuron-like computational units, to the event which triggered the tidal wave of interest in connectionist modelling on which much of cognitive science is still riding—the publication of *Parallel Distributed Processing* by McClelland, Rumelhart and the PDP Research Group in 1986.

In addition to introducing the principles and applications of connectionist modelling, there are exercises and demonstrations to give experience of running connectionist models, with the **tlearn** simulator. Appendix 3 is a User Manual for **tlearn** which will enable readers to build their own connectionist models of cognitive processes.

Part I
Principles

1   *The basics of connectionist information processing*

Connectionist modelling is inspired by information processing in the brain. A typical model consists of several layers of processing units. The unit can be thought of as similar to a neuron or a group of neurons. Each unit sums information from units in the previous layer, performs a simple computation on this sum, such as deciding whether it is above a threshold, and passes the result to units in the next layer. The pattern of activity on the first layer reflects the stimulus presented to the model. This pattern gradually becomes transformed to produce the pattern of activity on the final layer—the model's response. The influence of a unit in one layer on a unit in the next layer depends on the strength of the connection between them. Learning to produce the correct output in response to a given input is achieved by changing the strengths of connections between units. The aim of connectionism is to see whether models based on these principles can perform the computations which we know the brain can perform. That is, can a layered network of simple processing units transmitting information about the signals reaching them perform the transformation from stimulus to response which we produce when we read a written word aloud, or recognise a face from a new angle, or make a valid deduction from two premises.

Neurally inspired information processing

A casual perusal of the connectionist research literature (or even later parts of this book) may give an impression of dauntingly complex models, requiring advanced mathematical knowledge to be understood. Despite the complexity of the behaviour they can simulate, the principles on which connectionist models are based are simple. These are derived from observations of the organisation of information processing in the brain:

- The basic computational operation in the brain involves one neuron passing information related to the sum of the signals reaching it to other neurons.
- Learning changes the strength of the connections between neurons and thus the influence that one has on another.

- Cognitive processes involve the basic computation being performed in parallel by large numbers of neurons.
- Information, whether about an incoming signal or representing the network's memory of past events, is distributed across many neurons and many connections.

In this chapter we will discuss how the first two principles have been incorporated into connectionist models to determine the flow of information between processing units. In chapter 2 we will see how models based on the last two principles have many general properties which resemble those of human cognition.

The central principles of connectionist models are derived from our current knowledge of computation within the brain, so the models are said to be *neurally inspired*. This puts them in stark contrast to traditional models in cognitive psychology or artificial intelligence. Traditional models in cognitive psychology contain elements like limited capacity channels, articulatory loops and short-term memory stores. Models in Artificial Intelligence contain sets of rules. Either approach allows modelling of human cognitive capacities but in general no attempt is made to relate the operations these elements perform to the way the brain works at a neuronal level. The aim of a traditional model is to describe the performance of the subject, not the way that the performance is achieved. The connectionist approach is the reverse. It starts with a model that incorporates brain-like processing and sees whether behaviour emerges which mimics that shown by people.

Since the brain *does* compute with neurons it might seem to go without saying that neural plausibility is a virtue in modelling cognitive processes. But there are some drawbacks to this approach. We are far from having a complete understanding of the way that information is transmitted between neurons in the brain. The method of passing information from neuron to neuron in connectionist models certainly occurs, at least at a conceptual level, in the brain but there are other methods of inter-neuronal signalling which are not yet implemented in connectionist models. Also, as we shall see, some connectionist models contain procedures, especially learning algorithms, which are at present believed not to occur in the brain. Completely accurate neural models may be possible in the future. At the moment neural plausibility is a relative rather than an absolute virtue. Contemporary connectionist models are based on the assumption that although they make simplifications they can provide a useful starting point for understanding how cognitive computations might be performed.

An appealing aspect of the connectionist approach is that the models of cognitive processes are computational. That is, they actually produce a response to a stimulus. A connectionist model of reading aloud takes time to generate a response, and this varies with the frequency of the word; a connectionist model of children learning to produce the past tense form of verbs makes errors on a quantifiable number of occasions and the rate varies depending on when the verb was first learnt; a connectionist model of memory stores a specifiable number of events before interference between memories starts and the number changes as the structure of the memory is changed. The predictions that such models make about reaction time or error rate or interference can be compared at a *quantitative* level to the behaviour produced by subjects in experiments. If the predictions are wrong the model fails. The inability of many traditional models of cognitive processes to do more than make qualitative predictions about the effect of some experimental variable on performance has often made it difficult to choose between them because they make the same qualitative prediction.

This book contains the software to run a connectionist simulator called **tlearn**. The demonstrations and exercises at the end of each chapter will allow you to explore some of the models introduced in the book and find how changes of architecture or training regime lead to changes in the output of the model. Appendix 3 is a reference manual for the simulator which will allow you to build your own networks and start modelling cognition.

Five assumptions about computation in the brain on which connectionist models are based

In this section we will outline the basic principles of connectionist models and show how they are derived from observations about brain structure and the properties of neurons. Although much of the detail about computation by the brain is not yet understood, these principles are at a sufficiently abstract level that they seem a plausible starting point.

(1) Neurons integrate information. Many different types of neuron have been discovered. Three are shown in figure 1.1. Despite their bewildering variety in detail, they perform a common function—they integrate information about the firing of one set of neurons (their input) and pass information related to this input (their output) to a new set of neurons. In a 'classical neuron', a simplified approximation to a real one which captures the essence of its function, this operation takes place in three stages. First the neuron receives signals, either excitatory or inhibitory, from other neurons via synaptic connections onto its dendrites. If the sum of these signals exceeds a threshold, the neuron fires. This is communicated to other neurons by a signal passing down its axon. This signal acts in turn as part of the input to the dendrites of other neurons.

This view of neuronal function is represented in connectionist models by the computational unit on the right of figure 1.1. Connectionist models consist of a number of these simple units. Each line coming into the unit from above represents an input connection. These connections may be positive or negative, so activity on an

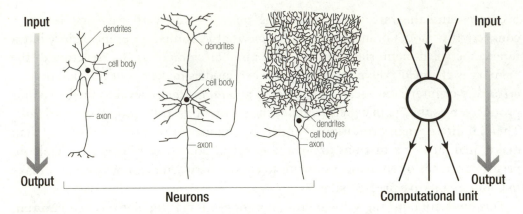

Figure 1.1   Three types of neuron. From left to right, a spinal motor neuron, a hippocampal pyramidal cell and a Purkinje cell of the cerebellum. Despite their structural differences the neurons perform a similar operation. Input is received on the dendrites from other neurons. If the sum of these inputs is sufficiently large the neuron fires, passing a signal down its axon to the other neurons to which it is connected. The last figure is a computational unit in a connectionist model. If the sum of the inputs exceeds the unit's threshold it passes a signal to the other units to which it is connected.

input line may increase or decrease the activity of the central unit. The central unit sums the inputs and passes information about the sum down the output connections to the other units to which it is connected. Thus the *functional* role of a unit in a connectionist model is the same as that of a classical neuron: It passes information about the pattern of activity of one set of units to another set.

(2) Neurons pass information about the level of their input. The output of a neuron communicates more than just the fact that it is receiving input. Its output varies systematically to convey information about the *level* of its input. In the classical neuron, information about the level of stimulation of the sending neuron is coded by the rate at which it fires.

Information transmission between connectionist units achieves the same end, conveying information about the level of input, but in a different way. Each unit has an activity level. The activity level is transmitted as a single value—not as a rate of production of pulses—to all the units to which it is connected. The activity level is related to the input level—the higher the input, the higher the activity.

(3) Brain structure is layered. Information is processed in the brain by a flow of activity passing through a sequence of physically independent structures. The organisation of part of the visual processing system is shown in the upper part of figure 1.2. If a word is presented to a child who is learning to read aloud, a pattern of excitation passes through a series of different structures. First the word stimulates receptors in the retina at the back of the eye. This produces a pattern of activity which passes along the optic nerve to the lateral geniculate body, a collection of cells about the size of a peanut in the middle of the brain. The pattern of firing from these

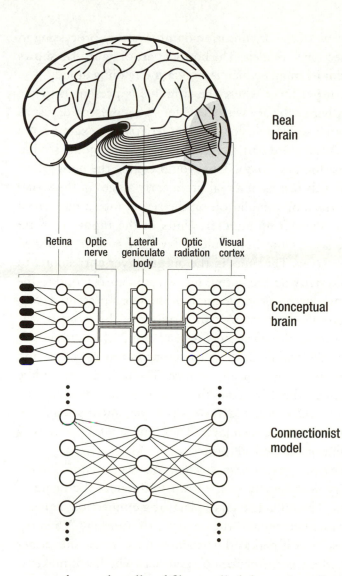

Retina | Optic nerve | Lateral geniculate body | Optic radiation | Visual cortex

Real brain

Conceptual brain

Connectionist model

Figure 1.2 The layered structure of information processing in the brain and connectionist models. Top: processing of visual information in the brain from retina to lateral geniculate body to visual cortex. Centre: this flow conceptualised as transmission of information through a series of processing layers. Bottom: a connectionist model with three layers of processing units.

passes along a bundle of fibres called the optic radiation to the visual cortex, a layer of cells a few millimetres thick at the back of the brain. The output from the visual cortex passes to a variety of other parts of the cortex, such as the motor cortex, which transform it in various ways, until it finally becomes a signal which stimulates the vocal muscles to produce an appropriate sound. At the retina a pattern of activity is produced by an external stimulus. At each subsequent stage, lateral geniculate body, visual cortex, motor cortex, there are millions of interconnected neurons which perform a transformation of the information carried by the incoming stream of nerve pulses. This transformed signal becomes the input to the next layer.

The first few layers of this transformation from a pattern on the retina to activation of vocal muscles are represented in figure 1.2 by the conceptual brain underneath the real one. This view of the organisation of information processing in the brain is represented in connectionist models. The bottom part of figure 1.2 shows a typical multi-layered connectionist model which is simulating reading aloud.[1] The row of units on the left is the input layer where the stimulus is presented to the network. The pattern of activity here will vary with the letter string presented, just as the pattern of activity on the retina is different for different letters. For example, the first unit might be switched on if the word had an A in the first position, the second one if it had a B in the first position and so on. This would enable the network to distinguish between different words just as in a real brain early stages in the visual pathway would convert the pattern of stimulation on the retina into a pattern of firing which distinguished one letter from another. Units in the input layer are connected to units in the middle layer. Units in the middle layer are in turn connected to units at the right, the output layer. The units in the output layer correspond to sound features. The pattern of activity on the output units would correspond to the network's attempt to produce the correct pronunciation of the word presented to it, just as in the real world the child would attempt to pronounce the word it was looking at. If the network has successfully learnt how to read aloud, the pattern here will vary with the input just as the child's does when she pronounces 'have' and 'nave' differently despite the similarity of their appearance. The units in the middle layer which neither receive input directly from the stimulus nor produce the network's response are called *hidden units*. As we shall see, most models of psychological processes contain at least one such layer. They have a vital role to play in allowing networks to find solutions to difficult problems.

(4) *The influence of one neuron on another depends on the strength of the connection between them.* A typical neuron in the brain influences the firing of several thousand other neurons. The influence takes place at a connection, called a synapse, between the axon of one neuron and the dendrite of another. When the axon on one side of the synapse fires it makes the neuron on the other side either more or less likely to fire. The effect of one neuron on another (whether it makes it much more or less likely to fire or whether it only slightly changes the probability) is determined by the strength of the synaptic connection between them.

This is represented directly in connectionist models. The effect that one unit has on another is determined by the strength of the connection between them. This is called the *weight* of the connection.

(5) *Learning is achieved by changing the strengths of connections between neurons.* Experience can change the behaviour of an organism in response to a

---

[1]To solve the problems involved in learning to read aloud it is not necessary to have the same number of layers of computing units as the brain. The minimum requirement for the solution of many psychologically interesting problems is that the network contains at least three layers of computing units with a layer of modifiable connections between each. (See chapter 5.)

particular stimulus. Although the mechanisms by which this happens in the brain are not fully understood, there is good evidence that learning involves changing the strength of synaptic connections between neurons.

Learning is implemented in connectionist models by rules which determine how the weights of the connections between units are changed. This idea is central to connectionism's contribution to understanding cognitive processes. A fundamental aspect of many connectionist models is that they are models of learning. They try to explain how a particular set of experiences could lead an initially unstructured system to the acquisition of knowledge. A model such as the one shown in the bottom of figure 1.2 would start with a random set of weights (i.e. strengths) for the connections between units in the different layers. When a word is first presented to the network, the pattern of activity on the output units—its attempt to pronounce the word—would be random, just like a child's. Just as with the child, an external teacher then tells the network what the correct pronunciation is. The network learns from this experience by changing the weights of the connections between the input and output units in such a way that the next time the word is presented at input it will produce an output which is closer to the correct pronunciation.

Symbols and elementary equations

We will now introduce some symbols and elementary equations to give quantitative definitions to the ideas described informally in the previous section. Since they will be repeated as a shorthand for the basic connectionist computation many times throughout the book, it is important to understand them. The equations are very simple and should not intimidate even the most numerophobic reader.

The upper part of figure 1.3 shows a typical net with three layers of processing units, input, hidden and output, joined by two layers of modifiable connections. The lower part of the figure focuses on a sub-part of the net outlined in the upper figure. It shows a typical processing unit, identified by the label i, in the hidden layer. Unit i receives input from units in the preceding layer. A typical unit in this layer has been identified with the label j.[2] The sum of the inputs from the preceding layer, via an activation function, determines the activity level of unit i. In its turn, unit i sends its activity level to units in the next layer.

The activity level of the units is the key to what a connectionist model can compute. A stimulus is applied to the network, resulting in the activity of some of its

[2]It would be hard to think of two more confusing labels than i and j for these units. Not only are the letters visually confusing when appearing as subscripts but j comes after i in the alphabet while unit j comes before unit i in the model. We have not selected these from a perverse desire to confuse. Unfortunately, the convention of calling a typical receiving unit i and a typical sending unit j has been adopted for many years in the connectionist literature, so you will just have to get used to it.

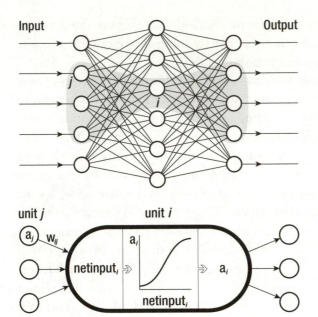

Input **Output**

unit *j* unit *i*

Integrate input from previous layer

Transform netinput to activity level (a_i)

Transmit activity level to units in next layer

Figure 1.3 The computational operation performed by a unit in a connectionist model. Upper: General structure of a connectionist network. Lower: A closer look at unit *i*. Its operation can be broken into three steps: (1) Integrate the inputs from the previous layer to create a netinput. (2) Use an activation function to convert the netinput to an activity level. (3) Output the activity level as input to units in the next layer.

input units. This produces a pattern of activity of the units in the next layer and so on until the units in the output layer become activated. The pattern of activity of the units in the output layer is the response of the net to this input. If the output units have the correct level of activity in response to the pattern of activity produced by any input in the problem domain, then the model has learnt the task it was set.

(1) Activity. The activity level of a unit is represented by the symbol *a*, with a subscript to denote which unit is referred to. Thus in figure 1.3 a_j refers to the activity level of unit *j* and a_i to the activity level of unit *i*.

(2) Weight. Unit *j* influences unit *i* by passing information about its activity level. The extent of this influence is determined by the weight of the connection between them, represented by the symbol *w*, which is given a subscript to indicate which unit is receiving the activity and which is sending it. We will follow the convention that the first subscript is the receiving unit and second is the sending unit.[3] Thus the strength of the connection shown in figure 1.3 by which unit *j* transmits information to unit *i* would be represented by the symbol w_{ij}. If w_{ij} is small, unit *j* has little effect on the activity level of unit *i*; if w_{ij} is large it has a large effect. The weight can be either positive or negative. If a_j is positive, it will increase the net input to all units to

[3]Although this is now the accepted convention, note that some influential early connectionist papers used the reverse convention.

which it is connected by a positive weight and reduce the net input to those units to which it is connected by a negative weight. (In the brain individual neurons are either excitatory or inhibitory, so allowing a single unit to have both negative and positive connections to other units is a simplification.)

(3) Input. The input from unit j to unit i (input$_{ij}$) is the product of the activity of unit j, a_j and the weight of the connection between them, w_{ij}:

$$\text{input}_{ij} = a_j w_{ij} \tag{1.1}$$

Thus the more active is unit j, or the stronger the connection between j and i, the greater the influence that unit j will have on unit i. Since the relationship is multiplicative there will be no input if either a_j or w_{ij} is zero.

(4) Netinput. The total input to unit i (netinput$_i$) is found by summing the inputs from all the units which send input to it. The mathematical symbol for summing across a number of inputs is Σ, so we express this as:

$$\text{netinput}_i = \Sigma_j a_j w_{ij} \tag{1.2}$$

where the subscript j on the summation sign indicates that netinput$_i$ is achieved by summing the input from all units indexed by j in the input layer.[4] (Netinput corresponds to the depolarisation or hyperpolarisation produced by the excitatory and inhibitory inputs received by a neuron.)

The exercises at the end of this chapter will allow you to explore the way that equations 1.1 and 1.2 define the flow of activity in a simple connectionist network.

(5) Activation function. To know what activity level unit i achieves, we need to know the relation between the net input and the activity level which this produces. This relationship is called the activation function. Figure 1.4 shows a number of possible activation functions with the net input to the unit (netinput$_i$) on the horizontal axis and the activity which this produces (a_i) on the vertical axis.

The simplest activation function is a linear relation between net input and activity level like that illustrated in figure 1.4(a). Real neurons have thresholds, with firing occurring only if the net input is above the threshold. A threshold linear activation function is shown in figure 1.4(b). Some non-linearity in the activation function, such as zero activity until the net input reaches a certain level, can be useful because it enables the effects of small inputs, produced perhaps by noise, to be minimized. Another simple activation function, which models neurons as two-state devices, either On or Off, is the binary threshold function shown in figure 1.4(d). This ensures that if the net input is below threshold there is no activity, but once the net input

---

[4]Note that the function we have called 'netinput' is sometimes called 'activation'. We have used netinput to avoid confusion with the unit's output which we refer to as 'activity'. You should be warned that some writers refer to the unit's output as its 'activation'. We only use the word 'activation' in the 'activation function' which is described in the next section.

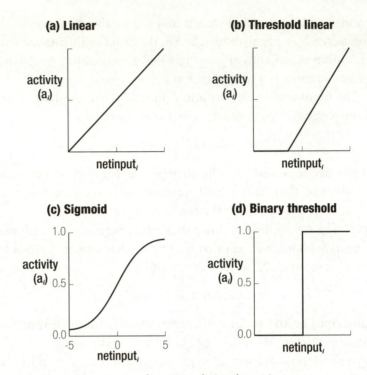

Figure 1.4   A variety of possible activation functions relating the net input to a neuron to the resulting activity level.

exceeds the threshold, the neuron becomes maximally activated. We will see an example of this activation function at work in the pattern associator analysed in chapter 3.

   An activation function frequently used in connectionist modelling is the sigmoid shown in figure 1.4(c). (This function is used in most of the models of cognitive processes described in chapters 8–12. It has some important properties which are described in chapter 5.) The range of possible activity has been set, arbitrarily, from 0 to 1. When the net input is large and negative the unit has an activity level close to zero. As the input becomes less negative the activity increases, gradually at first then more quickly. As the net input becomes positive the rate of increase in activity slows down again, asymptoting at the maximum value which the unit can achieve (1 in this case). This activation function effectively combines a threshold below which net input has little effect, a region in which the activity grows roughly in proportion to the net input, and then a region where further input has little effect as the unit approaches its maximum activity. This bears some relationship to the behaviour of neurons which have both lower thresholds and maximum firing rates, with a smooth transition between these two states.

   (6) Learning by weight change. A crucial aspect of connectionist models is their

ability to learn by experience. Various learning rules are described in chapters 3–5. Here we will give a flavour of the way that one particular learning rule, the Delta rule, works.

If the response of an output unit is incorrect then the network can be changed so that it is more likely to produce the correct response the next time that the stimulus is presented. Recall from figure 1.4 that the activity of unit i (a_i) is determined by the sum of inputs to it (netinput$_i$). From equation 1.2 we know that each input is given by the product of the activity of a unit connected to i multiplied by the weight of the connection between them. This means that any change in connection weights will change the activity level of units in the next layer. So an output unit which has too low an activity can be corrected by increasing the weights of connections from units in the previous layer which provide a positive input to it, and by decreasing the weights of the connections which provide a negative input. Output units which have too high an activity can be corrected by the opposite procedure. As a concrete example think of a network learning to read aloud. It should learn to pronounce the letter string HAVE with a short <a>. If it pronounces it with a long <a> (like the <a> in 'save') connections to the output unit representing a long <a> should be weakened and those to the output unit representing a short <a> should be strengthened.

Imagine that the unit i in figure 1.3 has an inappropriate level of activity when a particular stimulus pattern is presented to the net. Take the connection to i from j. The Delta rule for changing the weight of the connection, which will in turn change the activity level of i, is:

$$\Delta w_{ij} = [a_i(\text{desired}) - a_i(\text{obtained})]\, a_j\, \varepsilon \qquad (1.3)$$

where Δw_{ij} is the change in weight of the connection from unit j to unit i to be made after the learning trial.

To understand how this rule works, consider the three terms in the equation:

$[a_i(\text{desired}) - a_i(\text{obtained})]$ is the difference between the desired activity level of unit i (i.e. the correct activity) and the level which was actually produced by the flow of excitation and inhibition to it. Including this term in the weight change equation does two things. First, if the obtained activity is too low, $[a_i(\text{desired}) - a_i(\text{obtained})]$ is positive and the weight of the connection is increased. In consequence the activity of unit i will be higher if this stimulus is presented again. If the activity of i is too high, $[a_i(\text{desired}) - a_i(\text{obtained})]$ is negative and the weight will be reduced, with the opposite effect.[5] Second, $[a_i(\text{desired}) - a_i(\text{obtained})]$ ensures that the size of any weight change is proportional to the size of the error. When the obtained value of a_i

---

[5]This has been expressed loosely, assuming a positive a_j and a positive w_{ij}. In fact, as interested readers can work out for themselves, the Delta rule will produce an appropriate weight change whatever the polarity of a_j or w_{ij}.

is very inaccurate there will be large changes in the weights of the connections to unit *i* and thus large changes in its activity level the next time the stimulus is presented. But as a_i approaches the desired value these corrections, and the consequent changes in a_i become smaller. If a_i reaches the correct value, $[a_i(\text{desired}) - a_i(\text{obtained})] = 0$, and changes to the weight of the connection will cease. (The fact that the crucial term in this rule, $[a_i(\text{desired}) - a_i(\text{obtained})]$, represents a *difference* is the reason this is known as the Delta rule.)

a_j is the activity of unit *j*. To understand its role in the learning rule consider two units which both provide input to unit *i*. From equation 1.1 we know that the contribution which they each make to the activity of *i* is determined by the product of their activity and the weight of their connection to *i*. Other things being equal, the input unit with the higher activity will have the greater effect on the activity level of *i*. The learning rule recognises this, and concentrates the weight change on the connections from units in a high state of activity because these have the most effect on the state of unit with the incorrect activity level.

ε, the learning rate parameter, is a constant. It determines how large the changes to the weights will be on any learning trial.

(7) Bias. There is one special input unit connected to some units in many connectionist models. This is called the bias unit. The bias unit receives no input itself, and its activity is always set at $+1$. The weight from the bias unit to the unit of interest can be positive or negative and changes just like any other weight during learning. In the absence of strong input from other units, the effect of the bias is to make the unit it is connected to active if the weight is positive, or inactive if the weight is negative. A positive bias could be seen as representing the base firing rate of a neuron with a high spontaneous firing rate (i.e. one that is usually on). A negative bias can be seen as a threshold. Other input must exceed this before the unit will fire.

Connectionism in a nutshell

These, simple as they may seem, are the fundamental operations used in connectionist modelling. Imagine that the question is whether a connectionist network can learn to read English aloud. The problem is to find a set of weights which can represent the arbitrary mapping between letter strings and sounds which constitutes English pronunciation. The task is difficult (and interesting) because although English pronunciation contains many regularities, most of these have exceptions. For example, letter strings ending in -INT are usually pronounced as in *mint* but PINT is an exception; letter strings ending -AVE are usually pronounced as in *save* but HAVE is an exception, and so on. The net must find some way of representing both the general rules and the exceptions.

The modeller builds a network like that shown at the bottom of figure 1.2. The input units are activated with a pattern which represents the spelling of a particular word. Each input unit passes on its activity, multiplied by the weight of the connection, to all the units in the next layer. Each of these sums its inputs and converts this to an activity level with its activation function. The activity level is then passed on, multiplied by the appropriate weight, to all the units in the next layer. Eventually the activity reaches the output layer. Units in the output layer correspond to phonemes. So the activity of the output units is the network's response to the stimulus, its attempt to pronounce the word. An external teacher compares the output of each unit with its correct value. If the response is incorrect, a learning rule is applied to modify the weights of all the connections to the output units which were incorrect, and a new input is then presented. This procedure is repeated many times. If a time comes when the network produces the correct pattern of activity on the response units to all words presented to it, it has learnt the task. The modeller can then examine the performance of the network to see whether it resembles the performance of adult readers. Does the length of time it takes to pronounce a word depend on the frequency of the word? Can it pronounce non-words? Does it exhibit dyslexic symptoms when damaged? If it does resemble human readers in all these ways, examination of how the network solved the problem of learning English may shed some light on how people do it.

Intuitively it might seem implausible that such simple structures could ever do anything interesting, let alone simulate the richness of human intelligence. But, as Francis Crick once wrote: 'The results that can be achieved with such nets are astonishing.'

Exercises with `tlearn`

Setting up the simulator

We start the simulation exercises with a very simple demonstration of how a network simulator can be used to perform the computations described in this chapter. This will introduce you to the `tlearn` simulator which will be used throughout the book. We will not attempt to provide you with a complete introduction to the `tlearn` simulator or connectionist modelling. This can be found in Plunkett and Elman (1997).

The `tlearn` neural network simulator has been programmed to run on a variety of computing platforms including Macintoshes, PCs running Windows and most Unix machines that run X-windows. We have designed the user interface to look more or less the same across these different platforms. So the details involved in setting up your simulations will be similar irrespective of the type of computer system you are using. Where differences do occur they will be minor. The description we

```
Tlearn                                    _ □ ×
 File   Edit   Search   View   Network   Displays   Special   Help

 [□][🖿][🖫]  [✂][🗐][🗎]   [🖶][?]

 Ready
```

Figure 1.5   Startup menu for **tlearn**.

give here is for the Windows95 version of the application. For information on how to install **tlearn** on your computer system, refer to Appendix 1.

You start up **tlearn** on your computer in the same way as any other application, such as double-clicking on the **tlearn** icon or through a sequence of keyboard commands. We will assume that you have done this. When **tlearn** has started up, your monitor should display a set of menus like those in figure 1.5. These menus are accessed in the standard fashion for your computer system. For example, you may click on one of the menu items to display the options associated with that menu.

Propagating activity in linear feedforward networks

A neural network consists of a collection of units of the sort that we discussed earlier in this chapter. When we talk about the architecture of a network we are referring to the particular way in which that network is assembled, or its pattern of connectivity. A common architecture is one in which units are connected to each other in a layered fashion. For example, consider the network in figure 1.6. This consists of four units organized into two layers: an input layer and an output layer. The units in the input layer have connections to the output layer. There are no connections between units within a layer or back from output units to input units. Thus, in this network, the flow of activity is in one direction only, from the input layer to the output layer. We call these types of networks 'feedforward networks'.

Output nodes

Input nodes

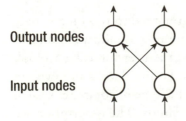

Figure 1.6   A simple feedforward network.

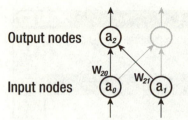

Output nodes

Input nodes

Figure 1.7 The input to the left-hand output unit via weighted connections from the input units.

We can now begin to consider just how the neural network performs its task. First, let us assume that each input unit has a certain level of activity associated with it. Our goal is to determine how the activity of the input units influences the output units. To simplify the explanation, we shall consider the process from the point of view of just one output unit, the left-hand output in figure 1.6. This is highlighted in figure 1.7. We refer to the two input units as $unit_0$ and $unit_1$, and to the two output units as $unit_2$ and $unit_3$. The activity values of the input units are denoted a_0 and a_1, respectively. Our goal is to calculate the activity of the leftmost output unit, a_2.

The only inputs to $unit_2$ come from the two input units. Each input is the product of the activity of the sender unit times the weight of the connection (equation 1.1). The net input to $unit_2$ is given by the sum of these two products (equation 1.2). As a concrete example, assume our network has the weights shown in figure 1.8, and the input units have the activities shown. What will be the net input received by $unit_2$?

The activity values of the two input units are both 1.0 and the connection weights are 0.75 and 0.5. The net input to $unit_2$ is the sum of the products of each weight and the activity coming in along that weight:

$$netinput_2 = (1.0 \times 0.75) + (1.0 \times 0.5) = 1.25$$

This is an extremely easy calculation to perform but imagine that you had to make thousands of these calculations to evaluate the performance of a network with many input and output units! Life would quickly become exceedingly tedious without a network simulator to do the calculations. Let us work through an exercise in which we use **tlearn** to perform these calculations for us. So we can check that the simulator is performing the calculations correctly, we will use the network shown in figure 1.6.

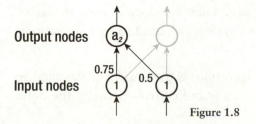

Output nodes

Input nodes

Figure 1.8

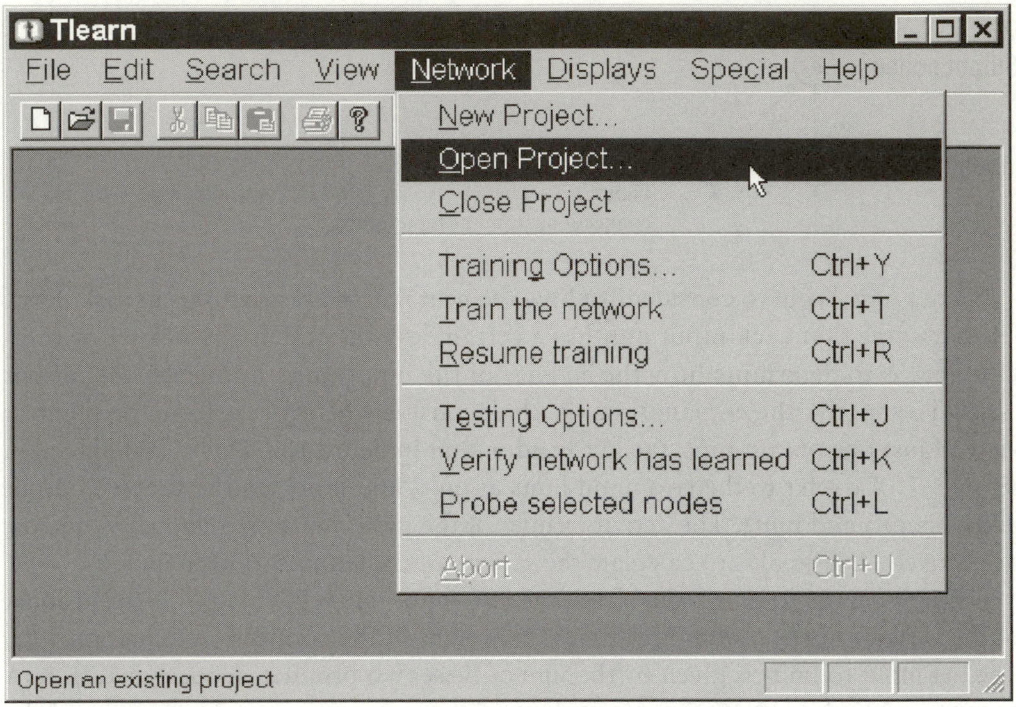

Figure 1.9   Select the **Open Project**... option from the **Network** menu.

You begin the process of opening a network from the **Network** menu. Select the **Network** menu and drag the mouse so that the **Open Project**... option is highlighted as shown in figure 1.9.

When you release the mouse button the **Open Project** dialogue box is displayed. In this dialogue box you can select the directory or folder in which your project files reside. You can move around the directory/folder hierarchy by clicking on the folders listed in the dialogue box until the display is as shown in figure 1.10.

Select the **NetInput** project file. The display on your monitor should now resemble that in figure 1.11.

tlearn has created 3 different windows—Netinput.cf, Netinput.data and Netinput.teach. You can view each window either by clicking on its header bar or by choosing the window from the **Window** menu. Each window is used to define information relevant to a different aspect of the network architecture or training environment:

- The **Netinput.cf** file (cf. stands for configuration) is used to define the number of units in a network and the initial pattern of connectivity between the units before training begins.

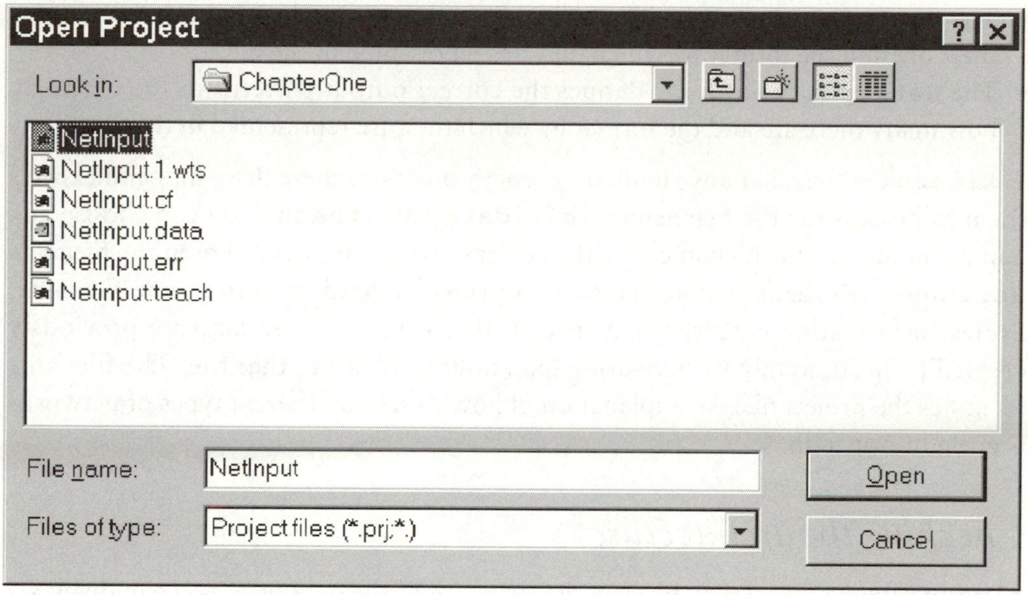

Figure 1.10 The **Open Project** dialogue box. Select the folder or directory in which the project called NetInput is located.

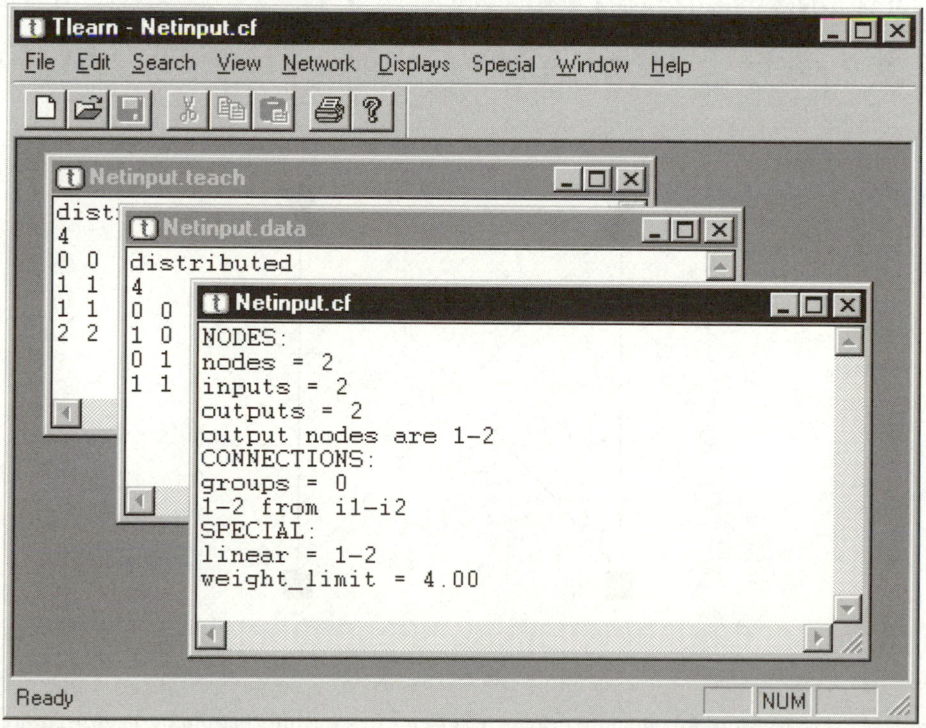

Figure 1.11 Startup files for the **tlearn** project include **.cf**, **.data**, and **.teach** files.

- The **Netinput.data** file defines the input patterns to the network, how many there are and the format by which they are represented in the file.
- The **Netinput.teach** file defines the correct output patterns to the network, how many there are and the format by which they are represented in the file.

tlearn requires that any simulation project possesses these three files and expects them to possess the file extensions **.cf**, **.data** and **.teach**. You can choose any name you like for the filename. For the current project, we have chosen the filename **Netinput**. All the files that belong to a project should have the same filename. Project information is stored in a special file so that you can activate previously created projects simply by activating (e.g. double-clicking) that file. The filename identifies the project file. An explanation of how to set up different types of networks is given in Appendix 3.

Checking the architecture

tlearn offers a useful way to view the structure of the network. You can display a picture of your network architecture using the **Network Architecture** option in the

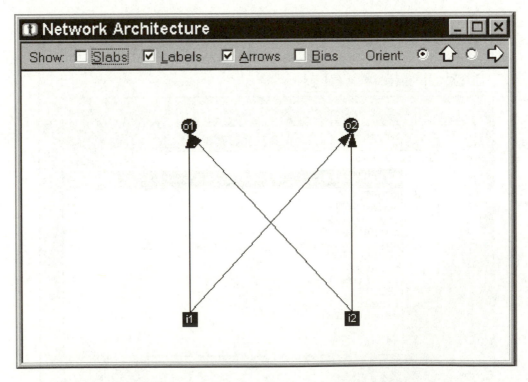

Figure 1.12 The Network Architecture display. **tlearn** reads the information in the **netinput.cf** file to construct this display.

Displays menu. The architecture for the **Netinput** network is shown in figure 1.12. This corresponds to the network depicted in figure 1.6. The buttons at the top of the display enable you to adjust your view of the network. Note, however, that the adjustments you make to the display do not affect the contents of the network configuration file.

Specifying the connections

Since we want to illustrate how `tlearn` can be used to calculate the netinput to a unit, you must specify the weights of the different connections in the network. This can be done by loading into the network a prespecified weights file. Go to the **Network** menu and activate **Testing Options...** The testing options dialogue box will appear as shown in figure 1.13.

Select the **Most recent** radio button and check that the highlighted **Weights** file is **NetInput.1.wts**.[6] Make sure that the other radio buttons and check boxes are as displayed in figure 1.13 and then press **OK**. This action will set the weights in the network to take on the values shown in figure 1.14.

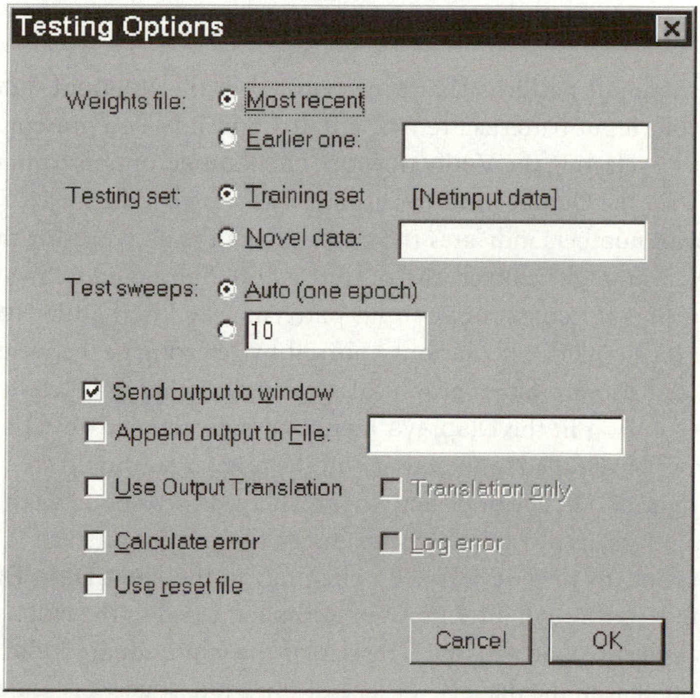

Figure 1.13   **Testing Options** dialogue box.

[6]On Macintosh installations you may need to select the 'earlier one' button and choose the file NetInput–1.wts.

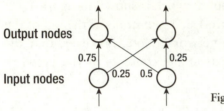

Figure 1.14

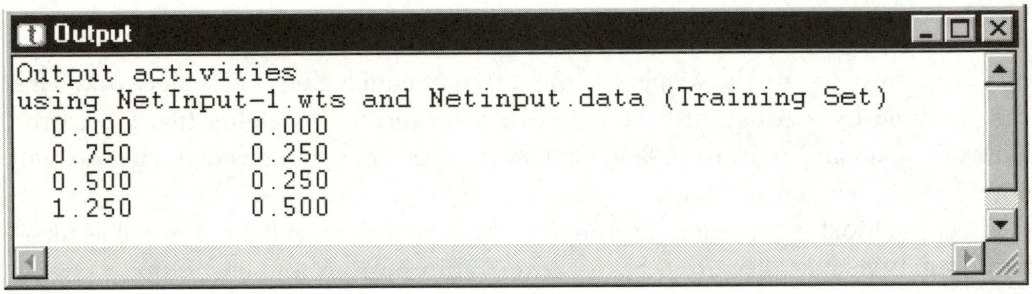

Figure 1.15   The Output window

Testing the network

Now present the input patterns that are specified in the Netinput.data file to the network. The four input patterns are 0 0, 1 0, 0 1 and 1 1. You present the patterns to the network by selecting the Verify network has learned option from the Network menu. You will see the Output window displayed as shown in figure 1.15.

   The first row of numbers indicates the output from the network for the first input pattern 0 0. As you might expect, the output is 0 0. Subsequent rows of numbers indicate the outputs for consecutive input patterns listed in the file Netinput.data. You can check the network calculations yourself by referring to the weights in figure 1.14. **tlearn** can also produce a graphical display of output unit activities using the Node Activities option in the Displays menu. ('Node activity' in **tlearn** corresponds to what we have called 'unit activity' in the text.) You should see a display like that shown in figure 1.16. The node activities displayed correspond to those obtained for the first input pattern 0 0, which produces the output pattern 0 0. The grey squares correspond to zero activity. By clicking on the Next Data Pattern radio button, you can step through all 4 input patterns indicated in the Netinput.data file. White squares indicate node activity. The size of the white square indicates the level of activity. (Note that in the display the size of the white squares is scaled to the size of the largest activity on display. So the Node Activities display only gives a rough idea of what is happening. The values in the Output and Netinput.data files give precise values.)

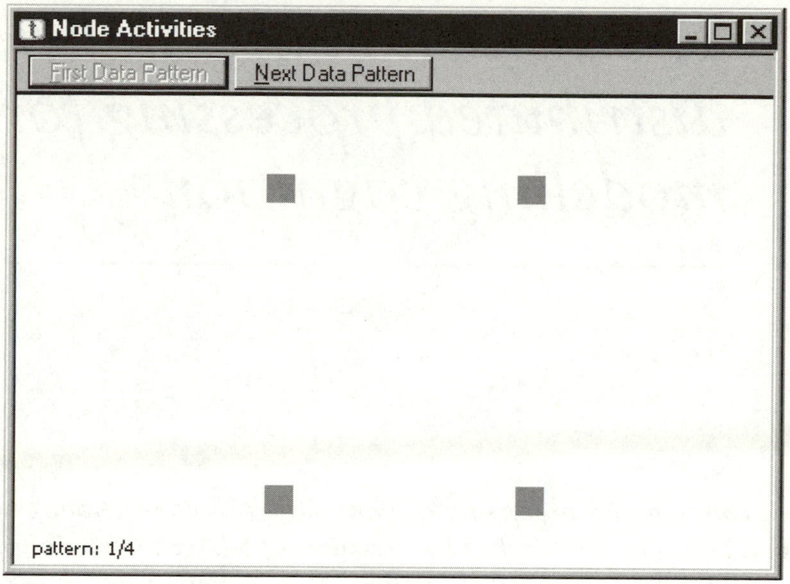

Figure 1.16 Node Activities display.

2 *The attraction of parallel distributed processing for modelling cognition*

The representation and processing of information in connectionist networks is distributed. Decisions are reached by consensus of a large number of simple computations taking place in parallel as stimulus information interacts with stored knowledge. In consequence, connectionist memories display many human characteristics: They are relatively immune to damaged components within the system or to noisy input; they allow retrieval by content; they are likely to retrieve typical instances from categories.

The last decade has seen an explosive growth in the connectionist modelling of cognitive processes, with simulation of most of the classical experimental paradigms of cognitive psychology. One reason for this enthusiasm is that, independent of their success at modelling human performance at any particular cognitive task, all connectionist models exhibit some general characteristics which are shown by human cognitive processes and distinguish them from non-biological computational systems such as computer programs: They still perform reasonably well after minor damage to components of the system; they still perform reasonably well if their input is noisy or inaccurate; they allow memory retrieval by content.

In this chapter we will look at two aspects of connectionist systems which are responsible for these characteristics. Like the principles of interneuronal communication described in chapter 1, these are based on general observations of brain structure. First, knowledge representation is *distributed* across many processing units. Second, computations take place in *parallel* across these distributed representations. The result is that conclusions are reached on the basis of a consensus of many calculations rather than depending on any particular one.

These principles put connectionist models in direct contrast to many traditional models in cognitive psychology or artificial intelligence where knowledge representation is local and computation is serial. In general, such models are not immune to damage or resistant to noisy input. So a traditional model of, say, syllogistic reasoning, might give as good a fit to the experimental data as a connectionist model, but it would do so without exhibiting the full range of human characteristics as it performed the task.

The representation of knowledge in connectionist networks is distributed

Traditional models of cognitive processing usually assume a local representation of knowledge. That is, knowledge about different things is stored in different, independent locations. In a traditional model of reading aloud, for example, information about how to pronounce the letter string DOG is stored in one place and information about how to pronounce the string CAT in another. What could be more natural? The two pieces of information are independent and would be required at different times. So storing them independently makes obvious sense. The information storage systems we are familiar with in everyday life—dictionaries, telephone directories, computer discs—use local representation. Each discrete piece of information is stored separately. How else could it be done?

In connectionist models information storage is not local, it is *distributed*. There is no one place where a particular piece of knowledge can be located. Consider the segment of network at the bottom of figure 1.2 in chapter 1, part of a larger network which is learning to read aloud. Any input, such as the letter string DOG, would excite units and connections all over the network. Learning takes place by changing the weights of the connections leading to all output units which have an incorrect level of activity. The knowledge of how to pronounce the input DOG is distributed across many different connections in different parts of the system. It is the sum total effect of all these connections which produces the pronunciation, not any single one of them.

The concept of distributed storage may be difficult to grasp at first because it is counter to our everyday experience of information storage systems. The connections which contain the system's knowledge about how to pronounce DOG are the same as those with the knowledge about how to pronounce any other letter string. All the knowledge that the network contains is superimposed on the *same* set of connections. Intuitively this may seem entirely implausible. How can the same set of weights store independent and even contradictory pieces of information? As we will see, it can be done, and some of the emergent properties of such systems are intriguingly similar to properties of human cognitive processes. But for the moment this will have to be taken on trust. There are no familiar information storage systems which use distributed coding, so analogy to a familiar system is not possible.

Distributed representations are damage resistant and fault tolerant

When one considers the structure of the brain it is remarkable that it ever manages to come to the correct conclusion about anything. By any conventional standards neurons are an entirely unsuitable medium for computation: they die throughout the brain's life, causing random loss of stored information; they have a finite probability of firing even when they are not engaged in signal processing; the response of a neuron to any particular input is probabilistic, not fixed.

If we look at the firing pattern of a single neuron the problem that probabilistic responses cause for the system will become clear. The upper part of figure 2.1 shows the average response of a single neuron in the visual cortex to a stimulus presented to the eye. The stimulus is presented at time 0. Time after the presentation of the stimulus is shown on the horizontal axis. The vertical axis shows the neuron's firing rate. It has an average background firing rate of a few spikes per second. When the stimulus is presented a signal is superimposed on this. About 50 ms after the stimulus appears the neuron fires strongly for about 30 ms. 100 ms later it fires again, rather less intensely, for about 50 ms. This is the signal that the neuron transmits to the other neurons to which it is connected, indicating what pattern of stimulation it has received.

This seems fairly straightforward. But the histogram was obtained by summing the spike patterns over a number of presentations of the stimulus. The lower part of the figure shows 12 different occasions on which the same stimulus was presented. Each time the neuron fires there is a vertical spike. If we look at these individual trials the pattern which emerges is much less clear than that suggested by the overall average at the top. On trial 5 the initial burst was missing. On trial 10 the second burst was missing. On trial 11 the neuron did not respond at all. It is clear that the 'signal' which the histogram at the top shows is an idealised average. On any given trial the output will only approximate this, sometimes quite closely, sometimes not at all. How can the system produce a reliable response on every trial when the individual components only produce their signal on average across trials?

If the processing components in a conventional digital computer produced random spontaneous output, a different response to the same stimulus on different occasions and suffered from random component drop-out, the system would be totally unpredictable! Sometimes it would work correctly, but if a computation required access to the contents of a missing memory unit, or a burst of noise obliterated a signal, the result would be garbage. Although the components in the brain can fire and die at random, the computations performed by the brain are not unpredictable. With minor damage it becomes a little slower and less accurate, but it still produces roughly the same answer. It has to suffer serious damage before it produces nonsense.

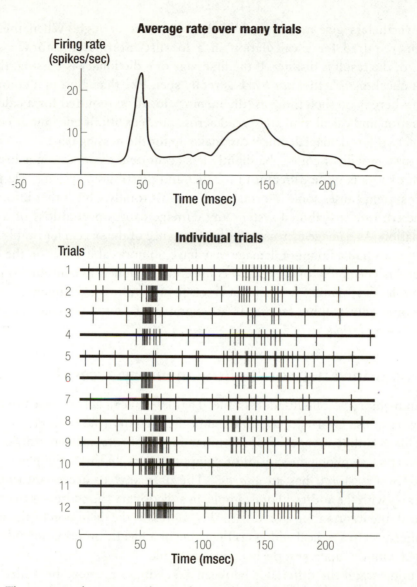

Figure 2.1   The response of a neuron in the visual cortex for 250 ms after stimulus presentation. Upper: The firing rate of the neuron summed over a number of presentations of the stimulus. Lower: The pattern on 12 of the trials which contributed to the average response shown at the top. Each vertical line represents the time at which the neuron fired. (Based on Morrell 1972.)

The brain escapes the consequences of the unpredictable behaviour of individual neurons because its computations are performed in parallel on representations which are distributed over many neurons. No one neuron plays a crucial role in processing. The overall result is the outcome of many distributed sub-computations. Even if individual components of the calculation are not accurate, the ensemble averaging can nevertheless give an answer which is accurate enough. When the memory location required for a calculation in a localist information storage system is damaged, the result is disaster. If the first page of a dictionary is missing, there is no way of checking whether *aardvark* is really spelt like that. But, in a connectionist system, there is no such thing as 'the memory location required for a calculation'. Information and calculation are spread across the network. If one unit or connection in the network is damaged, others can make up for the missing part.

The system will, of course, be slightly less accurate if a connection is lost. But the pattern of loss is quite different in localist and distributed systems. Damage to a localist system causes some information to be lost totally while other information is unaffected. In a distributed system any damage causes partial loss of a range of information. As damage increases, the performance of the system inevitably begins to drop. But a small amount of damage may have no noticeable effect on the output of the system. The ability of brains and connectionist models to continue to produce a reasonable approximation to the correct answer following damage, rather than undergoing catastrophic failure, is an example of fault tolerance referred to as *graceful degradation*.

Connectionist networks allow memory access by content

Human memory is content-addressable. That is, you can access a memory by using some part of the information contained in the memory (the *content*) as a retrieval cue. This is unlike retrieval from familiar forms of information storage, such as dictionaries, telephone directories or computer discs. In these, the place where the information is stored has an *address*. The only way to access information for retrieval is with the address. For example, in a dictionary the address is the spelling of the word; the information stored with this address is the definition of the word. In a computer system a typical address is the name of a file; the information which can be accessed with this address is the contents of the file.

To understand the difference between accessing a memory by address and by content, contrast retrieving information from a dictionary with obtaining the same information from a person. Imagine that you want to know the name of a man-made wall, built across a valley, to contain water to build up a head of pressure to generate electricity. With a dictionary, there is no way to access the location where this information is stored and extract the missing piece, the word 'dam'. If you start with the address (DAM) you can access all the information stored at the address. Without it you can access nothing. In contrast, a person given part of the information would probably be able to retrieve the rest. Unlike a dictionary, human memory allows access via any part of the information that forms the memory. One of the reasons why connectionist models of human memory are attractive is that content addressability follows as a natural consequence of their distributed structure. Content addressability can be built into localist storage but only by adding a complex cross-referencing system.

Any information processing system which works in the brain must be fault tolerant because the signals it has to work with are seldom perfect. There is a random component to neuronal firing; speech is usually heard against a background of other noises; objects rarely present the same image on different occasions. An attractive aspect of content-addressable memory is that it is inherently fault tolerant. Imagine someone asked you to guess who they were thinking of: 'This man was a British Conservative politician. He became Prime Minister in 1978 and was Prime Minister during the Falklands War. He was ousted from office by his own party, being held responsible for the fiasco of the Poll Tax. He was eventually replaced as Prime Minister by John Major.' You could probably suggest 'Margaret Thatcher' as an answer despite the fact that some of the information is incorrect. Mrs Thatcher did not become Prime Minister until 1979, of course. With content-addressable memory the weight of evidence pointing to one answer can overcome other evidence that is inconsistent. A best fit solution can be chosen even if it is not perfect. This is unlike memory systems in which access by address is the only possibility. Any error in the address will lead to failure. A search of *Who's Who* using the address 'Margaret Patcher' would discover nothing, despite the fact that most of the search term fits an existing entry.

Retrieving information from a distributed database

To see how a distributed system with parallel processing works in practice we will look at retrieval from a simple connectionist memory described by McClelland (1981).[1] This memory demonstrates content addressability and fault tolerance. It also shows typicality effects in retrieval—if asked to retrieve a random member of a category it will produce a typical member. Considering the simplicity of the simulation it demonstrates a remarkable range of human characteristics in memory retrieval.

Imagine that you live in a neighbourhood where many of your male acquaintances belong to one of the two rival local gangs, the Jets or the Sharks. Your knowledge about these characters will come from a succession of independent episodes. One night Fred emerges from behind a bush and offers you some white powder. You hear Dave and his wife trading insults as she drives off with a car full of suitcases. Everyone in the bar is laughing because Don has been admitted to college on the basis of forged examination results. Nick hangs out with Karl whom you know to be a Shark. All these pieces of information about your neighbours are gradually

[1]The Jets and Sharks memory system is not implemented in **tlearn** but its properties and the examples described in the text can be explored using the **iac** program in McClelland and Rumelhart (1988).

Table 2.1

Address	Contents				
	Gang	Age	Education	Marital Status	Occupation
Alan	Jets	30s	JH	Married	Burglar
Art	Jets	40s	JH	Single	Pusher
Clyde	Jets	40s	JH	Single	Bookie
Dave	Sharks	30s	HS	Divorced	Pusher
Don	Sharks	30s	Col	Married	Burlar
Doug	Jes	30s	HS	Single	Bookie
Earl	Sharks	40s	HS	Married	Burglar
Fred	Jets	20s	HS	Single	Pusher
Gene	Jets	20s	Col	Single	Pusher
George	Jets	20s	JH	Divorced	Burglar
Greg	Jets	20s	HS	Married	Pusher
Ike	Sharks	30s	JH	Single	Bookie
Jim	Jets	20s	JH	Divorced	Burglar
John	Jets	20s	JH	Married	Burglar
Karl	Sharks	40s	HS	Married	Bookie
Ken	Sharks	20s	HS	Single	Burglar
Lance	Jets	20s	JH	Married	Burglar
Mike	Jets	30s	JH	Single	Bookie
Neal	Sharks	30s	HS	Single	Bookie
Ned	Sharks	30s	Col	Married	Bookie
Nick	Sharks	30s	HS	Single	Pusher
Oliver	Sharks	30s	Col	Married	Pusher
Pete	Jets	20s	HS	Single	Bookie
Phil	Sharks	30s	Col	Married	Pusher
Ralph	Jets	30s	JH	Single	Pusher
Rick	Sharks	30s	HS	Divorced	Burglar
Sam	Jets	20s	Col	Married	Bookie

(Based on McClelland 1981.)

assembled over the years. Fred is a pusher; Dave is divorced; Don went to college; Nick is a Shark.

Table 2.1 shows how this information might be stored in a conventional information storage system. The system has a set of storage locations, corresponding to a set of cards in an index file or a set of files on disc in a computer, for example, each headed by an address. The address is the name of the person. Each new piece of information relating to him is stored at the location headed by this address. In this simple simulation we imagine that we have information about the **Gang** each person belongs to (*Jets* or *Sharks*), a rough idea of his **Age** (*20s*, *30s* or *40s*), the extent of his **Education** (*Junior High*, *High School* or *College*), his **Marital Status** (*Married*, *Single* or *Divorced*), and his **Occupation** (*Bookie*, *Burglar* or *Pusher*). The format used in table 2.1, address + contents, is a logical way of storing the information since the name *Alan* is the key which binds one set of information together, *Clyde* connects another set, and so on.

This form of storage is efficient for retrieving information in response to questions like 'Is Fred a pusher?'. The question contains the address, and the address leads directly to the place where the information which provides the answer is stored. But it is not so good for answering other enquiries. If you are asked 'Do you know the name of a pusher?', the only way is to search through the list of addresses until you find one where the information *Pusher* is stored under **Occupation**. Although the information *Pusher* is stored at many locations, it does not form part of the address. So an answer to this question cannot be extracted directly from the memory.

Admittedly, with this particular database it would not take long to find a pusher if you searched addresses at random. But a more realistic representation of knowledge of these people would include many unique pieces of information, such as the fact that Fred's grandparents came from Ballylickey. The only way to store this in a system like that shown in table 2.1 is as the fact 'grandparents came from Ballylickey' at the storage location with the address *Fred*. The question 'Whose grandparents came from Ballylickey?' could only be answered by random search of the addresses until the one containing that information was found. This might take a long time although you would get there in the end. But a human memory would not respond like that. If you could remember the information at all you would usually produce the answer reasonably quickly. This is because human memory can be accessed by *content*—any part of the knowledge base can be used to access any other part. 'Ballylickey' can be used as a cue, and will lead to *Fred*. The information storage system shown in table 2.1 is perfectly logical. Indeed, it is probably the sort of system you would use if you were asked to store the information about the Jets and Sharks. But human memory cannot be organised like this. A memory organised like table 2.1 does not allow content-addressable retrieval; human memory does.

Another way of seeing why human memory cannot be organised so that access is only possible by address is to consider how you would answer the question 'What are the Jets like?'. Table 2.1 allows easy access to information about individual Jets. But it offers no simple way to answer questions requiring generalisations across a number of entries. Human memory does allow generalisations across areas of memory. A person who knew these two gangs could probably tell you that the Jets were younger than the Sharks without having to think very hard. Although the method of information storage shown in table 2.1 seems natural, it cannot be the way that human memory is organised.

(1) Setting up a distributed database for the Jets and Sharks base. McClelland explored the consequences of storing the information about the Jets and Sharks in a distributed system. The architecture of his system is shown in the upper part of

figure 2.2. To store the information in table 2.1 we need to represent facts about **Name**, **Gang Membership**, **Age**, **Education**, **Marital Status** and **Occupation**. Within each of these areas of knowledge there is a node corresponding to the possible values that someone could have. So in the **Age** area there are nodes for *20s*, *30s* and *40s*, in **Occupation** for *Burglar*, *Bookie* and *Pusher*, in **Gang** for *Jet* and *Shark*, and so on. This model might seem to be localist rather than distributed because there are individual nodes to represent specific concepts. But, as we shall see, the underlying dynamics of the model are parallel and distributed. The result of any input is determined by interaction across the entire database. The localist coding of concepts is used to make it easy to see what the model is doing in the examples which follow.

A memory is formed by setting up a link between two nodes. If we discover that Sam is a bookie we set up a positive connection between the *Sam* node in the **Name** area and the *Bookie* node in the **Occupation** area. If we then discover that he is married we set up a positive connection between *Sam* in the **Name** area and *Married* in **Marital Status**, and between *Bookie* and *Married* (since we now know of a bookie who is married). To store all the information we know about Sam we would set up positive links between all the possible pairwise combinations of *Sam* in **Name**, *Jet* in **Gang**, *20s* in **Age**, *College* in **Education**, *Married* in **Marital Status** and *Bookie* in **Occupation**. The way that McClelland did this is shown in the middle of figure 2.2. He set up a Person node in the central region of the model and then made a positive connection between this and each fact that was related to that person. The result is similar to setting up all 15 links necessary to represent these facts individually, but requires fewer links. Person nodes were then set up for each of the people in table 2.1 and the necessary links formed to represent everything that is known about them[2].

The bottom part of figure 2.2 shows the connections between the various nodes building up as information about five of the people is added to the system. This also shows a second element of the model. There are mutually inhibitory connections between each of the exemplar nodes within a knowledge area. There must be some inhibitory links in a network like this where everything is interconnected or the result of activating any node would be that everything in the network would eventually reach its maximum activity level and no differential response to different inputs would be possible. These connections represent the fact that, for example, if someone is in his 20s, he cannot be in either his 30s or his 40s. This fact could have been implemented by making negative connections from each person node to all the things he is not. Building mutually inhibitory links between alternative instance nodes

---

[2]It might seem that the Person node corresponds to the address for the information just as the name Sam does in table 2.1. When information is retrieved from the net the Person node cannot be accessed, so it cannot be used as a retrieval address. It is just a convenience which reduces the number of connections required to set up the model and makes the operation of the model easier to follow.

within an area has a similar effect on the performance of the net but greatly reduces the number of connections required. As we shall see, the way that inhibition is built into this network has an important role to play in the way the model runs.

(2) Running the network. The nodes are the processing units of the model. They act like the one at the bottom of figure 1.3 which was described in chapter 1. Each has an activity level associated with it. When the model runs, each node passes activity to all the other nodes to which it is connected, in the way described in equation 1.1. That is, the input to the receiving node is the product of the activity level of the sending node and the weight of the connection between them. In this simple model the weight of all positive connections between nodes is $+1$ and that of negative connections is -1.[3] So, when the model runs, every node which has a positive activity level tries to increase the activity level of every node to which it has a positive connection, and to reduce the activity of every node to which it has a negative connection. The net input of each node is determined by summing these negative and positive inputs (as described in equation 1.2). The net input is then converted by an activation function to an activity level. The exact form of the activation function used by McClelland was not the same as any of those shown in figure 1.4 but had the same effect as the sigmoid function in figure 1.4(c) of limiting the maximum value which the activity level could reach, and of slowing the change in activity level with changes in net input as the unit's activity level approached its maximum value. In a single processing cycle the activity level of each unit is computed by summing its inputs and converting these to an activity level with the activation function. On the next cycle these new activity levels are used to compute the new net inputs to each unit, and thus their new activity level. This is continued until the net reaches a steady state. That is, until each node in the network reaches a constant activity level.

(3) Retrieval from the database. To test the memory performance of this system we ask it a question such as 'Can you remember the name of a pusher?'. This is done by activating the *Pusher* node in **Occupation** and waiting to see which unit becomes active in the **Name** area as activity passes round the network. The activity of all nodes starts at a level of -0.1. Activity of the *Pusher* node increases the activity level of all nodes to which it has a positive connection and decreases the activity of all those to which it has a negative connection. Once the activity level of a node rises

---

[3]There is no gradual learning phase in Jets and Sharks. Facts are given to the model complete. Therefore the weights do not develop as knowledge is acquired as they would in a conventional connectionist model. The way that information is entered into this system is an example of Hebbian learning (which will be discussed in detail in chapter 3). If two things are mutually consistent (e.g. being in your 20s and being a burglar) a positive connection (via the appropriate Person node) is made between them. If two things are mutually inconsistent (e.g. being in your 20s and 30s) a negative connection is made between them.

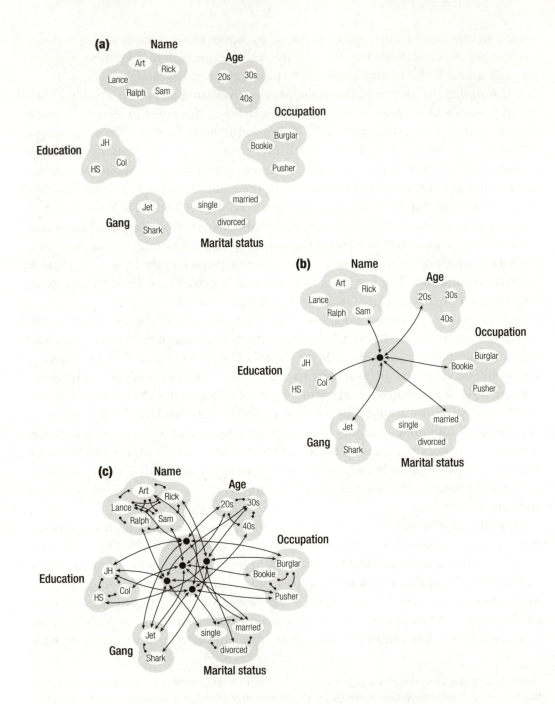

above 0 it excites all the nodes to which it has a positive connection and inhibits all those to which it has a negative connection. Eventually the system reaches a steady state in which the activity level of each node is constant, either because it has reached its maximum or minimum permitted value, or because its negative and positive

Figure 2.2 The architecture of McClelland's system for storing the information about the Jets and Sharks shown in table 2.1. (a) Each cloud represents an area of knowledge about the members of the two gangs, with the nodes within a cloud representing possible instances. (b) The information about Sam is represented by setting up excitatory connections between the facts that are known about him. This is done by setting up a Person node (the black node in the central circle) and linking this to all the instance nodes which represent his properties. If any one of these nodes becomes active these links will ensure that the nodes representing his other characteristics will be activated. (c) The excitatory connections necessary to represent all the information about five members of the gang have been entered. Inhibitory connections (links with filled circles on their ends) have been set up between competing instances nodes within each area of knowledge. When the model runs, any node which has a positive activity level will inhibit any other node to which it is connected by one of these links. (Based on McClelland 1981.)

---

inputs are exactly balanced.[4] The **Name** node which is most strongly activated when steady state is reached is the system's answer to the question.

Does such a system behave like human memory? Apart from being able to retrieve the information it had been given directly, by answering such questions as 'What does Fred do?', anyone who knew these people would find it easy to answer questions like 'Do you know the name of a pusher?' or 'What are the Jets like?'. These are the sort of questions which it is difficult to answer with a localist memory store organised like table 2.1. Will this distributed, connectionist memory system find them any easier?

With the aid of the bottom part of figure 2.2 it is possible to get some idea of what happens when the system runs. To see what answer the system will retrieve when it is asked: 'Can you remember the name of a pusher?' the *Pusher* node is activated. This activity passes along all the connections from the *Pusher* node. So the *Ralph* and *Art* **Person** nodes become excited because there is a positive connection to them from *Pusher*. (In the real model all the **Person** nodes of pushers would be excited. For simplicity we will just follow two of them.) The *Bookie* and *Burglar* nodes become inhibited because there are negative connections to them from *Pusher*. In the next processing cycle the *Ralph* **Name**, *Jet*, *30s*, *JH*, *Single* and *Pusher* nodes are excited by the *Ralph* **Person** node, and the *Art* **Name**, *Jet*, *40s*, *JH*, *Single* and *Pusher* nodes become excited by the *Art* **Person** node. At each succeeding cycle every node which is active influences every node to which it is connected by an amount which depends on its activity level and in a direction which depends on whether the connection between them is excitatory or inhibitory. So, for example, the fact that the *30s* node is excited by the *Ralph* **Person** node will in turn cause excitation of all the **Person** nodes connected to *30s*, and inhibition of the *20s* and *40s* **Age** nodes. At the same time the excitation of the *40s* **Age** node by the *Art* **Person** node may be sufficient to overcome

---

[4]In McClelland's model the activity of each unit also decays on each cycle by an amount proportional to its activity level. This affects the dynamic behaviour of the net but to understand why the net reaches a steady state it can be considered as another negative input contributing to the balance between positive and negative inputs to each unit.

this and cause excitation of all **Person** nodes connected to *40s* and the inhibition of the *30s* and *20s* **Age** nodes. After several processing cycles the activity level of every node in the system is being influenced by a mixture of positive and negative inputs. Obviously it soon becomes impossible to keep track of the patterns of excitation and inhibition and predict whether the system will reach a stable state, and if so, what will be excited and what depressed. The only way to find out what the system will do in response to stimulation of any of its nodes is to run a computer simulation of the whole system.

It should now be clear that a connectionist memory system is totally unlike a conventional memory such as a computer filing system. In a conventional system independent pieces of information are stored separately. When a specific piece of information is accessed, it and it alone is retrieved. But in a distributed connectionist system, an attempt to extract any information from the system leads to a flow of excitation and inhibition throughout the system to everything which has any relation to this information. This results in many different nodes becoming active. What is retrieved is the information which corresponds to the most active node(s) once this flow has stabilised. If one is accustomed to information retrieval from a con-ventional, non-connectionist system such as a telephone directory, this might seem very odd. If you looked up Tom Brown's number in a connectionist telephone directory the number retrieved would be influenced by the entries of everyone with a similar name or a similar number to Tom's. This would not be useful. You do not want the number retrieved to be influenced by the fact that there happens to be someone called Tim Brown who has a telephone number quite unlike Tom's. You want the information stored at the location with the address 'Tom Brown' and nothing else. But the interference which a connectionist system allows during retrieval between related items of stored information turns out to have some interesting and useful properties.

(4) Content-addressable memory in Jets and Sharks. To see whether this memory system allows access by content, we can ask it the question 'Do you know the name of a pusher?'. To do this we activate the *Pusher* node, leave it on, and see which **Name** nodes becomes activated. Figure 2.3 shows the activity level of three of the **Name** nodes as a function of the number of processing cycles for which the system has been allowed to run. All the pushers names initially become activated. Most of them, like *Oliver*, quickly return to their resting level. But *Fred* and *Nick* both become increasingly activated. After about 50 cycles *Fred* starts to dominate and soon the system enters a stable state with *Fred* activated and all the other names back at their resting level. The system answers the question with the reply: 'Err... Fred.' So, unlike the storage system of table 2.1, this system *does* allow information to be retrieved when it has been accessed by content rather than address.

The relative activity of the name *Fred* compared to the name *Nick* over the last 50

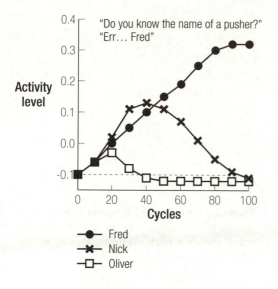

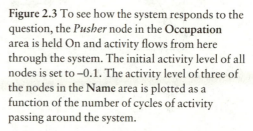

Figure 2.3 To see how the system responds to the question, the *Pusher* node in the **Occupation** area is held On and activity flows from here through the system. The initial activity level of all nodes is set to –0.1. The activity level of three of the nodes in the **Name** area is plotted as a function of the number of cycles of activity passing around the system.

cycles demonstrates an important characteristic of models with mutual inhibition between competing responses. When alternatives are equally activated they inhibit each other equally and everything is balanced. But once one gets ahead it inhibits the others more than they inhibit it. This reduces their activity and thus the extent to which they inhibit the one which is ahead. So it becomes more active and inhibits the others yet more. This rapidly results in the one that is a little more active consolidating its position in the lead and completely inhibiting the alternatives. The effect is sometimes referred to as 'the rich get richer' or 'winner takes all'.

Building positive feedback into the system in this way makes it likely that the system will quickly come to a definite conclusion, even if the difference between the evidence favouring one alternative rather than the other is small. But it makes the decision process vulnerable to noise. A random disturbance may be magnified and treated as a signal. This would generally be considered a drawback in a decision making system but it has one useful consequence. Figure 2.3 suggests that the system would always answer the question 'Do you know a pusher?' with the reply 'Fred'. If so, it would be an indifferent model of human memory. People would give a different answer to this question on different occasions, or if asked for an alternative answer, could provide the names of other pushers. It is straightforward to achieve this response variability with the model. If random noise is added to the starting activity levels the system will produce a different answer. Positive feedback ensures that a node that gets ahead is likely to consolidate its advantage. So a small change in starting conditions, or during processing, can make a radical difference to the outcome. Figure 2.4 shows the result of setting the initial activity level of Nick's **Person** node to −0.07 rather than −0.1 before activating the *Pusher* node. Now the system answers the question 'Do you know a pusher?' with the reply 'Err...Nick'.

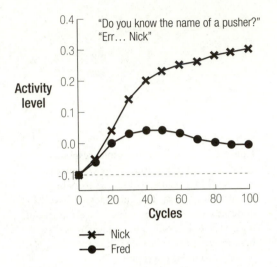

Figure 2.4 The effect of adding noise to the activity levels before asking the question. The initial activity of Nick's **Person** node is set to –0.07 rather than –0.1.

Given that we know the brain is a noisy system, it is appropriate to model it with an inherently noisy network. The result is the human characteristic of variability in response to the same input.

(5) Typicality effects in memory retrieval. If the information about the Jets and Sharks was stored in the manner of table 2.1 it would not be possible to retrieve the names of pushers directly, because pusher is not part of the address. But the information could be extracted by sampling addresses at random and giving the names of ones that turned out to contain the information *Pusher* under **Occupation**. In that case any pusher would have an equal chance of being produced as an example. But this is not how the network behaves when asked to name pushers. As figure 2.3 shows, it is more likely to retrieve the names of some pushers than others. It might retrieve Fred or Nick, but it is unlikely to produce Oliver's name.

Human memory retrieval has the same characteristic (see, for example, Rosch 1975). If you ask people to produce a list of birds (the equivalent of asking the network 'Tell me the names of all the pushers you know') most people will include Robin in their list but fewer will include Chicken. Some information is more easily available for retrieval from memory than other information from the same category. Since the answers which are most likely to be given to this question are the names of birds which would be rated as *typical* examples of the category, this result is called, unsurprisingly, a typicality effect.

The reason why the network is likely to retrieve Fred rather than Oliver in reply to the request for the name of a pusher can be seen in table 2.2. Pushers are more likely to be a Jet than a Shark, they tend to be in their 30s, to have been educated to High School level and to be single. So the **Person** nodes which get excited when *Pusher* is activated send more activity to the *Jet, 30s, HS* and *Single* nodes than to other nodes.

Table 2.2 The pushers

Gang	*Jets*	*Sharks*		
	5	4		
Age	*20s*	*30s*	*40s*	
	3	5	1	
Education	*JH*	*HS*	*College*	
	2	4	3	
Marital status	*Single*	*Married*	*Divorced*	
	5	3	1	
The prototypical pusher:	*Jet*	*30s*	*HS*	*Single*
Fred	Jet	20s	HS	Single
Nick	Shark	30s	HS	Single
Oliver	Shark	30s	Col	Married

The mutual inhibition between alternative instance nodes with an area means that *Single*, *HS* and *Jet* become more activated, and *Married*, *College* and *Shark* become less activated. This in turn means that the **Person** nodes connected to *Single*, *HS* and *Jet* get supported, and the **Name** nodes connected to these become activated but the **Person** nodes and hence the **Name** nodes connected to *Married*, *College* and *Shark* do not. Fred is a single, High School educated, Jet; Oliver is a married, College educated, Shark. So, as a result of Fred's similarity to a *prototypical* pusher, his **Person** and **Name** nodes become more and more active as processing continues. Oliver's dissimilarity to the prototypical pusher means that his become less and less active. The result is that when the system is asked to think of a pusher, Fred's name is retrieved but Oliver's is not. If asked to generate instances from a category, distributed connectionist nets automatically generate typical instances, just like people.

Constraint satisfaction in connectionist networks

When activity flows through a connectionist network in response to an input, each unit influences the state of all the units to which it is connected. If the connection weight is positive the sending unit tries to put the receiving unit into the same state of activity as itself; if the connection weight is negative it tries to put it into the opposite state. Since all activity changes are determined by these influences, each input can be seen as setting constraints on the final state (i.e. set of unit activities) which the system can settle into. When the system runs, the activities of individual units will change in a way which increases the number of these constraints which are satisfied. Thus connectionist networks are said to work by *constraint satisfaction*.

The ideal final state would be a set of activities for the individual units where all the constraints were satisfied. The network would then be stable because no unit would be trying to change the state of any of the units to which it was connected. This ideal solution is unlikely to exist because most units are connected to some units which are trying to increase its activity and others which are trying to reduce it. There is no way of satisfying both. But if the system can find a state in which any change in the activity levels of the units reduces the overall number of satisfied constraints, it will stop changing activities. That is, it will have found a stable state. For most networks there will be many possible stable states with a different pattern of activity, each one of which will be reached from a different pattern of input activity. The realisation that these stable states could be viewed as the network's memories—that is, the set of possible states that it could reach in response to different inputs—was an important step in the history of connectionism which will be discussed further in chapter 15.

In a conventional connectionist network where knowledge is distributed across many units, it is difficult to follow constraint satisfaction at work because it is difficult to see what role any particular unit is playing. In Jets and Sharks it is easy, because the concept coding is localist rather than distributed. Each node stands for an identifiable concept. The constraints on the system are the various facts in table 2.1, each one of which is represented by one of the links in the network. The fact that Clyde is a Jet in his 40s means that if either of the nodes representing these concepts is activated it will try to activate the other, and inhibit the *Shark*, *30s* and *20s* nodes. The fact that there are also both Jets and Sharks in their 30s and 20s means that a whole set of other, mutually contradictory constraints are influencing the way that the system changes the activity level of the units in response to any particular pattern of input. The key point is that the changes in activity on each cycle will increase the number of constraints which are satisfied.

A system which works by constraint satisfaction has a number of desirable characteristics for modelling human cognition. The main one is that it allows a decision to be reached by a consensus of evidence, a reasonable fit between input and memory, rather than requiring an exact match. We have already seen this as a virtue in any model of human cognition because the nature of the nervous system requires a degree of fault tolerance in the information processing system (remember figure 2.1). It is also desirable because of the nature of the input which the cognitive system has to work with in the real world. Consider what happens when you listen to one particular speaker in a crowded room. The signals arriving at your ear contain the sounds made by the person you are listening to, but superimposed on these are a jumble of sounds from different speakers, the whole thing obliterated from time to time by bursts of laughter and other noises. And yet, most of the time, what you perceive is words. The signal you receive bears *some* relationship to a prototypical representation of the word that you perceive but will be far from an exact match. The fact that you *perceive* words shows that the word recognition system must be looking for a *best fit* to the word patterns it has stored rather than for an exact match. This effect has been studied in the laboratory with an experimental paradigm called 'phoneme restoration'. In the original study by Warren (1970) the sound /s/ was removed from the word '*legislature*' and replaced with a cough. People then listened to a sentence containing the word '*legi<cough>lature*' and were asked what they heard. People reported the sentence correctly, adding that there was a cough before or after the word 'legislature'. In other words, the perceptual system does not necessarily give a veridical account of the stimulus, it gives a plausible *interpretation* of the input, given its knowledge of English words.

The same effect can be seen in the Jets and Sharks system. Figure 2.5 shows what happens when the system is probed with a variety of retrieval cues. The filled circles show what happens when the net is asked: 'Do you know a Shark, in his 20s, who went to High School, who is single and a burglar?' (i.e. the *Shark, 20s, HS, Single* and *Burglar* nodes are all switched On). The circles joined by solid lines show the activity of Ken's **Name** node and the circles joined by dashed lines the activity of the next most activated **Name** node. Not surprisingly, the net answers 'Ken' quickly.

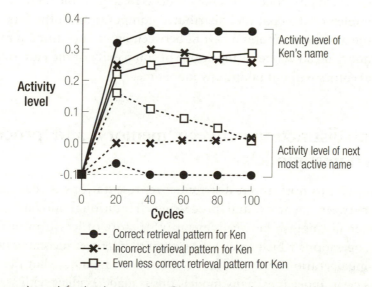

Figure 2.5 Constraint satisfaction in operation. Given a correct description of Ken as a retrieval cue, the system retrieves Ken's name. Given progressively less accurate retrieval cues, which are, nevertheless, closer to a description of him than to anyone else in the database, it still produces his name. Input activity levels:
($\bullet$) *Shark* = 1; *20s* = 1; *HS* = 1; *Single* = 1; *Burglar* = 1.
($\times$) *Shark* = 1; *20s* = 1; *JH* = 1; *Single* = 1; *Burglar* = 1.
($\square$) *Shark* = 1; *20s* = 1; *JH* = 1; *Single* = 1; *Burglar* = 0.5; *Pusher* = 0.25; *Bookie* = 0.25.

This is the equivalent of presenting a listener with a clear and unambiguous example of the word 'legislature' and asking her what word she heard. The crosses show what happens when *High School* is changed to *Junior High* in the input activity pattern. This input is no longer an accurate description of anyone in the database (the equivalent of presenting a listener with '*legi*<cough>*lature*'). A system which tried to find an exact match to the input would fail. There is no person who matches that input pattern in the database. But the network has no problem. It takes slightly longer to respond (i.e. Ken's name takes more time to become activated, and does not reach such a high level) but *Ken* still comes out as the clearly preferred item retrieved from memory. The squares show what happens with an even more ambiguous input. In this the *Bookie* and *Pusher* nodes have all been activated as well as *Burglar*. As long as the input pattern is closer to a description of Ken than to any alternative, the system makes a clear decision in favour of the response 'Ken'[5].

The fact that connectionist systems work by constraint satisfaction is the reason why they exhibit fault tolerance. No part of the input uniquely determines the outcome. The network's response is the best fit it can make between the current input and information it has acquired in the past. It would be possible to devise a system, based on address + contents information storage like table 2.1, which, if given an input that failed to match any stored information, could compute a best fit. However, this would be a time consuming process once possible inputs achieved any degree of complexity. The parallel distributed computation in the Jets and Sharks database automatically computes a best fit between input and stored information. It would continue to do so whatever the degree of complexity of the patterns describing the individual entries without taking any more time.

There is no distinction between 'memory' and 'processing' in connectionist models

One general point to note about distributed representations is that they blur the distinction between memory and processing. Traditional models of cognitive processes often distinguish between 'memory', a store of learnt information, and 'processing', operations which enable the system to interpret incoming information. The processing operations may use information from memory, but the conceptual distinction is clear. Indeed, in many models this is made explicit with separate parts of the model labelled 'memory' and 'processor'. Such models exploit the analogy to

---

[5]The interaction of information in the Jets and Sharks system produces some strange and unpredictable results which can only be appreciated by playing with the iac model. For example, figure 2.5 shows that if you wait long enough the *less* accurate description of Ken produces a stronger preference for his name than the more accurate description.

conventional digital computers where there are independent systems for storing information and for processing it.

There is no such distinction in connectionist models. All the information which the network has—its memory—is stored in the weights of the connections between units. All the processing that the net can do is determined by the same set of weights.

Problems for distributed representations

We have emphasised the advantage of distributed representations over localist representations in allowing the system some degree of resistance to damage and tolerance of noisy inputs. Given the unreliable nature of the matter which the brain uses for computation, it seems inevitable that it would use distributed representations. However, there are two properties of human memory which would not seem to be easy to account for with connectionist models but which would be expected with localist information storage: First, the addition of new information does not necessarily cause the loss of old. Second, learning can be immediate.

In a distributed system, any new information has to be added to the connections which already carry the system's current store of knowledge. To add the new information the strength of connections must be changed. If this is done in a single trial, addition of new information is likely to lead to some loss of old information. In a localist system, in contrast, the addition of new information is no problem. It is simply added to new storage locations and does not affect old information. At this point, however, we will just suggest that at an intuitive level there are different sorts of human learning.

At one extreme it seems clear that some sorts of knowledge can be acquired immediately, without interfering with other information. All young chess players are shown the smothered mate sequence with a queen sacrificed to a rook on g1 followed by mate of the king on h1 by a knight moving from h3 to f2. If you understand chess you only have to see this sequence once to remember it for ever, despite the fact that you may never have an opportunity to use it in a game. Similarly, if you knew anything about the British ex-Prime Minister Mrs Thatcher, and were told that her nickname at school was 'Bossy Roberts', you would be unlikely to forget it. A novel piece of information which you find interesting or amusing, in a domain where you already have sufficient knowledge to understand its significance, is likely to be remembered after a single presentation. And it can be retrieved as a specific item of information in future, independent of any other facts in the database. It is difficult to believe that such acquisition is accompanied by the loss of any other information. Quick, cost-free, addition of new information to existing databases characterises certain sorts of human knowledge acquisition. It is natural with localist representation of knowledge—you just add another entry to the database. But it is difficult to see how it can happen with a distributed system. (That connectionist models *can* perform one trial learning will be shown in chapter 13 which demonstrates a model of the role of the hippocampus in episodic memory formation.)

At the other extreme there are many areas of knowledge acquisition, such as learning to play tennis or learning to talk, where acquisition of new knowledge is gradual, and accompanied by the modification or loss of previous patterns. As your tennis serve improves or you learn to pronounce the language correctly you *want* to lose some aspects of your old response patterns because they were inaccurate. Later it is difficult to recall when a specific piece of information was added to the database. Such a pattern, where new information is inextricably interwoven with old, occurs naturally with a distributed system, but not with a localist one. Distinctions between different sorts of knowledge representation occur in many models of the cognitive system. Most of the connectionist learning algorithms we will look at are more appropriate for modelling the latter sort of acquisition and representation than the former.

3 *Pattern association*

This chapter will introduce the architecture and properties of one specific kind of network, a pattern associator, and the operation of one particular learning rule, the Hebb rule. During training a pattern associator is presented with pairs of patterns. If learning is successful then the network will subsequently recall one of the patterns at output when the other is presented at input. After training, a pattern associator can also respond to novel inputs, generalising from its experience with similar patterns. Pattern associators are tolerant of noisy input and resistant to internal damage. They are capable of extracting the central tendency or prototype from a set of similar examples.

The first two chapters introduced general principles which are shared by all connectionist networks. In this and the next four chapters we will look in detail at the structure and properties of a variety of specific network architectures: pattern associators, autoassociators, competitive nets and recurrent nets. Networks can be trained in a variety of ways. In this chapter we will look at one particular learning rule, the Hebb rule. In chapter 4 we will look at the Delta rule and in chapter 5 at backpropagation.

The examples and the networks in these early chapters have deliberately been kept very simple so that the principles involved in their operation can be seen at work. It may seem that the problems they solve are so trivial that they have little to do with human cognition. Don't worry. In chapters 8–14 we will look at networks which have been scaled up to the point where they can simulate realistic aspects of human behaviour. For example, in chapter 8 we will look at a model with roughly 1000 processing units and 200 000 connections which learns to pronounce all the monosyllabic words in the English language. In chapter 13 we will look at a model of episodic memory formation in the hippocampus with about 4000 processing units and about half a million connections. Exactly the same principles will be at work in these networks as in the examples which follow.

The architecture and operation of a pattern associator

A fundamental task for the nervous system is to discover the structure of the world by finding what is correlated with what. That is, to learn to associate one stimulus with another. For example, one stimulus might be the taste of chocolate and the other its appearance. Initially there is no connection between these two for a child. After the association between the patterns of neural firing caused by the two stimuli has been made, the sight of chocolate can recall responses originally associated with its taste. If the taste of chocolate caused salivation, then the sight of chocolate, which was initially neutral, could produce the same response. This form of pattern association was made famous by Pavlov and his dogs in some of the earliest investigations in experimental psychology. But similar mechanisms underlie far more than the control of autonomic nervous system responses like salivation. Learning that the letter string YACHT is pronounced /y/ /o/ /t/, that Mary has blonde hair or how hard you have to push the steering wheel of a car when you want to go round a corner are all examples of pattern association.

A pattern association network

A simple network which can perform pattern association is shown in figure 3.1. The upper network is drawn as a stylised version of a real neural network with axons from two sets of neurons synapsing onto the dendrites of a third. The lower figure is drawn in the standard format for a connectionist network, with two sets of computational units joined by weighted connections. These two ways of representing a pattern association network may look quite different but they perform exactly the same task. They are simply notational variants. By showing them together, the way that two different conventions represent what a network might compute should become clear.

   In the network in figure 3.1(a), the horizontal rectangular bars represent the dendrites of a set of neurons labelled r_{1-4}. During learning two patterns are presented to the network simultaneously. The first pattern is the output of a set of neurons which represents, say, the taste of chocolate. In figure 3.1(a) this pattern (P_1) is (1 1 0 0). It reaches the dendrites of neurons r_{1-4} via unmodifiable synapses (represented by the symbol ——<), forcing the neurons r_{1-4} into the same pattern of firing (1 1 0 0). The second pattern, P_2 (1 0 1 0 1 0), is the output of a set of neurons which represents the sight of chocolate. This reaches r_{1-4} along the axons shown by the vertical lines running downwards across the dendrites. This input connects to the dendrites of neurons r_{1-4} through the modifiable synapses represented by the black blobs. The synapse between axon j and dendrite i is w_{ij}. Learning (i.e. forming the association between P_1 and P_2) takes place by modification of these synapses.

   The process of pattern association in a single layer connectionist network (i.e. one with a single layer of modifiable connections between input and output) is shown in figure 3.1(b). P_2 (1 0 1 0 1 0) is presented to the input units. P_1 (1 1 0 0) is the pattern which the net has to learn to produce on the output units in response to the input of

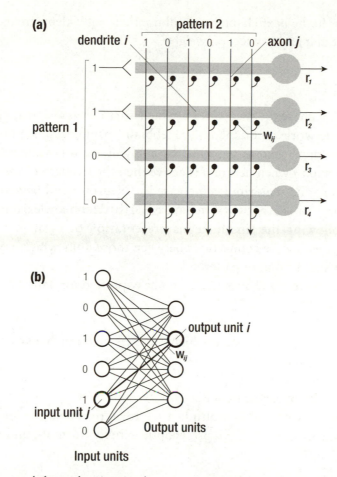

Figure 3.1 A network for performing simple pattern association. (a) The network is represented as it might appear in the nervous system with axons synapsing onto dendrites of cells r_1 to r_4. (b) The network is shown in the conventional connectionist format with an input presented to one set of units (indexed by j) producing an output on another set indexed by i.

P_2. The connection between input unit j and output unit i is represented by the line labelled w_{ij}. Pattern association takes place by modifying the strength of the connections between input units and output units.

The differences between these two ways of representing the same process should be carefully noted: First, the synapse at the junction of axon j and dendrite i in the upper figure has become a connecting line (shown in bold) between two processing units in the lower figure. Second, the way that pattern 1 reaches the network is explicit in the upper figure. In the lower figure it is a signal presented to the output units by an invisible 'teacher'. Despite these differences in presentation, the processes described are conceptually the same. In this chapter we will describe the process of learning with terms appropriate to figure 3.1(a)—axon, output neuron dendrite and synaptic strength. In the next chapter we will use their equivalents in figure 3.1(b)—input line, output unit and connection weight.

The Hebb rule

During the learning phase the two patterns which are to be associated, P_1 and P_2, are presented to the network simultaneously. Hebbian learning can be implemented in the network in the upper part of figure 3.1 by applying the following rule: If there is activity on input axon j when neuron i is active then the strength of the connection, w_{ij}, between axon j and dendrite i is increased.[1] (Neuron i will be active if the ith axon in P_1 is On.) In the network in figure 3.1(b) Hebbian learning would be implemented, following the simultaneous presentation of P_2 at input and P_1 at output, by strengthening the connections between those units which are On in both the input pattern and the output pattern.

The Hebb rule for weight change (Δw_{ij}) can be expressed formally as:

$$\Delta w_{ij} = \varepsilon \, a_i \, a_j \tag{3.1}$$

where ε is a learning rate constant which specifies how much a synapse alters on any one pairing of P_1 and P_2,

a_i is the activity of element i in P_1,

and a_j is the activity of element j in P_2.

The Hebb rule is expressed in multiplicative form to reflect the idea that, for a synapse to increase in strength, both presynaptic activity (from P_2) and postsynaptic activity (from P_1) must be present.

Learning with the Hebb rule

The following simple examples will demonstrate the basic principles of the operation of a pattern associator. They will show how the weight changes brought about by applying Hebbian learning give rise to some surprising and biologically useful properties. For simplicity the neurons will be treated as binary with an activity of 0 or 1.

A four neuron pattern associator with six input axons carrying P_2 and four input axons carrying P_1 is represented in figure 3.2. The sight of chocolate is represented by P_2 (1 0 1 0 1 0) and the taste by P_1 (1 1 0 0). The 6×4 weight matrix in figure 3.2 corresponds directly to the 6×4 matrix of synapses in figure 3.1(a). The first row of weights in figure 3.2 shows the strength of the connections from axons 1 to 6 of P_2 to

---

[1]That such an operation could be the basis for useful learning in neural structures was first suggested by the neurophysiologist Donald Hebb, hence Hebbian learning. Hebb's contribution to connectionism will be described in chapter 15.

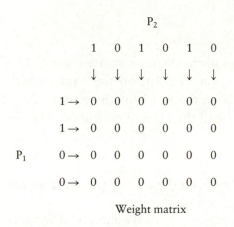

Weight matrix

Figure 3.2   The weight matrix in the pattern associator before learning takes place.

output neuron 1. Their equivalents in the network in figure 3.1(b) are the connections from the six input units to output unit 1. The second row of weights in figure 3.2 shows the connections from the six input axons in P_2 to output neuron 2; these are represented in figure 3.1(b) by the connections to the second output unit from the six input units, and so on. The synaptic weights are initially all 0 because no learning has yet occurred.

After pairing P_1 and P_2 for one learning trial, the synaptic weights are incremented according to the Hebb rule expressed in equation 3.1. That is, every synapse which connects an active axon in P_2 to an active dendrite will be strengthened. So, for example, the 1st, 3rd and 5th weights in the first row are incremented because the first element in P_1 and the 1st, 3rd and 5th elements in P_2 are all active. But the weights in the third row are not incremented because the third element in P_1 is inactive. Similarly the weights in the second column are not incremented because the second element in P_2 is inactive. The overall result following a single learning trial is shown in figure 3.3 (if $\varepsilon = 1$).

$$
\begin{array}{c}
\ \ P_2 \\
\ 1\ \ 0\ \ 1\ \ 0\ \ 1\ \ 0 \\
\ \downarrow\ \downarrow\ \downarrow\ \downarrow\ \downarrow\ \downarrow \\
1\rightarrow\ 1\ \ 0\ \ 1\ \ 0\ \ 1\ \ 0 \\
1\rightarrow\ 1\ \ 0\ \ 1\ \ 0\ \ 1\ \ 0 \\
0\rightarrow\ 0\ \ 0\ \ 0\ \ 0\ \ 0\ \ 0 \\
0\rightarrow\ 0\ \ 0\ \ 0\ \ 0\ \ 0\ \ 0
\end{array}
$$

P_1

Weight matrix

Figure 3.3   Weight matrix after one learning trial pairing (1 1 0 0) and (1 0 1 0 1 0).

Recall from a Hebb trained matrix

When learning has taken place, the effectiveness of the memory created is tested by presenting a recall pattern (P_R) to the matrix, on its own, on the axons which originally carried P_2. The consequence should be the recall of the pattern P_1 at output. That is, the sight of chocolate should recall the taste of chocolate. The net input to output neuron i is:

$$\text{netinput}_i = \Sigma_j \, a_j \, w_{ij} \qquad (3.2)$$

Σ_j indicates that the sum is over all the input axons indexed by j (i.e. over all the axons in P_R).

To discover what happens during recall we present P_R to the matrix of weights which were acquired on the learning trial. The net input to the four output neurons is found by applying the operation defined in equation 3.2 to each neuron in turn. That is, the activity on each of the input lines to neuron i is multiplied by the weight of the corresponding synapse and these products are summed down the dendrite. So, if the recall cue (1 0 1 0 1 0) is presented to the weight matrix in figure 3.3, the net input to neuron 1 will be $(1 \times 1 + 0 \times 0 + 1 \times 1 + 0 \times 0 + 1 \times 1 + 0 \times 0) = 3$ (figure 3.4).

The resulting pattern of net input to r_{1-4} is (3 3 0 0). If the output neurons have a binary threshold activation function (see figure 1.4(d) in chapter 1) with a threshold of 2, and we set the activity level of the neuron to 1 if it exceeds the threshold and 0 if it does not, then the output activity pattern is (1 1 0 0). Thus the pattern associator has correctly recalled P_1 when P_2 is presented as a recall cue.

Learning different associations on the same weight matrix

Application of the Hebb rule strengthens every connection between an axon and a dendrite where both are active. At recall that connection is then used to activate the

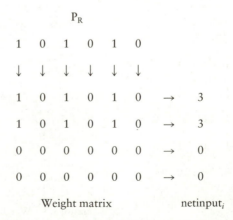

P_R

1	0	1	0	1	0		
↓	↓	↓	↓	↓	↓		
1	0	1	0	1	0	→	3
1	0	1	0	1	0	→	3
0	0	0	0	0	0	→	0
0	0	0	0	0	0	→	0

Weight matrix   netinput$_i$

Figure 3.4 Recall from the matrix after presentation of the pattern (1 0 1 0 1 0).

$$P_2$$

		1	1	0	0	0	1
		↓	↓	↓	↓	↓	↓
	0 →	0	0	0	0	0	0
	1 →	1	1	0	0	0	1
P_1	0 →	0	0	0	0	0	0
	1 →	1	1	0	0	0	1

Weight matrix

Figure 3.5   Weights acquired during one learning trial pairing (0 1 0 1) and (1 1 0 0 0 1).

dendrite when the axon in the recall cue is active. So it is hardly surprising that the pattern associator is capable of retrieving a pattern which was presented during the learning phase. But what happens if we try to store different associations on the same matrix? Can they still be recalled correctly or will they interfere?

Let us use the Hebb rule to store the association between the appearance and taste of apricots on the same connections. In this case P_1 is (0 1 0 1) and P_2 is (1 1 0 0 0 1). Equation 3.1 shows that the weights acquired by applying the Hebb rule during this learning trial will be as shown in figure 3.5.

Superimposing the weights acquired during learning to associate the taste and appearance of apricots on those acquired learning to associate the taste and appearance of chocolate (i.e. summing the weight matrices in figures 3.3 and 3.5) produces the combined weight matrix shown in figure 3.6.

The crucial test now is to see what happens when we present each P_2 in turn as a recall cue to the combined weight matrix. Presenting (1 1 0 0 0 1) produces the result (1 4 0 3) as shown in figure 3.7.

With the binary output thresholds set to 2 the activity pattern (0 1 0 1) is produced on the output neurons. So recall is correct. The appearance of apricots recalls the taste of apricots. If the pattern (1 0 1 0 1 0) is presented to the combined matrix the result will be as shown in figure 3.8.

With the threshold set at 2, the activity pattern (1 1 0 0) is produced. Thus the

1	0	1	0	1	0
2	1	1	0	1	1
0	0	0	0	0	0
1	1	0	0	0	1

Weight matrix

Figure 3.6   The combined weight matrix after learning two different P_1, P_2 pairs.

P_R

1	1	0	0	0	1

↓   ↓   ↓   ↓   ↓   ↓

1	0	1	0	1	0	→	1
2	1	1	0	1	1	→	4
0	0	0	0	0	0	→	0
1	1	0	0	0	1	→	3

Weight matrix   netinput$_i$

Figure 3.7 The result of presenting the recall cue (1 1 0 0 0 1) to the combined weight matrix.

P_R

1	0	1	0	1	0

↓   ↓   ↓   ↓   ↓   ↓

1	0	1	0	1	0	→	3
2	1	1	0	1	1	→	4
0	0	0	0	0	0	→	0
1	1	0	0	0	1	→	1

Weight matrix   netinput$_i$

Figure 3.8 Recall from the combined matrix with the cue (1 0 1 0 1 0).

appearance of chocolate still recalls the taste of chocolate even though the same connections are now also storing the association of the appearance and taste of apricots.

This simple demonstration shows that accurate recall of different associations from a pattern associator trained with the Hebb rule is possible even when the associations are stored on the same connections. However, with only two associations some interference between the patterns is already apparent—the recalled patterns do not exactly match the original patterns. In this example the differences have been removed by the threshold setting of the activation function. But there will obviously be a limit to the number of associations which can be stored in such a matrix before interference between the patterns becomes a problem. The effect of increasing the number of memories in a more realistic pattern associator will be explored in the section on the simulation of episodic memory formation in the hippocampus in chapter 13.

Recall reflects the similarity of retrieval pattern and stored patterns

Many operations within a connectionist network can be understood by treating the input patterns as vectors and the weights in the network as a matrix. To make connectionism accessible to the non-mathematical reader we have avoided explanations in terms of vectors. However, there is one crucial result, which explains retrieval in pattern associators (and also the operation of competitive networks described in chapter 6) that is most easily understood in terms of vector operations.[2] Before we can have the result we need the concept of the *dot product* (or *inner product*) of two vectors. A vector is an ordered set of numbers, such as [2 0 1 3]. The dot product of two vectors is found by taking the sum of the products of the numbers in equivalent positions in the two vectors. That is, the sum of the product of the first number in vector 1 and the first number in vector 2, the product of the second number in each vector and so on. If vector 1 was [2 0 1 3] and vector 2 was [1 1 0 4], the dot product would be $(2 \times 1 + 0 \times 1 + 1 \times 0 + 4 \times 3) = 14$.

The set of activities which constitute an input to a network is an ordered set of numbers. So they can be treated as the vector **p**. The activities are represented in equation 3.2 by a_j. An example is the set of activities [1 0 1 0 1 0] on the input lines representing the appearance of chocolate. The weights of the connections between the input and output neuron i, represented in equation 3.2 by w_{ij}, are another ordered set of numbers. So they can also be treated as a vector, $\mathbf{w}_i$. An example is the set of weights to output neuron 2 in the joint matrix in the previous example, [2 1 1 0 1 1]. Equation 3.2 shows that the net input to output neuron i is found by summing the product of the first activity in the input pattern and the first weight on the dendrite of output neuron i ($a_1 w_{i1}$), the second activity in the input pattern and the second weight ($a_2 w_{i2}$), and so on until the products of all pairs of activities and weights have been summed. So netinput$_i$ is the dot product of the vector representing the input pattern and the vector representing the weights of the connections from each input line to output neuron i.

The crucial result is this: For any given set of numbers representing the activities in one vector and the weights in the other, the more similar the numbers in vector 1 are to the numbers *in the corresponding positions* in vector 2, the larger will be the dot

---

[2]A more detailed analysis is given in Appendix 2. What follows is a simplification intended to help the understanding of a general result.

product. An intuitive grasp of the result can be obtained by taking the dot products of a set of vectors with 12 binary bits (1 or 0), half on and half off. Imagine that **p** is an input pattern vector and $\mathbf{w}_1$, $\mathbf{w}_2$, $\mathbf{w}_3$ and $\mathbf{w}_4$ are the vectors representing the weights on output units 1–4; $\mathbf{w}_1$ is identical to **p**; $\mathbf{w}_2$, $\mathbf{w}_3$ and $\mathbf{w}_4$ have patterns which are increasingly less like **p**:

    1 0 0 0 0 0 0 1 1 1 1 1 **p**
    1 0 0 0 0 0 0 1 1 1 1 1 $\mathbf{w}_1$
    0 1 0 0 0 0 1 0 1 1 1 1 $\mathbf{w}_2$
    0 0 1 1 1 1 0 1 1 0 0 0 $\mathbf{w}_3$
    0 1 1 1 1 1 1 0 0 0 0 0 $\mathbf{w}_4$

The dot product is taken by summing the product of corresponding elements in the two vectors. So where there is a 1 in the equivalent position on the two vectors, 1 will be added to the dot product; when there is a 1 in one vector and a 0 in the equivalent position in the other, nothing will be added. So the maximum dot product will be obtained when the two vectors are identical (**p** and $\mathbf{w}_1$). It will have a value of 6, each positive element contributing 1 to the dot product. Every dissimilarity between the vectors reduces the dot product.[3] The dot product of **p** and $\mathbf{w}_2$, which are quite similar, is reduced to 4 because there are four bits in pattern $\mathbf{w}_2$ which do not match those in **p**. The dot product between **p** and $\mathbf{w}_3$, which have little in common, is reduced to 2. **p** and $\mathbf{w}_4$ have no elements in common so their dot product is 0. **p** and $\mathbf{w}_4$ are said to be *orthogonal*.

During recall each output neuron in a pattern associator computes the dot product between the input pattern and its weight vector. What this does is to compute how *similar* the input pattern vector **p** is to the weight vector $\mathbf{w}_i$ which is stored on its dendrite. If this similarity is great, netinput$_i$ will be large and the neuron will be turned On. If they are dissimilar, netinput$_i$ will be small and the neuron will remain Off. Hebbian learning increments weights between elements of P_1 and P_2 which are both On. Over a series of learning trials therefore, a cumulative record of the correlation between individual elements in the different pairs of patterns builds up in the weight matrix. Thus the operation of a pattern associator trained by the Hebb rule can be summed up in the following way:

Learning—if neuron i is activated by P_1, an increment $\Delta\mathbf{w}_i$, that has the same pattern as P_2, is added to the weight vector of neuron i.

Recall—since the patterns presented during learning determine the weight vector on neuron i, the output of neuron i at recall reflects the similarity of the recall cue to the patterns presented during learning.

---

[3]The dot product is not the only way to calculate the similarity of two vectors. For example, zero elements in corresponding positions will contribute to the similarity of two vectors but not to their dot product.

Properties of pattern associators

Generalisation

During recall, pattern associators generalise. That is, if a recall cue is similar to a pattern that has been learnt already, a pattern associator will produce a similar response to the new pattern as it would to the old. This occurs because the recall operation on each neuron involves computing the dot product of the recall vector $\mathbf{p}_R$ with the synaptic weight vector $\mathbf{w}_i$. The result, netinput$_i$, thus reflects the similarity of the current input to the previously learnt input patterns. Small differences in netinput$_i$ for similar input patterns can be removed by a threshold at output. In the world faced by real biological systems, recall cues are rarely identical to the patterns experienced during learning. So a mechanism which automatically generalises across slight differences in input pattern has obvious adaptive value.

Generalisation can be illustrated with the simple binary pattern associator we have considered already. What happens when it is presented with the recall cue (1 1 0 1 0 0) which is similar, but not identical, to the pattern (1 1 0 0 0 1) which it learnt before?

With a threshold set at 2, the output pattern (0 1 0 1) would be recalled in response to the cue (1 1 0 1 0 0) (figure 3.9) just as it was to the cue (1 1 0 0 0 1). The network has treated the new pattern as a noisy version of one it already knew, and reproduced the response it learnt to that. The sight of a slightly bruised apricot still recalls the taste of an apricot. Generalisation has occurred.

Fault tolerance

Even if some of the synapses on neuron i are damaged after learning, netinput$_i$ following the presentation of a recall cue may still be a good approximation to the

$$\mathbf{p}_R$$

1	1	0	1	0	0		
↓	↓	↓	↓	↓	↓		
1	0	1	0	1	0	→	1
2	1	1	0	1	1	→	3
0	0	0	0	0	0	→	0
1	1	0	0	0	1	→	2

Weight matrix   netinput$_i$

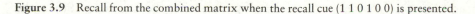

Figure 3.9 Recall from the combined matrix when the recall cue (1 1 0 1 0 0) is presented.

$$P_R$$

1	1	0	0	0	1		
↓	↓	↓	↓	↓	↓		
1	0	1	0	1	0	→	1
2	1	1	0	×	1	→	4
0	0	0	0	0	0	→	0
1	×	0	0	0	1	→	2

Weight matrix   netinput$_i$

Figure 3.10 Recall from a damaged matrix after presentation of the cue (1 1 0 0 0 1).

correct value. This is because netinput$_i$ represents the *correlation* of p_R with w_i. Provided the pattern carrying the recall cue consists of a reasonably large number of axons the correlation will not be greatly affected by a few missing items. After passing through the binary threshold activation function, the result may well be correct recall. The same result is achieved if some of the input axons carrying the recall cue are lost or damaged. Since real nervous systems are continually losing cells, fault tolerance is of great adaptive value.

We can illustrate this with the example shown in figure 3.10; x indicates a damaged synapse which now has no effect. Whatever information was stored in that synapse during learning has been lost. Presentation of the recall cue (1 1 0 0 0 1) to this matrix produces the net input pattern (1 4 0 2).

With the binary output threshold set to 2 this would produce the output pattern (0 1 0 1), the same as that produced by the complete matrix. The small difference between the net input to the output neurons produced by the damaged matrix and the complete one (shown in figure 3.7) illustrates graceful degradation. Minor damage will cause a small change in response to many inputs, rather than a total loss of some memories and no effect on others.

The importance of distributed representations for pattern associators

A distributed representation is one in which the activity of all the elements in the pattern is used to encode a particular stimulus. Comparing (1 0 1 0 1 0), (1 1 0 0 0 1) and the other P$_2$s which could be represented by a pattern of six 1s and 0s, we need to know the state of most of the elements to know which stimulus is being represented. No one element can be used to identify the stimulus. Since the information about which stimulus is present is distributed over the population of elements, this is called a distributed representation.

A *local representation* is one in which all the information about a particular stimulus is provided by the activity of one element in the pattern. One stimulus might be represented by the pattern (1 0 0 0 0 0), another by the pattern (0 1 0 0 0 0) and so on. The activity of element 1 would indicate that stimulus 1 was present, and of element 2 that stimulus 2 was present. If a particular element is active, we know that the stimulus represented by that element is present. If elements are taken to be equivalent to neurons, such coding is said to involve 'grandmother cells' because, in an extreme expression of localist coding, one neuron might represent a stimulus in the environment as complex and specific as one's grandmother. Where the activity of a number of cells must be taken into account in order to represent a stimulus the representation is described as using ensemble or distributed encoding.

The properties of generalisation and graceful degradation are only achieved if the representations are distributed. The recall operation involves computing the dot product of the input pattern vector p_R with the weight vector w_i. This only allows netinput$_i$ to reflect the *similarity* of the current input pattern to a previously learned input pattern if many elements of p_R are active. If local encoding were used [(1 0 0 0 0 0), (0 1 0 0 0 0) etc.] then a new p_R pattern would produce a dot product of either 1 or 0. Generalization and graceful degradation rely on a continuous range of dot products. They are dependent on distributed representations, for then the dot product can reflect *similarity* even when some elements of the vectors involved are altered.

Prototype extraction and noise removal

If a set of similar P_2s is paired with the same P_1 (e.g. a set of apricots which all look a little different are all associated with the taste of apricot) the weight vector becomes, with scaling, the average of the set of vectors appropriate for the individual P_2s. When tested at recall, the output of the memory is then best (i.e. the dot product is highest) to the *average* input pattern vector. If the average is thought of as a prototype, and the individual P_2s noisy exemplars of it, then even though the prototype vector itself may never have been seen, the strongest output of the network is to the prototype. Recognition of a prototype which has never been seen is a feature of human memory performance which will be explored in greater detail in chapter 4. This phenomenon is an automatic consequence of learning in a pattern associator with distributed representations.

Speed

Recall is very fast in a real neuronal network. The input firings which represent the recall cue P_R are applied simultaneously to the synapses, so netinput$_i$ can be accumulated in one or two time constants of the dendrite (e.g. 10–20 ms). If the threshold of the cell is exceeded, it fires. Thus in no more than a few tens of milliseconds all the output neurons of the pattern associator which will be turned On by a particular input pattern will be firing. The time taken to switch the output neurons On will be largely independent of the number of axons or dendrites in the pattern associator. This is very different from a conventional digital computer. Computing net input in equation 3.2 with one of these would involve successive multiplication and addition operations for each weight in the matrix. The time to compute the output pattern would increase in proportion to the product of the number of axons and the number of dendrites.

The pattern associator performs parallel computation in two senses. One is that for a single neuron, the separate contributions of the activity of each axon multiplied by the synaptic weight are computed in parallel and added simultaneously. The second is that this is performed in parallel for all neurons in the network. These types of neuronal network operate fast in the brain because they perform parallel processing.

Learning is also potentially fast in a pattern associator. A single pairing of P_1 and P_2 could, in principle, enable the association to be learnt. There is no need to repeat the pairing over many trials in order to discover the appropriate mapping. This is important for biological systems. A single co-occurrence of two events may provide the only opportunity to learn something which could have life-saving consequences. Although repeated pairing with small variations of the vectors produces the useful properties of prototype extraction and noise reduction, the properties of generalization and graceful degradation can be obtained with just one pairing. We will see one trial learning at work in the simulation of episodic memory formation in the hippocampus in chapter 13.

Interference is not necessarily a bad thing

In the elementary examples in this chapter we have demonstrated that independent events *can* be stored on the same connections of a distributed memory. However, it is obvious that there will be limitations on the number that can be stored without interference. Interference sounds like an undesirable property of a memory system. In the localised storage systems like computer discs and telephone directories which we are accustomed to, it *is* undesirable. So 'limitations to interference free storage' may sound like a problem. But remember that interference between responses to different but similar input patterns is the basis of many important properties of distributed memories. In this chapter we saw that it allowed generalisation, noise reduction and prototype extraction. In later chapters we will see how it enables a network to perform the generalisations which underlie many cognitive processes. The fact that interference is a property of connectionist pattern associator memories is of interest, for, unlike strictly localised forms of storage, interference is a major property of human memory. One reason that interference is tolerated in biological memory is presumably that the ability to generalize between stimuli is more useful than 100% accurate memory of specific past events.

Further reading

More detailed analysis of pattern associators and the Hebb rule can be found in Rolls and Treves (1997) and Hertz *et al*. (1991). Specific issues which go beyond the introductory account here are the types of pattern which can be easily learnt by one-layer pattern associators, the capacity of pattern associators trained with the Hebb rule and modifications to the Hebb rule which allow for decrease in synaptic weights as well as for increase.

Training a pattern associator with **tlearn**

Open the project called **pa** in the **Chapter Three** folder/directory. This project uses the **tlearn** network configuration file **pa.cf** that defines a network with 6 input units and 4 output units identical to that shown in figure 3.1(b). All the connections are set to zero. When you open the **pa** project, you will also open the **pa.data** and **pa.teach** files that will be used to train the network. These files are shown in figure 3.11. The two distributed data patterns defined in the **pa.data** file are those used to represent the appearance of chocolate and apricot earlier in the chapter. Similarly the two distributed teach patterns defined in the **pa.teach** file are those used to represent the taste of chocolate and apricot. You will use these files to train the network defined by the **pa.cf** file. You can confirm that you have the right network architecture by opening the Network Architecture display.

Training the network

In this exercise, you will train the network to associate the two sets of patterns described above. First, select Training Options… from the Network menu. The Training Options… dialogue box should appear as in figure 3.12. Set the number of training sweeps to 2 (we will train the network just once on each input pattern) and set the learning rate parameter to 10.0. If the other options in the dialogue box are not as shown, change them so they are. Now Train the network from the Network menu. The **tlearn** Status display will indicate when training is complete.

Testing the network

There are several ways to test whether the network has learnt the correct output patterns. First, open the Node Activities display as shown in figure 3.13. The top row

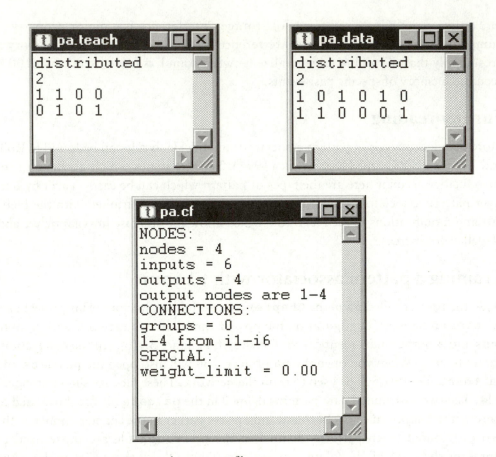

Figure 3.11 **pa.cf**, **pa.data** and **pa.teach** files.

represents the output units and the bottom row the input units. The size of the white squares indicates the level of activity of each unit. A grey square indicates no activity. The first input pattern, 1 0 1 0 1 0, should be displayed on the input units. If learning has been successful the output activities should correspond to the appropriate target for this input pattern, 1 1 0 0. Now click on Next Data Pattern. The second input pattern and its associated output are displayed. The input pattern is 1 1 0 0 0 1 and the correct output is 0 1 0 1. If these patterns are shown, the network has learnt to associate the correct inputs with the correct outputs.

Another way to test the network is to choose the Verify network has learned option from the Network menu. When you do this an Output window will be displayed as in figure 3.14. The two rows of numbers correspond to the activities of the 4 output nodes when the two input patterns are presented to the network. Notice that none of the activities is precisely 1.0 or 0.0. This is because we have used the non-linear sigmoid activation function for the output units shown in figure 1.4(c) of chapter 1.

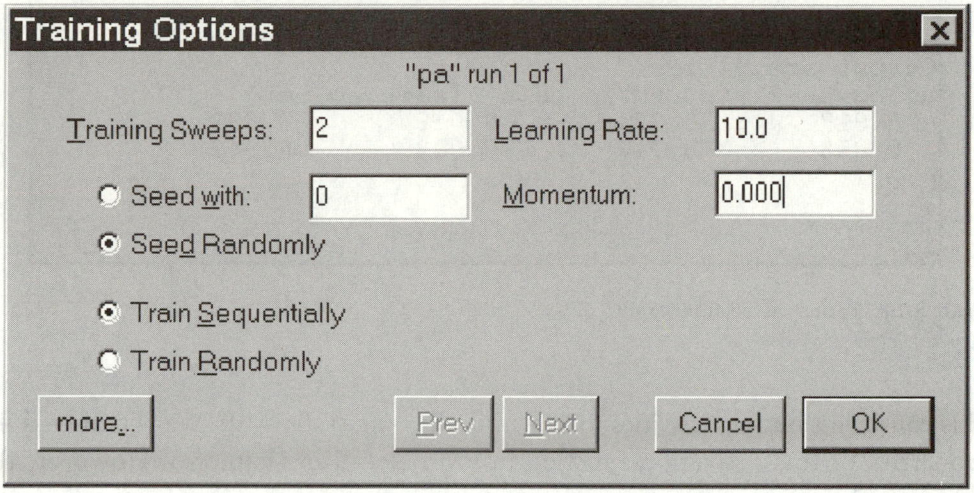

Figure 3.12   Training Options… dialogue box.

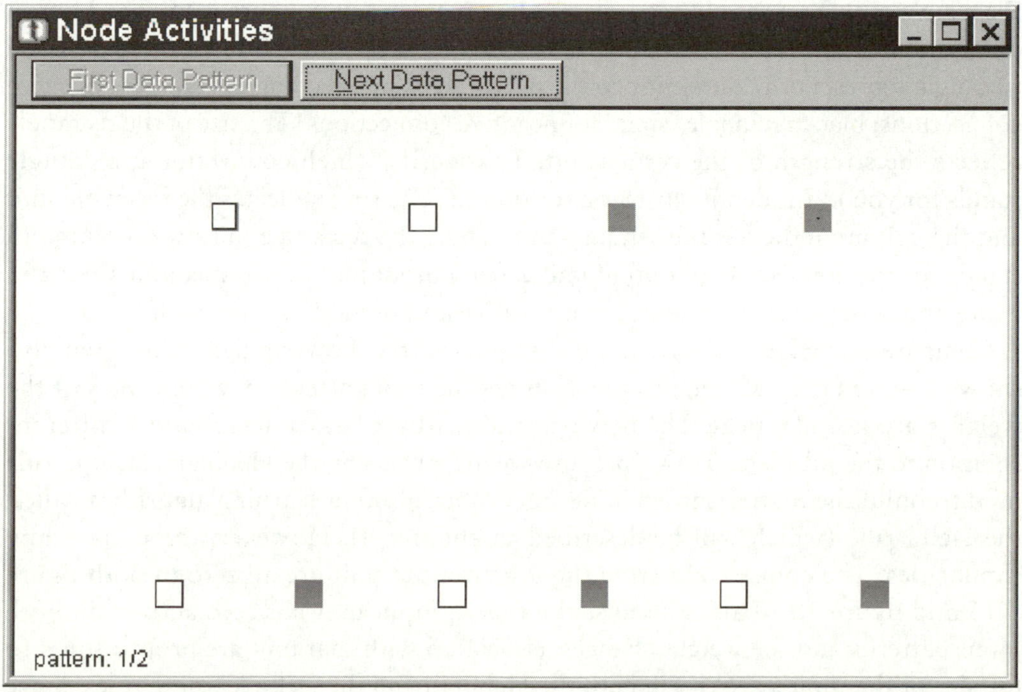

Figure 3.13   Node Activities display.

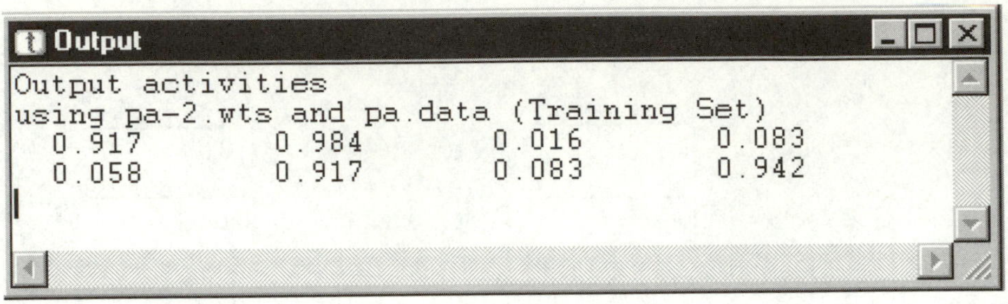

```
┌──────────────────────────────────────────────────────────────────┐
│ ⓘ Output                                              _ □ X │
├──────────────────────────────────────────────────────────────────┤
│Output activities                                              ▲   │
│using pa-2.wts and pa.data (Training Set)                          │
│   0.917        0.984        0.016        0.083                    │
│   0.058        0.917        0.083        0.942                    │
│▌                                                              ▼   │
│ ◄                                                         ►       │
└──────────────────────────────────────────────────────────────────┘
```

Figure 3.14   Pattern associator output.

This constrains output activities to be within the range 0.0 to 1.0. We will discuss the properties of this activation function in more detail in chapter 5. However, the output node activities are quite close to zero or one, depending on the required output. The sizes of the white squares in figure 3.13 reflect these values.

Looking inside the network

When you have trained the network, you can use **tlearn** to display the connection strengths using a *Hinton diagram*. Choose the Connection Weights option from the Displays menu. You should see a display like that shown in figure 3.15. The Hinton diagram is organised in rows and columns of black and white rectangles. Each rectangle represents a connection in the network. White rectangles stand for positive connections; black rectangles stand for negative connections. The size of the rectangle reflects the strength of the connection. To identify which connection a rectangle stands for you must identify its row and column. The row indicates the receiving unit and the column indicates the sending unit. Thus, the rectangle in row 2, column i3 stands for the connection to output unit 2 from input unit 3. It is medium sized and white, indicating that the connection is positive and of moderate strength.

Compare this Hinton diagram to the weight matrix shown in figure 3.6. That also shows a 4x6 matrix of weights which stores the two patterns but the values of the weights are not identical. The network trained by **tlearn** has found a different solution to the problem. This is because we are not using the Hebbian learning rule used to build the matrix shown in figure 3.6 but another learning algorithm called the Delta rule (which will be described in chapter 4). However, there are many similarities. The connections from the fourth input unit are all zero in both figure 3.15 and figure 3.6. This is because the fourth input unit has zero activity in both input patterns and the weight changes associated with that unit are proportional to the size of that unit's activity in both the Hebbian and the Delta learning rules. Since the activity is always zero, the connection is never changed and remains at zero.

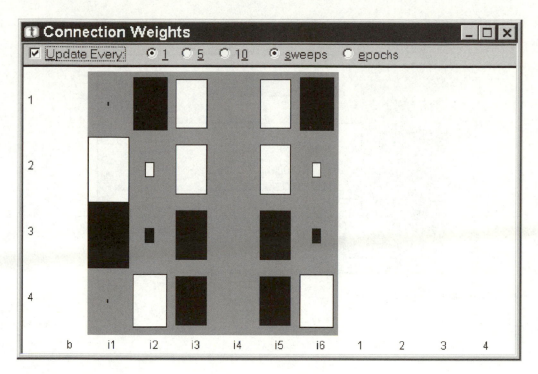

Figure 3.15 Hinton diagram for the pattern associator.

You can also examine the exact values of the connections of the pattern associator by opening a file called **pa-2.wts** which was saved at the end of training. You do this from the Open... option in the File menu. The format of the weights file is rather complicated and we will not describe it here. However, if you wish to investigate the weight values further, consult the description in the User Manual in Appendix 3.

Lesioning the network

You can use **tlearn** to examine the output activities when the network is damaged. To do this choose the Lesioning... option from the Special menu. You will see a dialogue box like that in figure 3.16. Select **pa-2.wts**—the weights file saved by **tlearn** at the end of training—in the Weights file area by double-clicking on the file selection box. Then make sure that the rest of the dialogue box is the same as that shown in figure 3.16. Notice that the settings in figure 3.16 request 100% removal of the connections (but no removal of nodes) from input node 5 to output node 2 and from input node 2 to output node 4. Click on the Lesion button. **tlearn** will suggest a file name for the lesioned weights file, e.g. **pa-2-lsn.wts**. You can accept this name or suggest another one. Save the lesioned weights file. **tlearn** will also display

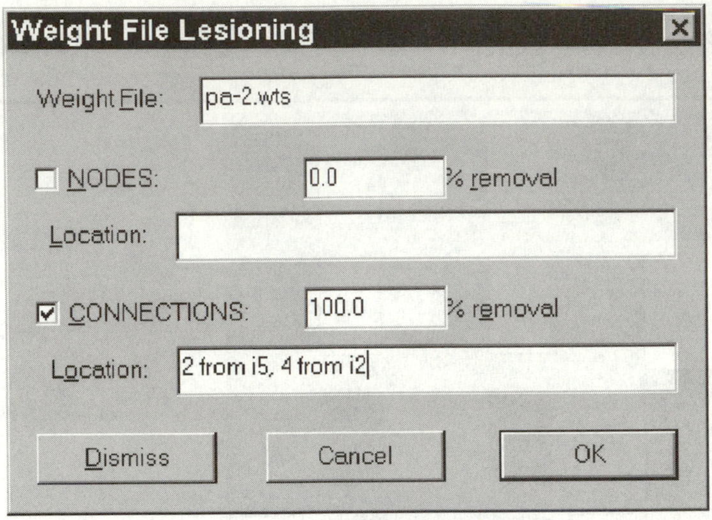

Weight File Lesioning   ☒

Weight File: pa-2.wts

☐ NODES: 0.0   % removal

Location:

☑ CONNECTIONS: 100.0   % removal

Location: 2 from i5, 4 from i2

[Dismiss]   [Cancel]   [OK]

Figure 3.16   Lesioning dialogue box.

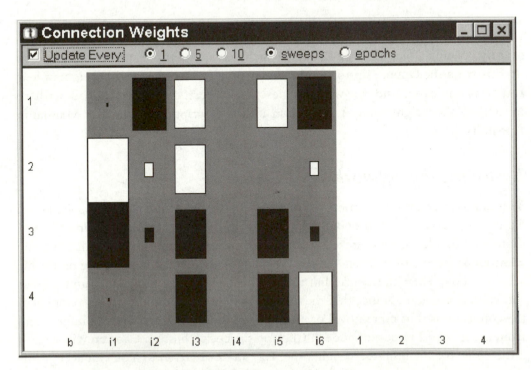

Figure 3.17   Lesioned weight matrix for the pattern associator.

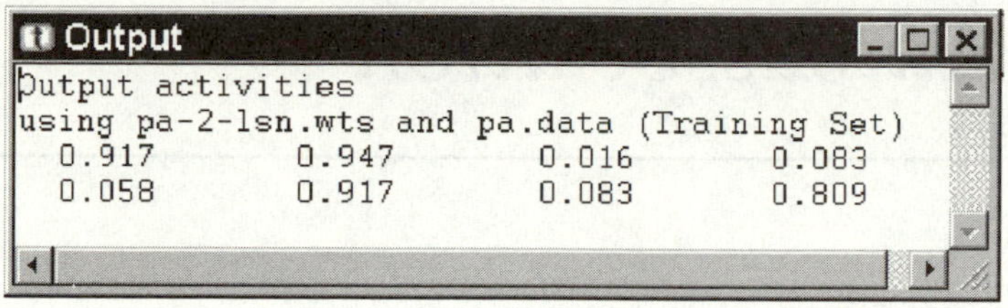

Figure 3.18   Output after lesioning the pattern associator's weight matrix.

the contents of the weights file itself. The format of this file is explained in the User Manual.

An easier way to examine the lesioned weight matrix is using the Connection Weights option from the Display menu. However, before you can do this you need to tell **tlearn** to use the lesioned weight matrix rather than the intact weight matrix. Choose Testing Options... from the Network menu and set the Weights File for Earlier one: to **pa-2-lsn.wts**. Make sure that the Send output to window box is checked. Now open the Connection Weights option in the Displays menu. The old intact weight matrix should still be displayed. Finally, Verify the network has learned. The Connection Weights display should update to show the lesioned network as in figure 3.17. Notice that the two medium sized positive connections from input unit 5 to output unit 2 and input unit 2 to output unit 4 have disappeared (compare with figure 3.10). **tlearn** also displays the activities of the output units when presented with the original input patterns as shown in figure 3.18. Although the output activities are not identical to those shown in figure 3.14, they show a similar pattern. You can also use the Node Activities Display to confirm this. The network has managed to produce an appropriate output despite the damage to connections in the network. Pattern associators show graceful degradation or fault tolerance.

4   *Autoassociation*

This chapter will examine the performance of a particular form of pattern associator, an autoassociator, trained with the Delta rule. An autoassociator reproduces at output the same pattern that was presented at input. It has many basic properties in common with the pattern associator taught with the Hebb rule. It can store independent memories on the same set of connections and it has the desirable property of 'cleaning up' incomplete or noisy inputs. When individual experiences, drawn from a set of different categories, are stored in an autoassociator memory, prototypical instances of each category are formed automatically. This offers a possible solution to the problem of how humans succeed in categorising the world without explicit teaching.

The architecture and operation of an autoassociator

The pattern associator described in chapter 3 learnt to produce a specified pattern at output in response to a particular pattern at input. Autoassociation is a special case of pattern association. The aim of the autoassociator is to reproduce the *same* pattern at output that was present at input. At first sight this may seem singularly pointless. Why have a complex structure if all it does is to reproduce at output the pattern which is already there at input? We shall see that an autoassociator network which has learnt about the statistical structure of previous inputs can perform some very useful operations on subsequent inputs.

Architecture

A typical structure for an autoassociator is shown in figure 4.1. It consists of a set of 8 processing units (numbered 1–8), each with a dendrite and an output line. The external input to the autoassociator comes from some previous stage of processing. The output lines take the transformation of this signal produced by the auto-associator on to the next stage of processing.

The difference between the structure of an autoassociator and that of the pattern associator discussed in the previous chapter is that the output line of each unit is

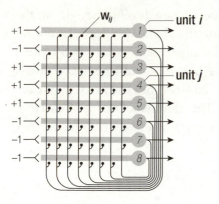
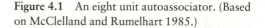

Figure 4.1 An eight unit autoassociator. (Based on McClelland and Rumelhart 1985.)

connected back to the dendrites of the other units. These are called *recurrent* connections. They are represented by the loop back from the output of each unit which connects to the dendrites of all the other units. At each meeting of recurrent feedback from one unit and the dendrite of another there is a modifiable connection. (Networks with recurrent connections have some special properties which will be described in chapter 7. In this chapter we will emphasise the general properties which are similar to those of the pattern associator described in the previous chapter even though the architecture of the network and the learning rule used to train it are different.)

The net input to unit i consists of the external input (extinput$_i$) and the internal input (intinput$_i$) generated by feedback from other units within the autoassociator. The internal input is calculated in the usual way, summing the products of the activity of each unit connected to unit i and the strength of the connection between them:

$$netinput_i = extinput_i + \Sigma_j a_j w_{ij} \tag{4.1}$$

where a_j is the activity of unit j. In this case j indexes the units other than i in the autoassociator,

w_{ij} is the strength of the connection between the recurrent input from unit j and the dendrite of unit i.

An input is presented to the autoassociator by clamping a pattern of stimulation, the external input, onto the dendrites. This is shown as a pattern of $+1$s and -1s in figure 4.1. This could represent the output from a prior stage of sensory processing following the presentation of some stimulus such as a word or a face. The external input produces an activity level in each unit determined by an activation function like one of those shown in figure 1.4 in chapter 1. Via the internal feedback connections, this activity, weighted by the strength of the appropriate connection, then starts to produce an internal input to all the other units. The net input to a unit is now the sum of the external and internal inputs. This produces a new level of activity in the unit, which feeds back to all the other units, changing their net input, and consequently their activity level, and so on. There is a danger that activity in a system with positive feedback can continue to grow. The use of a non-linear activation function such as the sigmoid shown in figure 1.4(c) ensures that the activity of each unit cannot grow beyond a fixed maximum value. The autoassociator is allowed to run for a number of cycles until it reaches a steady state where there is no further change in the internal input.

Learning with the Delta rule

The aim of the autoassociator is to reproduce at output the pattern presented at input. This is achieved during the learning phase by changing the weights so that the internal input to each unit matches the external input. This can be done by calculating the difference between the internal and external inputs and changing the weights of the connections in the direction which will reduce the difference. This is an example of the application of the Delta rule described in chapter 1.[1] If the internal input to a given unit is less than the external then the weights of connections carrying a positive input to the unit are increased, and those carrying a negative input are reduced. If the internal input is greater than the external, vice versa. The difference between the external and internal inputs to unit i is δ_i. So:

$$\delta_i = \text{extinput}_i - \text{intinput}_i \tag{4.2}$$

The rule for the weight change (Δw_{ij}) in the connection between unit i and the recurrent input from unit j is:

$$\Delta w_{ij} = \varepsilon \, \delta_i \, a_j \tag{4.3}$$

where ε is a constant which determines how large the weight change is on any individual trial,

δ_i is the error on unit i,

and a_j is the activity of unit j.

The inclusion of a_j in the weight change rule is a way of apportioning blame for δ_i. δ_i represents the failure of the internal input to unit i, $\Sigma_j \, a_j \, w_{ij}$, to match the external input. By making the weight change on a connection proportional to a_j, the activity of the unit sending input along that connection, the changes are concentrated on those connections where they will have most effect on the internal input to i.

This learning rule follows a different principle from the Hebb rule used with the pattern associator in chapter 3 (compare equation 4.3 with equation 3.1). The Hebb

---

[1]The aim of chapters 3 and 4 is to introduce a variety of architectures and learning rules. It is, of course, possible to train an autoassociator with the Hebb rule or a pattern associator with the Delta rule.

rule operated by strengthening connections between units which were both active. The rule represented by equation 4.3 starts by defining a desired state of affairs ($\delta_i = 0$) and operates by strengthening connections which would lead to a reduction in the difference between the desired and the actual state of affairs.

Chapter 5 will explore learning with the Delta rule in greater detail, in particular seeing how it can be used to train networks with more than one layer of modifiable connections. For now, we will see how the Delta rule works with a simple network. The weight matrix which results from the application of this rule turns out to have many of the same general properties as those which we saw resulting from use of the Hebb learning rule in chapter 3.

Properties of autoassociator memories

To demonstrate some of the properties of an autoassociator memory which apply to central problems in cognition we will follow some parts of a simulation which is described in greater detail in McClelland and Rumelhart (1985, 1986). The examples will be explored in the **tlearn** exercises at the end of the chapter. First we will use the simulation to show that, just like the pattern associator trained with the Hebb rule, an autoassociator trained with the Delta rule can store the individual memories of different events on a single matrix of connections. Then we will show that, again like the pattern associator, it has the biologically important properties of noise resistance and pattern completion if the recall cues for the memories are distorted.

What an autoassociator learns

The McClelland and Rumelhart exploration of autoassociator memory began with the 8 unit autoassociator shown in figure 4.1. Each unit had a maximum activity level of $+1$ and a minimum activity level of -1. Initially the weights were set to zero. They presented it with the external input pattern ($+1$ -1 $+1$ -1 $+1$ $+1$ -1 -1). Figure 4.2(a) shows the response of the autoassociator. Since the weights are zero there is no internal input to each unit. The unit activity, ± 0.5 in each case, reflects the result of feeding the external input value of ± 1 into the activation function. (The activation function was a sigmoid like that in figure 1.4(c) of chapter 1, but the range of activity it permitted was -1 to $+1$ rather than 0 to 1.)

What is the result of applying the learning algorithm represented by equation 4.3? Take unit 1. The change in the weights from units 2–8 to unit 1, Δw_{12} to Δw_{18}, will be equal to the product of ε, δ_1 and a_2 to a_8 respectively. Since the external input = 1 and the internal input = 0, equation 4.2 shows that δ_1 is positive. So the weights of the connections between unit 1 and units which have positive activity produced by the external input pattern (units 3, 5 and 6) will receive a positive increment, of a

(a)

External input	Initial unit activity	Unit
+1	+0.5	1
−1	−0.5	2
+1	+0.5	3
−1	−0.5	4
+1	+0.5	5
+1	+0.5	6
−1	−0.5	7
−1	−0.5	8

(b)

External input 1	Unit activity after training	Unit
+1	+0.7	1
−1	−0.7	2
+1	+0.7	3
−1	−0.7	4
+1	+0.7	5
+1	+0.7	6
−1	−0.7	7
−1	−0.7	8

(c)

External input 2	Unit activity after training	Unit
+1	+0.7	1
+1	+0.7	2
−1	−0.7	3
−1	−0.7	4
−1	−0.7	5
+1	+0.7	6
−1	−0.7	7
+1	+0.7	8

Figure 4.2 (a) The activity of the units in an untrained network like that shown in figure 4.1 after presentation of an external pattern. (b) The activity after training with the external input pattern. (c) The activity after training with a second external input pattern. (Based on McClelland and Rumelhart 1985.)

size determined by ε. Since these weights started at 0 they will become positive. Weights of connections between unit 1 and units with a negative activity (units 2, 4, 7 and 8) will receive a negative increment. Since they started at 0 they will become negative.

On the next trial the input to unit 1 will consist of the external input plus, since the weights are now non-zero, an internal input. The internal input is given by $\Sigma_j\, a_j\, w_{ij}$, the sum of the product of activity level and weight for each unit connected to unit 1. The units which have a positive activity level (3, 5 and 6) are connected to unit 1 by positive weights; the units which have a negative activity level (2, 4, 7 and 8) are connected by negative weights. So every unit makes a positive contribution to the internal input to unit 1. (If both a_j and w_{ij} are negative, $a_j w_{ij}$ is positive.) Since the aim of the autoassociator is to produce an internal input which matches the external input, and the external input to unit 1 is positive, the learning algorithm in equation 4.3 has produced a step in the right direction.

Now consider unit 2. Initially δ_2 is negative because the external input $= -1$ and the internal input $= 0$. So application of equation 4.3 will lead to the opposite result to that achieved for unit 1. The weights of connections to unit 2 from units which have a positive activity level (1, 3, 5 and 6) will be negative, and the weights of connections from units which have a negative activity level (4, 7 and 8) will be positive. Taking the product of these weights and the unit activities ($\Sigma_j a_j w_{ij}$) will produce a negative internal input to unit 2. So again the desired result will have been achieved since the external input to unit 2 is negative.

The learning rule develops a set of weights such that the internal input starts to match the external. So δ_i, the difference between external and internal inputs to unit i, will become smaller. Consequently the weight changes on each learning trial will become smaller. If the network achieves a set of weights such that the internal input matches the external input, $\delta_i = 0$ and learning (i.e. weight change) stops. Homing in on a set of weights which can perform the task, with gradually smaller changes of the weights, is typical of learning with the Delta rule. It is unlike learning with the Hebb rule where only one learning trial may be required to establish the necessary connections.

Acquiring a set of weights which would allow the internal input generated by pattern 1 to match the external input is straightforward. Autoassociation is potentially problematic because the same set of connections must also ensure that an appropriate internal input develops when a second, quite different pattern is presented. If the new pattern is $(+1 +1 -1 -1 -1 +1 -1 +1)$ the weights must now provide a positive internal input to units 1, 2, 6 and 8, and a negative internal input to units 3, 4, 5 and 7. In McClelland and Rumelhart's simulation these two patterns were presented to the autoassociator ten times. After each presentation the weights were changed according to equation 4.3. Figures 4.2(b) and (c) show that the learning algorithm developed a set of weights which produced a larger activity in the units than to the external input alone (0.7 vs 0.5). Thus the internal input has mimicked the external output in both cases. Just like the pattern associator trained with the Hebb rule, application of the Delta rule leads to a set of weights which can store an appropriate response to different patterns on the same connections.

Figure 4.3 shows how the network manages to produce the correct response to both patterns. Each part of the figure shows a weight matrix, that is, the weights of the connections in the autoassociator. The figure shows what the autoassociator shown in figure 4.1 would look like if the dendrites and feedback lines had been removed and only the modifiable connections remained. Each value in the matrix is the weight of the corresponding connection. (To understand this example the numerical values of the weights are not important, only the sign. So, for clarity, the numerical values have been omitted.) The eight rows in the matrix correspond to the input lines to the dendrites of the 8 units in the autoassociator; the columns show the weight of the connection from each other unit to the unit given by the row. (As usual the receiving units are indexed by i and the sending units by j.) Thus row 1 shows the weights of the recurrent connections from units 2–8 *to* unit 1. Column 1 shows the value of the weights of the connections *from* unit 1 to units 2–8. (Cells on the diagonal of the matrix are empty because there are no recurrent connections from any unit to itself—see figure 4.1.)

The matrix in figure 4.3(a) shows the weights that the autoassociator acquires on learning trials on which pattern 1 is presented. The aim of the learning rule is to ensure that the internal input to each unit matches the external input. Unit 1 receives a positive external input from pattern 1, so the set of weights from the other units (i.e. the values in row 1) should have a polarity which will generate a positive internal input to unit 1 when pattern 1 is presented. Pattern 1 also makes units 3, 5 and 6 positive. Their state is thus positively correlated with the desired state of unit 1. The positive weights between these units and unit 1 (i.e. weights 3, 5 and 6 in row 1) will tend to turn unit 1 on if units 3, 5 or 6 are active. In contrast, pattern 1 is making units 2, 4, 7 and 8 negative. The correlation between the state of these units and the state of unit 1 is negative. So negative weights develop at the connections between units 2, 4, 7 and 8 and the input line to unit 1. If any of these units are active, the negative weights will ensure that they also make a positive internal input to unit 1.

The second row shows the weights of the connections to unit 2 from units 1 and 3–8. The external input to unit 2 is negative, so the pattern of weight polarity is the reverse of the pattern to unit 1. There are positive weights to unit 2 from those units which have negative activity, and negative weights from those units which have positive activity. The third row shows connections from each unit to unit 3. Like unit 1 this has a positive external input in pattern 1. Thus the polarity of the weights from each unit to unit 3 is the same as it was to unit 1. And so on. Overall it can be seen that, just as with the pattern associator taught with the Hebb rule, a positive weight in the autoassociator reflects a positive correlation between the states of the two units it connects. In this case, because we have used –1 rather than 0 for non-positive inputs, negative weights have also developed to represent negative correlations.

Storage of different memories on the same connections

Figure 4.3(a) shows the matrix of weights which the autoassociator acquired as it learnt how to reproduce pattern 1. Figure 4.3(b) shows the weight matrix which the autoassociator acquired as it learnt to reproduce pattern 2. This is just like the matrix

(a) External Input 1

unit$_j$ →	1	2	3	4	5	6	7	8	Unit$_i$ ↓
+		−	+	−	+	+	−	−	1
−	−		−	+	−	−	+	+	2
+	+	−		−	+	+	−	−	3
−	−	+	−		−	−	+	+	4
+	+	−	+	−		+	−	−	5
+	+	−	+	−	+		−	−	6
−	−	+	−	+	−	−		+	7
−	−	+	−	+	−	−	+		8

Weight matrix

(b) External Input 2

unit$_j$ →	1	2	3	4	5	6	7	8	Unit$_i$ ↓
+		+	−	−	−	+	−	+	1
+	+		−	−	−	+	−	+	2
−	−	−		+	+	−	+	−	3
−	−	−	+		+	−	+	−	4
−	−	−	+	+		−	+	−	5
+	+	+	−	−	−		−	+	6
−	−	−	+	+	+	−		−	7
+	+	+	−	−	−	+	−		8

Weight matrix

(c)

unit$_j$ →	1	2	3	4	5	6	7	8	Unit$_i$ ↓
	·	·	−	·	+	−	·	1
·		−	·	−	·	·	+	2
·	−		·	+	·	·	−	3
−	·	·		·	−	+	·	4
·	−	+	·		·	·	−	5
+	·	·	−	·		−	·	6
−	·	·	+	·	−		·	7
·	+	−	·	−	·	·		8

Weight matrix

Figure 4.3 (a) and (b) The weight matrix acquired by the autoassociator when it has learnt to reproduce the external input pattern shown on the left. (c) The combined weight matrix formed when the two matrices acquired during learning to reproduce the two individual patterns are superimposed. (Based on McClelland and Rumelhart 1985.)

acquired to pattern 1, except that the pattern of positive and negative weights is different because the correlations between elements of the two input patterns is different. When the autoassociator is required to learn both patterns the weights learnt in response to input patterns 1 and 2 are superimposed on the same connections. The effect of learning both patterns is to produce the overall weight matrix shown in figure 4.3(c).

Figures 4.2(b) and (c) showed that the autoassociator produces the correct response when either pattern 1 or 2 is presented. Inspection of the combined matrix shows how it can do this. Where the weights in the two individual matrices [figures 4.3(a) and (b)] are opposite in sign they cancel out. Zero valued weights are represented by a dot. Where the weights are the same sign the combined matrix develops a weight with the corresponding sign. Thus for example, the connection represented in row 1 column 2 of the combined matrix is zero because there is a negative correlation between elements 2 and 1 in pattern 1 but a positive correlation in pattern 2. Row 1, column 4 in the combined matrix has a negative weight because there is a negative correlation between elements 4 and 1 in both patterns 1 and 2.

It should be clear why coherent memory retrieval is possible despite super-imposition of information about independent patterns. Each weight in the combined matrix represents something that is true about both pattern 1 and pattern 2. As the matrix learns more patterns the picture is, obviously, going to become more complex. But the fact that the weights can take any value allows the matrix to keep track of all the input correlations as more patterns are presented. If in all the patterns that are presented elements 1 and 4 are negatively correlated, the weight in row 1, column 4 will acquire a large negative value. If there is a negative correlation between elements 1 and 4 in many but not all patterns, the value will still be negative but with a lower value because the positive correlations will have reduced it. If there are only marginally more patterns in which the correlation is negative rather than positive, the value will still be negative, but now, because the positive and negative correlations will nearly cancel out, the magnitude will be close to zero. Each weight in the autoassociator reflects the correlation between the states of the two units it connects in the patterns which it has learnt—positive weights for positive correlations, negative weights for negative correlations. Now it is possible to see why this network has the properties of pattern completion and noise resistance.

Pattern completion

Figure 4.4 shows what happens when an incomplete fragment of pattern 1 is presented to the autoassociator rather than the pattern which it learnt. Part (a) shows the response to the full pattern $(+1 \ -1 \ +1 \ -1 \ +1 \ +1 \ -1 \ -1)$. Part (b) shows the response to the partial pattern $(+1 \ -1 \ +1 \ -1)$. Units 5–8 adopt the same polarity in response to the incomplete input (although at lower magnitude) as they did when the complete pattern was presented. The reason units 5–8 produce this pattern is that in pattern 1, positive activity in unit 5 is correlated with positive activity in units 1 and 3 and negative activity in units 2 and 4. These facts were recorded in the weights between units 1– 4 and 5 during the learning trials with pattern 1 (see row 5 of matrix (a) in figure 4.3). These facts are still preserved (up to a point) in the com-

(a)

External Input	Unit Activity	Unit
+1	+0.7	1
−1	−0.7	2
+1	+0.7	3
−1	−0.7	4
+1	+0.7	5
+1	+0.7	6
−1	−0.7	7
−1	−0.7	8

(b)

External Input	Unit Activity
+1	+0.6
−1	−0.6
+1	+0.6
−1	−0.6
	+0.4
	+0.4
	−0.4
	−0.4

(c)

External Input	Unit Activity
+1	+0.6
−1	−0.6
+1	+0.6
−1	−0.6
+1	+0.6
+1	+0.6
−1	−0.6
+1	+0.1

Figure 4.4 (a) The response of the network to an external input pattern. (b) The response to a fragment of this pattern. (c) The response to a noisy version of the pattern. (Based on McClelland and Rumelhart 1985.)

bined matrix (see row 5 in matrix (c) of figure 4.3). When the pattern (+ − + −) is presented to units 1–4, the internal input from these units achieves a positive activity level in unit 5. Similarly, *mutatis mutandis*, for units 6–8. The level of activity is less than it would be if the complete pattern had been presented because the external input is less for the fragment than for the complete pattern.

Noise resistance

Figure 4.4(c) shows what happens when a 'noisy' version of pattern 1 is presented to the autoassociator. When the pattern (+1 −1 +1 −1 +1 +1 −1 +1) is presented rather than pattern 1 (the polarity of the last input has been changed) the autoassociator nearly changes the polarity of the 8th unit to what it would have been if pattern 1 had been presented. It does this rather than reproducing the value in the external input for the same reason that it completes the partial pattern. When the noisy pattern is presented, the internal input to unit 8 from units 1–7 is trying to make unit 8 negative. This is nearly enough to overcome the positive external input.

It should now be clear why an autoassociator memory stage might be included in a processing system. It is not merely reproducing the input. If the external input is incomplete or noisy the internal input can clean it up before passing it on to the next stage of processing. Given that the brain is a noisy environment where signals are often distorted, either by random cell firing or by random cell death, this has obvious benefits. It is also the case that many signals reaching the brain *are* noisy versions of a prototype. Every example of a spoken word that you hear is slightly different because of the accent of the speaker, or the context it appears in, or the background noises which are superimposed upon it. Generally the distortions are not interesting in themselves—it is the prototype that the distortion came from which you wish to identify.

Despite its usefulness in some situations there is a cost to these cleaning up operations. The 'incomplete' or 'noisy' input in figure 4.4 may be neither—it may be a new signal, conveying some information different from that conveyed by pattern 1. Of course, the autoassociator cannot know which is the case. If an external input which it has not met before is presented to the autoassociator it will be altered to look more like whichever of its previously learnt signals the new one is most similar to.[2] If an unreliable transmission system is operating in a predictable world the inclusion of an autoassociation stage may be good system design—a novel signal is more likely to come from erroneous transmission of a known signal than from a novel signal. But it does force any part of the system beyond the autoassociator to see the present through a distorting filter of past experiences. This is, surely, a human characteristic. Everyone will recognise in other people (if not in themselves) a tendency to interpret novel experiences, not as they really are, but through a filter of preconceptions, determined by past experiences.

A dramatic example of the ability of an autoassociator to recall complete memories from partial or noisy cues, with more realistic stimuli than those used in figure 4.4, is shown in figure 4.5. Hertz *et al.* (1991) stored seven images in an auto-associative network. At recall they presented the network with either a noisy (upper left) or a partial (lower left) retrieval cue. In each case the complete original image was retrieved despite the poverty of the stimulus.

---

[2]This is an example of a general problem for autoassociators. If they are trained on patterns A, B and A+B they will have difficulty in recalling either A or B. Both will tend to complete and produce the output A+B. One way to reduce this problem is to recode the input pattern vectors, minimising their overlap, with a competitive network before they are presented to the autoassociator. (Competitive networks will be described in chapter 6.) We will see an example of this process at work in chapter 13 in a model of episodic memory formation in the hippocampus.

Input   **Output**

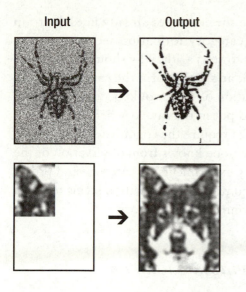

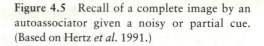

Figure 4.5 Recall of a complete image by an autoassociator given a noisy or partial cue. (Based on Hertz *et al.* 1991.)

Forming categories and prototypes from individual experiences

Experience comes in isolated incidents. One day a large brown Alsatian bites your leg; the next day a small sandy coloured terrier bites your ankle. By forming a memory of these experiences you can learn to keep your legs away from large brown Alsatians and your ankles away from small sandy coloured terriers. That's a good start. But on their own the memories will not suggest appropriate behaviour when you meet a medium sized black Rottweiler. The individual memories would be more useful if they could be pooled to form the *category* <dog>. Then the information <may bite> can be attached to the category. Provided you can recognise the black Rottweiler as an example of the *category*, you can benefit from your previous experiences with other members and take appropriate action even though this particular dog has not bitten you before. The human cognitive system is very good at recognising the similarities in individual experiences and forming general categories from them. People have no trouble recognising that Rottweilers are dogs even if they have never seen one before. Having formed a category we also know what a typical member of that category is like. Everyone would agree that while labradors and dachshunds are dogs, a labrador is a typical dog, but a dachshund is, frankly, a bit peculiar. How do people form categories from individual experiences?

Tutored category formation is not a problem. If a child has been taught a set of category names, dog, cat and bird, say, and is initially told which category to put each new experience in ('That's a dog', 'That's a cat' and so on) it is easy to see how each new example of an animal that it sees could be assigned to one of the categories.

Subsequent experiences could be compared to the examples already in each group and categorised accordingly. But *untutored* category formation seems to pose a serious problem. If the child has no categories to start with, why should it partition experiences in any particular way, or, indeed, at all? To form the category <dog> seems to require that you know that categorisation of dogs would be useful and that you know what sort of experiences you should put in the category before you start. In short, untutored category formation seems to require the cognitive system to pull itself up by its own bootstraps. And yet, as everyone knows from observation of the intellectual development of children, and many experiments on category and proto-type formation confirm, untutored category and prototype formation seems to be an inevitable consequence of entering experiences into human memory.

Discovering a prototype from exemplars with an autoassociator

McClelland and Rumelhart simulated the problem of forming categories and proto-types from individual experiences by imagining a child learning about dogs. The child sees many different dogs, all basically similar in appearance, although different in detail, but with unrelated names. We know that a child would form the category <dog> from such experiences, would know what a typical dog looked like and would recognise which new experiences could plausibly be dogs. Can a connectionist network do this if it is given no information about the existence of the category?

McClelland and Rumelhart used an autoassociator like that in figure 4.1 but with 24 units. Each experience of a dog was presented to it as an external input consisting of a string of 24 binary digits. The pattern of the first 8 digits represented the signal which would be generated by the dog's name; the next 16 represented the signal generated by its physical appearance. Despite their identifiably different appearance, alsatians, spaniels and labradors all look more like each other than like most other things in the world around the child. But their names are no more similar than any other words chosen at random from the English language. Since there is no prototypical name for different dogs, the first 8 elements, the *name* part of each pattern, were a random sequence of $+1$s and -1s. To represent the visual similarity of different dogs, the *visual* part of each pattern (elements 9–24) was a distortion of a particular pattern $(+1 \ -1 \ +1 \ +1 \ -1 \ -1 \ -1 \ -1 \ +1 \ +1 \ +1 \ +1 \ +1 \ -1 \ -1 \ -1)$ which represented the appearance of a prototypical dog. The distortions correspond-ing to the varying appearance of individual dogs were made by randomly changing the sign of each of the 16 elements with a probability of 0.2.

50 different patterns were constructed, corresponding to the child meeting 50 different dogs. The weights in the autoassociator were initialised to random values

```
          Unit_j  1   2   3   4   5   6   7   8     9  10  11  12  13  14  15  16  17  18  19  20  21  22  23  24
External
Input
  .                             .   .   .   .   +   .   .   .     .   .   .   .   .   .   .   .   .   .   .   .   .   .   .   .    Unit_i
  |                                                                                                                                 1
  N                         .   .   .   .   .   .   .   .     .   .   .   .   .   .   .   .   .   .   .   .   .   .   .   .    2
  A                         .   .   −   .   −   .   .   .     .   .   .   .   .   .   +   .   .   .   .   .   .   .   .   .    3
  M                         .   .   −   .   .   .   .   .     .   .   .   .   .   −   .   .   .   .   .   .   .   .   .   .    4
  E                         .   .   .   .   .   .   .   .     .   .   .   .   .   .   .   .   .   .   .   .   .   .   .   .    5
  |                         .   .   −   .   .   .   −   .     .   .   .   .   .   −   .   .   .   .   .   .   .   .   .   .    6
  .                         .   .   .   .   .   .   .   .     .   .   .   .   .   .   .   .   .   .   .   .   .   .   .   .    7
                            .   .   .   .   .   .   .   .     .   .   .   .   .   .   .   .   .   .   .   .   .   .   .   .    8

  .               +   .   .   .   .   .   .   .     −   +   .   .   +   .   .   −   .   +   +   .   .   .   .   +    9
  |               −   .   .   .   .   .   .   .     .   .   −   −   +   .   .   +   −   −   −   −   .   +   +   +   10
  |               +   .   .   .   .   .   .   .     +   −   .   +   −   .   −   −   +   +   +   +   +   .   −   −   −   11
  |               +   .   .   .   .   .   .   .     .   −   .   .   −   −   .   −   +   +   +   +   .   −   −   −   12
  |               −   .   .   .   .   .   .   .     .   +   −   −   +   +   +   −   −   −   −   .   +   +   +   13
  |               −   .   .   .   .   .   .   .     .   +   .   −   +   .   +   −   −   −   −   −   +   .   +   .   +   14
  V               −   .   .   .   .   .   .   .     −   −   +   .   +   −   −   −   −   .   +   +   +   15
  I               −   .   .   .   .   .   .   .     −   +   −   −   +   +   +   −   −   −   −   −   −   +   +   +   16
  S               +   .   .   .   .   .   .   .     .   −   .   +   −   −   .   −   +   +   +   .   −   −   −   17
  U               +   .   .   .   .   .   .   .     .   −   +   +   −   −   −   −   +   +   +   .   −   −   −   18
  A               +   .   .   .   .   .   .   .     +   −   .   +   −   −   .   −   +   +   +   .   +   −   .   −   19
  L               +   .   .   .   .   .   .   .     .   −   +   +   −   −   .   +   +   +   +   −   .   −   20
  |               +   .   .   .   .   .   .   .     .   −   +   +   −   −   .   −   .   +   +   +   −   .   −   21
  |               −   .   .   .   .   .   .   .     .   +   .   −   +   +   .   +   −   −   −   −   −   +   +   22
  |               −   .   .   .   .   .   .   .     .   .   .   .   .   .   .   .   −   .   .   .   .   +   23
  .               −   .   .   .   .   .   .   .     .   +   .   −   +   .   .   +   −   −   −   −   −   .   +   +   24


                  ↑
                 The
             prototypical
                visual
                pattern
```

Figure 4.6 The weight matrix which develops as a 24 unit autoassociator learns about the names and appearance of 50 dogs. The first 8 elements in the input string represent the name of the dog; elements 9–24 represent its visual appearance. The appearance of each dog is a random variation of the prototypical pattern. The rows show the weights from each other unit to unit *i*. Weights with a value close to zero are indicated by dots. (Based on McClelland and Rumelhart 1985.)

with a mean of zero. Each pattern was presented as an external input to the matrix, activity was allowed to cycle until a settled pattern was reached, and then the weights were changed in the manner represented by equation 4.3. Figure 4.6 shows the weights which the matrix acquires at the end of these learning experiences. Since the autoassociator has 24 units this matrix has 24×23 weights (no unit synapses to itself). As before, the rows represent the dendrites of each unit, with the weights of the connections from each other unit to the unit represented in that row. Units 1–8 receive the part of the external input which represents the name; units 9–24 receive the part which represents the visual image.

The matrix can be imagined as consisting of four blocks. (To help identify them a blank strip has been left around them in the matrix.) An 8×8 block in the top left hand corner shows the weights of connections from elements in the *name* part of the input pattern (units 1–8) to each other. The 16×16 block in the bottom right hand part of the matrix shows the weights of elements in the *visual* part of the external input pattern (units 9–24) to each other. The two rectangular 8x16 blocks show the weights of the connections from *name* to *visual* elements and vice versa.

It is immediately apparent that most of the cells in the blocks of the matrix representing the weights involving the *name* elements are close to zero. Remember that a weight in the autoassociator represents the correlation between the corresponding elements in the input, summed across all the 50 different input patterns. Since the 'name' elements in different patterns are random strings of $+1$s and -1s the correlation between any particular pair of elements summed across all input patterns is close to zero.

In contrast, for the block of the matrix corresponding to correlations between elements in the *visual* part of the pattern, positive and negative weights develop. Since all the *visual* patterns are derived from a common prototype, weights corresponding to the correlations between input elements in the prototypical pattern begin to emerge, despite the random variations from pattern to pattern. This can be seen by checking the weights along each input line against the value for that unit in the prototypical pattern shown to the left of the matrix. Consider, for example, the second element in the prototypical pattern. It is negative. Positive connections have developed to unit 10, which takes this element as its external input, from units 13, 16, 22, 23 and 24. These units have the same polarity as unit 10 in the prototypical pattern. Negative connections have developed from units 11, 12, 17, 18, 19 and 20 which have the opposite polarity to unit 10 in the original pattern. The external input which would give the strongest response on unit 10 would be the prototypical pattern itself because the whole of the internal input would be trying to push it in the same direction as the external input. Note that this happens despite the fact that the autoassociator has never had a chance to learn the prototypical pattern directly, because it has never been presented. The matrix has 'discovered' the structure of the prototypical pattern on which the different inputs were based. It did this not by some unspecified, high-level 'prototype extraction process' but as an automatic consequence of the way that the learning rule changed the weights after each stimulus presentation.

This result echoes a well-known experiment of Posner and Keele (1968). They presented subjects with patterns generated by random distortion of a prototypical pattern. Later the subjects were asked to judge whether patterns were old (i.e. in the first set) or new (i.e. a new set of random distortions). When presented with the prototype (which they had *not* seen before) subjects were as likely to claim it was old as they were when presented with a pattern they had seen before.

Learning different prototypes on the same matrix

The previous section showed how an autoassociator memory can come to represent the central tendency of a set of related examples without experiencing the prototype itself. Since people appear to do this, it is an important property of a memory system to simulate. But the simulation avoids the central problem which would face the human cognitive system in the real world. In the previous simulation the auto-associator was only shown dogs. So the fundamental problem of stimulus categorisation had been solved for it. Some part of the complete system would have to know what a dog was so that only examples of dogs were directed to this particular memory store. This can be done *after* the category is formed, but how did the category come to be formed in the first place? If this demonstration is to be a viable model of prototype extraction in people it must be capable of extracting prototypes when exemplars from different categories are presented to the same memory without any indication that they came from any predefined category.

McClelland and Rumelhart explored the autoassociator's ability to do this with a simulation in which they imagined that the child was learning about dogs, cats and bagels. They produced a visual prototype for each of these (a specific pattern for the units 9–24 which codes the prototypical object's appearance). The prototypes for dog and cat were quite similar but that for bagel unlike either of them. The prototypical patterns are shown in figure 4.7. The dog and cat prototype patterns share the same value for 12 of the 16 input elements. The bagel pattern is unlike either of them, sharing only 8 of the 16 elements with either of the other patterns (the number which would be expected by chance for two inputs that were not visually related.) The name input elements were left blank to simulate untutored visual experience.

As before, they then generated 50 distortions of each prototype to represent specific experiences of dogs, cats and bagels. These were presented to the matrix, with the weights incremented after each presentation. The 'probes' in figure 4.7 are test inputs applied to the autoassociator after the learning trials. In each case it is an incomplete pattern, resembling a distinctive part of one of the three prototypical input patterns. Figure 4.7 shows that pattern completion takes place for each frag-ment. In each case all 16 of the visual units in the autoassociator adopt the pattern of activity corresponding to the visual prototype pattern from which the fragment was taken.

As we saw earlier, pattern completion requires that the autoassociator has stored the information about the complete pattern from which the fragment was taken. So figure 4.7 shows that the autoassociator has stored a representation of all three prototypes simultaneously. It has done this without being given any information during acquisition that the patterns came from different prototypes. Thus the auto-

'Dog'	Probe	R	'Cat'	Probe	R	'Bagel'	Probe	R	Unit
+1		+0.3	+1		+0.3	+1		+0.2	9
−1		−0.3	−1		−0.3	+1		+0.3	10
+1		+0.3	+1		+0.3	−1		−0.4	11
+1		+0.3	+1		+0.3	+1		+0.3	12
−1		−0.3	−1		−0.3	−1		−0.3	13
−1		−0.4	−1		−0.3	+1		+0.3	14
−1		−0.3	−1		−0.3	+1		+0.3	15
−1		−0.3	−1		−0.3	−1		−0.3	16
+1	+1	+0.6	+1	+1	+0.6	+1	+1	+0.6	17
+1	+1	+0.5	−1	−1	−0.5	−1	−1	−0.6	18
+1	+1	+0.6	+1	+1	+0.6	−1	−1	−0.6	19
+1	+1	+0.5	−1	−1	−0.5	+1	+1	+0.6	20
+1		+0.3	+1		+0.3	+1		+0.3	21
−1		−0.2	+1		+0.2	+1		+0.3	22
−1		−0.3	−1		−0.3	+1		+0.3	23
−1		−0.2	+1		+0.2	−1		−0.3	24

Figure 4.7 'Dog', 'Cat' and 'Bagel' are the prototypical patterns from which the three sets of exemplars for training the matrix are derived. *Probe* shows the pattern fragments with which the matrix was tested after learning. R shows the activity pattern of the autoassociator to these inputs. (Based on McClelland and Rumelhart 1985.)

associator offers a solution to one of the central mysteries of cognition. With the right memory architecture, mere experience is enough to ensure that appropriate categorisation of stimulus events will take place without an homunculus to tell the system what would be an appropriate classification.[3] We will see an example of this in action in the section on vocabulary development in chapter 9.

Further reading

In this chapter we have looked at some of the central points covered by the McClelland and Rumelhart simulation. The original article investigates the ability of autoassociators to mimic a wider range of memory phenomena. An alternative approach to concept formation in connectionist networks can be followed in Dienes (1992).

Autoassociation exercises with **tlearn**

Open the project called **aa** in the **Chapter Four** folder/directory. This project uses the **tlearn** network configuration file **aa.cf** that defines a network similar to that shown in figure 4.1, i.e. 8 output units with feedback connections from each unit to

[3]This ability is not restricted to autoassociators. In chapter 6 we will see that competitive nets also perform untutored categorisation of inputs.

```
██ aa.cf                          _□✕
NODES:
nodes = 16
inputs = 8
outputs = 8
output nodes are 1-8
CONNECTIONS:
groups = 0
1-8 from i1-i8 = 1. & 1. fixed one-to-one
9-16 from 1-8 = 1. & 1. fixed one-to-one
1 from 10-16
2 from 9,11-16
3 from 9,10,12-16
4 from 9-11,13-16
5 from 9-12,14-16
6 from 9-13,15,16
7 from 9-14,16
8 from 9-15
SPECIAL:
linear = 9-16
bipolar = 1-8
selected = 1-8
weight_limit = 0.0
```

```
██ aa.data                        _□✕
distributed
20
1.0 -1.0 1.0 -1.0 1.0 1.0 -1.0 -1.0
1.0 -1.0 1.0 -1.0 1.0 1.0 -1.0 -1.0
1.0 -1.0 1.0 -1.0 1.0 1.0 -1.0 -1.0
1.0 -1.0 1.0 -1.0 1.0 1.0 -1.0 -1.0
1.0 -1.0 1.0 -1.0 1.0 1.0 -1.0 -1.0
1.0 -1.0 1.0 -1.0 1.0 1.0 -1.0 -1.0
1.0 -1.0 1.0 -1.0 1.0 1.0 -1.0 -1.0
1.0 -1.0 1.0 -1.0 1.0 1.0 -1.0 -1.0
1.0 -1.0 1.0 -1.0 1.0 1.0 -1.0 -1.0
1.0 -1.0 1.0 -1.0 1.0 1.0 -1.0 -1.0
1.0 1.0 -1.0 -1.0 -1.0 1.0 -1.0 1.0
1.0 1.0 -1.0 -1.0 -1.0 1.0 -1.0 1.0
1.0 1.0 -1.0 -1.0 -1.0 1.0 -1.0 1.0
1.0 1.0 -1.0 -1.0 -1.0 1.0 -1.0 1.0
1.0 1.0 -1.0 -1.0 -1.0 1.0 -1.0 1.0
1.0 1.0 -1.0 -1.0 -1.0 1.0 -1.0 1.0
1.0 1.0 -1.0 -1.0 -1.0 1.0 -1.0 1.0
1.0 1.0 -1.0 -1.0 -1.0 1.0 -1.0 1.0
1.0 1.0 -1.0 -1.0 -1.0 1.0 -1.0 1.0
1.0 1.0 -1.0 -1.0 -1.0 1.0 -1.0 1.0
```

Figure 4.8 **aa.cf** and **aa.data** files.

the input of each other unit. All the connections are initially set to zero. Do not worry about the details of the **aa.cf** (network configuration) file. It simply reveals the gymnastics we have performed to make **tlearn** behave like an autoassociator.[4] To see what the network looks like and work out how it simulates the autoassociator in figure 4.1 use the Network Architecture display. (It is easier to see what is happening if you activate the bias button.)

When you open the **aa** project, you will also open the **aa.data** and **aa.teach** files that will be used to train the network. These files are shown in figure 4.8. The **aa.data** file contains the two patterns presented to the autoassociator in the section 'Properties of autoassociator memories' $(1 -1 1 -1 1 1 -1 -1)$ and $(1 1 -1 -1 -1 1 1 -1 1)$. Each pattern is repeated 10 times for each of the cycles of processing necessary for the output units to reach a stable level of activity. The **aa.teach** file is identical to the **aa.data** file since we are doing autoassociation.

Training the network

Activate the Training Options dialogue box from the Network menu. Use the expanded version of the Training Options dialogue box as shown in figure 4.9. If you do not see this, press the More button. Set the number of training sweeps to 20 so

---

[4]**tlearn** does not implement the autoassociation learning algorithm described in the earlier part of this chapter. We have simulated the autoassociator by creating feedback connections to other units via a bank of 8 linear units that keep an updated record of the activities of the output units on the previous cycle. This is equivalent to having 8 units with feedback connections to each other.

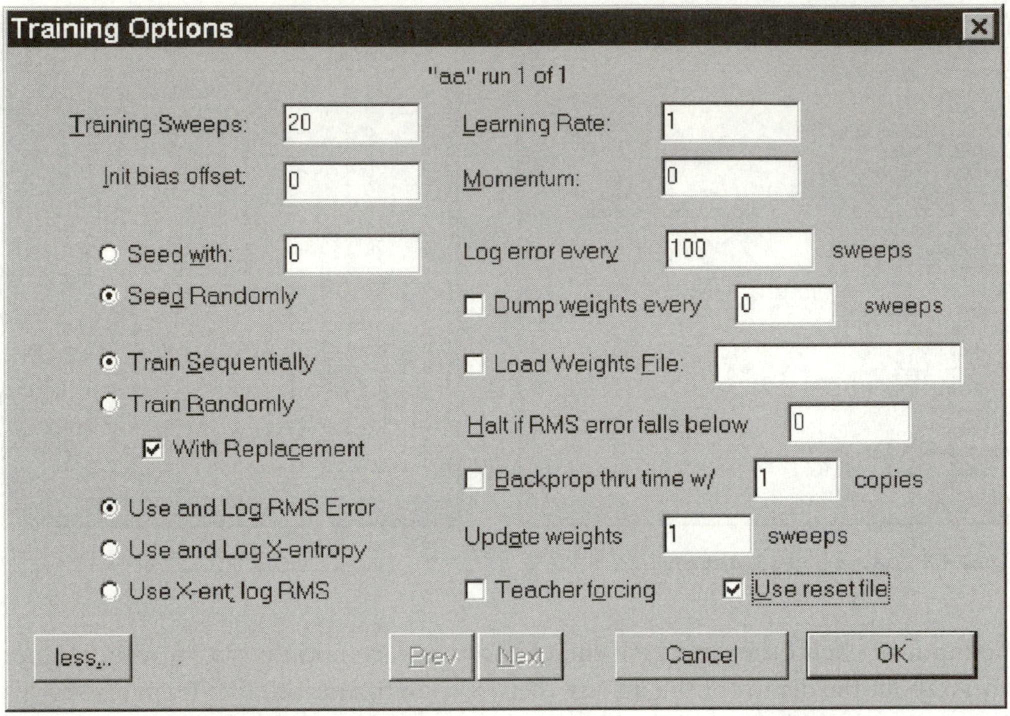

Figure 4.9 Training Options dialogue box.

that the network cycles through each pattern 10 times and set the learning rate parameter to 1.0. If the other options in the dialogue box are not as shown, change them so they are. In particular, make sure that the network is Trained Sequentially so that the patterns are presented in the right order and make sure that the Use reset file box is checked. The reset file (**aa.reset**) ensures that the activities of the output units are neutral when a new pattern is presented to the network. Now Train the network from the Network menu. The **tlearn** Status display will indicate when training is complete.

Testing the network

Open the Testing Options dialogue box and ensure that all the available options match those in figure 4.10. In particular, make sure that you have selected the Most recent weights file (**aa-20.wts**) and that you are testing the Training set (**aa.data**). Finally, ensure that the reset file box is checked.

   Now activate the Node Activities display. You should see a display like that shown in figure 4.11. The first pattern $1 \; -1 \; 1 \; -1 \; 1 \; 1 \; -1 \; -1$ from the **aa.data** file is

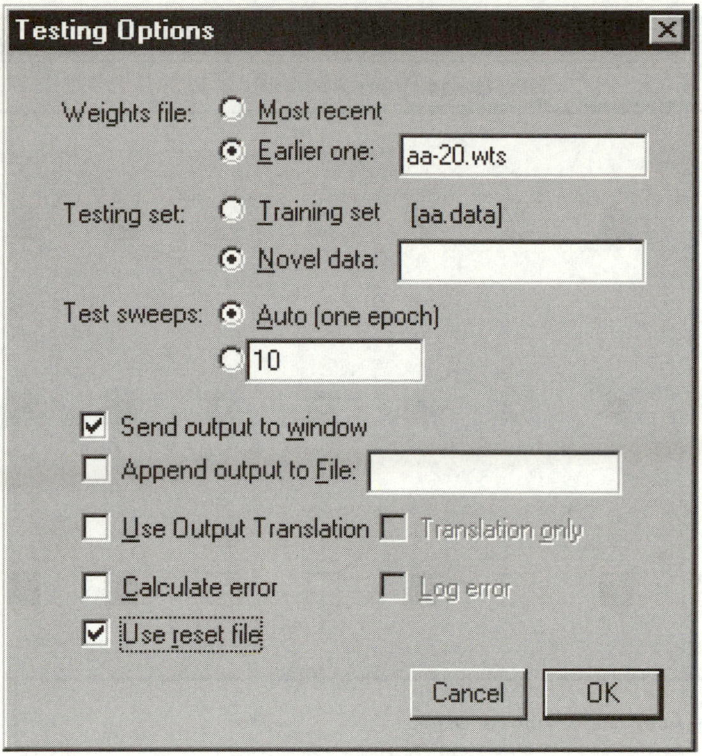

Figure 4.10   Training Options for autoassociation.

displayed on the bottom row.[5] The top row displays the activities of the output units. These are all close to ±0.5 because the autoassociator has not cycled through the patterns yet. (You can ignore the intermediate row of units with the same activities as the output units. These represent the feedback process we have implemented to make `tlearn` behave as an autoassociator.) The size of the squares indicates the level of activity of each unit. A grey square indicates no activity. White indicates positive activity and black indicates negative activity.

Now click on Next Data Pattern. You will see that the output units change their activity. You have not presented a new data pattern—just the next cycle of the same input pattern. Repeat until you reach the tenth cycle. You will see the output units update their activities so that they look more and more like the inputs. By the tenth cycle the output activities should have stabilised to produce a pretty good replica of the input. On the eleventh cycle, the network presents the first cycle for the second pattern 1 1 −1 −1 −1 1 −1 1. The input activities change accordingly and the

---

[5]Note that if you have activated the bias in Network Architecture display, the bias will also be displayed (as an active input in first postion) in the Node Activities display.

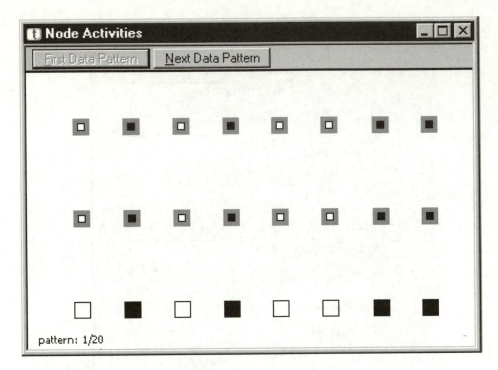

Figure 4.11   Node Activities for autoassociator.

output unit activities (as well as their feedback units) are reset. Again, with further cycles the activity on the output units builds up to resemble that of the input units representing the second pattern. In other words, the network has learnt to autoassociate the two patterns.

Pattern completion and noise reduction

Now you can run through a demonstration of noise reduction and pattern completion with the autoassociator. Open the Testing Options dialogue box and select the Novel data: option by double-clicking on its box. Choose the file **noise.data** from the list of options presented. This file contains a corrupted version of the first training pattern in **aa.data**. Deactivate the reset file check box (we are only presenting a single pattern) and make sure that the weights file **aa-20.wts** is still selected for testing. Now reactivate the Node Activities display. You should see a noisy version of the first training pattern at the input as shown in figure 4.12. The activity of the last unit has been flipped. Now cycle through successive presentations of the noisy pattern by clicking on Next Data Pattern. Observe how the output units gradually converge on a pattern of activity which is more similar to the first training pattern than the noisy input pattern. Autoassociators perform noise reduction.

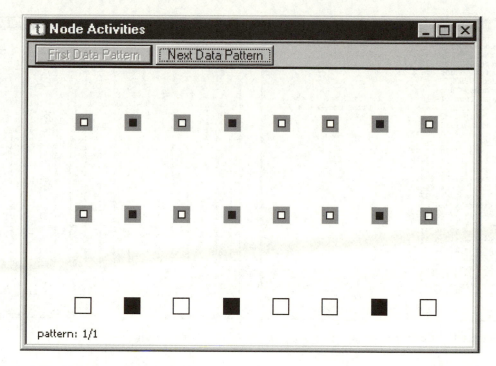

Figure 4.12   Noisy input for autoassociator.

Close the Node Activities display and repeat the testing process with the file **partial.data** which contains just 4 active units from the first training pattern. The remaining units are set to zero activity. As you present successive cycles of this incomplete pattern to the network, you should observe that the output units converge on a pattern of activity very similar to that for the complete training pattern. Autoassociators perform pattern completion.

Prototype extraction

Close the **aa** project and associated windows and open a new project called **dcb**. This project activates the necessary files to replicate the dog, cat, bagel project discussed earlier in this chapter. The **dcb.cf** file and part of the **dcb.data** files are shown in figure 4.13.

The **dcb.cf** file configures a network like that for the **aa** project except that there are 16 output units instead of 8. The **dcb.data** file contains distortions of the dog, cat and bagel prototype vectors:

dog: 1 −1 1 1 −1 −1 −1 −1 1 1 1 1 1 −1 −1 −1
cat: 1 −1 1 1 −1 1 −1 −1 1 −1 1 1 −1 1 1 −1 1
bagel: 1 1 −1 1 −1 1 1 1 −1 1 −1 −1 1 1 1 1 −1

```
dcb.cf                                    _ □ X
NODES:
nodes = 32
inputs = 16
outputs = 16
output nodes are 1-16
CONNECTIONS:
groups = 0
1-16 from i1-i16 = 1. & 1. fixed one-to-one
17-32 from 1-16 = 1. & 1. fixed one-to-one
1 from 18-32
2 from 17,19-32
3 from 17,18,20-32
4 from 17-19,21-32
5 from 17-20,22-32
6 from 17-21,23-32
7 from 17-22,24-32
8 from 17-23,25-32
9 from 17-24,26-32
10 from 17-25,27-32
11 from 17-26,28-32
12 from 17-27,29-32
13 from 17-28,30-32
14 from 17-29,31-32
15 from 17-30,32
16 from 17-31
SPECIAL:
linear = 17-32
bipolar = 1-16
selected = 1-16
weight_limit = 0.1
```

```
dcb.data                                  _ □ X
distributed
750
-1 -1  1  1 -1 -1 -1 -1  1  1  1  1  1 -1 -1 -1
-1 -1  1  1 -1 -1 -1 -1  1  1  1  1  1 -1 -1 -1
-1 -1  1  1 -1 -1 -1 -1  1  1  1  1  1 -1 -1 -1
-1 -1  1  1 -1 -1 -1 -1  1  1  1  1  1 -1 -1 -1
-1 -1  1  1 -1 -1 -1 -1  1  1  1  1  1 -1 -1 -1
 1 -1  1  1 -1 -1 -1 -1  1 -1  1  1  1 -1 -1  1
 1 -1  1  1 -1 -1 -1 -1  1 -1  1  1  1 -1 -1  1
 1 -1  1  1 -1 -1 -1 -1  1 -1  1  1  1 -1 -1  1
 1 -1  1  1 -1 -1 -1 -1  1 -1  1  1  1 -1 -1  1
 1 -1  1  1 -1 -1 -1 -1  1 -1  1  1  1 -1 -1  1
-1 -1 -1  1 -1  1  1  1  1  1 -1  1  1  1  1 -1
-1 -1 -1  1 -1  1  1  1  1  1 -1  1  1  1  1 -1
-1 -1 -1  1 -1  1  1  1  1  1 -1  1  1  1  1 -1
-1 -1 -1  1 -1  1  1  1  1  1 -1  1  1  1  1 -1
-1 -1 -1  1 -1  1  1  1  1  1 -1  1  1  1  1 -1
-1 -1  1  1 -1  1 -1 -1  1  1  1  1  1 -1 -1  1
-1 -1  1  1 -1  1 -1 -1  1  1  1  1  1 -1 -1  1
-1 -1  1  1 -1  1 -1 -1  1  1  1  1  1 -1 -1  1
-1 -1  1  1 -1  1 -1 -1  1  1  1  1  1 -1 -1  1
-1 -1  1  1 -1  1 -1 -1  1  1  1  1  1 -1 -1  1
-1  1  1  1 -1 -1 -1  1  1 -1  1 -1  1  1  1  1
-1  1  1  1 -1 -1 -1  1  1 -1  1 -1  1  1  1  1
-1  1  1  1 -1 -1 -1  1  1 -1  1 -1  1  1  1  1
-1  1  1  1 -1 -1 -1  1  1 -1  1 -1  1  1  1  1
-1  1  1  1 -1 -1 -1  1  1 -1  1 -1  1  1  1  1
 1  1  1  1 -1 -1  1 -1  1 -1 -1  1  1 -1 -1 -1
 1  1  1  1 -1 -1  1 -1  1 -1 -1  1  1 -1 -1 -1
 1  1  1  1 -1 -1  1 -1  1 -1 -1  1  1 -1 -1 -1
 1  1  1  1 -1 -1  1 -1  1 -1 -1  1  1 -1 -1 -1
```

Figure 4.13   Configuration and data files for **dcb**.

50 distortions of each prototype are produced by randomly flipping each element in the prototype vector with a probability of 0.1. The **dcb.data** file contains 5 copies of each of these distortions so that the network can cycle through each distortion 5 times. Since there are 3 prototype vectors, 50 distortions of each vector and 5 copies of each distortion, the training set contains 750 pattern vectors. The training data lists the files (with 5 replications of each) in the order dog, cat, bagel, dog, cat, bagel, and so on.

Training the network

Open the Training Options dialogue box and set the parameters to the values shown in figure 4.14. In particular, make sure that you have set Training Sweeps: to 750, Learning Rate: to 0.25, that you Train sequentially and that you Use reset file. Now Train the network. It might take some time because the network has to process 750 patterns. The **tlearn** Status display will indicate how far it has reached in the training process.

Testing the network

Test the network using the latest weights file, **dcb-750.wts** and the training data, **dcb.data**. Also make sure that the you use the **reset** file in the Testing Options

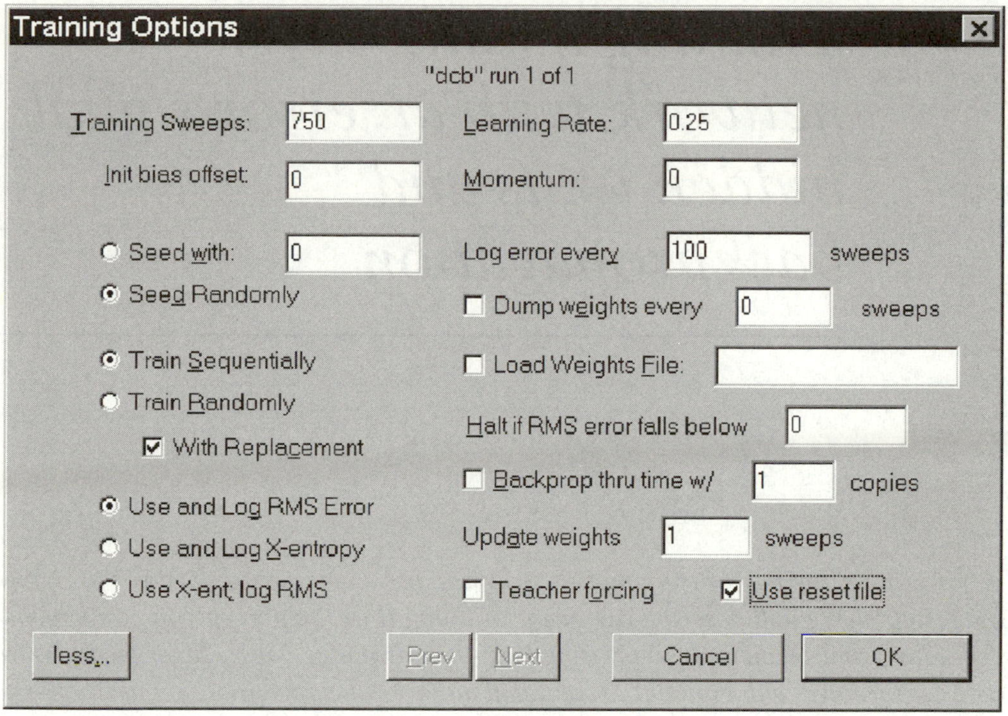

Figure 4.14 Training Options parameters for **dcb**.

dialogue box. Evaluate network performance using the Node Activities display. You will find that for most of the distortion patterns, the output is not quite the same as the input. In fact, the output tends to be a cross between the input distortion and the prototype from which it was generated.

Now test the network on the prototypes themselves. Do this by setting the Testing set: option to Novel data in the Testing Options dialogue box and choose the file **bagel.data**, **cat.data** or **dog.data**. Remember also to turn off the reset check box and the Calculate error check box. When you test the network on the prototype vectors for dog, cat and bagel, you should find that the response is pretty accurate. Autoassociators are good at extracting prototypes from a training set consisting mostly of distortions.

Finally, test the network on incomplete versions of the dog, cat and bagel prototype vectors. These are found in the files **bagel probe.data**, **cat probe.data** and **dog_probe.data**. Each file contains only 4 active elements of the prototype vectors—all the rest are set to zero. Nevertheless, when you test the network, you will see that it does a reasonable job of producing lookalikes of the appropriate prototype at the output.

5   *Training a multi-layer network with an error signal: hidden units and backpropagation*

A powerful technique for training networks is to use a measure of the error to change the weights. We will describe two ways of doing this: the perceptron convergence procedure, and gradient descent using least-mean-squares. Single layer feedforward networks trained with gradient descent will discover an appropriate set of weights to solve the problem of mapping a given set of input patterns onto a given set of output patterns if such a set exists. But for many problems no set does exist for a single layer network, only for a multi-layer network. However, multi-layer networks cannot be trained in the same way as single layer networks because the error term required for gradient descent learning is not available at the hidden units. The backpropagation learning algorithm suggests a way of estimating a plausible value for the error of the hidden units, allowing multi-layer networks to be trained by gradient descent. Hidden units can re-represent the input patterns in a novel way which is appropriate to the problem which the network has to solve. This makes multi-layer networks very powerful problem solving devices.

The discovery that networks with hidden units could be trained with the back-propagation algorithm is probably the single most important factor in the growth of interest in connectionist networks which began in cognitive science in the mid-1980s. Most of the models described in chapters 8–12 are trained using this procedure. In this chapter we will describe the problem that the learning rule overcame and how it works. The aim is to show why backpropagation was needed and, at an intuitive level, how it works, using as little mathematics as possible. Stripped of their mathematical formalism, the *ideas* involved in backpropagation are simple, indeed so simple that, admittedly with the benefit of hindsight, it is difficult to see why it took the cognitive science community so long to discover the power of this technique. A formal derivation of the backpropagation learning algorithm, which requires an understanding of calculus, can be found in chapter 8 of Rumelhart and McClelland (1986a) or chapter 3 of Bechtel and Abrahamsen (1991).

A number of separate problems must be understood before the point of the backpropagation algorithm can be appreciated. We will take these one at a time. But since, on their own, their relationship to the final goal may seem somewhat obscure, we will start by making the structure of the chapter explicit:

(1) Using the error of the output to adjust the weights is a powerful way to teach a network. The technique of *error gradient descent* is particularly effective, guaranteeing to find a set of weights to perform the task (i.e. produce the correct output pattern in response to all input patterns) if one exists.

(2) But with single layer networks a set of weights which will produce zero error only exists if the input–output mappings to be learnt are *linearly separable*. Unfortunately many problems of interest in cognitive science do not satisfy this condition.

(3) Multi-layer networks can solve problems which are not linearly separable by forming a novel representation of the input patterns on the *hidden units*. The ability to reorganise a problem into a form which is soluble makes multi-layer networks extremely effective problem solving devices.

(4) But error gradient descent learning requires the error on all units in a network to be known. The error on the output units of a multi-layer network is known but the error on the hidden units is not.

(5) The backpropagation algorithm suggests a plausible way to estimate a value for the error on the hidden units given the error on the output units. So all is well. The powerful technique of error gradient descent can be used to train a multi-layer network.

An important point to note en route to this conclusion is that error gradient descent requires the units in the network to have a *differentiable (i.e. continuous) activation function*. We will show that the connectionist modeller's favoured activation function, the logistic, meets this requirement. The section 'Hidden units and internal representation' is a digression from the main line of the argument to illustrate the nature of the representations which can form on hidden units, and to show how they allow networks to draw inferences which go beyond the information they have been given in individual training examples.

The perceptron convergence rule

The aim of a learning rule is to find a set of weights for the connections in a network which ensure that the correct pattern appears at output for every input. Consider the

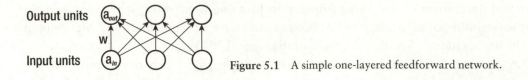

Output units

Input units

Figure 5.1   A simple one-layered feedforward network.

simple perceptron[1] shown in figure 5.1. We will focus attention on two units, one in the input layer and one in the output layer, linked by a connection of weight w. The activities of the two units are a_{in} and a_{out}. The net input to the output unit is given by:

$$netinput_{out} = \Sigma_{in}\, w\, a_{in} \qquad\qquad (5.1)$$

Let us assume that the output unit has a binary threshold activation function. It will fire if and only if the net input exceeds a threshold value, θ. This activation function is shown in figure 1.4(d) in chapter 1. It can be expressed as:

$$a_{out} = 1 \text{ if } netinput_{out} > \theta \qquad\qquad (5.2)$$
$$= 0 \text{ otherwise}$$

Let t_{out} be the desired target value for the activity, a_{out}, of the output unit. The perceptron convergence rule (Rosenblatt 1958) attempts to reduce the discrepancy between the actual activity and the desired activity by adjusting both the threshold of the output unit and the strength of the connection from input to output. If the activity level is too low then the threshold value is decreased and the connection strength is increased. If the activity level is too high then the threshold is increased and the connection strength decreased. This is a straightforward approach to learning: if the activity of the output unit is too low you make it more likely to fire; if it is too high make it less likely to fire. This is an example of the general class of learning algorithm referred to earlier as the Delta rule.

If $\Delta\theta$ and Δw are the adjustments to the threshold and the connection weight respectively, the learning rules are:

$$\Delta\theta = -\varepsilon\, \delta \qquad\qquad (5.3)$$

$$\Delta w = \varepsilon\, \delta\, a_{in} \qquad\qquad (5.4)$$

where δ is $(t_{out} - a_{out})$, the discrepancy between the desired and actual activity level of the output unit,

and ε is the learning rate constant which determines how large the changes are on each trial.

---

[1]A 'perceptron' is not a precisely defined kind of network. The term is typically, but not exclusively, used to refer to a single-layered, feedforward network, with threshold activation functions for the output units, trained by gradient descent.

Figure 5.2   Boolean OR in a one-layered network.

Note that the corrections have opposite signs. If the activity is less than the target value, δ is positive. So the threshold is decreased and the weight increased. If the activity is greater than the target value the opposite happens. Note also that the threshold of the output unit will always change if the activity differs from the target. But a change in the connection strength will occur only if the input unit is active. If $a_{in} = 0$, then $\Delta w = 0$. No attempt is made to teach a connection which is attached to an input unit which is inactive and so does not affect a_{out}.

The computations of $\Delta\theta$ and Δw involve only known quantities, a_{in}, a_{out} and t_{out}, so the learning rule can be implemented. However, it is not obvious what effect it will produce. As different patterns are applied to the network the weights and threshold value might oscillate up and down and never settle on a stable set of values. In fact, the perceptron convergence rule can reach a stable solution as we will see by applying it to the problem of computing Boolean OR.

The computation of Boolean OR can be demonstrated in a network with two input units and a single output unit as shown in figure 5.2. The network has to map four input patterns (00, 10, 01, 11) onto two output patterns (0 and 1). Boolean OR can be thought of as a classification problem—input pattern 00 should be classified into category 0; input patterns 10, 01 and 11 into category 1. Let us set the initial values of $\theta = 1$, $w_{20} = 0.2$ and $w_{21} = 0.1$. Table 5.1 shows the changes of the connections and threshold as the perceptron convergence rule (equations 5.3 and 5.4) is applied after presentation of an input pattern. In this example, the learning rate $\varepsilon = 0.5$. After one cycle through each of the four input patterns the network has found a set of values for the two weights and the threshold which solve the problem. $\delta = 0$ for all four problems and there are no further changes in θ, w_{20} or w_{21}. The perceptron convergence rule is a powerful learning algorithm. In fact, as we will see, it guarantees to find a suitable configuration of weights and thresholds to solve any mapping problem *provided such a configuration exists*. We shall describe the classes of problems for which the perceptron convergence rule succeeds or fails to find the right network configuration in the section 'Linear separability'.

Gradient descent

Another technique for adjusting the weights in a network is called the least-mean-squares (LMS) learning procedure (Widrow and Hoff 1960). Consider the two units

Table 5.1. Training the network in figure 5.2 on Boolean OR. The first row of numbers shows what happens when the pattern 00 is applied to the untrained network. The net input to the output unit, $a_0 w_{20}$ + $a_1 w_{21}$, is zero because a_0 and a_1 are both 0, so $a_{out} = 0$. $t_{out} = 0$, so $\delta = 0$, and there is no change in the weights or the threshold. The second row shows what happens when a new input pattern, 10, is applied. The net input to the output unit is now $1 \times 0.2 + 0 = 0.2$. This is less than the threshold so $a_{out} = 0$. t_{out} = 1, so $\delta = 1$ and learning takes place. Equation 5.3 is applied to the threshold, giving $\Delta\theta = -0.5$. Equation 5.4 is applied to the weights, giving $\Delta w_{20} = 0.5$ and $\Delta w_{21} = 0$. So for the next cycle $\theta = 0.5$, w_{20} = 0.7 and $w_{21} = 0.1$. The next row shows the application of the third pattern, 01, to the network with its new values, and so on.

In	w_{20}	w_{21}	θ	a_{out}	t_{out}	δ	$\Delta\theta$	Δw_{20}	Δw_{21}
0 0	0.2	0.1	1.0	0	0	0	0	0	0
1 0	0.2	0.1	1.0	0	1	1.0	−0.5	0.5	0
0 1	0.7	0.1	0.5	0	1	1.0	−0.5	0	0.5
1 1	0.7	0.6	0.0	1	1	0	0	0	0
0 0	0.7	0.6	0.0	0	0	0	0	0	0
1 0	0.7	0.6	0.0	1	1	0	0	0	0
0 1	0.7	0.6	0.0	1	1	0	0	0	0
1 1	0.7	0.6	0.0	1	1	0	0	0	0

in the simple network shown in figure 5.1 again. If t_{out} is the desired target value for a_{out}, we can define an error score E_p following input pattern p:

$$E_p = (t_{out} - a_{out})^2 \tag{5.5}$$

$a_{out} = F(\Sigma_{in}\, w\, a_{in})$, where F represents the activation function of the output unit. So as w is varied, E_p will vary. The square of a real number is always positive, so E_p will be positive. If, in a single layered network, we hold all the other weights constant and vary w, then the plot of E_p against w will always look like figure 5.3. That is, it will have a single minimum. The lowest point on the curve corresponds to the minimum error that can be achieved in the network for the input pattern p by adjusting w. The aim of the learning rule is to find the value of w which corresponds to the lowest point on the curve.

Figure 5.3 suggests a different approach to the problem of finding the desired value of w from that used by the perceptron convergence rule. The network will always be

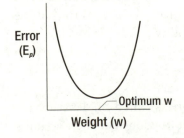

Figure 5.3 The relationship between error and weight for a single connection in a network.

at some point on the error curve dependent on the current value of w. If the slope of the curve at its current position can be calculated we can change w in the direction which will reduce the error. If the slope is negative, w is less than the optimum value and should be increased. If the slope is positive, the value of w is above the optimum and should be decreased. The change in w on any one learning trial can be as small as you like. But if this operation is repeated enough times, eventually the target value of w which corresponds to the minimum error will be reached. At this point the slope is zero and the weight change procedure will stop. This approach to learning is, naturally, called *gradient descent*.

If the change to be made to the weight on any one trial is Δw, then:

$$\Delta w = -\varepsilon \frac{dE}{dw} \qquad (5.6)$$

where dE/dw is the calculus expression which stands for the rate of change of E with w, that is, the slope of the curve in figure 5.3,

ε is a constant which determines how large the change to w is on any trial,

and the negative sign ensures the desired result that the weight will be increased when the slope is negative and decreased when it is positive.

$E = (t_{out} - a_{out})^2$, so equation 5.6 can be rewritten as:

$$\Delta w = -\varepsilon \frac{d(t_{out} - a_{out})^2}{dw} \qquad (5.7)$$

$a_{out} = F(\Sigma_{in}\, w\, a_{in})$, so equation 5.7 can be rewritten as:

$$\Delta w = -\varepsilon \frac{d[t_{out} - F(\Sigma_{in}\, w\, a_{in})]^2}{dw} \qquad (5.8)$$

Calculus allows us to perform the operation represented by d/dw. If you do not understand calculus you will just have to accept that the result is:

$$\Delta w = 2\,\varepsilon\,[t_{out} - F(\Sigma_{in}\, w\, a_{in})]\, F'(\,\Sigma_{in}\, w\, a_{in})a_{in} \qquad (5.9)$$

where F' stands for the differential of F with respect to w, that is, the slope of the activation function at the point corresponding to the net input, $\Sigma_{in}\, w\, a_{in}$.

Since $\delta = (t_{out} - a_{out})$, and letting F^* stand for $F'(\Sigma_{in}\, w\, a_{in})$, equation 5.9 becomes:

$$\Delta w = 2\,\varepsilon\,\delta\, F^*\, a_{in} \qquad (5.10)$$

Equation 5.10 is similar to equation 5.4, which expressed the weight changes required by the perceptron convergence procedure. However, it now contains the term F^*, the slope of the activation function of the output unit. If the unit has the binary threshold activation function, which we considered in the previous example, we are in trouble. The function has a slope of either 0 or ∞ [see figure 1.4(d)] so it is not possible to compute a meaningful value for Δw. Gradient descent cannot be used to train a network where the output units have a threshold activation function.

However, many other activation functions are possible. The simplest is the linear activation function shown in panel (a) of figure 1.4. In this the activity of the output unit is a constant proportion of the net input. The slope of a linear activation function is a constant, so equation 5.10 becomes:

$$\Delta w = k \, \delta \, a_{in} \qquad\qquad (5.11)$$

where k is a constant representing the learning rate and the slope of the activation function.

Δw can now be calculated because we know the values of δ and a_{in}. Surprisingly, given that their approaches appear to be quite different, gradient descent in a network with a linear activation function and the perceptron convergence procedure lead to the same learning rule (i.e. equation 5.11 is the same as equation 5.4). In both cases, the learning algorithm leads the network to perform gradient descent to the bottom of the error curve. Δw is proportional to δ, so as the activity level approaches the target value the changes become smaller and stop when the correct value has been found.

Feedforward networks with a single layer of modifiable connections always have an error curve with a single error minimum. So, if the network employs a learning algorithm that performs gradient descent, it will always find the global minimum of the curve. It is now possible to understand the claim that the perceptron convergence rule (or the LMS rule) will always find a solution to a mapping problem provided such a solution exists. This corresponds to saying that the network will always descend to the lowest point on the error curve. If that point is at zero error then the network has solved the problem. If the error curve is still above the x-axis, as in figure 5.3, then an exact solution to the mapping problem is not possible with a single-layered feedforward network.

Training networks using a gradient descent learning algorithm corresponds to moving the network through a space of states that we can think of as a landscape. In figure 5.3 this landscape was defined by calculating the error as a single weight was varied. If we included two weights in the calculation of error then the landscape would become three-dimensional as in figure 5.4. With more weights the surface acquires more dimensions and becomes difficult to visualise. But training would still correspond to the state of the network moving through a landscape. In the 2- or 3-dimensional case one can think of the state of the network as a ball bearing moving down hillsides and along valleys. It is always seeking the lowest potential energy.

Gradient descent with a sigmoid activation function

Connectionist models of cognitive function seldom use a linear activation function. One reason is that there is always a single layer network which is equivalent to any

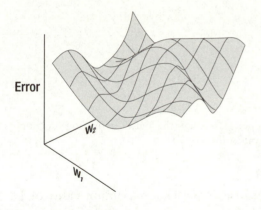

Figure 5.4 Error landscape in a network with two weights.

multi-layer *linear* network (see Appendix 2) and single layer networks cannot solve certain classes of problems. Another reason is that there is no way to keep the activity of units under control in a linear network. If the net input increases or decreases, so will the activity, without limit. Apart from the undesirable consequences that this might have in the network, this is unlike real neurons. They operate over a fixed range. Increasing the input has little further effect as the neuron approaches its maximum firing rate. Similarly, increasing inhibitory input can have no further effect once the neuron has stopped firing.

In practice, most modellers use a sigmoid activation function such as the logistic function shown in figure 5.5 to relate activity to input. This constrains the maximum activity of the unit to 1, however large the positive net input is, and produces a minimum activity of 0 however large a negative net input is. So at its extremes this is like a threshold function which constrains the range of activity between 1 and 0, but the crucial difference is that the activity moves smoothly and continuously from maximum to minimum as the net input changes.

The logistic activation function defines the relation between the net input to a unit and its activity (a_i) as:

$$a_i = \frac{1}{(1 + e^{-\text{netinput}_i})} \qquad (5.12)$$

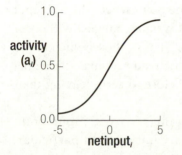

Figure 5.5 The logistic activation function relating a unit's net input to its activity level.

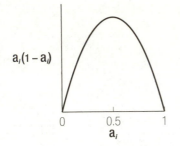

Figure 5.6   The slope, $a_i(1 - a_i)$, of the logistic activation function over the range of a_i values from 0 to 1.

a_i has a value of 0.5 when netinput$_i$ = 0 (because e^{-0} = 1), a maximum value of 1 when netinput$_i$ has a large positive value, and a minimum value of 0 when netinput$_i$ has a large negative value. What will happen if we try to do gradient descent in a network where the units have a sigmoid activation function? The relevant component of equation 5.10 is F^*, the slope of the activation function. If we are to be able to use equation 5.10 as the basis of a learning rule, the activation function must be continuous so that its slope is defined (i.e. it must have no discontinuities like the binary threshold activation function). Also F^* must be defined by terms which we know the value of.

The slope of the logistic function given in equation 5.12 can be shown to be $a_i(1 - a_i)$. Remember that the logistic function constrains a_i to lie between 0 and 1, whatever the value of netinput. In figure 5.6 $a_i(1 - a_i)$ is plotted against a_i. $a_i(1 - a_i)$ has a value of 0 when a_i = 0, increases steadily up to a maximum value when a_i = 0.5, and then declines steadily to zero again as a_i approaches 1.

So the logistic activation function creates no problems when using gradient descent to compute weight changes—it is continuous, and it is computable because we know a_i. However, the inclusion of the slope of the logistic function in the gradient descent weight change algorithm (equation 5.10) does influence learning in the network in a number of important ways:

(1) The logistic function outputs a value of 0.5 when its net input is zero. Units can therefore participate in the learning process (i.e. experience weight change) even though they are not receiving any input.
(2) The slope of the logistic function is steepest around the point where the net input is zero. This means that most learning (i.e. the largest weight changes) will occur for those units which receive a net input around zero. That is, those which are as yet uncommitted to the task. Conversely, units which already receive a large net input will change little because F^*, for them, will be close to zero, leaving their current role in the mapping problem unchanged.
(3) These properties of the logistic function around the zero net input point determine the manner in which many simulations are initiated. In particular,

networks are initialised (before any training) with a set of random weights that are constrained within the range ±0.5. As a result, the net input to any unit is likely to sum to zero and learning is maximised.

These properties of sigmoid activation functions will be discussed further in chapter 10 where we will see that they allow modellers to simulate critical periods in the acquisition of cognitive skills.

Linear separability

Single-layered, feedforward networks trained by gradient descent can solve a given mapping problem provided the classification inherent in the mappings is linearly separable. The concept of linear separability can be represented graphically by examining three simple and apparently similar mappings, two of which turn out to be linearly separable (and so can be learnt by a single layer network) and one of which does not.

Consider the three Boolean functions AND, OR and XOR shown in table 5.2. Each function takes a two-value input (0 or 1) and classifies it along one dimension (0 or 1). AND requires both inputs to be On to produce the output 1; OR will produce the output 1 if either input is On; XOR will produce the output 1 provided only one input line is On. Can the network in table 5.2 find a suitable pair of weights so that the output represents the AND, OR or XOR of the input? In a real network the numbers of units and set of patterns to be learnt would usually be much larger, of course. But, at a scale which is possible to follow, these mappings are typical of the problems which networks have to solve.

The mappings can be considered as a projection from a two-dimensional (input) space to a one-dimensional (output) space. We can represent the two dimensional input space on a simple x,y graph. The four possible input patterns (00, 10, 01, 11) are shown as points in this space in figure 5.7(a). The one-dimensional output space

Table 5.2. Boolean AND, OR and XOR.

Input	Output		
	AND	OR	XOR
0 0	0	0	0
1 0	0	1	1
0 1	0	1	1
1 1	1	1	0

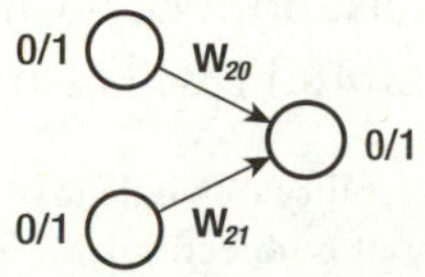

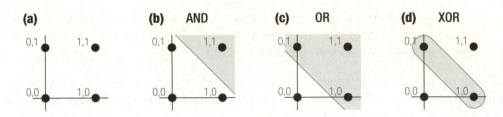

Figure 5.7 Boolean functions in two dimensions. (Based on McClelland and Rumelhart 1988.)

can be represented by a straight line partitioning the input space into two categories, the shaded portion representing the output 1 and the unshaded representing the output 0. In figure 5.7(b) the partitioning corresponds to Boolean AND. Input 1,1 falls in the region corresponding to the output 1, and the others in the region corresponding to the output 0. There are an infinite number of lines, with different slopes, which could partition the space in this manner. The different lines correspond to the variety of solutions (i.e. the different values of w_{20}, w_{21} and θ) that could solve the problem represented by Boolean AND in a single-layered, feedforward network.

A different partitioning of the space is required for Boolean OR. This can also be achieved by separating the space with a straight line as shown in figure 5.7(c). Now the input 0,0 is the only point in one of the partitions. Again, there are an infinite number of such lines (and weights in the network) that can do the job. The Boolean functions AND and OR are *linearly separable*. The functions inhabit a two-dimensional space where it is possible to divide the space appropriately with a single line. If the target function inhabited a three-dimensional space (i.e. a set of patterns which required three units to code them) then the condition for linear separability would be that it was possible for the problem space to be partitioned by a plane. In more than three dimensions the condition for linear separability would be that the partitioning must be achievable with a hyperplane.

A partitioning of the two-dimensional space which would solve XOR (i.e. produce the output 1 to inputs 10 and 01 and the output 0 to inputs 00 and 11) is shown in figure 5.7(d). It is not possible to achieve this partition with a single straight line. Hence Boolean XOR is a function which is not linearly separable. There is no pair of weights for the connections in the network in table 5.2 which will allow the output to represent the XOR of the input. The reason for this is easy to understand. w_{20} and w_{21} must both be positive to ensure that 10 and 01 respectively produce the output 1. Inevitably 11 will also produce the output 1.[2]

[2]The inability of single layer perceptrons to solve XOR has a significance of mythical proportions in the history of connectionism. This is discussed in the sections on Rosenblatt and on Minsky and Papert in chapter 15.

Solving the XOR problem with hidden units

A network that *can* perform Boolean XOR is shown in figure 5.8. The network consists of three layers of units: an input layer of two units to represent the activities for the four input patterns, and an output unit to provide the classification of the input patterns (as before), and a layer of hidden units (so-called because they are connected only to other units and are thus hidden from the external environment of the network). The hidden units accumulate net input in the same fashion as the output units in single-layered networks. The hidden units and output unit are threshold units where $\theta = 1.0$. A set of weights which can solve the problem has been given to the connections because the perceptron convergence procedure will not work with a multi-layer network. We cannot discover suitable values for the weights starting from a set of random values in the way we found a set of weights to solve the Boolean OR problem in table 5.1. (If you cannot see the problem you may find it instructive to start with a random set of weights and try applying equation 5.4 just as we did in table 5.1.)

Table 5.3 shows the activity level of the units as the four input patterns pass through successive layers of the network. The crucial point to note is that while there are four patterns of activity at the input layer, there are only three at the hidden layer. The input patterns 00 and 11 are both represented as 00 at the hidden layer. So 00 and 11 both produce the same output, 0.

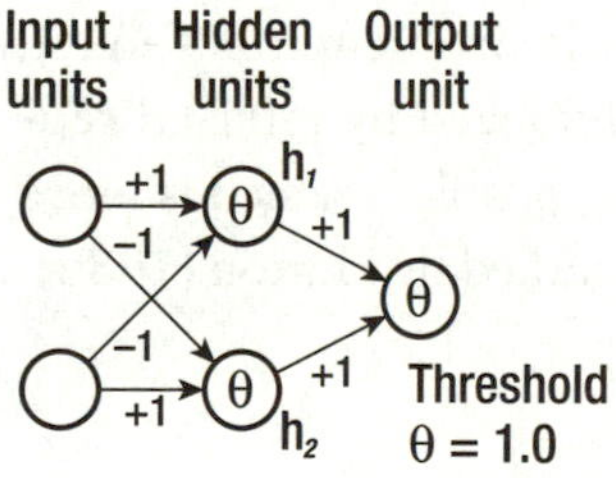

Input **Hidden** **Output**
units **units** **unit**

Figure 5.8 A multi-layered perceptron for solving the XOR problem.

Table 5.3. Representing similarity relations in the hidden units of an XOR network.

Input	Hidden		Target
	h_1	h_2	
0 0	0	0	0
1 0	1	0	1
0 1	0	1	1
1 1	0	0	0

In terms of the two-dimensional representation of the problem shown in figure 5.7, the input space has been folded so that the point 11 has been transformed into 00. The similarity structure of the problem has been changed. In the hidden units the representation following the input 11 is now more similar to 00 than it is to either of the points 10 or 01. It is possible to draw a straight line with 10 and 01 on one side and 00 and 11 on the other. The problem, as represented in the hidden units, is now linearly separable. So it will be possible for the final layer of connections between the hidden units and the output unit to transform the hidden activities into the correct response pattern for the problem. In the exercises at the end of the chapter you will be able to watch the representation on the hidden units change as a network acquires a set of weights which will solve the XOR problem.

Hidden units and internal representation

The XOR example demonstrated that a multi-layered network can form novel representations of a set of input patterns on its hidden units. For obvious reasons these are referred to as 'internal representations'. The freedom to alter the similarity structure of the input patterns makes multi-layer networks very powerful. They do not require inputs to be linearly separable, like single layer networks trained with gradient descent. If the input patterns have some characteristic which makes the correct transformation to output patterns unlearnable, the network can reorganise the inputs into a form where the transformation is learnable. XOR is a simple example of what hidden units can do, which is easy to follow. But the problem it is solving may seem a little abstract. As an example of what can be achieved by internal rep-resentations on the hidden units of a network trying to solve a problem which is more obviously cognitive we will look at a multi-layered network studied by Hinton (1986).

Hinton's family tree problem

Consider the two family trees shown in figure 5.9, one representing an extended English family and the other an isomorphic Italian family. All the information in the trees ('Andrew's wife is Christine', 'Sophia's mother is Lucia' and so on) can be represented as propositional triplets of the form (person$_1$, relationship, person$_2$). The 12 relationships used were *mother, daughter, sister, wife, aunt, niece* and their masculine equivalents.

Hinton trained a network to learn the information in the tree expressed in propositional triplet form. During the learning phase the net was presented with (person$_1$) and (relationship) as inputs, and the appropriate (person$_2$) as target output. Discrepancy between the target and actual output was treated as error and used to adjust the weights in the network. The test for the network after training was to

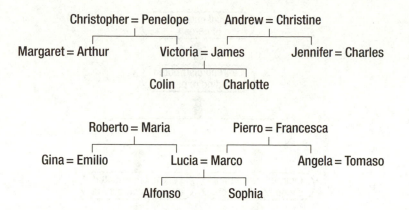

Figure 5.9 Two isomorphic family trees. (Based on Hinton 1986.)

switch on the appropriate output unit for (person$_2$) when the input units corresponding to (person$_1$) and (relationship) had been activated. Thus, for example, if the input units <Victoria> and <father> were switched on, the equivalent of asking the network 'Who is Victoria's father?', the network should respond by switching on the output unit <Christopher>.

The network was trained on 100 of the 104 possible relationships. Naturally the network learnt the 100 examples it had been trained on, but it also succeeded in giving the correct answer to questions about the four relationships which it had not been taught. At first sight this may seem a trivial achievement, just the sort of generalisation which we might expect a network to be good at. But in fact it shows that something very significant has happened in the network during training. Imagine that 'Victoria's son is Colin' is one of the facts that the network was not given during training. When the network is given the question 'Who is Victoria's son?', activity would pass down every connection stemming from the inputs <Victoria> and <son>. If the network were a single layer one, positive connections would have developed during training from the <Victoria> input unit to all the output units corresponding to the people she was related to. These would include James and Arthur, for example, because the net was taught that 'Victoria's husband is James' and 'Victoria's brother is Arthur'. But there would be no connection from <Victoria> to the output unit <Colin> because the net was not taught about their relationship. Similarly there would be positive connections from the input unit <son> to James and Arthur because the network was taught that 'Christine's son is James' and 'Christopher's son is Arthur'. There will also be a positive connection from <son> to Colin because the network was told that he is James's son. But the network would not get the right answer to the question 'Who is Victoria's son?' if output is driven by the strength of connections between input and output. Both <James> and <Arthur> would get more excitation than <Colin> if the input units <Victoria> and <son> were activated.

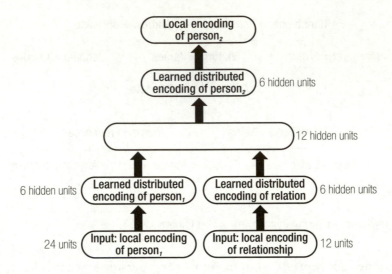

Figure 5.10   The structure of the network used to learn the family tree. (Based on Hinton 1986.)

The problem can only be solved by deduction from the structure of the family tree: James is the husband of Victoria and his son is Colin, so Colin must also be Victoria's son. Or, Charlotte is Victoria's daughter and Colin is Charlotte's brother, so Colin must be Victoria's son. Correct answers to the untaught problems require that the network is not merely memorising the family relationships by rote. It must have discovered enough about the structure of the family tree to be able to do what, if we were doing it, would be called 'drawing inferences'. The structure of the tree is transparent to us because we can look at figure 5.9. But this structure was not given to the network. It was only given exemplars drawn from the structure. How has it discovered the structure of the family tree and how is this information represented in the network?

The network used by Hinton is shown in figure 5.10. Each person is represented by the activity of a single unit at input or output. The 12 relations are represented at input by the activity of a single unit. In addition there are several layers of hidden units to enable the network to construct its own internal representations of the individuals and their relationship to each other. There are 6 hidden units to form an internal representation of (person$_1$) and 6 to form an internal representation of (relationship). These feed into a layer of 12 hidden units which can form an internal representation of the combination [(person$_1$),(relationship)].

What the hidden units represent in the family tree task

Hinton analysed the strength of the connections leading from the (person$_1$) input units to the first layer of hidden units. These are shown in figure 5.11. Each block

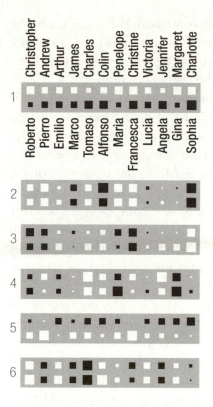

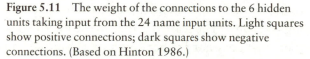

Figure 5.11   The weight of the connections to the 6 hidden units taking input from the 24 name input units. Light squares show positive connections; dark squares show negative connections. (Based on Hinton 1986.)

represents the strength of the connections feeding into one hidden unit from the 24 input units. The top row shows the connections from the input units representing members of the English family; the bottom row the corresponding connections from the Italian family. Since there are 6 hidden units and 24 people, there are 6 blocks with 24 squares in each block. The size of the square reflects the strength of the connection and the shading reflects whether the weight is excitatory or inhibitory.

Hidden unit 1 has developed excitatory connections from all members of the English family and inhibitory connections from all members of the Italian family. It will be switched on by any English (person$_1$) and switched off by any Italian (person$_1$). It represents the fact, discovered from the training examples, that the nationality of (person$_1$) allows predictions to be made about (person$_2$) independent of any other characteristic, either specific such as their name, or general such as their generation. What it has discovered is that if (person$_1$) is English, so is (person$_2$). So when this unit receives an input from any English name it sends positive activity to all English names at output and inhibition to all Italian names. Unit 5 encodes the corresponding conclusion which can be drawn when (person$_1$) is Italian. The other four units have roughly the same pattern of activity whether (person$_1$) is English or Italian. This reflects the fact that any inference to be drawn from the generation, gender or side of the family of (person$_1$) holds equally for both the English and the Italian families. Thus units 1 and 5 do not represent information from a specific training example, as the strengths of the individual connections in a network do, they represent an inference drawn by pooling across all the training examples.

Hidden unit 2 encodes (more or less) which generation (person$_1$) belongs to. It is maximally active when (person$_1$) is any member of the oldest generation, has medium activity when (person$_1$) is from the middle generation and minimum activity when (person$_1$) is from the youngest generation. Unit 3 has acquired the reverse pattern of activity. Coding of generation could be used in conjunction with the coding of relationship to represent, for example, that (person$_2$) should be a member of the same generation as (person$_1$) when (relationship) is <brother> and a member of a different generation when (relationship) is <son>. Units 4 and 6 encode which branch of the family tree an individual belongs to. This can be used to bias the output units towards choosing a (person$_2$) who comes form the same branch of the family as (person$_1$), which is true of the majority of relationships.

Why do none of the units appear to encode gender? That is, why do none of the units have positive connections from the female half of the tree and negative from the male, or vice versa? Gender seems (to us) one of the most obvious ways of categorising (person$_1$). The reason is that in the microworld of these family trees the gender of (person$_1$) does not predict anything about (person$_2$). So, however salient gender may appear to us, because of all the knowledge about male–female differences which we cannot help bringing to bear, it is not relevant to the task of categorising (person$_1$) in a way which allows prediction of (person$_2$).[3]

In no cases has the network been told explicitly about the organisational principles of the family tree. It has discovered them because they happen to be true of the training examples. Nationality, generation and family branch of (person$_1$) can all be used to predict (person$_2$). By using the appropriate microinferences the network can make correct predictions about (person$_2$) in examples which it has never met before. In fact, by the level of the hidden units direct information about (person$_1$) (i.e. information represented in specific training examples) seems largely lost. It has been replaced by a representation which consists of the inferences about (person$_2$) which can be drawn from (person$_1$).

Backpropagation

Hidden units add greatly to the power of connectionist networks. Multi-layered networks are not constrained like single layer networks just to record the correlation

---

[3]Gender *is* represented in the hidden units in the relationship channel. The strength of the connections from input to hidden units are shown in figure 5.12. Unit 4 codes gender. (person$_1$) does not predict the gender of (person$_2$) but (relationship) does.

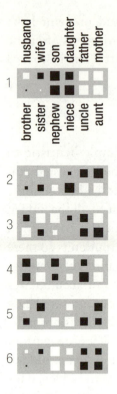

Figure 5.12 The weight matrix for input to the 6 hidden units taking input from the 12 input units representing (relationship). (Based on Hinton 1986.)

between input and output. In the XOR example we saw that they can reorganise the input in any way which is suitable for solving the problem. In Hinton's family tree example we saw that they can represent the structure of the input in a way which allows inferences to be drawn which go beyond the data given. We will now introduce a learning algorithm that is able to adjust weights in a network with hidden units. The algorithm is called backpropagation or the generalised Delta rule.

The problem

Backpropagation uses the discrepancy between the desired output of a unit and its actual output to determine the changes to the connections feeding into the unit. This is the procedure described earlier in LMS learning. Indeed, adjustment to the connection between hidden units and output units is the same as the adjustments to the connections between input and output units in a single layer network. But the adjustment of the connections between the hidden units and the units in the previous layer appears to pose an insoluble problem. In order to compute Δw using equation 5.10, we need to know the error, δ. But there is no predefined target (i.e. t_{out}) for the hidden units—only for the output units. So we cannot say what the activity level of a hidden unit *should* be and hence cannot specify an error for it. This problem restricted gradient descent learning to single layer networks and prevented the widespread application of perceptrons to interesting cognitive problems after the initial discovery of the perceptron convergence rule by Rosenblatt. (The historical angle is discussed in chapter 15.)

An informal account

The designers of the backpropagation algorithm proposed a simple heuristic to establish an appropriate value of the error at the hidden units. They suggested that the error on an output unit can be assumed to arise from error in the hidden units which activate it. They *assign blame* for the error on the output unit to all the hidden units to which it is connected, in proportion to the strength of the connection between them. A hidden unit will usually be connected to many output units so there will be an attributed error term from each of them. The hidden unit accumulates error from the output units in the reverse of the way an output unit accumulates input from the hidden units. The algorithm works as if the error at output were being propagated backwards through the network in the same way that activity is normally propagated forward. Hence the name of the learning algorithm—backpropagation. In the conventional forward pass through the network, activity flows from hidden units to output; in the backward pass, error flows from output units to hidden. This analogy between forward propagation of activity and backward propagation of error is represented in figure 5.13. In the forward pass the flow of activity is represented by:

$$a_{out} = F(\Sigma_{hidden} \, w \, a_{hidden}) \qquad (5.13)$$

For the reverse flow the corresponding equation is:

$$\delta_{hidden} = F(\Sigma_{out} \, w \, \delta_{out}) \qquad (5.14)$$

δ_{out} and all the values of w are known so δ_{hidden} can be computed. Once the hidden units have been assigned an error signal, the changes to the connections between the hidden units and the units in the layer preceding them can proceed in the usual fashion using equation 5.10. That is, weight changes will be proportional to the product of the error on the hidden units and the activity of the input units. The same process can continue backwards one layer at a time for as many layers as there are in the network.

Local minima

It turns out that a multi-layered network can, in principle, learn any mapping function. This is unlike single layer networks, which are constrained by the require-

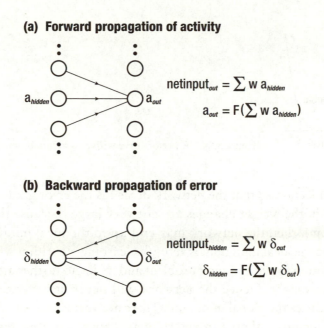

(a) Forward propagation of activity

a_{hidden} a_{out}

$netinput_{out} = \sum w \, a_{hidden}$

$a_{out} = F(\sum w \, a_{hidden})$

(b) Backward propagation of error

δ_{hidden} δ_{out}

$netinput_{hidden} = \sum w \, \delta_{out}$

$\delta_{hidden} = F(\sum w \, \delta_{out})$

Figure 5.13   Backpropagation of error represented as the reverse of forward propagation of activity.

ment that inputs must be linearly separable. However, while the perceptron convergence procedure guarantees to find a solution to the mapping problem if such a solution exists, backpropagation guarantees that a solution exists but does not guarantee to find it. To understand why this is the case, we need the concept of a local minimum.

In figure 5.3, we plotted the error curve for a single-layered, feedforward network trained with the LMS algorithm. The curve has no bumps in it and consequently has only a single global minimum which will eventually be attained if training with a gradient descent algorithm is continued for long enough. It turns out that the error surface for a multi-layered perceptron looks rather different. A hypothetical example is shown in figure 5.14. There is a local dip or minimum in the curve at a higher error than the global minimum. In general, there will be many such dips in the error curve for a multi-layered perceptron, but one will illustrate the problem. Recall that gradient descent algorithms adapt the weights in the network by calculating the slope of the curve at the position that corresponds to the current state of the network. The learning algorithm can only calculate the slope at the place where it is—rather like determining the slope in mountainous terrain at night. The algorithm changes the connections in the network in proportion to the steepness of the slope. If the slope is shallow the connections will not be changed very much and if the slope is zero the connections will not be changed at all. Now suppose that the initial state of the network corresponds to the point A in figure 5.14. Backpropagation will increase the

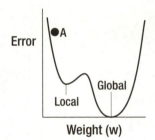

Figure 5.14   An error curve with a local minimum.

value of the connection so that the network descends the error gradient. However, if the increments in the weight changes are not very large (because the learning rate parameter is low), then the network may end up in the local minimum. Since the error gradient at the local minimum is zero, the learning algorithm will behave as if it has found a solution to the mapping problem and make no further attempt to change the value of the weight. Hence the network will never discover the value for the weight that produces the global minimum. There are various fixes that can be applied to reduce the chances that a network gets caught in this fashion (such as manipulating the learning rate) but they are not perfect solutions.

Backpropagation and biological plausibility

Backpropagation requires connections to carry signals in two directions—activity level in one direction and error in the other. Since it was first proposed as a learning algorithm it has seemed implausible that backpropagation could be implemented in the brain because axons are basically unidirectional transmitters of information. However, the technique is so effective that it has been widely used as a way of training connectionist networks in the simulation of cognitive processes. The use of backpropagation has led to polarisation of the connectionist modelling community depending on whether biological plausibility or effective simulation is seen as more important. Here we will set out typical arguments for and against the use of back-propagation. Undoubtedly the force of these arguments will change as, on the one hand, we learn more about information transmission in the brain and, on the other, new learning algorithms are discovered. Individual readers will have to come to their own conclusion about the relative merits of the different arguments.

A response favoured by some connectionists using backpropagation to train their networks is that they are studying *what* networks learn rather than *how* they learn it. Their assumption is that although backpropagation may not used by the nervous system, the representations it forms are similar to those that would be formed by any gradient descent learning algorithm. Therefore the behaviour of any net trained on a gradient descent learning algorithm would be similar irrespective of the way gradient descent is achieved. As yet we do not know enough about neurons to know how the learning of higher cognitive functions is achieved in the brain. Backpropagation is a technique which may turn out to be biologically implausible. Similarly, other connectionist learning techniques will require modification as we discover more about synaptic modifiability. For the time being, the issue is whether it is reasonable to assume that the behaviour of any net trained on a gradient descent learning algorithm will be similar irrespective of the way gradient descent is achieved. Support for the position that nets trained with backpropagation are helpful in the study of cognitive function would come from showing that the pattern of acquisition of skills by nets trained with gradient descent mimics that of children, and that the pattern of breakdown of nets trained with gradient descent matches that of patients. Evidence from these areas will be explored in chapters 8–11.

However, some neural networkers do not use backpropagation because it seems implausible that the brain uses it. First, it requires a single hidden unit to receive information from all the neurons to which it is connected about their error, and to know the relevant strength of every synapse involved, to compute an error term. Second, for backpropagation networks to work correctly, the number of neurons in the hidden layer is crucial. If there are too many, the network fails to generalise; if there are too few, the network fails to learn correctly.[4] There is no evidence (as yet) about how the brain could set the number of hidden units available to solve a cognitive problem to an appropriate value. Modellers who find these arguments persuasive use learning rules such as the Hebbian. The Hebbian is an example of a *local* learning rule—so-called because the information required to implement it is believed to be present at the synapse where the learning takes place. Thus they are considered more biologically plausible than backpropagation. Many classes of neural network, such as pattern associators, autoassociators and competitive networks, can learn with a local rule rather than backpropagating error. Future work will show whether complex learning problems can be solved by networks with local learning rules. In chapters 13 and 14 we will see examples of what can be achieved without backpropagation—formation of episodic memories, creation of position invariant representation of faces and the development of speech recognition devices.

Learning Exclusive OR with **tlearn**

To train a network to compute the XOR of two binary inputs you need a multi-layered perceptron like the one shown in figure 5.15. There are two input nodes, two hidden nodes and an output node. The hidden and output nodes each have a

---

[4]An example of this problem will be discussed in chapter 10. Algorithms for allowing a neural network to allocate an appropriate number of hidden units to solve a problem are discussed in Fahlman and Lebierre (1990), and in Quartz and Sejnowski (1997).

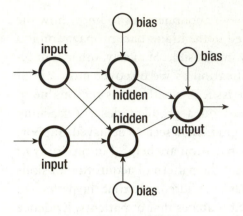

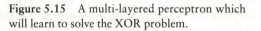

Figure 5.15   A multi-layered perceptron which will learn to solve the XOR problem.

connection from a bias node. Connections propagate activity forward from the input nodes to the hidden nodes and from the hidden nodes to the output node. There are no connections between nodes within a layer or feedback connections to nodes in previous layers. During training, error is assigned to the hidden nodes by back-propagating the error from the output. The error on the output and hidden nodes is used to change the weights on the second and first layer of connections respectively. Before starting the exercises in this chapter, make sure that you are familiar with the procedure described in the previous section by which backpropagation adapts the weights in a network in response to an error signal.

Network configuration

Start up **tlearn** and Open the Project called **xor. tlearn** opens three windows called **xor.cf**, **xor.data** and **xor.teach**. Examine the **xor.cf** file to determine how **tlearn** creates a network with the same architecture as that shown in figure 5.15.

   Once you are confident that the configuration, data and teach files are specified correctly, open the Training Options... dialogue box via the Network menu. Set the Learning rate parameter to 0.3 and the Momentum parameter to 0.9. (Momentum takes into account the size of the weight changes on previous learning trials. See Appendix 3 for further details.) Select a seed of 5 and set **tlearn** to Train randomly for 4000 sweeps. Check that Log error is set to 100.

Training the network

When you have specified all these training options open the Error Display and Train the network. If you have set all the training options as suggested, then you should observe an error display identical to that shown in figure 5.16. Check your training options if you do not observe this learning curve!

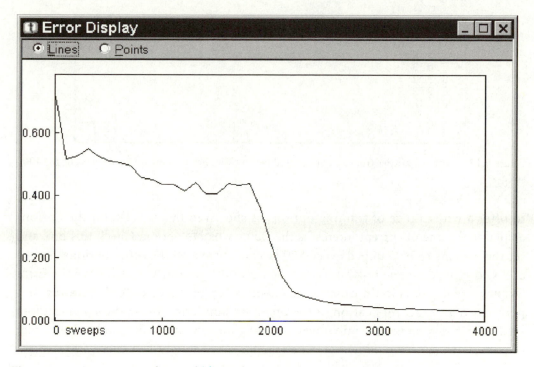

Figure 5.16 An error curve for a multi-layered perceptron trained on the XOR problem.

The error curve shows a sharp drop around the 2000 sweep mark. What has happened? First, examine the output activities for each of the input patterns after 4000 sweeps. The easy way to do this is to use the Verify network has learned option in the **Network** menu. The output from the network is shown in figure 5.17. Again, if you do not observe these values in your own simulation, check that you have set the options in the **Testing Options...** dialogue box correctly. Now consult the **xor.teach** file for the target activity values. The teacher signals for the four input patterns were 0, 1, 1, 0 respectively. So the network has found a good solution to the problem.

But why is there a sudden drop in error around the 2000 sweep mark? To answer this question, it would be useful to examine output activities prior to this point in training. We can achieve this by saving weight files during training of the network and then testing network output with these weight files instead of the network's final (mature) state.

Testing at different points in training

Open the Training Options... dialogue box in the **Network** menu. Click on the more... button in the bottom left-hand corner of the dialogue box. The dialogue box expands

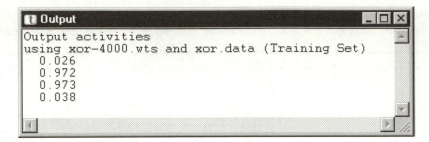

Figure 5.17   Output activities from a multi-layered perceptron after training on Boolean XOR for 4000 sweeps.

to offer a wider range of training options as shown in figure 5.18. Of the options available the one of current interest is the Dump weights option. Check this box and set the weights to be dumped every 500 sweeps. Leave all the other options as they are. Close the dialogue box and Train the network again. If you still have the Error Display open, you should observe an identical error curve unfold. **tlearn** has performed an exact replication of the previous simulation using the same random seed (which determines the initial weight configuration) and same randomized order of pattern presentation. However, **tlearn** has saved weight files every 500 sweeps.

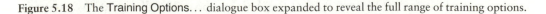

Figure 5.18   The Training Options... dialogue box expanded to reveal the full range of training options.

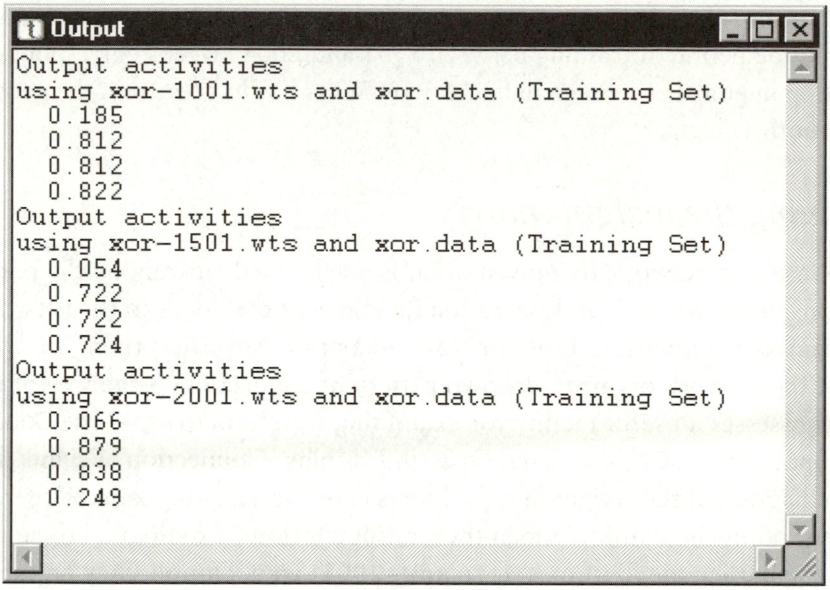

Figure 5.19   Sample output activities after 1001, 1501 and 2001 sweeps of training on XOR.

Since the network has been trained for 4000 sweeps, 8 weight files will have been saved.

Next, open the Testing Options… dialogue box and select the Earlier one: button. Double click in the box to the right of the button to activate the dialogue box. Choose the **xor-1501.wts** file. Close the dialogue box and Verify the network has learned. **tlearn** will now display the output activities for the four input patterns after it has been trained for 1501 sweeps. By resetting the weights file in the Testing Options… dialogue box and Verifying the network has learned, you can determine output activities at any point in training. Figure 5.19 shows the output activities after 1001, 1501 and 2001 sweeps respectively. Rounding off activities, we observe that the network has already learned the first three patterns correctly after 1001 epochs. Overall, however, the network is behaving as though it was supposed to learn Boolean OR. It is categorizing the fourth input pattern in the same fashion as the second and third input patterns. By the 1501 sweep mark the output activities on the first and fourth patterns have been reduced—a move in the right direction. However, the reduction in error on these two patterns has been achieved (apparently) at the expense of the second and third patterns. Notice that the output activities for the second and third patterns have reduced instead of increasing. The network is still behaving like Boolean OR. Finally, after 2001 sweeps of training the output activity for the fourth pattern has decreased considerably and the activity for the second and third patterns has increased again. Activity patterns have begun to move in the right direction and using a rounding off criterion, the network has now solved XOR. Notice that the period of training between 1501 and 2001 sweeps corresponds to the sudden drop in global error seen in figure 5.16. What has happened in the network to bring about this change?

Examining the weight matrix

The response of a network to a given input is determined entirely by the pattern of connections in the network and activation functions of the nodes in the network. We know what the activation functions are—**tlearn** specifies them in advance. However, the network organizes its own pattern of connections—the weight matrix. **tlearn** possesses a useful facility for examining weight matrices—the Connection Weights option in the Display menu. Open this display. **Connection Weights** displays a Hinton diagram of the weight matrix. In this case, we want to examine the weights at different points in training. Open the **Testing Options...** dialogue box and make sure that the **Earlier one:** button is set to **xor-2001.wts**. Double click on the box to activate the dialogue box permitting you to select the **xor-2001.wts** file. Close the **Testing Options...** dialogue box and select the **Verify network has learned** option. **tlearn** will display the output activities again and update **Connection Weights** to display a Hinton diagram for the state of the network after 2001 sweeps. You should obtain a diagram identical to that shown in figure 5.20.

As we saw in figure 5.10, a Hinton diagram represents the strengths of the connections within a network. White squares represent positive weights. Black squares stand for negative weights. The size of the square reflects the absolute value of the connection. The display organizes connections by rows and columns. The row identifies the receiving node and the column identifies the sending node at either end of a connection. In the network shown in figure 5.15 there are three nodes which *receive* input—the two hidden nodes and the output node—so there are three rows in the Hinton diagram. The first two correspond to the hidden units and the third to the output unit. There are five nodes which *send* input, the two input nodes, the two hidden nodes, and the bias node.[5] So there are five columns. The column labelled b shows connections from the bias node; the columns labelled i1 and i2 from the two input nodes; the columns labelled 1 and 2 from the two hidden nodes. Row 1 in figure 5.20 identifies all the connections going into the first hidden node. There are three connections—from the bias node and the two input nodes. Figure 5.20 shows that the first hidden node has a mildly positive connection from the bias node, so it is disposed to become active in the absence of any other input. In contrast, the first hidden node receives strong inhibitory connections from both input nodes. Thus, any activity coming on the input lines will tend to turn the first hidden node off.

[5]All bias nodes have the same activity (1.0) so they are treated as a single node.

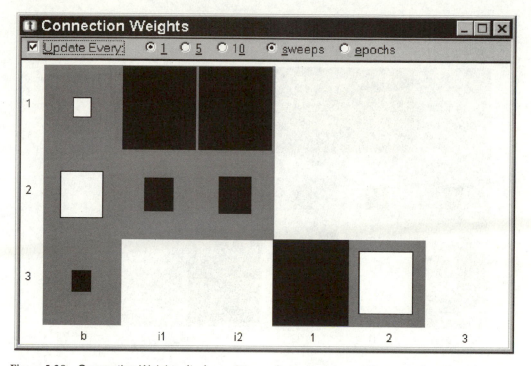

Figure 5.20 Connection Weights displays a Hinton diagram of the weight matrix for XOR after 2001 sweeps.

In a later section we will examine how this network connectivity manages to provide a solution to the XOR problem. For the time being however we are concerned with the *changes* that occur in the network between 1501 and 2001 sweeps that enable the network to solve the problem. Now examine the weight matrix after 1501 sweeps of training. Open the Testing Options... dialogue box and set the **Earlier one:** option to `xor-1501.wts`. Close the dialogue box and Verify the Network has learned. The Connection Weights diagram will be updated to show a Hinton diagram for the weight matrix at 1501 sweeps as shown in figure 5.21.

How does the weight matrix shown in figure 5.21 change into the weight matrix shown in figure 5.20? The most significant changes take place in the connections from the bias node to the hidden and output nodes, and from the second hidden node (column labelled 2) to the output node (row 3). The remaining connections do not change much. In particular, the bias connections to the hidden nodes grow in strength to provide positive excitation to their target nodes while the bias connection to the output node switches to inhibit its activity. The connection from the second hidden node to the output node increases in strength to excite the output node. These changes take place in unison, as they must if they are to permit the fourth input pattern to be classified correctly.

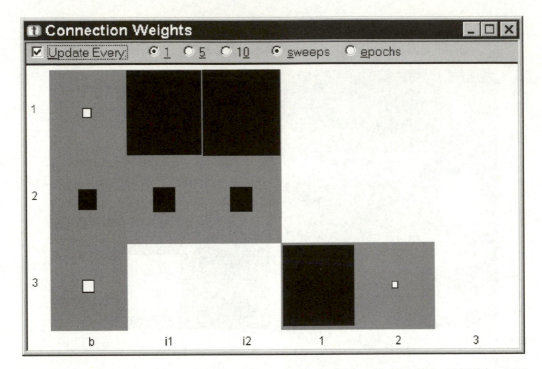

Figure 5.21 Connection Weights displays a Hinton diagram of the weight matrix for XOR after 1501 sweeps.

Hinton diagrams provide a convenient overview of the connectivity in the network. You can even request that **tlearn** displays changes in the weight matrix on-line. Make sure that the Connection Weights diagram is displayed and then Train the Network. Initially, you will observe substantial swings in the weight values in the network. However, weight values will gradually stabilize. If you have the Error Display active then you can also observe how changes in the global root mean square (RMS) error coincide with changes in the weight matrix.

Hidden node representations

The next stage in analysing network performance involves examining hidden node activities. The activities of the hidden nodes provide an important clue as to how the network has solved XOR. In general, we may consider the hidden unit activity resulting from an input pattern to be the network's *internal representation* of that pattern. We shall discover that patterns that are dissimilar at the input layer can be almost identical when we view the activity at the hidden node level. Conversely, patterns that are similar at the input layer can end up looking quite different at the hidden layer. Hidden nodes and the connections feeding into them have the capacity

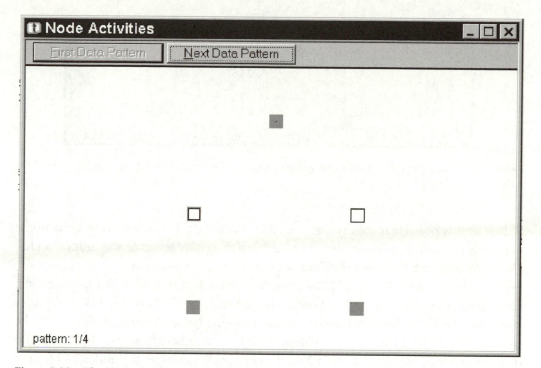

Figure 5.22   The Node Activities display shows the activity of all nodes in the network (excluding the bias nodes). The level of activity of each node determines the size of the white square. A grey node indicates an inactive node.

to transform the similarity relations of the patterns in the input space so that the nature of the problem itself is changed.

We shall investigate several ways of examining these activities in the network. To begin with open the Testing Options... dialogue box and set the Earlier one: option to `xor-2001.wts`. Close the dialogue box and open the Node Activities display in the Display menu. The display should update to look like figure 5.22. This represents the pattern of activity in the network when the first input pattern 0 0 is presented to the network. The current pattern is identified in the bottom left-hand corner of the display. All the nodes in the network are represented (except for the bias nodes). The activity level of a node is represented by the size of the white square—large squares reflect high activity. Grey squares indicate dormant nodes. Input nodes are displayed at the bottom of the diagram. Subsequent layers in the network are shown at higher levels in the display. Hence, in figure 5.22, the input nodes are dormant, the output node is dormant (as it should be for correct performance) and the hidden nodes are active. By clicking on the Next Data Pattern button, you can display node responses to each of the four input patterns. You can see how the representation on the hidden units has transformed the patterns on the input units.

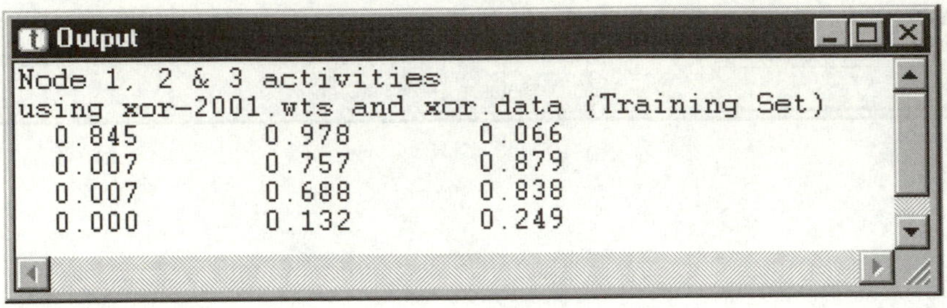

```
Node 1, 2 & 3 activities
using xor-2001.wts and xor.data (Training Set)
   0.845        0.978        0.066
   0.007        0.757        0.879
   0.007        0.688        0.838
   0.000        0.132        0.249
```

Figure 5.23 Node activities in the Output window for nodes 1–3 in a network trained on XOR for 2001 sweeps.

Just as it is possible to determine the exact values of the connection weights in the network, it is also possible to determine the exact activity levels of the hidden nodes. Open the **xor.cf** file using the Open option from the File menu (if it is not already open). Observe that in the SPECIAL: section there is a line with the instructions: selected = 1–3. This line tells **tlearn** to output the activity of the selected nodes whenever the Probe Selected Nodes option from the Network menu is chosen. Make sure that the Testing Options... is still set to use the weights file **xor-2001.wts** and then select Probe selected nodes. **tlearn** will display activities for nodes 1–3 for the four input patterns as shown in figure 5.23. Notice that the third column of activity values is identical with the activity levels displayed in figure 5.19 for 2001 sweeps. The first two columns in figure 5.23 list the activity level of the two hidden nodes for the four input patterns. These values give the precise values used to calculate the Node Activities display in figure 5.22. The hidden unit representations of the second and third patterns are very similar so they produce a similar response (1) at the output. In contrast, the hidden unit activity for the first and fourth patterns are quite different—approximately (11) and (00) respectively. Nevertheless they produce the same response (0) at output because the connections from the hidden units to the output unit are almost equal but opposite in size. This results in the hidden unit activities for the first pattern cancelling each other out. The negative bias on the output unit then ensures a zero response for both patterns.

6 Competitive networks

When an input pattern is presented to a competitive network the output units compete with each other to determine which has the largest response. This unit is the 'winner' for that input pattern. The connections to the winning output unit from the input units which were active in that pattern are strengthened and those from input units which were inactive are weakened. When this learning algorithm has been applied to the different winning units following a range of input patterns, the network will come to categorise input patterns into groups, with one output unit firing in response to each. Competitive learning is unsupervised. There is no external teacher signal which knows in advance what categorisation is appropriate. The network finds a categorisation for itself based on the similarity between input patterns and the number of output units available. We will illustrate this by showing how a competitive network presented with patterns of letters can come to categorise them on the basis of features, individual letter values, letter position or letter combinations as the number of output units is changed.

In previous chapters we have looked at ways to teach a network to produce a specific output in response to a specific input. In chapter 3 we saw how two patterns presented to a network simultaneously can be associated by the Hebbian learning rule. Subsequent input of one will lead to output of the other. In chapters 4 and 5 we looked at networks taught by the Delta rule. The desired response of the network acted as an explicit teacher signal. During training any discrepancy between the current output and the desired output was used to adjust the weights until the desired output was obtained. Both methods are examples of *supervised* learning because the response that the network is required to learn is presented to the network during training. Useful knowledge can also be acquired by networks when there is no predetermined target for each output unit. This is called *unsupervised* learning. In this chapter we will consider an example called competitive learning. A competitive network learns to categorise input patterns into related sets, with one output unit firing for each set.

The architecture and operation of a competitive network

Competitive learning can be demonstrated with the simple network shown in figure 6.1(a). Three input units are connected in a fully feedforward fashion to two output units which have inhibitory connections with each other. Excitation propagates from the input units to each of the output units. These compete with each other via the inhibitory connections until only one remains active. This is the winner. (In some competitive networks there is a gradation of success for different units, not just one winner. But the principles are similar, so for simplicity we will consider networks with a single winner.) The strengths of connections to the winning output unit from active input units are then increased and those from inactive input units are decreased. Connections to units which did not win the competition are not altered. This procedure does not involve an external teaching signal. Learning is determined by which output unit produces the biggest response to the input signal, the outcome resulting from the interaction between the input signal and the weights on each output unit. The weights are set by the prior learning of the network, not by an explicit external teacher.

We can divide competitive learning into three phases: excitation, competition and weight adjustment.

Excitation

Excitation of the output units proceeds in the usual fashion. The net input to each output unit is computed by summing the products of the activity of each input unit and the weight of its connection to the output unit:

$$\text{netinput}_i = \Sigma_j\, a_j\, w_{ij} \tag{6.1}$$

Remember that netinput$_i$ is the dot product of the vector representing the input pattern and the vector representing the weights of the connections from each input unit to output unit i.

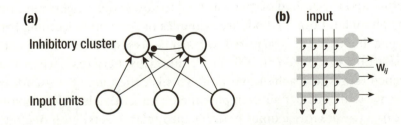

Figure 6.1 A simple competitive learning network. (a) A single layer connectionist network with inhibitory connections between the output units. (b) A competitive network as it might be implemented in the nervous system (without the inhibitory connections) using the same conventions as the pattern associator in figure 3.1.

Competition

To keep the calculations simple in the following examples we will assume that the output units have a linear activation function, so the activity is proportional to the net input. The activities of the output units are compared to determine the winner. The identification of the winner may be achieved by selecting the unit with the highest activity value. Alternatively, units may be set in direct competition with each other through their inhibitory connections. The more active unit will force the other to become inactive. This operation identifies which output unit had the largest net input, that is, the largest dot product between its weight vector and the input vector.

Weight adjustment

Weight adjustment is only made to connections feeding into the winning output unit. Let the change, Δw_{ij}, of the weight of the connection between input unit j and output unit i when input pattern p is presented be:

$$\Delta w_{ij} = 0 \text{ if unit } i \text{ loses}$$
$$= \varepsilon (a_j - w_{ij}) \text{ if unit } i \text{ wins} \tag{6.2}$$

where ε is a learning rate parameter,
a_j is the activity of input unit j when pattern p is presented,
and w_{ij} is the strength of the connection from j to i before the trial.

The learning rule results in adjustment to the strengths of the connections to the winning unit until each weight has the same value as the activity of the corresponding input unit in that input pattern, that is, until $w_{ij} = a_j$. If w_{ij} is smaller than a_j it is increased; if it is larger it is reduced. ε determines how quickly this process takes place. The result is that the winning unit's weight vector is changed to make it *more similar* to the input vector for which it was the winner.

We will illustrate this process with the network shown in figure 6.1(a). Let us assume that the weights are currently at the values shown in figure 6.2. (The units have been numbered 0–4 so that indexing of the weights can be followed.) Consider what happens when the pattern (0 1 1) is presented to the network. The net input to an output unit is found by taking the dot product of the vector representing the input pattern and the vector representing the weights on the connections to the unit. So for unit$_3$ the net input will be $(0 \times 0.3 + 1 \times 0.2 + 1 \times 0.5) = 0.7$. The net input to unit$_4$ will be $(0 \times 0.2 + 1 \times 0.3 + 1 \times 0.5) = 0.8$. So unit$_4$ wins. Now we will apply the learning algorithm from equation 6.2. Since the second output unit was the winner there will only be changes in the connections to this unit. The activity of the first input unit is 0 when the pattern (0 1 1) is presented, so the weight change,

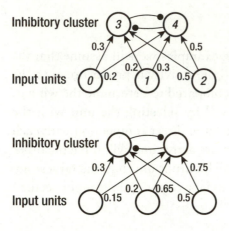

Figure 6.2 The weights in the network before a learning trial with the input pattern (0 1 1).

Figure 6.3 The weights in the network after a learning trial with the pattern (0 1 1).

$\varepsilon(a_j - w_{ij})$, for the connection from this unit is $-\varepsilon \, w_{40}$. If $\varepsilon = 0.5$ then $\Delta w_{40} = -(0.5 \times 0.2) = -0.1$. So w_{40} decreases from 0.2 to 0.1. The other two input units have an activity of 1 in the pattern (0 1 1) so $\Delta w_{41} = 0.5(1 - 0.3) = 0.35$, and $\Delta w_{42} = 0.5(1 - 0.5) = 0.25$. So w_{41} and w_{42} increase from 0.3 and 0.5 to 0.65 and 0.75 respectively.

Implementing these weight changes we obtain the new matrix of connections shown in figure 6.3. The vector representing the weights of the connections into unit$_4$ has changed from (0.2 0.3 0.5) to (0.1 0.65 0.75). The result of applying the competitive learning rule is that the weights of the connections to the second output unit have changed in a manner that causes them to resemble the input vector (0 1 1) more closely.

The crucial result which explains what competitive networks can achieve comes from vector mathematics. With a proviso which we will come to later, the result is that the more similar two vectors are, the larger is their dot product.[1] The output unit whose weight vector makes the largest dot product with the input vector wins the competition. So making the weight vector of the winning unit more like the input vector which caused it to win on this trial makes it likely that it will win in the future when this pattern, or one like it, is presented again. Before the learning trial the weight vector for unit$_3$ was (0.3 0.2 0.5) and for unit$_4$ was (0.2 0.3 0.5). The unit$_4$ weight vector was closer to the input vector (0 1 1) so it won the competition. The weight adjustment made it even closer so it is likely to win if this pattern is presented again. If the same output unit won after presentation of a different input pattern then the weight vector would attempt to mimic that input pattern as well. One weight vector cannot mimic two distinct input vectors exactly. So it will compromise and end up with a vector intermediate between the input vectors it attempts to

[1]This result was introduced in chapter 3. As in that chapter, we have simplified the issue to concentrate on the central point. Vector similarity is discussed in more detail in Appendix 2.

duplicate—in fact, it will produce an average which reflects the frequency of presentation of the different input patterns.

Similar input patterns are likely to cause the same output unit to win the competition because the dot products of similar vectors are larger than those of dissimilar vectors. The weight vectors for different units will come to look like the averages of the input patterns for which they won the competition. If there are natural groupings of patterns in the input set, the network will discover them. The weight vectors for each output unit will come to look like the average vector of one of the groups of related input patterns. The competitive learning network will thus perform a categorisation of the input patterns in the absence of any teacher signal which knows in advance what would be appropriate. If there are no natural groupings then the weight vectors may never stabilise, changing as new patterns are presented to the network. Alternatively, the network may reach a stable state but the final state may be sensitive to the order in which the input patterns are presented.

Figure 6.4 expresses these ideas pictorially. It represents a multi-dimensional space compressed into two dimensions. The crosses represent the end-points in this space of vectors corresponding to a set of nine input patterns which will be presented to a competitive network. The similarity of the input patterns is represented by the closeness of the crosses. The weight vectors of the output units have the same dimensionality (i.e. number of elements) as the input pattern vectors so they can be represented in the same similarity space (the circles in the figure). Figure 6.4(a) shows the similarity before training. The input patterns form a number of natural groupings, two, three or four depending on how finely one wants to divide them. The weight vectors are random, and have no particular relationship to the input vectors.

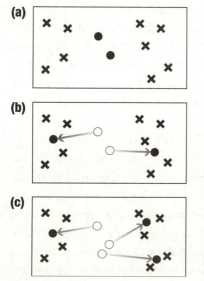

Figure 6.4 A similarity space for the vectors corresponding to a set of nine input patterns (x) and the vectors corresponding to the weights of the output units in the network (•). (a) Before competitive learning the weight vectors for the two output units have a random relation to the input patterns. (b) The competitive learning algorithm changes the weight vectors (along tracks indicated by the arrows) so that each one resembles a subset of the input vectors. (c) With more output units the weight vectors come to resemble subsets of the input patterns more closely.

Figure 6.4(b) shows the effect of training with the competitive learning algorithm. The weight vectors for the output units will move in the directions shown by the arrows. One will come to resemble the group of input patterns on the left quite closely; the other will form a compromise between the two groups on the right, not looking quite like either, but looking more like them than like the group on the left. Figure 6.4(c) shows what would happen if a third output unit were added to the network. The extra unit will share the job of representing the group of patterns on the right. Each of the three weight vectors will now come to resemble one of the three natural groupings of the inputs quite closely. This illustrates the fact that the way in which a competitive network will categorise the input patterns presented to it will depend on the number of its output units.

Limiting weight growth

There is a potential problem for a competitive network. Imagine that by chance one particular output unit won the competition for the first few patterns that were presented to the network. In terms of figure 6.4(a) this would simply mean that the first few input patterns selected were all ones which were closer to one of the weight vectors than to the other. The early learning would result in increasing the magnitude of elements representing some of the individual weights within that weight vector. It might become so much bigger than the weight vector for the other unit that it would win, whatever input pattern was presented subsequently. That is, it would produce the larger dot product with any input, not because of similarity to the input pattern, but because individual elements were much larger than those for the weight vector of the other output unit. A vector with large individual elements can produce larger dot products than one with small individual elements, irrespective of their relative similarity to the vector with which a dot product is being computed. It would continue to become stronger and stronger, winning all future competitions. The same output unit would be turned on by any pattern and the network would have achieved nothing. This is the proviso mentioned earlier. The result that similar vectors will produce a larger dot product than dissimilar vectors is only true if the vectors are of comparable magnitude (or length). (See Appendix 2.)

To prevent this problem the size of the individual elements of any weight vector in a competitive net must be limited. The learning rule in equation 6.2 decreases some weights while increasing others so it helps with this problem. If all the input patterns had the same magnitude, equation 6.2 would be sufficient with no other mechanism to control the magnitude of the weight vector. Another way to control the weights is to start with the sum of the weights to any unit equal to a constant and not to allow this to change when the learning rule is applied. In both cases the learning process is one of *redistribution* of weight among the connections to the winning unit (i.e. taking weight from connections to inactive input units and reallocating it to connections to active input units). A comparison of various methods can be found in Hertz *et al.* (1991) or Rolls and Treves (1998).

Competitive learning in the brain

Competitive learning is biologically plausible because it uses a local learning rule. That is, the information required to change the weight of a connection is available at the axon and the dendrite on either side of the connection. It is also of interest in brain computation because it can perform feature analysis without an explicit teacher. Figure 6.1(a) showed a single layer competitive network in the conventional connectionist format. Figure 6.1(b) shows a network drawn in a way which represents how competitive learning might be realised in a real neural network. Four axons, carrying the input, synapse onto a set of output neurons via modifiable excitatory synapses, w_{ij}. The only difference between this and the pattern associator shown in figure 3.1(a) is the absence of the external input driving the output neurons because there is no external teaching input in competitive learning. The output neurons are activated in the usual way by the pattern of activity on the input axons— netinput$_i = \Sigma_j \, a_j \, w_{ij}$. They then compete with each other (in the brain by using inhibitory interneurons, for example) until the most strongly activated neuron is the only one firing. Hebbian learning is then applied—synapses between input lines which are active and output neurons which are active are strengthened. Since the only output neuron which is active is the winning unit, the only synapses which are strengthened are those between the active input lines and the winning output unit. This achieves the basic goal of competitive learning ensuring that the winning output neuron is more likely to win if the same or a similar pattern is presented in future. Ways in which the unfettered growth of the weights of connections to individual output units might be constrained and normalisation of input patterns (i.e. keeping them the same size) might be achieved in real neural networks are discussed in Rolls and Treves (1998).

Competitive networks are a feature of many real brain circuits. This is not surprising as they have a number of potentially useful properties. First, they can remove redundancy from a set of inputs by allocating a single output neuron to represent a set of inputs which co-occur. This reduces the number of active units required to represent an input pattern without a loss of information. This can be a helpful preprocessing operation in networks which require a sparse input to operate efficiently. Second, they can produce outputs for different input patterns which are less correlated with each other than the inputs were. In the limit they can turn a set of partly correlated patterns at input into a set of orthogonal (i.e. uncorrelated) patterns at output. This is a useful function because pattern associators can work more

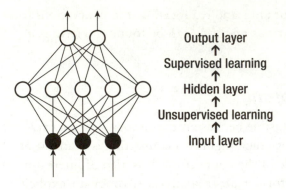

Output layer
↑
Supervised learning
↑
Hidden layer
↑
Unsupervised learning
↑
Input layer

Figure 6.5 A multi-layer network in which the first layer is an unsupervised competitive network and the second layer is a supervised pattern associator.

efficiently if the input patterns they have to learn are not highly correlated. The efficiency of a pattern associator can thus be improved by allowing a competitive network to act as a preprocessor on its input. An example of this architecture is shown in figure 6.5 where an unsupervised competitive layer precedes a supervised pattern associator layer. Such a net can solve problems which would be too hard for a single layer net (for example, because the inputs were not linearly separable) without introducing the complexities associated with teaching a multi-layer net which were described in chapter 5. (See, for example, Schyns 1991.)

We shall see examples of sparsification, redundancy removal and orthogonalisation at work in the simulation of memory formation in the hippocampus in chapter 13. The use of competitive networks to perform feature analysis is described in the section on the formation of view invariant representations in the temporal cortex in chapter 13.

Orthogonalisation and categorisation might seem to be entirely different processes. The first involves producing outputs which are less similar to each other than the input patterns which generated them. The second involves producing the same output to inputs which are not identical. But both operations can be performed by competitive networks. By allocating *separate* output units to somewhat related input patterns, a competitive network can produce a set of outputs which are less correlated than the inputs—orthogonalisation. By allocating the *same* output unit to more related patterns a competitive network can produce outputs which are more correlated than the inputs—categorisation. The balance between the number of output units and the number of patterns presented to the network will determine which process takes place, as we will see in the examples below.

A common competitive architecture is to have a succession of layers, each operating as a competitive net, as shown in figure 6.6. Within each layer small circles represent individual units, with filled circles representing active units and unfilled circles representing inactive units. After the initial input layer the units within a layer are collected into competitive clusters. Within each cluster only one unit, the winner,

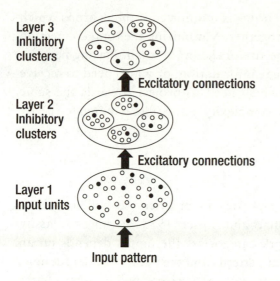

Layer 3
Inhibitory
clusters

Excitatory connections

Layer 2
Inhibitory
clusters

Excitatory connections

Layer 1
Input units

Input pattern

Figure 6.6 A network consisting of a succession of layers, each operating as a competitive net. (Based on Rumelhart and Zipser 1985.)

will be active. (A biologically plausible way of implementing competitive clusters within layers would be to limit the distance over which inhibitory processes between units can operate.) Any unit within a layer can have an excitatory connection to any unit in the next layer so the input to each successive layer will be the winner from each of the clusters in the previous layer. A series of competitive transformations will take place, with the potential for discovering successively higher order patterns in the original input. An example of what can be achieved by a multi-layer competitive net will be demonstrated with the development of position and view invariant representations of images of faces in the simulation of processing of visual information in the temporal lobe in chapter 13.

Topographic map formation

Topological organisation is found in many cortical processing areas. That is, similar input features are processed in adjacent cortical regions. A simple modification to the competitive networks described so far enables them to develop topological maps. The modification is to add short-range excitation and long-range inhibition between the units. The effect of this connectivity between units, which need not be modifiable, is to encourage units which are close together to respond to similar features in the input space, and to encourage units which are far apart to respond to different features in the input space. When these response tendencies are present during learning, the feature analysers which are built by modifying the connections from the input to the activated units tend to be similar if they are close together, and different if far apart.

The biological utility of developing topology-preserving feature maps may be that if computation requires neurons with similar types of response to exchange information more than neurons involved in different computations, then the total length of the connections between the neurons is minimized if the neurons which need to exchange information are close together. Minimizing the total connection length between neurons helps to keep the size of the brain small. Placing neurons close to each other which need to exchange information, or which need to receive information from the same source, or which need to project towards the same destination, may also help to minimize the complexity of the rules required to specify cortical connectivity.

Pattern classification

To see how an unsupervised network operates in practice we will look at a competitive network described by Rumelhart and Zipser (1985) learning to classify patterns of letters.[2] The way the network categorises the inputs depends on an interaction between the nature of the input patterns and the number of output units given to the network. Depending on this balance the network will become a letter position detector, a letter combination detector, or a letter feature detector.

The input to the network is the pattern of stimulation produced by the letters when they are superimposed on a 'retina' consisting of a 7×14 grid. Each point on the grid feeds to one input unit in the network. Three examples of the pattern of stimulation produced when a pair of letters falls on the retina are shown in figure 6.7. Highlighted points are those input units which receive activation following the input pattern.

First the network is presented with letter pairs drawn from the set AA, AB, BA and BB. The network is trained with a procedure similar to that described in equation 6.2. The weight vector for each of the two output units has 96 elements representing the strength of the connections from each input unit so it can be represented by a 7×14 matrix. Figure 6.8 shows how the weight matrix develops for the two output units, with the darkness of each blob representing the strength of the weight. The left hand side of each matrix develops a set of weights which are positive for the points in the input matrix representing A and B respectively, with all other weights at zero. It can be seen that the output units have developed into position specific letter detectors, one unit coming on when there is an A on the left and the other coming on

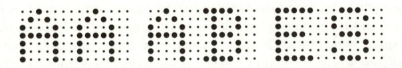

Figure 6.7 Letter pair stimuli presented to a competitive network with a retina of 7×14 input units. (Based on Rumelhart and Zipser 1985.)

[2]Examples of competitive learning can be studied using the **cl** program in McClelland and Rumelhart (1988).

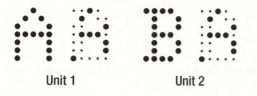

Unit 1   Unit 2

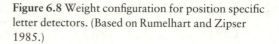
Figure 6.8 Weight configuration for position specific letter detectors. (Based on Rumelhart and Zipser 1985.)

when there is a B on the left. Competitive learning has led to the network classifying the four input patterns into two groups, with the combinations AA and AB in one group and BA and BB in the other group. The right hand side of the matrices develops weights on connections to features which are common to both A and B because both of these will be present on the right of the input grid on half the occasions when the unit won the competition. Had we started with a different random set of weights the net might have found the equally plausible partition (AA + BA) and (AB + BB). The patterns in the weight matrices would then be reversed, but the output units would still be acting as position specific letter detectors.

Now suppose the same set of input patterns is presented to the network but it is given four output units instead of two. In this case, the network develops units which are sensitive to letter combinations rather than to letters in specific positions. That is, given there are four letter combinations in the input set and four units in the inhibitory cluster, the natural classification for the network to make is one set of letters per output unit. Thus one unit responds to AA, another to AB, etc. This illustrates one of the fundamental features of the competitive learning regime. The number of output units determines the degree of differentiation which will be performed on the input set. Higher resolution classifications are achieved as the number of output units increases.

Finally, consider a simulation in which we require the network to categorise individual letters instead of letter combinations. We will use the four letters A, B, E and S, shown in figure 6.7, as input and a cluster of two output units. This means that the four letters will be classified into two groups. What grouping will the network discover? Examination of the fonts in figure 6.7 shows that A and E are quite similar and B and S are quite similar. Competitive learning networks look for a similarity structure in the input patterns (see figure 6.4). Therefore, the cluster units organise themselves in a fashion such that one turns on if an A or an E is presented and the other turns on if a B or an S is presented. The output units have become detectors for features within letters.

Correlated teaching

It is possible to create sets of input patterns which force the network to look for unnatural classifications. Consider a network with two output units which has to

Unit 1   Unit 2

Figure 6.9 Correlated weight matrices. (Based on Rumelhart and Zipser 1985.)

classify the input patterns AA, BA, SB and EB. A simple solution for the network is to develop position specific letter detectors with one output unit responding when A is in second position and the other when B is in second position. Indeed, this is what the network does. However, notice that the identity of the second letter also classifies the patterns across another dimension: If A is in second position then A or B must be in first position and if B is in second position then S or E must be in first position. In effect, A and B are being forced into the same group and S and E into the same group—the opposite of the natural similarity structures that we saw in the previous example.

Figure 6.9 shows the weight matrices which develop for the two output units. The position specific letter detectors are clearly marked for the second position. But the first position for each of the cluster units has developed feature detectors which are common to either A and B in one case, or to E and S in the other—an unnatural classification. The correlation between second position and first position has overwhelmed the natural pairings of A and E, and B and S, and forced the weight vector to represent whatever it can find in common between A and B, and between E and S. In effect, the letter in second position has functioned as teacher for deciding what information should be represented in the first position.

The correlated input patterns used in this section demonstrate how a selected training set can force a network into an organisational structure which it would not otherwise have been able to discover. This finding has implications for training networks on problems that are difficult, such as linearly inseparable problems.

Further reading

A variety of competitive learning problems similar to the classification of letter patterns are discussed in chapter 5 of McClelland and Rumelhart (1986).

A more detailed and technical account of competitive learning can be found in chapter 9 of Hertz *et al.* (1991).

The implementation of competitive learning in the brain is discussed in Rolls and Treves (1998).

7   Recurrent networks

In a recurrent network, output from later layers feeds back to provide new input for earlier layers. Such networks can produce sequences of output following a single initial input or predict the next input in a sequence. They can also form attractor networks in which the output in response to an input changes with time.

Controlling sequences with an associative chain

Much of human activity involves the coordination of motor sequences to achieve goals. For example, the production of a word involves the utterance of a sequence of phonemes in the appropriate order. If the sequence is lost, the word changes its identity or becomes nonsensical. One possible mechanism for controlling sequencing in behaviour is the associative chain. Suppose that three actions ABC are to be performed in that order. An associative chain consisting of three states, each state representing the execution of a given action, could control the sequence. This is shown in figure 7.1(a). The sequence ACB could be controlled by the associative chain in figure 7.1(b).

This approach works well until we realise how many such associative chains will be required to control all of the sequences that humans are capable of performing. Lashley (1951) recognised this problem and argued that it was endemic to any associative account of the organisation of serial order in human behaviour. Furthermore, associative chains do not seem to capture the repetition of actions in an intuitive fashion. Consider the sequence AABC. We might represent the control of this sequence by the associative chain shown in figure 7.2(a). However, this mode of representing the repetition of the action A does not capture the intuition that the repeated occurrences of A are identical actions. We are using two separate states to represent A just as we are using two separate states to represent A and B. Of course, it is not difficult to fix the associative chain so that it can capture this intuition. This is achieved by adding a feedback loop, or recurrent connection, as shown in figure 7.2(b).

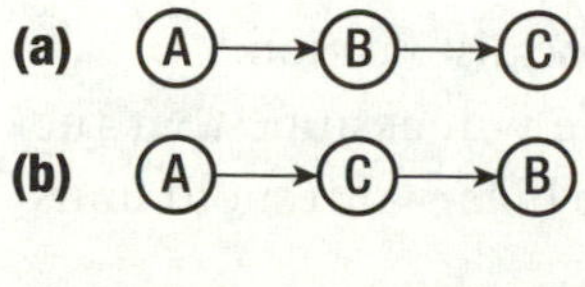

(a) (A) ⟶ (B) ⟶ (C)

(b) (A) ⟶ (C) ⟶ (B)

Figure 7.1   Simple associative chains.

(a)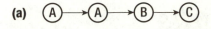

(b)

Figure 7.2   Repetition in associative chains.

Figure 7.3   Associative chains for complex sequences.

The augmented associative chain is now, in principle, capable of producing sequences containing any number of repetitions of A, all represented by the same state. Repetition of other actions can be achieved by introducing feedback loops on other states. Different sequences of the same set of actions can be achieved in a single associative chain by introducing bi-directional links between states as shown in figure 7.3. The connectivity of the associative chain shown in figure 7.3 enables it to produce all possible combinations of A, B and C. This overcomes the problem of having distinct associative chains for each possible sequence.

However, this compactness of representation is purchased at a price. We have lost the power to determine which sequence the chain is to perform. Consider the simple associative chain that permits the repetition of an unlimited number of As [figure 7.2(b)]. The system contains no mechanism for determining how many As to produce before moving on to B. We could choose which associative link to follow in a probabilistic fashion but then we have lost the ability to determine the execution of a particular sequence at a particular time. Associative chains by themselves are not adequate to explain how humans are able to sequence their actions.

Controlling sequences with a recurrent net

Jordan (1986) has shown how an associative network augmented with a planning structure can be used to sequence actions. Figure 7.4 shows a network that will produce the sequence AAAB where A is represented by the output pattern (1 1) and B is represented by the output pattern (0 0). The network contains two input units, a hidden unit and two output units. The output units are also connected to the input units in one-to-one fashion and the input units are connected to themselves—that is, they have feedback loops. The desired action is now represented by a pattern of activity on the output units rather than a single state node as in the associative chain. In other words, states are represented in a distributed fashion rather than in a localist fashion.

Consider the network starting with inputs set to zero. We will assume that the input units are linear and that the hidden and output units are binary threshold units

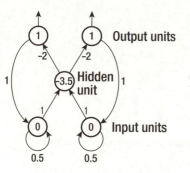

Figure 7.4 A one-sequence recurrent network.

with an output of 1 for positive net input and an output of 0 for negative net input. The weights and biases of the network are shown in figure 7.4. The patterns of activity in the nodes at different time steps are shown in table 7.1. Initially, the negative bias of the hidden unit results in no activity being propagated through the network. Consequently, the positive biases of the output units turn the units on and the output of the system is (1 1) (i.e. A). The activity of the output units is fed back to the input units ready for the next cycle of network activation. Since the input units had zero activity on the first time step, the recurrent connections provide no new information. However, because the input units are receiving positive input from the output units, they pass on this activity to the hidden unit. This still does not fire because the negative bias is too high (a bias of −3.5 vs a net input of 2.0). Thus, the output units continue to fire on the current processing cycle because of their positive bias. Hence, another A is produced. By working through the activations over several time steps as shown in table 7.1, you can determine that the network will produce the sequence AAAB. You might like to consider what the network does after it has finished producing this initial sequence.

State units and plan units

The input units in figure 7.4 gradually build up their activity, then suddenly the activity drops (after a B output is produced) and a new activity build-up commences.

Table 7.1 The input and output of each of the five units in figure 7.4 at four consecutive time steps.

Time	Input 1		Input 2		Hidden		Output 1		Output 2		Resp
	In	Out	In	Out	In	Out	In	Out	In	Out	
1.	0+0	0	0+0	0	0−3.5	0	0+1	1	0+1	1	A
2.	1+0	1	1+0	1	2−3.5	0	0+1	1	0+1	1	A
3.	1+0.5	1.5	1+0.5	1.5	3−3.5	0	0+1	1	0+1	1	A
4.	1+0.75	1.75	1+0.75	1.75	3.5−3.5	1	−2+1	0	−2+1	0	B

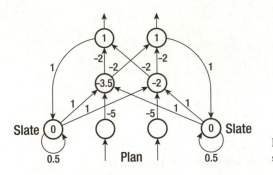

Figure 7.5   A recurrent network for multiple sequences.

The activity of the input units carries the information about where in the current sequence of actions the network has reached. They are thus akin to the single state nodes in associative chains. Jordan referred to these as *state* units. The advantage of this type of network is that it can produce indefinitely long sequences of actions in a deterministic fashion. However, given an initial start state only one sequence of actions is produced—unless we introduce a probabilistic factor, but then we are back where we started, not knowing which sequence will be produced at which time.

Jordan's solution to this problem was to introduce another set of input units that modified the start state. Changing the start state results in a different sequence of actions being performed. To see how this works consider the network in figure 7.5. This is identical to the network in figure 7.4 except that there are two additional input units and an additional hidden unit. Consider what happens if the two additional input units are set to have constant input activities of (0 1) respectively. This results in the second hidden unit being strongly inhibited and the network functions just as before. However, if the initial input is (1 0) then the second hidden unit becomes active after just one cycle and turns off the output units. In other words, one input results in the output sequence AAAB and the other input results in the sequence AB. Because these extra hidden units modulate the effects of the two state units, they are referred to as *plan* units. The conceptual separation between the plan and state units in a recurrent networks provides a system capable of learning a wide variety of complex sequences.

Simple recurrent networks (SRNs)

The incorporation of planning units into a network allows the execution of arbitrarily complex sequences. But it is not always easy to see how a network should be designed to perform a particular task. So we will introduce a network which is capable of *learning* any sequence which is given as input. The measure of learning is the ability to predict the next item in the sequence.

A simple recurrent network (SRN) contains connections from the hidden units to a

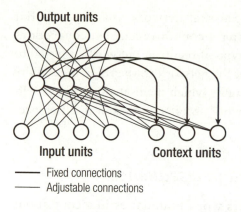

Output units

Input units   **Context units**

—— Fixed connections
—— Adjustable connections

Figure 7.6   A simple recurrent network (SRN).

set of context units. These store the hidden unit activities for one time step, and then feed them back to the hidden units on the next time step. They are the equivalent of state units, storing the network's memory of the state of the network on the previous time step. Because the hidden units have an input which includes a record of their prior activity, they are able to carry out tasks which extend over time. Note that this sort of network is not merely a tape-recording of the past. The hidden units continue to recycle information over multiple time steps. The input to the hidden units at time $t + 1$ includes information from t and $t + 1$. At time $t + 2$ the input includes information from $t + 2$, $t + 1$ and t. And so on. If there are sequential dependencies in the training data, an SRN can discover them. Anticipation plays a key role in early learning, so learning to predict is an important aspect of cognition.

In figure 7.6 the activities of the context units are direct copies of the hidden unit activities on the previous time step. Connections from the hidden units to the context units are fixed while connections from the context units to the hidden units are adjustable, in the same manner as all the other connections in the network. That is, they will be adjusted by the learning procedure. Context units can be thought of as providing the network with a dynamic memory. Identical input signals can be treated differently depending on the current status of the context.

Recurrent networks are trained in the same way as feedforward networks. First, an input pattern results in activity being propagated through the network to the output units. The actual pattern of activity at output is then compared to the desired output (usually the next pattern in the sequence) and the discrepancy between the two is used to drive a backpropagation learning algorithm to adapt the weights in the network. If the desired output is the next pattern in the sequence the network is being trained to predict the next input. Weight adaptation occurs in just the same way as in a feedforward network, except that the connections from the hidden units to the context units are never changed since their function is to establish copies of the hidden unit activities on the context units.

It is possible to create different types of recurrent network architectures. For example, the autoassociator described in chapter 4 contains recurrent connections between all the units in the network. Another type of recurrent network, referred to as a Jordan net, uses the activity of the output of the network (rather than the activity of the hidden units) to feed back to the context units which themselves may have self-recurrent connections. These differences in network architecture result in differences in computational properties.

Learning to predict the next sound in a sequence

Elman (1990) discussed an SRN that discovers word boundaries in a continuous stream of phonemes. Elman used a network like that shown in figure 7.6 to simulate the child's task of identifying words from a continuous sequence of input phonemes. The network is fed one phoneme at a time and has to predict the next input (i.e. the next phoneme in the sequence). The difference between the predicted input and the actual one was used by the learning algorithm to adjust the weights in the network at each time step. The context units ensure that at time t the hidden layer processes both the input of time t and the results of its processing at time $t - 1$. In this way the network can capture the sequential nature of the input.

The input corpus consists of sequences of phonemes. The phonemes themselves go together to make up English words and the words make up sentences. In attempting to predict the next phoneme in the sequence, the network must exploit the statistical regularities in the language. It is not given any explicit information about the structure of the language. Figure 7.7 shows the average error for predicting individual letters in the string:

manyyearsagoaboyandgirllivedbytheseatheyplayedhappily...

The error tends to be high at the beginning of a word and decreases until the word boundary is reached. The error for any phoneme can be interpreted as a measure of the level of confidence with which the network is making its prediction. Before it is exposed to the first phoneme of the word it is unsure what is to follow. However, the identity of the first two phonemes is usually enough to enable the network to predict the next phonemes in the word with a high level of confidence. Of course, when the input string reaches the end of the word the network cannot be certain which word is to follow, so it cannot predict the next phoneme with any confidence. Consequently the error curve has a saw-tooth shape with words falling into the teeth. The increased error at the beginning of a word shows that the network has discovered a word boundary.

Sometimes the network makes segmentation errors. For example, in figure 7.7 the string 'aboy' is treated as a single unit by the network—the error continues to decline

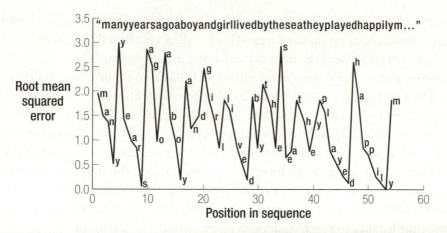

Figure 7.7 The error for a network trained on phoneme prediction. Error is high at the beginning of a word and decreases as the word is processed. (Based on Elman 1990.)

across the boundary. This reflects the fact that the article 'a' and the noun 'boy' often occur together just as the phonemes within a word occur together. The network also makes 'undershooting' segmentation errors. For example, in figure 7.7 the error curve for the sequence 'they' rises after 'e' because it recognises 'the' as a legal sequence and leaves the 'y' stranded unattached to any word. Children have been shown to make these kinds of segmentation errors (see Plunkett 1993).

The network can learn to rectify some of these segmentation errors. On exposure to further training examples where the indefinite article 'a' combines with a wider range of nouns, it will eventually learn to split 'aboy' into two separate words. In contrast the network will continue to have difficulty deciding whether 'the' should be continued into 'they' since the former is a legal unit. To solve this problem the network would require higher order information about whether it should be expecting a pronoun or an article. Since sentences can begin with either word, it would never be able to decide which was appropriate at this point in the sentence. That could only be resolved if the restriction on processing the sentence from left to right were dropped and it were allowed to backtrack to resolve ambiguity as subsequent information became available.

In chapter 9 we will examine other work by Elman with SRNs in greater detail. We will see how recurrent nets are able to assign words to grammatical categories and to implement syntactic rules.

Attractors

The output of a simple recurrent network changes over time in a well-defined way so it can learn to produce or predict sequences. It is also possible to devise networks where the change of the output over time causes the network to settle into one of several states depending on the input. This is called an *attractor* network. The set of possible states into which the network can settle are the attractors.

Consider the network shown in figure 7.8. It has two input units and two output units. The two input units are linear and can have activities in the range 0 to 1. The input patterns to the network span a square 2-dimensional region bounded by the points (0 0), (1 0), (1 1) and (0 1) as shown in figure 7.9. The hidden and output units have a logistic activation function so their activities are also constrained to the range 0 to 1, but in a non-linear fashion (see chapter 5). As the network processes the input, the pattern of activity at the output always converges on either (0.1 0.1) or (0.9 0.9). These states are the attractors for this network. The final output pattern, and the time it takes to reach it, depend on the identity of the input.

The way that the network operates can be understood by considering the attractor space shown in figure 7.10. The square represents the possible input patterns that can

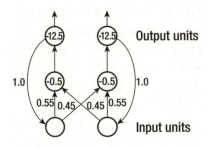

Figure 7.8   An attractor network.

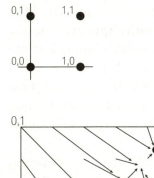

Figure 7.9   The input pattern space for the network in figure 7.8.

Figure 7.10   An attractor space with two basins of attraction.

be presented to the network. The arrows in the figure indicate how the input patterns are transformed to output patterns at each successive time step as activity cycles round the network. All the arrows below the diagonal line connecting inputs (1 0) and (0 1) home in on the point representing the output (0.1 0.1). All the arrows above the line home in on the output (0.9 0.9). So the region on one side of the diagonal can be seen as a *basin of attraction*. An input landing anywhere in the basin will eventually end up at the attractor. The diagonal forms a dividing line between the two basins. An input which lies exactly on this diagonal would move to the point (0.5 0.5). However, in a real system this would not be a stable state as any random noise would take the input off the diagonal and into one basin or the other, from where it would move to the attractor. The length of each arrow shows how much the input pattern is transformed on each time step. Points that are close to the diagonal require several steps (i.e. processing cycles) before they reach the attractor. Points close to the attractor reach the final state more quickly.

Attractor networks have a number of properties which make them very useful in the simulation of cognitive processes. First, they produce a simulation of reaction time. A stable output (i.e. which would be required for a response) will require the network to settle into one of the attractor states. The 'reaction time' of the network is the length of time (i.e. number of cycles) it takes to reach a stable state. The time it takes to do this will depend on the shape of the basin and the position within the basin where the initial input landed. Second, attractor networks are relatively immune to noisy input. Provided an input falls within a basin, the exact position does not matter. The response will eventually be the same—the state corresponding to the attractor.[1] In chapter 2 we discussed the importance of noise resistance in cognitive activity. Third, and perhaps most important, attractor networks allow an arbitrary mapping between input and output. In the example above, the mapping between input and output was straightforward. The output pattern bore an obvious relation to the input pattern. But imagine we wanted the network to learn a mapping where an arbitrary set of inputs, some of which were close to (0.1 0.1), must produce the output (0.9 0.9) and vice versa. Such a desired mapping is illustrated in figure 7.11(a). The points marked + indicate input patterns which must produce the output (0.9 0.9); points marked − indicate input patterns which must produce the output (0.1 0.1). A recurrent network can learn to produce a boundary between two attractor basins like that shown in figure 7.11(b) such that the appropriate mapping will be achieved. The arrow shows the state of the output units as an input which initially produces an output close to (0.1 0.1) is gradually transformed to (0.9 0.9) on successive processing cycles. The ability to do this is important because many

---

[1]This will be discussed further in chapter 15 where we will derive Hopfield's (1982) proof of this important point. This paper had a key historical role in stimulating interest in neural nets as models of brain and cognitive function in the wider scientific community.

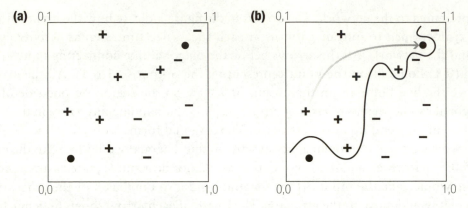

Figure 7.11 (a) An arbitrary mapping problem. The input patterns represented by + must all produce the output (0.9 0.9); the inputs represented by – must all produce the output (0.1 0.1). (b) This problem could be solved by a recurrent network creating the two basins of attraction separated by the curved line. As activity cycles around the network after an input falls in the upper basin, the output pattern will gradually home in on (0.9 0.9) as shown by the arrow.

cognitive tasks involve arbitrary mappings. One which we will study in detail in chapter 11 is the mapping of a word's spelling pattern onto its meaning.

Learning sequences with `tlearn`

In this exercise you will:
- Train a simple recurrent network to predict the next letter in a sequence of letters.
- Test how the network generalizes to novel sequences.

The task

Imagine a letter sequence consisting of only three unique strings:

    `ba dii guuu`

For example, part of the sequence might look like this:

    `babaguuudiiguuubadiidiibaguuuguuu....`

Note that the sequence is only semi-random: the consonants occur randomly but the identity and number of the vowels is regular—for example, whenever a **d** occurs, it is always followed by exactly two **i**s. If we trained a recurrent network to predict successive letters in the sequence, the best we could expect would be for the network to say that all three consonants are equally likely to occur in word-initial position; but once a consonant is received, the identity and number of the following vowels should be predicted with certainty.

A file called `letters` exists in the `Chapter Seven` folder. It contains a random sequence of 1000 words, each word consisting of one of the 3 consonant–vowel combinations shown above. Open... the **letters** file. Each letter occupies its own line. Translate these letters into a distributed representation suitable for presenting to a network. Create a file called **codes** which contains these lines:

b	1	1	0	0
d	1	0	1	0
g	1	0	0	1
a	0	1	0	0
i	0	0	1	0
u	0	0	0	1

You do this by selecting New from the File menu and enter the data in the new window. Remember to include spaces between the elements of each line. Save the file as codes. Now with the **letters** file open and active, select the Translate... option from the Edit menu. The Translate dialogue box will appear as shown in figure 7.12. Set the Pattern file: box to codes and check that the Direction of Translation is from left to right. Then click on OK. Your **letters** file is translated into rows and columns of binary digits. (Note that both the **letters** and **codes** files must be in the same directory or folder.) Each row consists of one of the sequences of 4 digits taken from the **codes** file. Translate has replaced every letter in the **letters** file with a pattern vector. Every occurrence of a letter in the **letters** file which corresponds with a letter in the first column of the **codes** file is replaced by the sequence of binary digits to the right of the first column in the **codes**

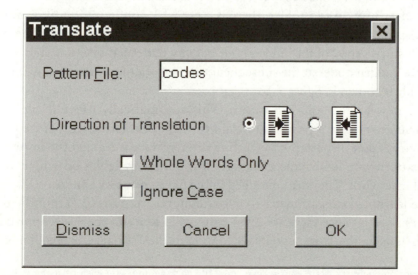

Figure 7.12 The Translate dialogue box.

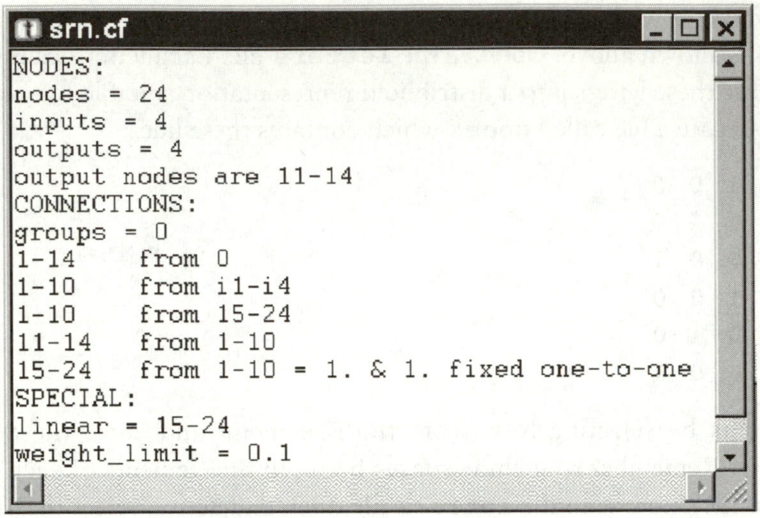

```
srn.cf                                      _ □ ✕
NODES:
nodes = 24
inputs = 4
outputs = 4
output nodes are 11-14
CONNECTIONS:
groups = 0
1-14      from 0
1-10      from i1-i4
1-10      from 15-24
11-14     from 1-10
15-24     from 1-10 = 1. & 1. fixed one-to-one
SPECIAL:
linear = 15-24
weight_limit = 0.1
```

Figure 7.13   The **srn.cf** file.

file.[2] **tlearn** asks you for the name of a file in which to save the translated data. To avoid overwriting the existing **letters** file, call it **srn.data**. Next copy this file to a file called **srn.teach** and edit the file, moving the first line to the end of the file. The **srn.teach** file is now one step ahead of the **srn.data** file in the sequence. Complete the **teach** and **data** files by including the appropriate header information. This involves adding the word 'distributed' on the first line of the files and the total number of pattern vectors on the second line (2993).

In the **Chapter Seven** folder, there is a network configuration file—**srn.cf**— that defines a 4x10x4 simple recurrent network with 10 context nodes. These special nodes will store a copy of the hidden node activity pattern at one time step and feed it back to the hidden nodes at the subsequent time step (along with the new input). The **srn.cf** file is shown in figure 7.13.

Open a new project and call it **srn**. This automatically uses the files describe above. You are now in a position to train the network. However, before you do so you will need a set of patterns for testing after you have trained the network. The testing patterns are just single instances of the three syllables on which you have trained the network. They are contained in the file **predtest.data**.

Set the learning rate parameter to 0.1 and momentum to 0.3. Train the network for 70 000 sweeps (since there are 2993 patterns in **srn.data**, this is approximately 23 epochs), using the Train sequentially option in the Training Options dialogue box.

---

[2]Notice that you could translate your transformed file back again if you wish by using the alternative Direction of translation in the Translate... dialogue box.

To see how the network is progressing, keep track of the RMS error using the Error Display. Why do you think the RMS error is so large?

Test the network using the **predtest.data** file. How well has the network learned to predict the next element in the sequence? Given a consonant, does it get the vowel identity and number correctly? What does it predict when a consonant is the next element in the stream?

Run through these test patterns again but plot a graph of the error (using the Error Display) as the network processes the test file. To do this you will need to construct a **predtest.teach** file and make sure that the Calculate error box is checked in the Testing Options dialogue box. You should be able to see how the error declines as more of a word is presented. Thus, error should be initially low (as we predict an **a** following the first **b**, then increases when the **a** itself is input and the network attempts to predict the beginning of a new sequence. If you look at the bit codes that were used to represent the consonants and vowels, you will see that the first bit encodes the C–V distinction; the last three encode the identity of the letter. When individual output bits are interpretable in this way, you might wish to look not only at the overall error for a given pattern (the sum-squared error across all bits in the pattern) but at the errors made on specific bits. What do you notice about the network's ability to predict the occurrence of a vowel versus a consonant as opposed to specific vowels and consonants?

Part II
Applications

8   *Reading aloud*

Models of reading aloud have traditionally contained a lexicon, a store of specific information about particular words with which the reader is familiar, and some other mechanism, such as a set of general rules of pronunciation, to allow pronunciation of novel letter strings. We describe a connectionist model of reading aloud which has neither a lexicon or explicit pronunciation rules. The model succeeds in learning the correct pronunciation for all monosyllabic English words, regular and irregular. Once the model has learnt this vocabulary it is tested in simulations of experiments which measure the speed at which normal adult readers can read words aloud. It proves remarkably good at mimicking the effect on word naming latency of variables such as word frequency and consistency of spelling pattern. However, it is worse than normal adult readers at reading non-words, and at recognising whether a letter string is one it has learnt or not (lexical decision). A change in the form of input coding appears to solve these problems. When recurrent connections are added to this model to give it attractor structure it retains the ability to read both words and non-words while gaining the desirable property of being able to cope with a noisy environment.

A child learning to read aloud has to discover how to match the letter strings it is looking at to an oral vocabulary it already possesses. To do this quickly the child needs to discover general rules of pronunciation so that it can make a reasonable guess when it meets a new word rather than having to learn every new word as a specific pronunciation.

Learning to read aloud in English is complicated by the anarchy of English pronunciation—most spelling-to-sound 'rules' have exceptions. For example, the A in monosyllabic words ending -AVE is usually long (CAVE, GAVE, NAVE, PAVE, RAVE, SAVE and WAVE) but short in HAVE; the I in monosyllabic words ending INT is usually short (DINT, HINT, LINT, MINT, TINT) but long in PINT. Some pattern matches are completely unpredictable—THROWN, GROWN, MOWN and SOWN, but FROWN, BROWN, TOWN and GOWN. And some matches, such as -ACH- in YACHT, are just arbitrary. The child has to try and discover the regularities in an environment where there *are* regularities but also many exceptions.

The traditional '2-route' model of reading aloud

Many traditional box-and-arrow models of the information processing involved in skilled reading have two independent mechanisms which can lead to the pronunciation of a letter string. The assumption that independent mechanisms are required follows from two simple observations:

(1) People have no difficulty pronouncing letter strings they have never seen before such as SLINT or MAVE. So it is assumed that skilled readers must possess some mechanism, such as a set of general rules of pronunciation, which can generate a plausible pronunciation of any letter string.

(2) But people have no difficulty producing the correct pronunciations for words which break the general rules, such as PINT or HAVE. So it is assumed that there must also be a store of specific knowledge about the pronunciation of individual words.

It is common to have these two methods, the rule based and the lexical or word based, represented as two separate pathways (hence '2-route' models). An example of such a model is shown in figure 8.1. The lexical route uses a store of information about specific words to generate the correct pronunciation (directly or via semantics); the non-lexical route consists of a set of pronunciation rules.

To see the difference between the lexical and the non-lexical way of pronouncing a letter string, consider how the model would generate the pronunciation of KINT, MINT or PINT. KINT is not a word so it has no entry in the lexicon; it can only be pronounced by the pronunciation rules. MINT can be pronounced correctly either by

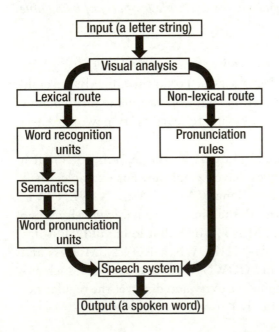

Figure 8.1 A typical '2-route' model of reading aloud with lexical and non-lexical routes from input to output.

the lexical route or by the rule based route. PINT can only be read correctly if it is read by the lexical procedure. The rule based route would be likely to pronounce it to rhyme with MINT.

One line of evidence consistent with the sort of model shown in figure 8.1 comes from neuropsychology. There is a striking contrast between the pattern of reading errors made by two groups of patients who have become dyslexic as a result of brain damage acquired after they have learnt to read. One group (called phonological dyslexics) reads words without difficulty, but cannot produce a pronunciation for non-words. A second group (called surface dyslexics) pronounces regular words and non-words correctly but makes errors on irregular words, tending to regularise them (e.g. pronouncing PINT to rhyme with 'mint'). This contrast is easily explained by 2-route models. It is assumed that phonological dyslexics can still use the lexical route but have lost the rule based route; surface dyslexics are assumed to have the rule based route, but to have lost the lexical route.

Although non-connectionist models of reading aloud differ in many details, there is general agreement on two issues. First, the reality of a privileged status for words is not in doubt—all models contain a lexicon, a store of specific information about particular words with which the reader is familiar. And, consequently, there must be another mechanism, such as a set of general rules of pronunciation, to allow pronunciation of novel letter strings.

The connectionist approach

Connectionist models of reading challenge both these assumptions. There is no place in a distributed connectionist model for something like a *lexicon* where specific information about particular inputs is stored, independent from other information. Information in a connectionist model is distributed across the storage space, superimposed on the information associated with other inputs. Similarly, there is no distinction between specific information and general rules in most connectionist models. There is only one kind of knowledge—the weights of the connections which the model has acquired as a result of its experiences during training—and this is all stored in a common network. (You could have a dual route connectionist model in which qualitatively different processes operate in different routes to store different sorts of knowledge, but we shall not consider such a model here.)

Attempting to simulate reading aloud without storage of specific information or a distinction between two different sorts of knowledge about converting print to sound might seem to be flying in the face of the received wisdom of decades of research into reading. On the other hand learning to read aloud is the sort of skill which seems ideally suited to connectionist modelling. First, the task is to learn a set of mappings from one domain (print) to another (sound). Multi-layer connectionist nets are good at learning mappings between domains even if they are somewhat arbitrary (see chapter 5). Second, teaching a child to read seems much like the typical process of teaching a net. It is a gradual process, improving over a long period, in which attempts are corrected by a teacher who gives feedback about the desired response. If connectionist modelling cannot capture this process it is hard to imagine what cognitive skill it would be appropriate for.

As an example of the connectionist approach to learning to read we will look at a 2-layer feedforward model, presented by Seidenberg and McClelland (1989). This is trained to pronounce all the monosyllabic[1] words in the English language using the backpropagation learning algorithm. Once the model has learnt this vocabulary it can produce an impressively accurate quantitative fit to many empirical findings about the factors which influence the speed at which skilled readers pronounce different words. For example, it correctly predicts the effects that the consistency of the spelling to sound pattern and the number of words with similar spelling pattern have on the time it takes to pronounce an individual word. However, although this model reproduces the words it has been taught in a way which accurately mimics the performance of skilled readers, it is poor at generalising to new ones—it does not read non-words as well as skilled readers. Nor is it as good as skilled readers at lexical decision (deciding if a letter string is a word or not).

Opponents of the connectionist approach to modelling cognitive processes have argued that these failures are due to the fundamental differences between connectionist networks and conventional wisdom about the modelling of reading. They suggest that the network is poor at pronouncing new words *because* it does not have specific rules about pronunciations and it is poor at lexical decision *because* it lacks representations of information about specific words. (We will explore the same criticisms of a connectionist model of learning the transformation required to form the past tense of a verb in chapters 9 and 12.) However, we will see that a change in the form of input coding can give the model an ability to read non-words which matches that of normal readers. Finally we will look at what happens when recurrent connections are added to the model. Its ability to read exception words and non-words is retained, but by giving it attractor structure, the model acquires the desirable characteristic of resisting noisy or degraded inputs.

The Seidenberg and McClelland model of reading aloud

The model is shown in figure 8.2. It is a conventional 2-layer feedforward model in which 400 input units, responsive to orthography, map onto 460 output units, representing phonology, via 200 hidden units. It embodies the standard connectionist

[1]One limitation of the model is that it has no representation of time. It simply switches on a set of phoneme units in response to an input string of letters. So it cannot pronounce polysyllabic words.

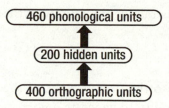

Figure 8.2   The structure of the Seidenberg and McClelland model. (Some connections which are not relevant to points made in the text have been omitted.)

principles for simulating cognitive processes: distributed representations at input and output, distributed knowledge within the network and gradient descent learning.

Input and output

The input units are activated by the letters in the words presented to the model. The output units represent the set of phonological features generated by the model in response to the pattern of activity on the input units.[2] The relationship between letters and input units and between output units and phonemes is complex and not easy to understand (or explain!). Any given unit is activated by a large number of different words. On average a word activates 20% of the input units and the model's response activates 12% of the output units. However, the particular form of coding adopted does not seem to be crucial to the main success of the model—its ability to mimic patterns of naming latency shown by normal readers. Indeed, it probably contributes to the model's main failing—its inability to pronounce non-words as successfully as normal readers. So we will leave discussion of the coding until the section on the Plaut *et al.* model, where we will describe an attempt to improve the performance of the model by changing the input coding.

Processing

Processing follows the conventions for a 2-layer net described in chapter 1. The input from unit j to unit i (input$_i$) is the product of the activity level of unit j and the strength of the connection between units j and i:

$$\text{input}_i = a_j\, w_{ij} \tag{8.1}$$

The net input to unit i (netinput$_i$) is the sum of all the inputs from the units it is connected to, plus a bias term:

$$\text{netinput}_i = \Sigma_j\, a_j\, w_{ij} + \text{bias}_i \tag{8.2}$$

The activity level of unit i, a_i, is determined by passing the net input through the logistic activation function shown in figure 1.4(c) of chapter 1. This produces a

---

[2]A phonological feature defines a contrast that distinguishes speech sounds. For example, the phonological feature 'voicing' distinguishes the phonemes /b/ and /p/. The vocal chords vibrate for /b/ and not for /p/.

sigmoidal relationship between netinput and activity, constraining the activity of the unit to lie between 0 and 1.

Learning

Connection strengths and biases are initially random, so the first attempt of the model to pronounce a word is random. The model's ability to generate a correct phonological code comes about through learning. After a word has been presented to the system a 'teacher' computes the difference between the actual value of each phonological unit and its correct value. Weights are then changed, using the backpropagation procedure, so that the output of each unit will be closer to the correct value the next time that the word is presented. (Training a multi-layer net by backpropagation is explained in detail in chapter 5).

Training

The model was trained on all the monosyllabic words with three or more letters in American English, except proper nouns and foreign words—a set of about 3000 words. In each epoch the net was trained with a sub-set taken from the complete corpus, with words which occur more frequently in written American being presented to the net more often. Over 250 training epochs the most common word (THE) was presented 230 times while the least common was presented 7 times. (In reality, THE is about 100 000 times more common than the least frequent monosyllabic word in the language, but subsequent studies suggest that this compression has no significant effect on the performance of the model (Plaut *et al.* 1996)).

The model's response is the pattern of activity of the phonological units. Many units are at least partially active in response to any input. The pattern was considered to be correct if the most active output units were closer to those of the correct pronunciation than to any other word. After 250 training epochs the model could pronounce 97% of the words in its training set correctly.

Naming latency

Experiments on normal reading measure the reaction time (latency) to name a word as a function of variables such as the frequency of occurrence of the word in the language or the regularity of its spelling pattern. The test of the model as a simulation of adult reading is whether it can mimic these results once it has learnt all the words in its training corpus.

The model does not represent processes which could generate a *latency* directly. The output comes on after one computational pass through the network, whatever the input. That is, the output is produced after the same amount of processing time. Seidenberg and McClelland simulated latency with the *phonological error score*. This is the difference between the activity pattern actually achieved in response to an input and the correct pattern. They assumed that the error score would correlate with naming latency, with a lower error score being equivalent to a short reaction time and a large error score equivalent to a long reaction time. If you imagine the output units feeding to an equivalent of the motor neurons and muscles controlling the human articulatory system, this is probably reasonable. Vocal production requires various parts of the articulatory system to move to particular places. So pronunciation cannot start until there is a clear pattern of signals to the vocal muscles. With an ambiguous pattern (which would produce a high error score) the system would have to wait until the ambiguity had been resolved before a word could be pronounced.

Replicating the results of word naming experiments

The first result to note is that the model *does* learn most of the words in its training corpus, whether their spelling follows a regular or an exception pattern. Therefore, despite the assumptions of most non-connectionist models of reading, it is not necessary to have word specific memory locations to ensure that exception pronunciations like HAVE or PINT are learnt in an environment where most words with this spelling pattern are pronounced differently. But the model can do much more than this. Skilled readers show a bewildering set of effects of frequency and spelling-to-sound consistency on the speed with which they name written words. We will look at some examples of the model displaying behaviour remarkably similar to that of normal adult readers when asked to retrieve information from the data base it acquired as it learnt to read.

The word frequency effect

Common words are pronounced more quickly than uncommon words. This is an example, with words as stimuli, of a ubiquitous result in experiments on human information processing—reactions to stimuli which have been encountered frequently are quicker than to those which, although similar in other ways, have been encountered less frequently. No model of information processing would be taken seriously unless it could produce this result.

The conventional explanation in models which have localist representations of individual words is that the threshold of activity required for a word recognition device to fire reflects the word's frequency—high frequency words have a low threshold and are thus recognised more quickly, low frequency words have a high recognition threshold and are thus recognised more slowly. The Seidenberg and McClelland model has no lexical entries so an explanation of this sort is not possible. However, it does produce this result (with error rather than reaction time). The number of training trials on a particular word is proportional to its frequency.

Phonological error is reduced by training trials. Thus high frequency words will produce a lower phonological error than less frequent words. Since reaction time is deemed to be proportional to phonological error, naming latency will be proportional to word frequency.

This result is an inevitable consequence of the structure of the model, the choice of learning algorithm and the training schedule. So perhaps the model does not gather much credit for getting it right. On the other hand this explanation is no more ad hoc than the explanation of traditional models which can set thresholds to reproduce the right result without any constraint.

The frequency×regularity interaction

A more subtle result than the basic word frequency effect is the *interaction* between frequency and regularity. *Regular* words are those like GAVE or MUST which follow the common pronunciation for their spelling pattern. *Exception* words are those like HAVE or PINT which represent an unusual pronunciation for that spelling pattern. Overall, people pronounce regular words faster than exception words. But this effect interacts with word frequency. The effect only shows with low frequency words.

The interaction is shown, with data from an experiment on naming latency with normal subjects, at the left of figure 8.3. The filled circles show the average latency at which subjects name words with regular spelling-to-sound correspondence which are of high (e.g. MUST) or low (e.g. MODE) frequency. There is a small effect of frequency—on average it takes a little longer to start pronouncing a low frequency word than a high frequency word. The open squares show equivalent data for words with an exception spelling-to-sound correspondence. Here there is a large effect of frequency. It takes considerably longer to start pronouncing a low frequency exception word (e.g. LOSE) than a high frequency exception word (e.g. HAVE).

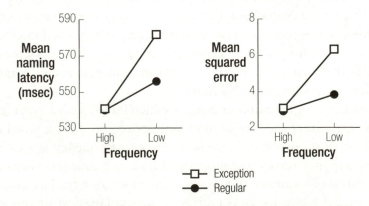

Figure 8.3   Left: The time it takes subjects to start naming words as a function of their frequency and spelling regularity. Right: The error produced by the model when reading the same words. (Based on Seidenberg and McClelland 1989.)

The right of the figure shows what happens when the same set of words used in the experiment with normal subjects was presented to the model. The model does not just show the interaction between frequency and regularity found with normal adult readers, it reproduces the normal data with startling precision. The 'precision' is partly illusory as the model does not actually produce reaction times—it produces an error score. (Note the vertical scale on the graphs.) So a particular value on the reaction time scale of the experiment with normal subjects does not correspond to a particular error score. But if the error score in any one condition (say, high frequency regular) is taken as an arbitrary reference point, the *relative* error score in the other three conditions is proportionately similar in the model to those produced by the subjects.

How does a traditional reading model such as that shown in figure 8.1 explain this result? In such a model the lexical and the rule based routes generate a pronunciation for each word. They produce the same pronunciation for regular words but competing pronunciations for exception words. For example, the lexical route would specify one pronunciation of the O in LOSE (the correct one) while the rule based route would specify a different one (to rhyme with ROSE). The confusion caused by these competing commands to the speech output system is proposed as the reason why exception words are pronounced more slowly. To explain the interaction with frequency such models have to assume that high frequency exception words produce their (correct) pronunciation by the lexical route too quickly for the competing (incorrect) pronunciation generated by the grapheme → phoneme conversion rules to cause confusion. But the lexical route takes a little longer to produce a pronunciation for a low frequency word, and this is not produced before the competing pronunciation from the non-lexical route starts to cause confusion. Such an explanation can give a qualitative account for the data. But, given the small difference in latency between high and low frequency words, the assumption that this slowing should be just enough to allow competition from the non-lexical route to appear requires a somewhat implausible coincidence. In contrast, the precise quantitative fit to the data produced by the connectionist model seems genuinely impressive.

The frequency × neighbourhood size interaction

The 'neighbourhood size' of a word is defined by the number of other words which can be made from it by changing one letter. Figure 8.4 shows that neighbourhood size (N) has an effect on naming latency which interacts with word frequency in the same way as regularity—it has little effect on the speed of naming high frequency words, but low frequency words with many neighbours are pronounced more quickly than those with few.

The neighbourhood effect for low frequency words shows cooperation over the information learnt in response to many different inputs. If the model has not seen a

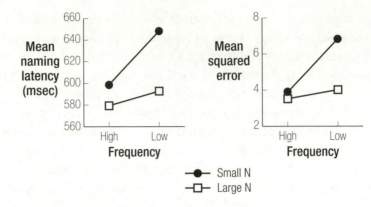

Figure 8.4   Left: The time it takes subjects to name words as a function of their frequency and the number of words with similar spelling in English. Right: The error produced by the model when reading the same words. (Based on Seidenberg and McClelland 1989.)

word very often, it has had little opportunity to develop the weights required to produce the phonology accurately. But if it has seen many similar words, what it knows about their pronunciation can make up for the absence of experience with the word itself and a pronunciation with relatively low error is produced. One of the strengths of connectionist modelling is that it has a natural way of explaining effects which require pooling over many individual experiences. (This is explored in the analysis of prototype extraction in chapter 4.) Models with a lexicon require the addition of ad hoc mechanisms for pooling across the localist representations of specific experiences to account for such effects.

The effect of spelling-to-sound consistency on the pronunciation of non-words

Consistent spelling-to-sound patterns are ones like -UST where all words have the same pronunciation. Inconsistent patterns are those like -AVE where there are exceptions to the general pronunciation pattern. Adult readers pronounce non-words derived from consistent patterns (e.g. NUST) more quickly than non-words derived from inconsistent patterns (e.g. MAVE). Figure 8.5 shows that the model produces this effect when pronouncing letter strings it has never seen before. The inconsistency of the pronunciation of -AVE as opposed to the consistency in the pronunciation of -UST is recorded in the weights and affects response production.

This effect is difficult for 2-route models to account for. NUST and MAVE must both be pronounced by the non-lexical route using the pronunciation rules. So their pronunciation should take the same time. To explain the result one would have to say that the rule box has flags attached to inconsistent rules, warning the system to slow down. Although one can imagine some justification for such a proposal, the absence of any control on the ad hoc additions which can be made to accommodate any empirical result makes such models seem dangerously unfalsifiable.

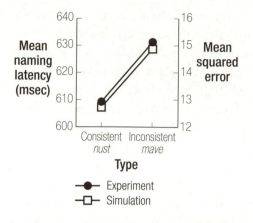

Figure 8.5 The length of time subjects take to pronounce non-words based on consistent or inconsistent spelling to sound patterns and the error produced by the Seidenberg and McClelland model pronouncing the same letter strings. (Based on Seidenberg and McClelland 1989.)

The precision fit of the connectionist model to the data is again impressive. Indeed, it seems almost too good to be true. Why should phonological error and reaction time show exactly the same proportional change when dealing with non-words derived from consistent or inconsistent spelling patterns when the relationship between them is arbitrary? Although the model has learnt a large chunk of English vocabulary it has only a fraction of the lexical experience of a normal adult reader. If the results are determined by the sum total of lexical experience why should a model with a partial database give a perfect fit to the normal adult data?

What has the model learnt?

Seidenberg and McClelland's model contains no lexical entries and no explicit rules. How does it produce effects like the reading of exception words and pronunciation of non-words which have traditionally been assumed to require these?

The entire set of weights is used in computing the phonology of every letter string presented to the model. So the response to any particular input is a function of the network's entire experience. The pronunciation of an input string depends both on what it learnt on previous trials with that string and on what it learnt on all trials with any word which has any resemblance to that string. The representation in the weights of specific information, such as that the A in HAVE is short, is strong enough to overcome the general information that the A in _AVE sequences is usually long. At the same time the representation in the weights of general information is strong enough to produce a plausible pronunciation for MAVE even though it has never been seen before. This is a concrete example of the claim, discussed in chapter 4, that a single connectionist network can represent both specific and general information.

Given that the network's response to any letter string is a function of its entire experience, perhaps it is not surprising that the model can account for effects of word frequency, spelling-to-sound regularity and the number of other words with a similar spelling pattern on word naming. But what is impressive about the model is that it does not just make vague qualitative predictions about these effects. It gives precise, quantitative matches to data obtained from normal adult readers. Moreover it accounts for the relative effects of frequency, consistency and neighbourhood size without any additions to the model. This suggests that the connectionist approach to learning and the representation of knowledge may indeed mimic some aspects of the way the people learn.

Limitations of the model

Despite the successes of this model it does not match every aspect of adult readers' performance. First, the model's knowledge of what it has seen before is not nearly as good as that of skilled readers. Skilled readers know that FRAME is a word and FRANE is not. But the model often gets this sort of decision wrong. The problem is that although FRANE is not a word it is similar to many letter strings which are (FRANK, FRAME, CRANE and so on). The process of superimposing similar information, which is central to the way the model works and which underlies its ability to reproduce naming latency data so effectively, makes it difficult for the model to know whether it has actually seen a specific string before if it is similar to many others which it has seen. To critics of the connectionist approach this high-lights the inadequacy of a model of reading which has no lexical units. With these, deciding whether FRANE is a word or not is straightforward—you just check whether there is a lexical unit for FRANE. If there is, it's a word; if there isn't, it isn't. Second, although the model can read non-words, it is not as good at this as normal adult readers. For example, in experiments reported by Besner *et al.* (1990) the model performed at about 60% correct on a set of non-words of which adults read more than 90% correctly. To critics of the connectionist approach, failure to pronounce non-words is what would be expected of a model which lacks pro-nunciation rules. It can pronounce the words it knows but cannot generalise to new ones.

These failures cut right to the heart of the connectionist enterprise. They appear to show that the inability to simulate the performance of adult readers can be ascribed precisely to the lack of two things a connectionist model does not have—localist storage of knowledge about specific experiences, and explicit rules. One difficulty with evaluating the failures is that the model, as it stands, is not a complete model of reading. The most obvious lack is that it has no representation of the semantics of the words it has learnt. Skilled readers do not just know how to read words, they also know what they mean. The problem is that semantic knowledge might well help in tasks like lexical decision. If FRANE generates no activity in semantics, then it's probably not a word. But without knowing the relative contribution of semantic and non-semantic components to lexical decision it is impossible to know whether the model is adequate or not.

Seidenberg and McClelland's model was an attempt to see how far a simplified approach to reading aloud, based on connectionist principles, could get. The answer appears to be 'Quite a long way'. The fit to the normal data in figures 8.3–8.5 is most impressive. But this does not tell us whether the problems with pronouncing non-words and with lexical decision are fatal flaws or not.

The Plaut, McClelland, Seidenberg and Patterson model

The general approach of Seidenberg and McClelland was extended by Plaut *et al.* (1996) in two ways. First they explored the effect of a different form of input coding. Then they examined the effect of adding attractor structure to the model by including recurrent connections. (Attractors and recurrent connections are described in chapter 7.)

Input coding

If a child is to learn quickly to read aloud, the ability to generalise from past experiences to novel letter strings is essential. The traditional assumption in cognitive psychology has been that this is done by applying general rules of pronunciation. Since connectionist models have no explicit rules, their ability to generalise is a crucial test of the approach.[3] A test of the ability to pronounce novel letter strings seems a fair test since this task does not involve knowledge of semantics, and the Seidenberg and McClelland model contains no representation of semantics. Normal subjects have no difficulty producing a pronunciation of strings like SLINT or MAVE based on the pronunciation of similar real words. If the model cannot match this performance, then it is probably a failure.

If the network is to generalise well to novel inputs it must capture the regularities in the inputs to which it is exposed during learning. The most direct way to organise the input units might seem to be to have a set of 26 input units, one for each letter of the alphabet, with a set for each letter position up to the longest word in the training set. This will produce a unique input pattern for every possible word. But a problem with this sort of organisation can be seen by considering the words LOG, GLAD, SPLIT, GRILL and CRAWL. The model is trying to learn pronunciation regularities, such as the correspondence between the letter L and the phoneme /l/. There is no connection between the input units activated by L in different positions in the arrangement for input coding outlined above, so the model could not generalise from

---

[3]The ability of connectionist networks to represent knowledge which would naturally seem to be expressed as a rule will be a recurring theme in the following chapters.

learning that L corresponds to /l/ in LOG, to help it pronounce the L in GLAD. Thus this sort of coding works against the model discovering pronunciation regularities. Although the coding system used by Seidenberg and McClelland used a distributed representation rather than a slot based coding system like the one described above, it suffered from the same sort of problem. Information it had learnt about the pronunciation of a letter in one context would not generalise easily to that letter occurring in other contexts.

The opposite extreme to the coding of letters by position would be to have a single set of position independent letter units mapping onto a single set of position independent phoneme units, with all input units simultaneously activating all output units. Learning about a particular grapheme → phoneme correspondence would then accumulate across different words, even if the letter appeared at different places or with other combinations of letters in different words. But this will not work because it fails to preserve the order information which is required to distinguish different words composed from the same letters. Such a system could not distinguish between RAT, ART and TAR. However, it turns out there are strong constraints in English about the ordering of phonemes in monosyllabic words.

This allows a modified version of such a scheme to work. The structure of monosyllabic words is an initial consonant (or cluster), one vowel and a final consonant (or cluster). Monosyllabic words contain only one vowel sound so only one set of letter to phoneme units is required for vowel correspondences. Most consonants can appear in both the letter cluster before the vowel (the onset) and the cluster after it (the coda). So there must be a separate set of units coding letter-to-phoneme correspondences for each of these positions to preserve order information. But within each of these clusters there turn out to be very strong order constraints if more than one letter is present. For example, if S and T are both present in the onset cluster, S always precedes T; if T and R are both present, T always precedes R. So only one set of consonant-to-phoneme units is required for the letters in each group. Thus the grapheme → phoneme correspondences that have to be learnt can be pooled across different words even if the letters appear in different positions in the different words. The information that the input T should generate the output /t/ will accumulate on the same units when the net is learning to pronounce TRAIN or STAIN. This goes some way towards condensing the grapheme → phoneme learning problem. (The nature of the input and output coding in this model may become clearer when you have run the **tlearn** simulation at the end of the chapter.)

Pronunciation

The model with the new form of input coding succeeds in learning both regular and exception words, just like the Seidenberg and McClelland model. It also produces the frequency×regularity interaction. So it passes the basic test of learning to read, and subsequently demonstrates the same influences of frequency and neighbourhood size on its word reading latency as adult readers.

But the acid test is its ability to pronounce non-words. With a set of non-words based on words with a consistent pronunciation (e.g. HEAN derived from DEAN) it produced the regular pronunciation for 98% compared to 94% by normal adult readers. With non-words based on words with an inconsistent pronunciation (e.g. HEAF derived from DEAF or LEAF) it produced the regular pronunciation for 72% compared to 78% by normal adult readers. Both normal readers and the model produce a mixture of the two possible pronunciations with these words. Thus a model with a form of input coding which condenses grapheme → phoneme regularities across words shows a similar pattern of non-word pronunciation to normal readers. Overall, then, the results show that a model without either lexical units or explicit pronunciation rules *is* capable of learning to read both exception words and non-words.

The success of Plaut *et al.*'s simulation highlights one problem of explicit computational models. Some input coding system must be chosen to get the model to run. But the appropriate form of input coding is not likely to be an issue about which connectionism has anything to say. Seidenberg and McClelland chose one which prevented the model from simulating a key aspect of normal behaviour. But the failure was not of the connectionist principles which were under investigation. It was of an arbitrary component of the model which was irrelevant to the central issue of whether the connectionist approach to cognition is a useful one.

Reading with an attractor network

Having shown that a connectionist model *could* cope with the non-word naming problem, Plaut *et al.* looked at the consequences of introducing recurrent connections to the network. Seidenberg and McClelland's simple feedforward network involved no interactivity between units within a layer or between layers. The response is generated in a single computational pass through the net. Recurrent connections allow units to constrain each other as the network settles on the most plausible overall interpretation of the input. One consequence is the formation of *basins of attraction*—a set of input states which will all converge on one particular final state, the attractor, during the settling period of inter-unit interaction.

Attractor structure means that the network can produce the correct response even when the input is degraded. The brain frequently has to cope with degraded input— think of trying to listen to a conversation in a noisy room. Also, the brain is an inherently noisy environment—its computational units have a spontaneous, random, background firing rate. So the natural ability of attractors to produce the right answer even when the input is degraded would appeal to anyone trying to produce a realistic model of a cognitive process.

Despite the general desirability of attractor structure for modelling cognitive processes, there is a problem when the task is one like reading. Attractors offer a solution to the problem of dealing with a novel input when the novelty is, in reality, just a noisy version of something the system already knows about. But where the correct response to a novel input *is a novel output* they will cause problems. Ideally you want the system to *generalise* (i.e. produce the same response) across noisy exemplars of the same input but to *discriminate* (i.e. produce a different response) when the inputs represent different words. The tendency to generalise, inherent in attractor architecture, would seem to lead to the problem of inappropriate lexicalisation of non-words (i.e. producing a word at output in response to a non-word at input). In order to pronounce non-words the network must be able to generalise from the knowledge it acquired as it learnt words. This knowledge resides in the attractors. So non-words must access attractors to gain pronunciation information, but they must avoid capture by them. If offered FRANE as an input, an attractor network might treat it as a degraded version of one of the similar words it already knew and produce one of these as output. This seems like an insoluble problem.

Figure 8.6 shows the architecture of the model. The crucial difference from the previous one is represented by the recurrent connections. Output activity is fed back to the hidden units and all phonological units are connected to each other. After a letter string is input to the network activity cycles around these connections while the system gradually settles into a stable state which represents its response. The network was taught in the same way as the previous network. It successfully learnt to read both regular and exception words, and produced the frequency×regularity interaction. So in the basic tests of reading ability it performs as well as the feedforward nets discussed before. Surprisingly, the model also passed the crucial test of non-word reading ability. Its performance was similar to normal readers, producing regular pronunciations for ~95% of the non- word strings presented to it. Given that the network formed attractors for words, how did it manage to read non-words? To generate a pronunciation for the letter string MAVE it must have accessed an attractor with knowledge about how to pronounce _AVE. Why didn't the input get caught and produce the word represented by the attractor?

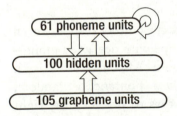

Figure 8.6 The structure of Plaut *et al.*'s model.

Componential attractors

The solution to the net's paradoxical ability to read non-words is that the attractors developed for regular words are *componential*. They have separate attractors representing knowledge about how to pronounce the onset cluster, vowel and coda. A novel letter string can use the knowledge held about some parts of the pronunciation while allowing for the difference that makes it a novel string. This is illustrated by Plaut *et al.*'s analysis of the extent to which production of the correct response in each phonological cluster (onset, vowel, coda) depends on the input from each of the orthographic clusters.

Consider the pronunciation of a regular word like GAVE. The activity of the orthographic units corresponding to G, A and VE was manipulated to see what effect they have on the phonological units for producing /g/, /A/ and /v/. The result is that only G affects /g/, only A effects /A/, and only VE affects /v/. The attractors for onset, vowel and coda are independent. Thus if M is substituted as the initial letter—the network is asked to read the non-word MAVE—the network has no problem. /A/ is still produced as the vowel sound, /v/ as the coda, and the attractor built up over practice with words for pronouncing M has no difficulty in dealing with it in a non-word.

But this leaves the problem of exception words. Why doesn't the network respond with a long /A/ to the input HAVE? It turns out that non-componential attractors develop for exception words. When the influence of orthographic clusters on phonology was tested with words such as HAVE, the H and VE had a large influence of the vowel pronunciation. More, in fact, than the orthographic unit corresponding to the vowel. So in the presence of an H and a VE, a short /a/ will be produced as the vowel sound in response to A. The attractor which develops for HAVE represents the fact that in the specific context of H_VE, A requires a particular unusual pronunciation. By building componential attractors for the individual parts of regular words and non-componential attractors for exception words, the model can achieve the crucial results—non-words are given a regular pronunciation, and exception words are pronounced correctly.

What have these models achieved?

These models have shown that it is possible for a connectionist model of a real, complex cognitive process to produce a precise quantitative fit to data produced in experiments with normal subjects. The success of the model with attractor structure suggests that this approach might continue to work in a realistic noisy environment.

The fact that a distributed model can work shows that neither localist information storage nor knowledge represented as an explicit set of rules is a requirement for modelling cognitive processes. However, the Plaut *et al.* model suggests that localist and distributed information storage do not necessarily have to be seen as polar opposites. The attractor basins which emerge as the dynamic state of the model interacts with specific inputs seem to have some of the characteristics of lexical units. Furthermore, the distinction between componential and non-componential attractors seems to offer a way in which what might be regarded as rules of pronunciation could be instantiated. The way in which rules and symbols might be represented in connectionist networks will be examined at greater length in chapter 12.

Further reading

Sejnowski and Rosenberg (1986) is the original classic paper on teaching a network to pronounce English text.

Besner *et al.* (1990) attack Seidenberg and McClelland's model on the grounds of its inability to mimic normal data on non-word reading or lexical decision, and defend the claim that models of reading require explicit lexical units.

Coltheart *et al.* (1993) attack Seidenberg and McClelland's model on the grounds of its inability to explain patterns of reading deficit found in patients, and defend 2-route models of reading.

Reading aloud with `tlearn`

In this exercise you will replicate part of the Plaut *et al.* (1996) feedforward model of word reading.

Preparing the reading aloud simulation

The training environment
The first task is to define a training environment for the network. The network's task is to learn to map a set of orthographic representations to their phonological forms. That is, it must discover the regularities (and exceptions) that enable readers to pronounce English written words. Plaut *et al.* used a special type of coding scheme to represent the orthography and phonology of English monosyllabic words. The codes they use are shown below:

ORTHOGRAPHY
onset
y s p t k q c b d g f v j z l m n r w h ch gh gn ph ps rh sh th ts wh
vowel
e i o u a y ai au aw ay ea ee ei eu ew ey ie oa oe oi oo ou ow oy ue ui uy

coda

h r l m n b d g cxf v j s z p t k q bb ch ck dd dg ff gg gh gn ks ll ng
nn ph pp ps rr sh sl ss tch th ts tt zz u e es ed

Each orthographic input (i.e. written word) is defined in terms of an onset (the first letter or consonant cluster), a vowel and a coda (the final letter or consonant cluster). There are 30 possible onsets, 27 possible vowels and 48 possible codas. Monosyllabic English words are spelt by choosing one or more candidates from each of the 3 possible groups. For example, the orthographic form THROW would activate the onsets 'th' and 'r', the vowel 'o' and the coda 'w'.

The phonological output (spoken word) is similarly defined in terms of an onset, vowel and coda. There are 23 possible onsets, 14 possible vowels and 24 possible codas. The onsets and codas are classified into subgroups that capture the phonotactics (legal sound sequences) of the language. The onsets are divided into 3 groups, each group containing mutually exclusive members. For example, 't' and 'k' cannot be simultaneously active in the onset of a word. The codas are divided into 9 mutually exclusive groups. There is only 1 vowel group, indicating that only 1 vowel is ever pronounced, as you would expect in a monosyllabic word. Using this coding scheme, the word 'scratch' would be pronounced 's k r a _ _ _ _ _ _ _ C'. The blanks indicate where none of the possible phonemes should be articulated.

PHONOLOGY
onset
s S C
z Z j f v T D p b t d k g m n h
l r w y
vowel
a e i o u @ ^ A E I O U W Y
coda
r
l
m n N
b g d
ps ks ts
s z
f v p k
t
S Z T D C j

The vowels are sounded as in the following words with American pronunciation: a – pot; e –bed; i – hit; o – dog; u – good; @ – cat; A – make; E – keep; I – bike; O – hope; U – boot; W – now; Y – boy; ^ – cup.

Since there is a total of 105 possible orthographic onsets, vowels and codas, the network has 105 input units. Since there is a total of 61 possible phonological onsets, vowels and codas, the network has 61 output units. Plaut *et al.* used 100 hidden units in their simulation, giving a 105×100×61 network architecture.

Defining the network and the training set

Start up the simulation by opening the project **plaut** either by double-clicking on the project icon or opening the project through the Network menu. It might take a while for the project to initialise as the files are rather large! Plaut *et al.* trained their network on 2998 monosyllabic words. The orthographic representations of these words (in binary format) are contained in the file **plaut.data**. The corresponding phonological representations can be found in the file **plaut.teach**. The network architecture is defined in the file **plaut.cf**.

Training the network[4]

Set the learning rate and momentum parameters in the Training Options dialogue box to 0.001 and 0.0, respectively. Set the network to Train randomly (i.e. to select training pairs at random from the training set). Set the network to train with the cross-entropy version of backpropagation (**x-ent**). Cross-entropy tends to work better than ordinary sum-squared error on problems where most of the output units are zero. Finally, set the network to update the weights after every 2998 training sweeps. This forces the network to perform 'batch update' of the weights rather than 'pattern update'. Now train the network for 10 epochs (i.e. 29 980 sweeps). This is not enough training for the network to solve the problem but we want to start out without using any momentum term to avoid magnifying the effects of initial weight changes. These tend to be very large at the beginning of training and potentially unrepresentative of the problem to be solved. We introduce momentum after 10 epochs of training by opening the Training Options dialogue box again, setting momentum to 0.9 and loading in the weights file **plaut-29980.wts**. Now continue training for a further 290 epochs. The weights files are called **plaut-29980.wts** and **plaut-899400.wts**. To load a weights file into **tlearn**, open the Training Options dialogue box and click on the More button if it is displayed. Now check the Load weights file box, double-click on the name space and select the appropriate weights file or simply type in the name of the weights file. Remember that you need to be in the correct folder.

---

[4]Warning! Do not attempt to run this simulation unless you have a computer with plenty of memory running at a minimum of 100 MHz. It took 24 hours to run on a PowerMac 8100 running at 110 MHz. For users who do not have access to powerful machines we have provided the weights files obtained from the training process.

Analysing network performance

The precise way to determine the performance of the network on the reading task is to examine the output activities on a node by node basis. You can do this by specifying the latest weights file in the Testing Options dialogue box and Verify the network has learned on the training set. However, when you have 2998 patterns to examine and 61 nodes in each pattern, this can quickly become a tedious business! So we will consider a shortcut to evaluating network performance on this task.

Using the Output Translation utility

A utility program called Output Translation... in the Special menu enables you to determine the phonemic output of the network from the node activities. Before you can use this utility, you will need a reference file that tells **tlearn** how to translate the real-numbered output vector into a string of phonemes. This reference file is contained in **plaut.out**. Open the file in **tlearn**. Ensure that the file is identical to that shown in figure 8.7.

The Output Translation file follows a strict format:

MAPPINGS: The first section of the file tells **tlearn** how to divide up the output vector into meaningful chunks. In the current example, chunks represent the phonological codings shown above. The MAPPINGS section of the file is always at the beginning of the file and the line MAPPINGS: is always the first line of the file (remember the colon). Subsequent lines identify groups of units and the codes that will be used to translate them. There are 13 GROUPS corresponding to the 13 output clusters. You may only use CODENAMEs that are defined in subsequent sections of the file.

<CODENAME>: Subsequent sections of the file define the binary codes for the ASCII characters. Output Translation will decipher the network's ASCII output by referring to these codes. You can define as many sections as you wish but the binary vectors within a section must all be of the same length. Make sure that the number of elements in the binary vector agrees with the number of output units you have assigned to this CODENAME in the MAPPINGS section. The CODENAME must be in uppercase letters and end with a colon.

When you are confident how the reference file operates, choose Output Translation... from the Special menu. Click on the Pattern file: box and select the **plaut.out** reference file. Check the Euclidean Distance button and then OK the translation. Finally, check the Use Output Translation box in the Testing Options dialogue box. Now when you attempt to Verify the network has learned, the Output display will include an ASCII representation of the output units together with the target output. The output display will continue to include this ASCII output until you uncheck the Use Output Translation box in the Testing Options dialogue box. You

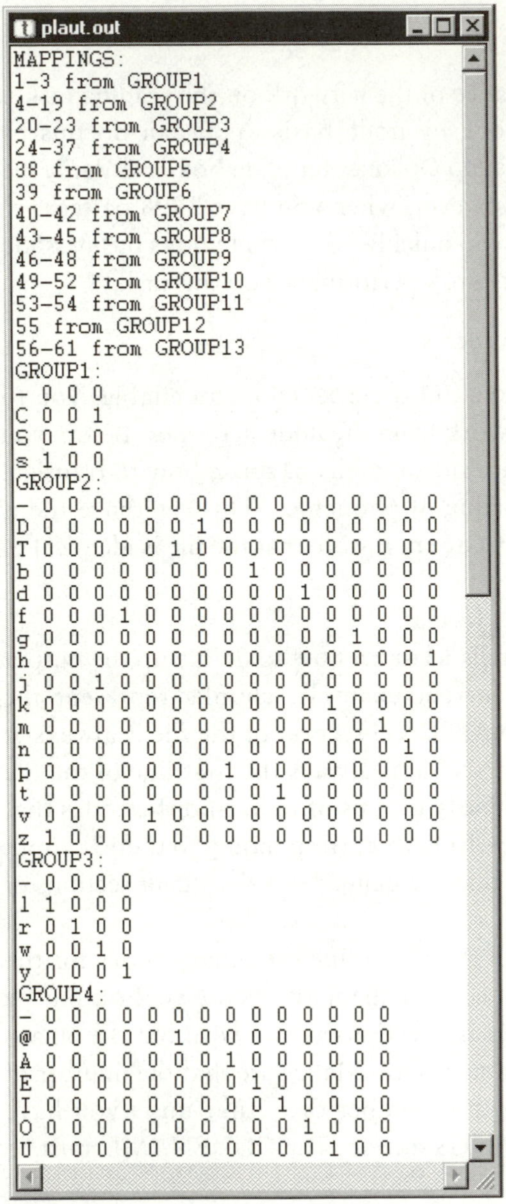

```
plaut.out

MAPPINGS:
1-3 from GROUP1
4-19 from GROUP2
20-23 from GROUP3
24-37 from GROUP4
38 from GROUP5
39 from GROUP6
40-42 from GROUP7
43-45 from GROUP8
46-48 from GROUP9
49-52 from GROUP10
53-54 from GROUP11
55 from GROUP12
56-61 from GROUP13
GROUP1:
- 0 0 0
C 0 0 1
S 0 1 0
s 1 0 0
GROUP2:
- 0 0 0 0 0 0 0 0 0 0 0 0 0 0 0 0
D 0 0 0 0 0 0 1 0 0 0 0 0 0 0 0 0
T 0 0 0 0 0 1 0 0 0 0 0 0 0 0 0 0
b 0 0 0 0 0 0 0 0 1 0 0 0 0 0 0 0
d 0 0 0 0 0 0 0 0 0 1 0 0 0 0 0 0
f 0 0 0 1 0 0 0 0 0 0 0 0 0 0 0 0
g 0 0 0 0 0 0 0 0 0 0 0 1 0 0 0 0
h 0 0 0 0 0 0 0 0 0 0 0 0 0 0 0 1
j 0 0 1 0 0 0 0 0 0 0 0 0 0 0 0 0
k 0 0 0 0 0 0 0 0 0 0 1 0 0 0 0 0
m 0 0 0 0 0 0 0 0 0 0 0 0 1 0 0 0
n 0 0 0 0 0 0 0 0 0 0 0 0 0 1 0 0
p 0 0 0 0 0 0 1 0 0 0 0 0 0 0 0 0
t 0 0 0 0 0 0 0 0 0 1 0 0 0 0 0 0
v 0 0 0 0 1 0 0 0 0 0 0 0 0 0 0 0
z 1 0 0 0 0 0 0 0 0 0 0 0 0 0 0 0
GROUP3:
- 0 0 0 0
l 1 0 0 0
r 0 1 0 0
w 0 0 1 0
y 0 0 0 1
GROUP4:
- 0 0 0 0 0 0 0 0 0 0 0 0 0 0
@ 0 0 0 0 0 1 0 0 0 0 0 0 0 0
A 0 0 0 0 0 0 0 1 0 0 0 0 0 0
E 0 0 0 0 0 0 0 0 1 0 0 0 0 0
I 0 0 0 0 0 0 0 0 1 0 0 0 0 0
O 0 0 0 0 0 0 0 0 0 1 0 0 0 0
U 0 0 0 0 0 0 0 0 0 1 0 0 0 0
```

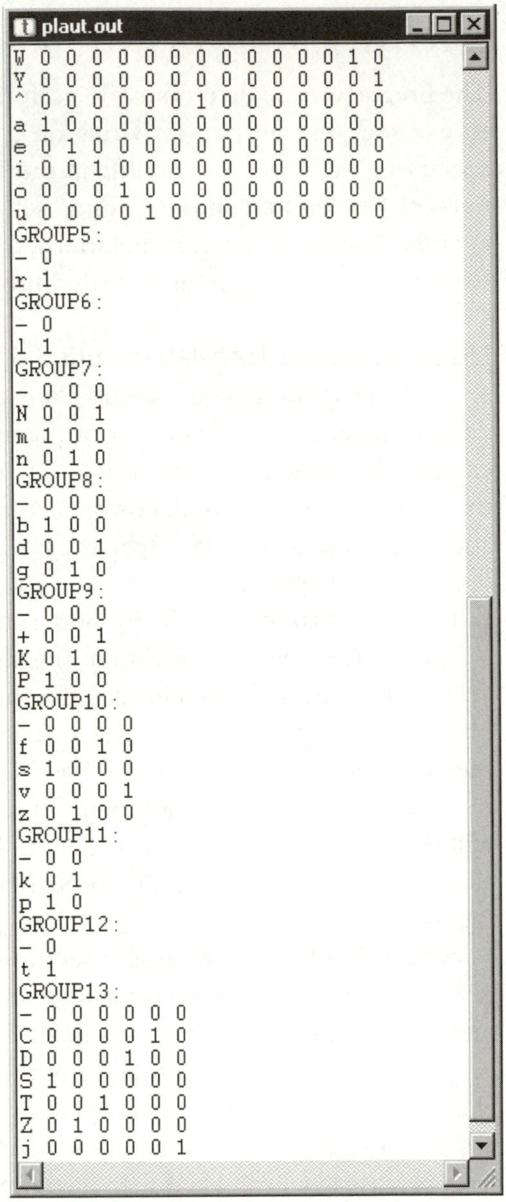

```
plaut.out

W 0 0 0 0 0 0 0 0 0 0 0 1 0
Y 0 0 0 0 0 0 0 0 0 0 0 0 1
^ 0 0 0 0 0 1 0 0 0 0 0 0 0
a 1 0 0 0 0 0 0 0 0 0 0 0 0
e 0 1 0 0 0 0 0 0 0 0 0 0 0
i 0 0 1 0 0 0 0 0 0 0 0 0 0
o 0 0 0 1 0 0 0 0 0 0 0 0 0
u 0 0 0 0 1 0 0 0 0 0 0 0 0
GROUP5:
- 0
r 1
GROUP6:
- 0
l 1
GROUP7:
- 0 0 0
N 0 0 1
m 1 0 0
n 0 1 0
GROUP8:
- 0 0 0
b 1 0 0
d 0 0 1
g 0 1 0
GROUP9:
- 0 0 0
+ 0 0 1
K 0 1 0
P 1 0 0
GROUP10:
- 0 0 0 0
f 0 0 1 0
s 1 0 0 0
v 0 0 0 1
z 0 1 0 0
GROUP11:
- 0 0
k 0 1
p 1 0
GROUP12:
- 0
t 1
GROUP13:
- 0 0 0 0 0 0
C 0 0 0 0 1 0
D 0 0 0 1 0 0
S 1 0 0 0 0 0
T 0 0 1 0 0 0
Z 0 1 0 0 0 0
j 0 0 0 0 0 1
```

Figure 8.7　Output Translation file—**plaut.out**—for converting the output vector back to an ASCII representation of phonemes.

probably want to check the Translation Only check box to prevent **tlearn** printing out all the binary activity patterns. Use the Output Translation technique to assess the performance of the network on the training items. Note that you can also use the Node Activities display to investigate actual and target output when you have activated the Output Translation utility.

Changes to the Plaut et al. simulation

There are several discrepancies between the way you have run this simulation and the original Plaut *et al.* work. First, there is no *weight decay* feature implemented in **tlearn** so it is possible that the network will not generalise quite so well as the original network. Second, and more importantly, no account is taken of the token frequencies of different words in the current simulation. This will have important implications for the network's pronunciation of irregularly pronounced words like 'have'. Nevertheless, you should find that your network does very well on the task and reads over 90% of the words correctly.

How well does the network generalise?

Test the network using the file **test.data** which contains the three words *mave*, *save* and *have*. Select the **test.data** file in the Novel data: option in the Testing Options dialogue box. Use the Output Translation utility and then Verify the network has learned. You should find that *mave* is pronounced with a long /A/ (as in save) rather than a short /a/ (as in have).

9 *Language acquisition*

This chapter examines three aspects of language learning by children—learning the past tense, the sudden growth in vocabulary which occurs towards the end of the second year, and the acquisition of syntactic rules. First we will look at a three layer net, trained to produce the past tense from a verb stem by backpropagation. Under certain training conditions its pattern of production of correct and erroneous past tenses is similar to that of a number of children whose production over the first five years of life has been studied in detail. Then we will look at a model that learns to associate a name with the visual image of an object. It produces a sudden increase in production similar to the vocabulary spurt observed in many children around 21 months. Also, like children at this stage, it demonstrates over- and under-extension errors, and a production–comprehension asymmetry. In the final example we will look at a recurrent network which is given sentences (i.e. strings of words rather than individual words) as input. It is given no explicit information about syntactic rules, but the hidden units come to represent words in a way which corresponds to their syntactic class. Nouns are represented differently from verbs, verbs which take a direct object differently from those which do not, and so on.

In this chapter we will continue to explore the modelling of language skills but the emphasis will shift from adult performance to the way that children acquire language. A crucial aspect of connectionist modelling, which distinguishes it from much of traditional cognitive modelling, is that it models learning. A connectionist model is not just a model of a skill, but a model of how the skill is acquired. To evaluate their success as models of learning they can be tested against developmental data. (The potential of the connectionist approach to developmental psychology will be discussed further in chapter 10 where we will look at connectionist models of the acquisition of cognitive and perceptual/motor skills.)

As in chapter 8 we will see that the connectionist approach to language acquisition offers a direct challenge to much received wisdom in cognitive psychology. Many traditional models assume that language learning involves the acquisition of *rules*. For example, overregularisation errors occurring in children's early attempts to produce the past tense (saying 'eated' instead of 'ate') are seen (not surprisingly) as evidence for the possession of the rule 'to form a past tense add -ed to the verb stem'. The fact that children can make subject and verb agree in a sentence they have never produced or heard before is assumed to reflect the possession of a general rule about the relation of subject and verb which can be applied in any sentence. And so on.

Connectionist models do not have explicit declarative rules like 'to form a past tense add -ed to the verb stem'. Neither is there a place for a specific memory to store the list of exceptions which would be required to override application of this rule to exception verbs. Knowledge about all verbs, regular and irregular, is stored in the same general matrix of information. So a challenge for connectionism is to show how a pattern of behaviour which appears to require a database of rules and exceptions can be produced without one.

Developmentalists try to characterise the nature of the start state that allows the acquisition of skilled behaviour. Connectionist modelling allows a theory about the mechanisms present in the start state to be implemented. The first and third examples in this chapter, the acquisition of inflectional morphology[1] and syntactic rules respectively, show that a relatively unstructured start state can support the learning of a complex skill. However, in both cases we will see that the nature of the training environment to which the unstructured start state is exposed is crucial. Behaviour which mimics that of children will only emerge under certain conditions.

A common view in developmental psychology (which will be explored further in chapter 10) is that a sudden change in performance reflects the acquisition of a new cognitive mechanism. In the second example, the modelling of the vocabulary spurt in young children, we will see how a system with a constant architecture and learning rule can, nevertheless, produce a sudden change in behaviour. Connectionist modelling shows that discontinuous performance does not necessarily imply a discontinuity in the underlying mechanisms.

Learning the English past tense

Young children add the past tense suffix 'ed' to form the past tense of irregular verbs, producing errors like *goed*. Since this would have been appropriate were the verb regular, such errors are known as overregularisations. These have been cited as evidence that in learning a language, children are acquiring a system of rules. Overregularisation errors are assumed to result from the inappropriate application of a rule. They cannot be explained in terms of imitation. The child is not exposed to overregularisation errors in the adult language. The errors are the child's own

---

[1]A suffix which modifies the information carried by a stem, such as -s to indicate plural or -ed to indicate past tense is known in psycholinguistics as an *inflection*. So learning how to apply an appropriate suffix to form the past tense is called 'acquisition of inflectional morphology'.

creation. Children would be expected to make errors as they acquire a skill. But over-regularisation errors are surprising because they often occur *after* children have succeeded in producing the correct past tense of the verb. For example, children may correctly produce the past tense form *went* early in their third year and then produce *goed* at the beginning of their fourth. Developmentalists have sought an explanation for this U-shaped profile of learning.

A symbolic account of past tense learning

A natural interpretation of this pattern of performance is to suggest that early in development, children learn past tenses by rote, storing in memory the forms that they hear in the adult language. At a later stage, they recognise the regularities in the inflectional system of English and reorganise their representation of the past tense to include a new device that does the work of adding a suffix. Subsequently they will not need to memorise new forms. During this stage, some of the originally learnt irregular forms may suffer inappropriate generalisation from the addition of the regular suffix. Finally, they sort out which forms cannot be generated with the new rule-based device and these are stored as a list of exceptions.

This approach identifies errors as a consequence of the transition from pure rote learning to partly symbolic rule-governed behaviour. Recovery from error occurs when the representations of the irregular forms are sufficiently strong to resist interference from the rule-governed process. Representational strength is achieved by continued exposure to the language, so infrequent irregular forms will be more susceptible to overregularisation than frequent forms. Frequent forms will also recover more quickly from error. The symbolic account identifies the recovery from overregularisation errors with the consolidation of an associative memory for the representation of irregulars. The associative process operates in parallel and in competition with the rule-governed process. So the mature state of the adult inflectional system can be characterised as a dual-route device (see figure 9.1).

This account of the representation and development of inflections in English assumes that two qualitatively different types of mechanism are needed to capture the profile of development in children—a rote memory system to deal with the irregular forms and a symbolic rule system to deal with the rest. The behavioural dissociation between regular and irregular forms—children make mistakes on irregular forms but not on regular forms—makes the idea of two separate mechanisms appealing. In some language disorders children preserve performance on irregular verbs but not on regulars, while in other disorders the opposite pattern is observed (see Pinker 1994). This double dissociation between performance on regular and irregular forms in disordered populations adds to the strength of the claim that separate mechanisms are responsible for different types of

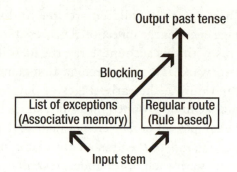

Figure 9.1 The dual-route model for the English past tense (based on Pinker and Prince 1988). The model involves a symbolic regular route that is insensitive to the phonological form of the stem and a route for exceptions that is capable of blocking the output from the regular route. Failure to block the regular route produces the correct output for regular verbs but results in overgeneralisation errors for irregular verbs. Children must strengthen their representation of irregular past tense forms to promote correct blocking of the regular route.

errors.[2] The dual-route approach to inflectional morphology can account for several aspects of the observed data. It offers an explanation of the U-shaped profile of development. It also offers an account of why some irregular forms are over-regularised and others are not: Irregular forms differ in representational strength and therefore exhibit variability in the reliability of their retrieval from memory. So, for example, it can explain why overregularisation of high frequency verbs is uncommon.

The dual-route approach is typical of the symbolic approach to cognition in general. On this view, cognitive and linguistic processing consists of the manipulation of symbolic structures by rules (themselves symbolically defined). Exceptions require special treatment, usually involving some extra machinery like the associative memory needed for irregular verbs. The goal of the symbolic cognitivist is to find the most parsimonious characterisation of these rules and their exceptions compatible with the facts of human behaviour and ultimately with what we know about the brain. However, there is a missing component to the symbolic account of the acquisition of the English past tense. It does not tell us how children *learn* the rule that the past tense of English is formed by adding 'ed' to the stem of the verb. It could be argued that children do *not* learn this rule. Knowledge that an inflectional process is required to form the past tense of a verb may be part of an innate language capacity. The emergence of the past tense suffix in language development may reflect the onset of a process of maturation, triggered by some biological or environmental

[2]When one group of patients performs well on task A and poorly on task B and a second group shows the opposite pattern, a double dissociation is said to exist. This has traditionally been interpreted as evidence that the two tasks are controlled by functionally independent processes. The interpretation of double dissociation within connectionist networks is discussed in detail in chapter 11.

event. Once this event has occurred, children are free to discover the manner in which their native language encodes the inflectional process for past tense.

There are two problems with this account. First, the identification of the rule in English is not as straightforward as it might seem at first glance. Many of the verbs that are learnt by children during the early stages of development are irregular. Furthermore, the irregulars can be grouped into sub-classes that show patterns of family resemblance. For example, all of the verbs in English that do not change from the stem to the past tense (e.g. *hit→hit*) end in an alveolar consonant (a 't' or a 'd'), and some verbs that rhyme with each other undergo similar changes to the vowel (e.g. *ring→rang, sing→sang*). Children learning the past tense might pick up on one of these sub-regularities and mistakenly construe it as the rule for English. In fact, children produce past tense errors that suggest a sensitivity to these subtle characteristics of past tense formation, so-called *irregularisations,* such as *pick→puck.* However, these tend to occur late in development. How do children avoid or reject these spurious hypotheses in favour of the correct one?

The second problem comes from considering patterns of inflection in different languages. The English past tense is unusual in possessing a large class of regular verbs. There are thousands of regular verbs but only around 180 irregular. In other languages the proportion is quite different. For example, the regular form of the Arabic plural (the so-called *sound plural*) constitutes less than 20% of the plurals in the language. In other languages, there is more than one regular process of past tense formation. For example, Norwegian has two ways of forming the past tense in regular verbs (add a consonant suffix 'te' or add a vowel suffix 'ede'[3]) in addition to about 100 irregular verbs. In Norwegian, it would appear that children need to adopt a three-route approach rather than a dual-route approach—one route for the irregulars and one for each regular form of the verb. If it is assumed that the child does not know at the outset of language acquisition how many routes will be needed, then some explanation of how children partition their inflectional system will be needed. The combined possibilities of cross-linguistic variation and the existence of sub-regularities in the irregular verbs makes the partitioning problem particularly difficult for the child. It might be very difficult to decide for any particular language whether the sub-regularity associated with irregular verbs is a property of a rule or an exceptional form.

We will outline an alternative approach that uses a connectionist network. The system does not make any initial distinctions between regular and irregular forms but gradually learns to identify patterns of regularity based on the forms it encounters. The model does not require any rules to be built into or mature in the system.

---

[3]These suffixes are not allophonic variants of one another, nor are they phonologically predictable—children cannot 'hear' which suffix should be applied on the basis of some phonological characteristic of the verb stem. They have to know to which regular class a verb belongs.

Regular behaviour emerges from the demands that the learning environment imposes on the system. This offers a more parsimonious account of inflectional learning than the symbolic account in that it minimises the structural complexity of the start state and places the burden of learning on a general learning device that can exploit the structure of the environment.

A connectionist account of past tense learning

Rumelhart and McClelland (1986b) were the first to apply a connectionist model to the problem of learning inflectional morphology (and indeed the first to attempt to apply connectionist modelling to developmental issues). They assumed, as did the symbolic approach, that children attempt to construct a representation of the relationship between verb stems and their past tense forms, and that overregularisation errors emerge from the inappropriate representation of this relationship. The Rumelhart and McClelland model was successful at mimicking a number of the facts associated with children's learning of the English past tense, including U-shaped learning. However, the model was flawed in a number of important respects which seemed to undermine the authors' claim to have offered an alternative to the smybolic account of the acquisition of the English past tense (see Pinker and Prince 1988). More recently, a number of researchers have responded to the criticisms of the Rumelhart and McClelland model and demonstrated that although some of the assumptions of their model were incorrect, these do not undermine the general applicability of connectionist models to an understanding of the acquisition of inflectional morphology.

Plunkett and Marchman (1993; 1996) used a feedforward network with one layer of hidden units to map a phonological representation of the stem of the verb to a phonological representation of its past tense (see figure 9.2). The network consists of a layer of 20 input units fully connected to a layer of 30 hidden units which are fully connected to a layer of 20 output units. The pattern of activity at input is a phonological representation of the stem of a verb. This pattern uniquely identifies each verb stem presented to the model. Activity propagates along the connections through the hidden layer to produce a pattern of activity over the output units. The output pattern is interpreted as a phonological representation of the past tense of the input verb.

Initially the model is required to learn the past tense of 10 regular and 10 irregular verb stems. This proportion reflects current estimates of the balance between regular and irregular verbs in children's early vocabularies. At the start of training the weights of the connections in the network are randomised. When a verb stem is first presented to the network, an erroneous pattern of activity is produced at the output. This output pattern is compared to a teacher signal which specifies the correct past

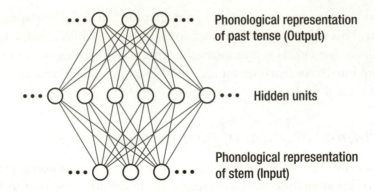

Phonological representation
of past tense (Output)

Hidden units

Phonological representation
of stem (Input)

Figure 9.2 The Plunkett and Marchman (1993) model of the acquisition of the English past tense. The input is a distributed representation of the stem of the verb and the output a distributed representation of the appropriate past tense.

tense form for the current verb stem. The discrepancy between the actual output from the network and the teacher signal is used as the error signal for the backpropagation learning algorithm.[4]

The task of the learning algorithm is to find a configuration of connection weights that suits all the verbs presented to the system. In other words, the learning algorithm must discover a set of connections that will activate the units for the 'ed' suffix when a regular verb is presented to the network but switch them off when an irregular verb is presented. This may not be a straightforward task since regular verbs and irregular verbs can sound very similar (e.g. *hit→hit* but *pit→pitted*). Multi-layered networks that use the backpropagation learning algorithm are able to form internal representations of the input patterns at the hidden unit layer, so patterns that look similar at input may have distinct internal representations (see chapter 5). These can produce the required differences at output. However, considerable training may be required before the network learns the appropriate internal representations. The competition between regular and irregular verbs (and between different types of irregular verbs) over the same matrix of connections in the network will lead to temporary patterns of interference in which some irregular verbs will be treated as if they were regular or vice versa.

Plunkett and Marchman trained their network on a sample of 500 verb stems. After the initial period with 10 regular and 10 irregular the size of the verb vocabulary was gradually increased, to mimic the gradual uptake of verbs by

---

[4]It is sometimes thought that the use of a teacher signal falls foul of the 'no negative evidence' assumption. That is, it is assumed that young children are not usually told that what they have said is grammatically incorrect. In fact, the model is exposed to positive evidence alone—the teacher signal itself. The child is assumed to generate an error signal from a comparison of the past tense it has just heard with its own current hypothesis about the verb's past tense, just like the model.

children. The sample as a whole contained about 90% regular verbs, similar to the relative frequency of regular verbs in English. Verbs introduced early in training had a higher frequency than verbs introduced later in training and so were presented more frequently throughout training. The model succeeded in learning the verbs in the training set. However, it made a number of errors *en route* to mature performance. The errors are produced by interference between the different patterns of regular and irregular mappings that the network is required to learn. The errors disappear as the learning algorithm discovers a set of connections which is compatible with all the verb patterns presented to the network. The network learns to satisfy the constraints imposed upon it by its training environment. The general character of the network's performance can be summarised as follows:

(1) Early acquisition is characterised by a period of error-free performance.
(2) The overall rate of overregularisation errors is low—typically between 5% and 10%.
(3) Overregularisation errors are not restricted to a particular stage of development. Once errors begin to appear, they recur throughout the training period.
(4) Common irregular verbs do not experience overregularisation. Errors like 'goed' are particularly rare.
(5) Errors are phonologically conditioned. For example, irregular 'no change' verbs which end in a alveolar consonant (/t/ or /d/) are robust to overregularisation. Thus, errors like 'hitted' are rare.
(6) A very small number of irregularisation errors are observed. For example, the network produces 'bat' for the past tense of 'bite'.

This profile of development is similar to that reported in a study by Marcus *et al.* (1992) of the overregularisation errors in the spontaneous speech of 83 English children. Figure 9.3 is a comparison of the production of overregularisations of irregular verbs in the Plunkett and Marchman simulation and by Adam, one of the children analysed by Marcus *et al.*. The general pattern of development in child and network is very similar—errors occur after an initial period of error free performance; once errors have occurred they continue to occur at random; the error rate is never more than 5%.

The Plunkett and Marchman model demonstrates how patterns of regularity and irregularity might be represented in a cognitive system without appealing to an innate pre-wiring of the system. The model challenges the orthodoxy that learning a language consists of learning a system of symbolic rules. Of prime importance to developmentalists is the demonstration that a homogenous computational system can learn to perform a complex task that was thought to require a heterogeneous architecture. The model demonstrates that you do not need as much pre-wired, innate structure to learn the past tense as the dual-route approach supposes.

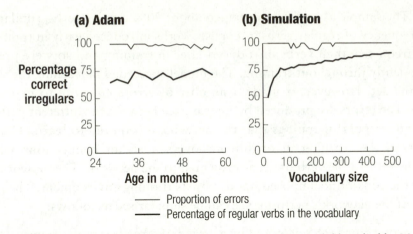

Figure 9.3 A comparison of the overregularisation errors of Adam, a child studied by Marcus *et al.* (1992), and those produced by the Plunkett and Marchman (1993) simulation. The thin lines shows the proportion of errors as a function of age (Adam) or vocabulary size (simulation). The thick lines indicate the percentage of regular verbs in the child's/network's vocabulary at various points in learning.

The fact that a multi-layered network can perform the task does not prove that children use the same type of mechanism—only that they might. Evaluation of the plausibility of the model rests on its behavioural predictions. For example, one might ask if the model predicts whether particular types of error should predominate over others at different stages of learning or how the network copes in languages with several regular forms of the verb (e.g. the Norwegian past tense) or in languages where an inflectional system is dominated by irregular forms (e.g. the Arabic plural). (The way that connectionist models deal with such problems is explored in chapter 12.) Connectionist models are slaves to their training environments. Their performance reflects the distribution of examples they encounter. For example, current connectionist models predict that the onset of overregularisation errors, heralding the discovery of the regularities underlying the inflectional system, is closely yoked to the achievement of a *critical mass* of regular verbs in the child's vocabulary. A critical mass effect in children acquiring the English past tense has been demonstrated by Plunkett and Marchman (1996).

Connectionist modelling of past tense acquisition shows that inferring dissociations in mechanism from dissociations in behaviour (in this case, performance on regular versus irregular verbs) is hazardous. It is not necessary to invoke a separate symbolic system to explain the processing of regular verbs. Instead, it is possible that both regular and irregular verbs are processed in the same fashion, and perhaps even in the same mechanism. This result reinforces the view that the start state for language learning (at least for inflectional morphology) may not require as much initial structure as has been supposed. Instead, the additional constraints necessary for learning inflectional systems may be found in the learning environment itself—in this case, English verbs and their past tense inflections. One of the strengths of connectionist networks is their ability to extract and represent the patterns of regularity inherent in a structured training environment. In this respect, they act like statistical inference machines. But they can go beyond mere surface regularities to extract and represent the abstract structure of the input. Their use in modelling development provides the researcher with a tool for examining the trade-off between initial architectural and computational constraints on the one hand and environmental information on the other.

Early lexical development

A dramatic increase in vocabulary is observed in many children towards the end of their second year—the so-called vocabulary spurt (see figure 9.4). The sudden acceleration in vocabulary size appears to signal the beginning of a new stage of development in children's language acquisition. Since most of the new words acquired by children at this point are names for objects, the vocabulary spurt has often been interpreted as evidence for the development of a naming insight, though other explanations relating to children's developing phonological skills or semantic representations have also been proposed. All these explanations assume that the discontinuity is associated with the emergence of a new cognitive mechanism.

Children produce over- and under-extension errors at this stage. The ability to say the word 'dog' does not necessarily show that the child has a complete understanding of what it means. The word may be used when referring to a cat—an overextension error. Or it may be used only when referring to the family dog—an underextension error. Such errors are assumed to arise because children base their use of words on the *prototype* of the concept associated with the word. The overextension error of

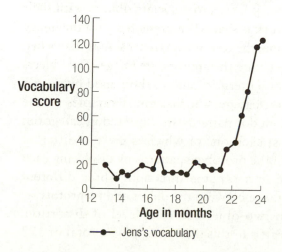

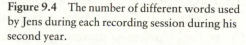

Figure 9.4 The number of different words used by Jens during each recording session during his second year.

using the word 'dog' to refer to a cat could arise because cats share certain features with the prototypical dog. The underextension error of a child who fails to use the word 'dog' the first time it encounters a dachshund could arise from the fact that it lacks some of the features of the prototypical dog.

Children also appear to understand words that they do not themselves produce. This asymmetry has prompted some researchers to postulate the existence of separate mechanisms for comprehension and production of words. Others maintain that comprehension and production exploit the same underlying knowledge base and that the asymmetry can be explained by the difference of the tasks. For example, production involves recall whereas comprehension involves recognition. It is often difficult to decide between non-computational theories. Does a production–comprehension asymmetry mean that there must be separate processes for each, maturing at different times, or not? A connectionist model can help to answer such a question.

A connectionist model of early lexical development

We will look at a connectionist model of lexical development, that is, a model which learns to name objects, which produces a vocabulary spurt, over- and under-extension errors, prototype effects and a comprehension–production asymmetry. (The model is described in detail in Plunkett *et al.* 1992.) The success of this simulation shows that these effects can all be accommodated within a system that maintains the same basic architecture and learning process throughout training. The discontinuities in the performance of the model result from a process of continuous and progressive change in the network, not from the appearance of new mechanisms. The simulation also demonstrates how the connectionist approach can simplify cognitive modelling by showing that an apparently diverse set of behavioural phenomena emerge from the same structure.

Like the child learning to talk, the network learns to associate objects with their names. The test of production for the network is that when presented with the image of an object, it can generate the correct name; the test of comprehension is that when presented with a name, the network can generate the appropriate image. The objects categorised by the network are random dot patterns similar to those used by Posner and Keele (1968) in their experiments on category formation. Examples of the objects are shown in figure 9.5. The random dot patterns are clustered in categories based on prototype random dot patterns, each one of which is given a different name. Each object is generated from one of the prototype patterns by displacing each of the nine dots by a specified distance in a random direction. Three different distortion levels, corresponding to the distance between the object and its prototype, are generated from each prototype with two objects at each level of distortion. Thirty-two clusters of patterns are generated in this manner, giving a total of 192

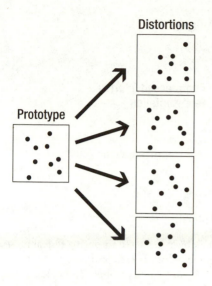

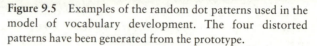

Figure 9.5 Examples of the random dot patterns used in the model of vocabulary development. The four distorted patterns have been generated from the prototype.

different objects. Thus the network operates in a world in which there are 32 prototypical objects which it learns about through experiencing six different, distorted, examples of each, each distortion carrying the name of the prototype on which it was based. No prototype pattern has more than two dots in positions common with any other prototype pattern. A degree of overlap between distortions of different prototypes is permitted.

Each of the 32 clusters of related patterns is associated with a discrete label which represents the name of the prototypical object. Labels are 32 bit patterns in which only a single bit is active. Thus all label patterns are orthogonal to each other. (This simulates the fact that the letter string d-o-g has no more in common with the string c-a-t than it does with the string b-a-l-l even if the appearance of cats has more in common with that of dogs than that of balls.) There is no internal categorial structure to the set of labels and there is an arbitrary relationship between a label and its associated cluster of images. The label associated with each image provides the network with information necessary to perform a conceptual classification of the objects it encounters. That is, it enables the network to know that the distortions are related. Without a label, images would be classified purely on the basis of their perceptual similarity.

The world of the network is obviously much simpler than that of the child. But it simulates some of the problems facing the child who is trying to learn to use words such as 'dog', 'cat' or 'ball' to name the objects around it. First, the relationship between name and object is arbitrary. (There is nothing inherently dog-like about the word 'dog'; the word 'cat' would have done just as well to describe the image of a dog.) Second, although all the objects which have the name 'dog' have some

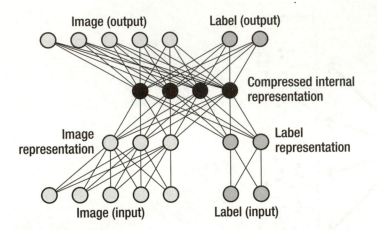

Figure 9.6 A simplified version of the network architecture. The object is filtered through a retinal pre-processor which constructs a distributed representation of the random dot patterns prior to presentation to the image units in the network. There are 32 label units and 171 image units at input and output, 30 and 32 hidden units for image representation and label representation respectively, and 50 hidden units for the joint representation.

similarities, each exemplar from the category which the network meets is different. Third, some members of other sets of objects which have a different name (e.g. 'cat' or 'toy') may have some similarities with members of the group which have the name 'dog'.

The network architecture is shown in figure 9.6. The task for the network is to reproduce on the output units the object representation (the image of the object) and the label representation (the name of the object) that are presented to the network on the input units. (This type of learning, autoassociative, was discussed in chapter 4, although in that chapter a recurrent network was used. Although the architecture is different the networks must solve the same problem. They must find an internal representation which will allow the input pattern to be reproduced at output.) Separate input channels are reserved for the random dot patterns (the images) and the label patterns (the names). Each modality projects to a separate bank of hidden units before converging on a common set of hidden units. The first banks of hidden units permit the network to organise its own representation of the input patterns. The penultimate layer of hidden units forms a compressed, composite representation of the image and label patterns. Since there are fewer hidden units in this layer than in the input layer, the network has to discover an efficient code to represent both the image and label across the same set of units.

The network is trained in a three-phase cycle. First, an object is presented at the image input units and activity is propagated through the network to the output units. The activity on the image output units is compared to the initial object representation. Any discrepancy is recorded as an error signal. A backpropagation learning algorithm then adjusts the weights on the image side of the network only. A similar learning trial is conducted for the label associated with the object, except that weight adjustment now occurs only on the 'label' side of the network. Finally, both image and label are presented simultaneously and error signals are used to adjust weights on both sides of the network. A useful mnemonic for interpreting the three-phase training cycle is as an attention-switching process. First, the network attends to the image, then to the label, and finally associations between the two are constructed. Likewise, we can think of the child as identifying the object in the world, recognising a word in speech and then attempting to associate the two. This three-phase learning sequence is applied to all object–label pairs in the training set. During training only distorted images and their associated labels are used. The network is never trained on a prototype object. Neither is the network ever trained to produce an output image given an input label alone or an output label given an input image alone.

The performance of the network in producing labels and image representations at output is evaluated during training. Both comprehension and production are measured. 'Production' is the capacity of the network to output the appropriate label in response to the presentation of an image pattern at input—that is, its ability to name an object. 'Comprehension' is the ability of the network to produce the appropriate image representations at output in response to the presentation of a label at input—that is, its ability to recognise what object a word refers to.

Two other types of measure are used to evaluate the network's performance throughout the training period. First, the network's comprehension and production of patterns it has experienced in training is compared with its performance on the prototype patterns which were not presented during training. Performance on prototypes can be interpreted as a measure of the network's ability to generalise from its prior experience. Correct production corresponds to the activation of the appropriate name at output when the image of a prototype object is presented at input. Correct comprehension corresponds to the generation of the image of the prototype on the output units when the label is applied to the input units. Second, overextension (calling all animals 'dog') and underextension (calling only the family dog 'dog') can be examined by seeing whether the network uses labels inappropriately. The range of objects that elicit a given label, and the range of objects that are elicited by a given label, are evaluated after each training cycle. These measures indicate when a label is over- or under-extended in production, and when a label is over- or under-extended in comprehension.

Figure 9.7 provides a summary of the comprehension and production scores for the distortions and prototype during the first 100 epochs of training. The first aspect of the network's performance to note is that production (output of the appropriate name in response to the input of an image) exhibits a sudden increase after about 35 epochs of training. The network shows a vocabulary spurt. It occurs both for the objects that the network has been trained on (the distortions) and for the prototypes

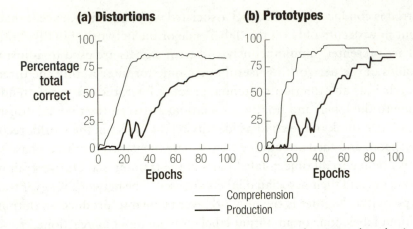

Figure 9.7 Performance on distorted and prototype images in comprehension and production.

which it has never seen before. Successful performance on the prototype indicates that the network is not just memorizing the training set. It is able to generalise from its previous experience to generate a plausible name for an object it has never seen before. Secondly, the network is better at comprehension (generating the correct image at output in response to a name at input) than it is at production—there is a comprehension–production asymmetry. The asymmetry holds for the objects on which it was trained and for novel objects (the prototypes). Over- and under-extension errors occur in both production and comprehension. In production, underextension errors are most likely to occur before the vocabulary spurt and overextension errors after the spurt. Children show the same pattern with under-extension errors tending to occur earlier than overextension errors. In compre-hension, the model produces overextension errors before the vocabulary spurt as well as after. Finally, the network exhibits a prototype effect. As figure 9.7 shows, the performance in both comprehension and production is in general better for the prototype patterns than the trained patterns. The network has abstracted a prototype (or central tendency) from the distorted training patterns in the same way that Posner and Keele showed adults do.

Evaluation of the model

When this model was first run it did more than just mimic facts about early lexical development. It predicted new results. For example, the model suggested that children should show a comprehension spurt as well as a production spurt.[5] This was

[5]In figure 9.7 the comprehension spurt is difficult to see because it starts after about five training trials. The modeller can make this period any length by adjusting the learning rate. But whatever the learning rate the production spurt will always appear later than the comprehension spurt.

a genuine prediction—it was an emergent property of the network, not one that was 'designed in' before the model was built. At that time behavioural data had only identified a production spurt. The comprehension spurt was subsequently confirmed as typical of children's early lexical development (Goldfield and Reznick 1992; Fenson *et al.* 1994). The model's prediction that overextension errors in comprehension should occur before the vocabulary spurt has yet to be tested with children.

The model also suggests novel theoretical interpretations of familiar facts. The vocabulary spurt is not due to the triggering or maturation of a new mechanism. The same network architecture and the same learning algorithm is used throughout training. All that changes is the strength of the connections in the network. Initially, the connections in the network are randomised so the system knows nothing about the relationship between objects and labels. Early learning consists in a tentative exploration of the error landscape in an attempt to improve performance on as many input patterns as possible. During the early stages of training, the network is still attempting to make sense of the problem domain to which it is exposed. Solutions for some inputs will be discovered before others. However, as the number of isolated solutions increases, the structure of the problem domain emerges. The network discovers the natural clustering of the objects and the fact that the objects within a cluster tend to possess the same label. The achievement of a critical mass of label–image associations makes the business of learning new associations relatively easy. Hence, a vocabulary spurt is obtained. This explanation illustrates the role of computational models in the understanding of cognitive development. Gopnik and Meltzoff (1987) proposed that the vocabulary spurt emerges from children's understanding that objects belong in categories and that the discovery of specific semantic domains (such as 'animals') helps the child discover which names are associated with which objects. Such a proposal may seem eminently reasonable but without a computational model there is no way of knowing whether it would predict a vocabulary spurt, a steady growth in vocabulary size, or anything else. The fact that the network's successful categorisation of the objects can be shown to provide the foundations for the vocabulary spurt is the quantitative evidence that Gopnik and Meltzoff's proposal needs.

The comprehension–production asymmetry is a direct outcome of the different representational formats used for the images and the labels—distributed for the images, localist for the labels. This suggests that it may be unnecessary to invoke separate processes or mechanisms to account for the comprehension–production asymmetry. The explanation might lie in the differences between the modes of representation in the visual system and the auditory/linguistic system. The model also provides an account of how the timing of over- and under-extension errors are related to the vocabulary spurt. In the model, the extension of a given label is closely linked to the internal representation of the objects and the accuracy with which other labels are processed. Underextensions (only referring to a sub-set of distortions in a group by the label for the group) go with a period in the training of the network when labels are imperfectly projected onto limited regions of the image space. That is, when only a few labels are used appropriately and then only applied to a subset of possible images. So these occur before the vocabulary spurt. Overextension errors (using a single label for more than one group) are associated with the period of training when the image space has already been roughly charted and fine-tuning of the partitioning of the space is taking place. So these occur after the vocabulary spurt. High-distortion images are most prone to overextension in the network. These are also the type of objects on which children are most likely to make mistakes.

The behavioural characteristics of the model are a direct outcome of the inter-action of the label and the image representations that are used as inputs to the network. The vocabulary spurt is a consequence of the learning process that sets up the link between the label and image inputs, and the asymmetries in production and comprehension can be traced back to the types of representation used for the two types of input. The essence of the interactive nature of the learning process is under-scored by the finding that the network learns less quickly when only required to perform the production task. Learning to comprehend image labels at the same time as learning to label images enables the model to learn the labels faster.

This simulation is, obviously, a simplification of the task that the child has to master in acquiring a lexicon. Words are not always presented with their referents and even when they are it is not always obvious (for a child who does not know the meaning of the word) what the word refers to. Nevertheless, within the constraints imposed upon the model, one message from the simulation is clear: New behaviours do not necessarily require new mechanisms. Systems integrating information across modalities can reveal surprising emergent properties that would not have been predicted on the basis of exposure to one modality alone. We will come to this point again in the modelling of the development of object permanence in chapter 10.

The acquisition of syntax

Consider the sentences:

'The *boy* who lived in the little house at the end of the lane bought some flowers for *his* mother.'

'The *boys* who lived in the little house at the end of the lane bought some flowers for *their* mother.'

In each sentence, the form (singular or plural) of the first italicised word determines the form of the next italicised word. Behaviourist accounts of language attempt to explain grammatical agreement in terms of chains of stimulus–response associations. However, the further apart that words are in a sentence, the weaker should be the learnt associations between them. Chomksy demonstrated that sentences can be indefinitely long yet still require grammatical agreement between words at the beginning and end of the sentence—so-called *long distance dependencies*. An alternative to the behaviourist approach is to see language production in terms of the use of rules. An appropriate rule would ensure agreement between the noun and a following pronoun irrespective of the distance between them.

But how does the child learn these rules? The rules of language vary from one culture to another in terms of the words and concepts expressed, and in the syntactic rules which convey information by word order. How does the young English language learner come to recognise the difference in the message conveyed by the two strings 'The boy bit the dog' and 'The dog bit the boy' when they do not know what a subject, verb or object is? Another difficulty facing the child is that adults often fail to speak in well-formed grammatical sentences. Their linguistic performance is characterised by false starts, slips of the tongue and half-completed sentences, all of which make the grammatical structure of the sentence more difficult for the child to decipher. Acquiring a grammar, given these impoverished learning conditions, would seem an almost impossible task.

Chomsky's solution was to propose that the child comes equipped with innate knowledge that directs her to look for the special type of rules that underly the language that she hears. Of course, this innate knowledge cannot be specific to any particular language. A Japanese child brought up by English speaking parents will learn English just as quickly as an English child. Chomsky proposed that children come equipped with a *Universal Grammar*—a grammar which underlies all the languages of the world. Knowledge of Universal Grammar enables the child to avoid the traps posed by the impoverished stimulus and assists the child in discovering the rules that are particular to her native tongue. More specifically, Universal Grammar predisposes the child to search for hierarchical structures in her language of the type depicted in figure 9.8. These 'tree' diagrams are called *phrase structures*. They capture the structural relationships between the words in sentences that are necessary to interpret the meaning of the sentence. They are constructed out of rules such as:

S (sentence) → NP (noun phrase) + VP (verb phrase)

NP → Art (article) + N (noun)

VP → V (verb) + NP

N → boy, ball, etc.

V → kicked, etc.

Art → the, etc.

By applying such rules in the correct order, it is possible to construct a very large number of phrase structure descriptions of sentences. Furthermore, it is quite easy to elaborate on these rules to show how they can account for a wide range of sentence types as well as long distance dependencies. In essence, it is possible to insert new

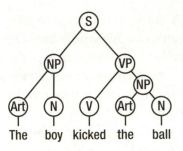

Figure 9.8 A simple phrase structure for the sentence 'The boy kicked the ball.'

elements into the sentence hierarchy while maintaining information that binds together the early and late elements in the sentence.

The computational machinery that is needed to drive this learning process would seem to rely on built-in parts. In fact, it is often assumed that some kind of pre-wired symbol manipulating system, rather like a traditional computer program, is exploited by the child during the process of language learning. The symbol manipulating system embodies the child's knowledge of Universal Grammar. Recently, however, the idea that the child might be able to extract grammatical knowledge from the language that she hears without prior knowledge of Universal Grammar has re-emerged. The perspective has been stimulated by connectionist modelling using *simple recurrent networks* (SRNs). These take *sequences* of items and extract the underlying regularities that are inherent in the sequences (see chapter 7). In this section, we will examine the capacity of a recurrent network to extract structural information from sequences of words that make up sentences of the sort traditionally described by a phrase structure tree. We will see that structural representations need not be defined in terms of hierarchies. We shall also examine the conditions under which recurrent networks are capable of extracting sequential structure from an ordered input and the manner in which such information is represented within the network.

Elman (1990; 1993) described a simple recurrent network that succeeded in assigning words to grammatical categories (such as noun and verb) on the basis of distributional evidence extracted from strings of words which followed a set of grammatical rules. In later work he demonstrated that recurrent networks are able to learn long-distance grammatical dependencies. The networks used by Elman involve the use of recurrent connections from the hidden units back to themselves via a set of *context* units. Hidden units in feedforward networks without recurrent connections develop internal representations of inputs which are determined by the current input alone. In the recurrent networks the hidden units take on the additional task of representing sequential structure, and do so in surprisingly subtle ways. The hidden unit representations which encode temporal information are also able to represent, in a distributed fashion, hierarchical organisation.

Figure 9.9 shows a recurrent network in which context units receive input from a

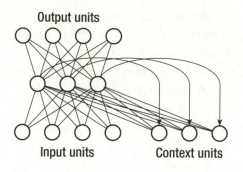

Output units

Input units   **Context units**   Figure 9.9   A simple recurrent network.

layer of hidden units. The activities of the context units are direct copies of the hidden unit activities. Connections from the hidden units to the context units are fixed while connections from the context units to the hidden units are adjustable, in the same manner as all the other connections in the network. Context units provide the network with a dynamic memory. Identical input signals may be treated differently depending on the current status of the context units, that is, depending on what the previous input processed by the network was.

The task involves presenting the network with sequences of words, one at a time, and training it to output a prediction of the next word. The order of the words in each sequence conforms to a simple grammar like that illustrated in figure 9.8. The training corpus consists of thousands of different sentences covering a range of structural types, including simple active sentences like 'boy kicks ball' and sentences with embedded clauses like 'boy who chases dogs kicks ball'. The words themselves are represented as orthogonal patterns of activity at the input. This means that only one or two input units are active in the representation of a given word. Furthermore, there is no semantic information indicating meaningful relationships between words. As far as the untrained network is concerned, the word 'boy' is as similar to 'cat' as it is to 'boys'.

When a word is presented to the network, activity is propagated through the connections in the usual fashion to produce a pattern of activity across the output units. If the network is accurate, the output activity should correspond to the representation for the next word in the sequence. At the beginning of training the error obtained at the output is used to drive the backpropagation learning algorithm to adapt the connections to improve the predictive power of the network. When the next word is presented to the network, the hidden units receive activation from the input units *and* the context units, which are themselves a copy of the hidden unit activities on the previous time step. The output prediction is contingent upon the current input word and the network's internal representation of the previous word. As the network sees more words, it builds up a deeper and deeper context for predicting the next word in the sequence.

In fact, Elman's network was not particularly successful at predicting the next word in the input sequence, even after considerable training. This result is not surprising given that there are often a wide variety of possible word candidates in a sentence string. Try predicting the next word in the sentence 'The boy in the black shirt ...'. In this sense, the problem confronting the network is indeterminate and so it is bound to fail. However, the type of predictions the network ends up making is illuminating. Rather than the precise word, the network predicts the right grammatical category of the word. The network partially activates a range of possible candidates at its output layer, all of which belong to the appropriate grammatical category for the current position in the sentence. In other words, the network is capable of inducing the grammatical structure of the input sentences from the input strings themselves without any prior knowledge of the type of grammar that was used to generate the training set or even that words fall into grammatical classes. It is important to note that the training sentences include verbs that vary in their argument structure (transitive and intransitive), nouns that can occur in the singular and plural and, importantly, embedded clauses. The inclusion of embedded clauses requires the network to remember whether the subject of the sentence is singular or plural in order to predict the correct form of the verb in the main clause occurring after an embedded clause. For example, it must remember that the subject was singular to choose the correct form of the verb *chase* in the sentence:

The boy who likes dogs chases the cat.

The network was able to predict the correct third person singular form of the verb even though the noun immediately preceding the verb was plural. Clearly, the network is not just remembering simple associations between consecutive words. Performance in predicting long distance dependencies deteriorates as the distance between a subject and its main verb increases. However, it is not just a question of the distance between the main verb and its subject. Centre-embedded sentences like 'The boy the cat the dog the rat saw chased likes' were more difficult for the network to process than right-branching sentences like 'The boy likes the cat that chased the dog that saw the rat'—as is true of people.

Why was the network so successful at learning the structural characteristics of the language? A useful technique for analysing the internal organisation of a trained network is to examine how the hidden unit activities change over time as a sentence is processed. The hidden unit representations constitute the internal state of the network. The possible configurations of hidden unit activities define the state space of the network. It is possible to construct state-space trajectories of the network's internal representations as it processes sentences. In reality these trajectories move in a multi-dimensional space, but they can be represented in two dimensions to give some idea of patterns of similarity or difference during the processing of different sentences. Figure 9.10(a) shows the state space trajectories for the network while it is processing the two sentences:

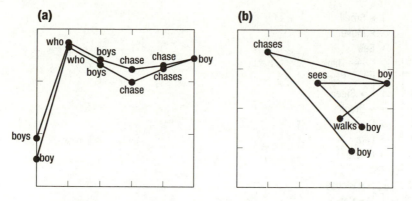

Figure 9.10   A representation of hidden unit activities while processing individual words from different sentences. (Based on Elman 1993.)

Boys who boys chase chase boy.

Boy who boys chase chases boy.

Although these two sentences contain identical embedded clauses, the network is able to maintain a memory trace of the subject's number while processing the embedded clause and predict the correct form of the verb when it exits the embedded structure. The memory trace is manifest in the slightly different trajectories for the network through the two sentences. Figure 9.10(b) shows state space trajectories for sentences starting with the word 'Boy' but continuing with verbs with different argument structures. The three sentences are:

Boy chases boy.

Boy sees boy.

Boy walks.

The first verb takes a compulsory direct object; the second one takes an optional direct object; the third cannot take a direct object. The regions of state space occupied by verbs depend on their argument structure. The representation of constituent syntactic structure is reflected by the shape of the network's trajectory through the state space. Grammatical boundaries are reflected in characteristic turns in the trajectory, and verb argument structure is reflected by the regions in state space to which trajectories are attracted.

How a network represents individual words can be investigated using a *cluster analysis*. When a word is presented to the network the pattern of activity produced across the hidden units corresponds to a point in the state space of hidden unit activity. By averaging the hidden unit activities produced by individual words in many different sentence contexts, it is possible to investigate how different words cluster together in the state space. Figure 9.11 shows the results of a cluster analysis of hidden unit activities in a network for all the words in the network's vocabulary. This reveals that the network's internal representations are highly structured.

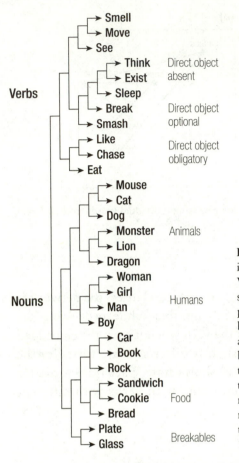

Figure 9.11 A cluster analysis of hidden unit activities for individual words averaged across many sentence contexts. Words which are on the same branch of the tree produce similar patterns of activity. For example, 'mouse' and 'cat' produce similar patterns of activity so they are on the same branch. Going up a branch we can see that these patterns are closer to that produced by 'dog' than to that produced by other nouns. Going up one more branch shows that all the animals produce patterns more similar to each other than to any other words. The animals produce patterns more similar to that produced by humans than to the other nouns, and nouns produce patterns which are more similar to each other than to those of verbs. (Based on Elman 1990.)

Individual words are clustered (i.e. produce similar patterns of hidden unit activity) in a manner that reflects both the unique identity of the word and the grammatical role of that word in the sentence. Verbs are clustered together, as are nouns. Within these clusters, verbs are clustered in a way which reflects whether they take a direct object, and nouns from separate semantic classes are clustered together. (These groupings reflect what the network discovered about the set of sentences Elman trained the network on. They are not necessarily true for the English language.) Elman was also able to show that hidden unit activities corresponding to different presentations of the same word will reflect whether the word plays the role of, say, subject or object in the current sentence. These analyses are very impressive. They demonstrate that a recurrent network is able to discover something which corresponds to a word's grammatical category simply by attempting to predict the next word in sequences in which the word appears. It does not need to be told ahead of time anything about nouns or verbs. This suggests that the apparently intractable problem of how the child can get grammar learning off the ground without knowing about grammatical categories in advance may not be quite so intractable as it seems.

The success of simple recurrent networks in correctly predicting long distance dependencies is determined by the way in which the system is trained. Elman (1993) found that exposing the network to the complete range of sentence structures in the corpus resulted in poor performance on the complex forms. For example, it failed to master verb agreement across clause boundaries. However, application of an incremental training technique resulted in success. If the network is exposed at the start of training only to simple syntactic forms and then gradually exposed to an increasing proportion of complex structures, final performance on complex forms improves dramatically. The simpler sequences provide the network with an opportunity to discover the basic building blocks of the sentence structure. Once the network has derived these regularities from the training corpus and encoded them in the weight matrix, more complex sentences, which otherwise are structurally opaque, become amenable to analysis.

However, it is by no means clear that children are exposed to simplified input or that such input is beneficial to the child. Therefore Elman (1993) investigated an alternative procedure that might benefit the network in its efforts at syntactic discovery. Instead of manipulating the training set, Elman manipulated the memory span of the network for previously processed words. Specifically, he flushed the activities of the context units after every third or fourth word by resetting their activities to zero. This removed any memory for words occurring more than three or four items earlier in the sentence. This prevents the detection of structure in long sentences. In early training this had the effect of limiting the network to discovering short distance dependencies such as the structure of basic sentences like *boy kicks ball*. Once the network discovers the dimensions of simple structural variation, it can exploit them to discover more complex dependencies. As training proceeded, Elman gradually increased the memory span of the context units until there was unlimited feedback. Eventually the network was able to master the training corpus to a level comparable to that achieved by controlling the length of the sentences presented to the network. In this manner, Elman was able to demonstrate an *advantage* of limited memory span in simple recurrent networks for the initial extraction of syntactic structure and suggested that 'starting small' may be crucial for children's acquisition of syntax.

The complementary nature of the solutions that Elman discovered to the problem of learning long-distance agreement between verbs and their subjects highlights the way that nature and nurture can trade off against one another in the search for solutions to complex problems. In one case, environmental factors assisted the network in solving the problem. In the other case, processing factors pointed the way to an answer. In both cases, though, the solution involved an initial simplification in the service of long term gain. In development, big does not necessarily mean better.

Elman's work represents an important first step in understanding how compositional lexical structure and hierarchical syntactic constituents might be represented in a connectionist network. This is not to suggest that the problem of learning syntactic structure has been solved. For example, these networks were all trained on well-formed grammatical sentences. It is not at all clear that children have access to such pristine input. Nor is it clear how well these networks would perform if they were exposed to false starts, slips of the tongue and half-completed sentences. However, this work does demonstrate that some of the initial pessimism about the ability of networks to deal with hierarchical structure in language or in cognition in general may be ill-founded.

Further reading

Inflectional morphology

Plunkett, K. and Juola, P. (1999). A connectionist model of English past tense and plural morphology. *Cognitive Science* 23(4), 463–90.
A detailed review of the debate between symbolic and connectionist approaches can be found in Plunkett (1995). Languages in which the default process is only applied to a relatively small number of forms would appear to be a particular problem for a connectionist network learning inflectional morphology. Such minority default mappings are found in the Arabic and German plural systems. This is discussed in chapter 12.

Vocabulary spurt

The model is described in detail in Plunkett *et al.* (1992). The timing of over- and under-extension errors in children is discussed in Barrett (1995).

Acquisition of syntax

A fuller description of Elman's work on the acquisition of syntactic relationships by simple recurrent nets can be found in Elman (1993).

Learning the English past tense with `tlearn`

In this exercise you will replicate some of the Plunkett and Marchman (1991) simulations and evaluate the level of performance and pattern of errors produced by a network trained on a task analogous to the acquisition of the English past tense.

Preparing the past tense simulation

The training environment

The first task is to define a training environment for the network. We will assume that the network's task is to learn to map a set of verb stems to their past tense forms. This corresponds to the assumption that children attempt to discover a systematic relationship between the sound patterns that characterize verb stems and their past tense forms.

Plunkett and Marchman trained their network on four types of verbs:

1. Regular verbs that add one of the three allomorphs[6] of the /-ed/ morpheme to the stem of the verb to form the past tense (e.g. /pat/ → /patted/).
2. No-change verbs where the past tense form is the same as the stem (e.g. /hit/ → /hit/). Note that all no-change verbs end in an alveolar consonant, a /t/ or a /d/.
3. Vowel change verbs where the vowel in the stem is changed while the past tense form retains the same consonants as the stem form (e.g. /come/ → /came/). Note that the vowel change is often conditioned by the vowel and final consonant in the stem (/sing/ → /sang/, /ring/ → /rang/). Vowel change stems can thus be considered to form a family resemblance cluster of sub-regularities in the language (Pinker and Prince 1988). A set of sub-regularities that was omitted from this model was the blend family (/sleep/ → /slept/, /weep/ → /wept/, /creep/ → /crept/) where both the vowel is suppleted and a suffix is added. (You can add some to the training set if you wish.)
4. Arbitrary verbs where there is no apparent relation between the stem and the past tense form (e.g. /go/ → /went/).

We will use a similar classification of verbs for our training set.

Input and output representations

Each phoneme will be represented as a distributed pattern of activity across a 6 bit vector. The first bit identifies whether it is a vowel or a consonant, the second whether it is voiced or unvoiced, the next two the manner of articulation (high, middle or low), and the last two the place of articulation (front, middle or back). The coding scheme is shown in table 9.1. You will find a file called **phonemes** in the **tlearn** folder containing this coding scheme. ASCII characters are used to represent each phoneme. The ASCII characters W, X, Y and Z are used to represent the absence of a suffix and the three allomorphs of the suffix [d], [t] and [ed] respectively. Non-phonological codes are used for these past tense endings. They are the 2-bit patterns 0 0, 0 1, 1 0 and 1 1 respectively.

---

[6]The suffix used for the past tense of regular verbs in English depends on the final phoneme in the stem of the verb. If the final phoneme is voiced (as in *arm*) then the [d] allomorph is used (*arm–[d]*). If the final phoneme is unvoiced (as in *wish*) then the [t] allomorph is used (*wish–[t]*). If the final phoneme is an alveolar stop (as in *pit*) then the epenthesised allomorphy is used (*pit–[ed]*).

Table 9.1 Phonological coding used in the Plunkett & Marchman (1991) simulation. Suffix activations are not represented here

Phoneme	Example	ASCII	Cons/Vow #1	Voicing #2	Manner #3	Manner #4	Place #5	Place #6
/b/		b	0	1	1	1	1	1
/p/		p	0	0	1	1	1	1
/d/		d	0	1	1	1	1	0
/t/		t	0	0	1	1	1	0
/g/		g	0	1	1	1	0	0
/k/		k	0	0	1	1	0	0
/v/		v	0	1	1	0	1	1
/f/		f	0	0	1	0	1	1
/m/		m	0	1	0	0	1	1
/n/		n	0	1	0	0	1	0
/h/		G	0	1	0	0	0	0
/d/		T	0	0	1	0	1	0
/q/		H	0	1	1	0	1	0
/z/		z	0	1	1	0	0	1
/s/		s	0	0	1	0	0	1
/w/		w	0	1	0	1	1	1
/l/		l	0	1	0	1	1	0
/r/		r	0	1	0	1	0	1
/y/		y	0	1	0	1	0	0
/h/		h	0	0	0	1	0	0
/i/	(eat)	E	1	1	1	1	1	1
/I/	(bit)	i	1	1	0	0	1	1
/o/	(boat)	O	1	1	1	0	1	1
/^/	(but)	^	1	1	0	1	1	1
/u/	(boot)	U	1	1	1	1	0	1
/U/	(book)	u	1	1	0	0	0	1
/e/	(bait)	A	1	1	1	1	1	0
/e/	(bet)	e	1	1	0	0	1	0
/ai/	(bite)	I	1	1	1	0	0	0
/æ/	(bat)	@	1	1	0	1	0	0
/au/	(cow)	#	1	1	1	1	0	0
/O/	(or)	*	1	1	0	0	0	0

Create an input set of verb stems

We will simplify the problem by training the network on verb stems that have a constant length—this will make it easier for you to analyse the output from the network and yet still capture the essence of the past tense learning problem. Each verb will consist of three phonemes ordered in a sequence that conforms to the phonotactics (legal sound sequences) of English. A list of 500 verbs can be found in the file called **stems** in the **Chapter Nine** folder. Use the Translate... facility under the Edit menu to convert **stems** to a binary representation of the verb stems that obeys the phonological coding scheme stored in the **phonemes** file. Save the resulting file as **phone.data** and format with the appropriate header information for **tlearn**. (There is a set of files already prepared for you in the **Chapter Nine** folder if you want to avoid creating the files yourself.)

Create an output set of past tense forms

Now you need to create a file called **phone.teach** that contains all the corresponding past tense codes for the verb stems in **phone.data**. The file **pasts** contains a list of 2 arbitrary past tense forms, 410 regulars, 20 no-change verbs and 68 vowel change verbs, in that order. Each line in the **pasts** list is simply the past tense form of the verb stem in the corresponding line of the **stems** list. Convert this list into a binary representation of phonological features of the past tense and save the files as **phone.teach**. Finally, open a New Project and call it **phone**. This will automatically open the appropriate network configuration file (**phone.cf**) as well as the training files **phone.data** and **phone.teach**.

Training the network

Set the learning rate and momentum parameters in the Training Options dialogue box to 0.3 and 0.9 respectively. Set the network to Train randomly (i.e. to select verb stem–past tense pairs at random from the training set). Now train the network for 50 epochs (i.e. 25 000 sweeps).

Analysing network performance

The performance of the network can be assessed by examining the output activities on a node by node basis. You can do this by specifying the latest weights file in the Testing Options dialogue box and Verify the network has learned on the training set. However, just as we saw in the previous chapter, this would be very time consuming with 500 patterns to examine with 20 nodes in each pattern.

One way to get a quick idea of how the network is performing on individual patterns is to calculate the error for individual patterns in the training set and display the error in the Error Display. To do this you must check the Calculate error box in the Testing Options dialogue box. When you attempt to verify that the network has learnt, **tlearn** will display the RMS error for each pattern in the **phone.data** file, in the order that it appears in the file. Since you know the order of the verbs in this file it is relatively easy to determine which verbs are performing poorly and which verbs are performing well. Figure 9.12 displays the individual errors for the **phone** verbs after 50 epochs of training. The verbs with the largest errors are those at the

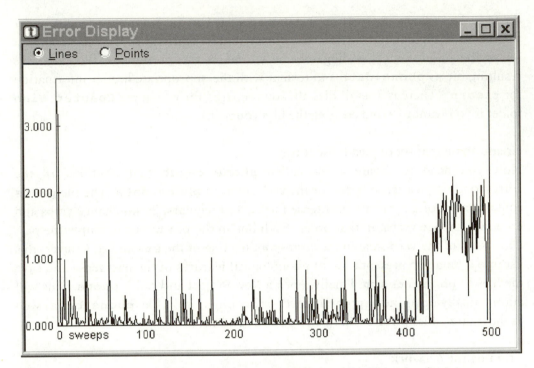

Figure 9.12   RMS error for individual verbs in the **phone** project after 50 epochs of training.

beginning of the training set and those towards the end. Recall that the arbitrary verbs are placed at the beginning of the **phone.data** and **phone.teach** files while the no-change verbs and vowel change verbs are placed at the end of these files. Clearly, the irregular verbs are performing the least well in this simulation.

Using the Output Translation *utility*

Ideally, we would like to be able to determine the phonemic output of the network from the set of node activities we obtain for past tense forms in the training set. Just as in chapter 8, we can use the Output Translation... utility in the Special menu to do this. Before you can use this utility, you will need to create a reference file that helps **tlearn** translate the real-numbered output vector into a string of phonemes. This reference file will be based on the **phonemes** file you used to translate the original verbs into binary vectors. Make a copy of the **phonemes** file (call it **phonemes.out**) and open the file in **tlearn**. Now edit the file and make sure it is identical to that shown in figure 9.13.

MAPPINGS: The first section of the file tells **tlearn** how to divide up the output vector into meaningful chunks. In the current example, the first 6 output units represent a single phoneme, as do the next two sets of 6 output units. Output units

```
phonemes.out                    _ □ ×
MAPPINGS:
1-6 from PHONEMES
7-12 from PHONEMES
13-18 from PHONEMES
19-20 from SUFFIXES
PHONEMES:
E 1 1 1 1 1 1
i 1 1 0 0 1 1
O 1 1 1 0 1 1
^ 1 1 0 1 1 1
U 1 1 1 1 0 1
u 1 1 0 0 0 1
A 1 1 1 1 1 0
e 1 1 0 0 1 0
I 1 1 1 0 0 0
@ 1 1 0 1 0 0
# 1 1 1 1 0 0
* 1 1 0 0 0 0
b 0 1 1 1 1 1
p 0 0 1 1 1 1
d 0 1 1 1 1 0
t 0 0 1 1 1 0
g 0 1 1 1 0 0
k 0 0 1 1 0 0
v 0 1 1 0 1 1
f 0 0 1 0 1 1
m 0 1 0 0 1 1
n 0 1 0 0 1 0
G 0 1 0 0 0 0
T 0 0 1 0 1 0
H 0 1 1 0 1 0
s 0 0 1 0 0 1
z 0 1 1 0 0 1
w 0 1 0 1 1 1
l 0 1 0 1 1 0
r 0 1 0 1 0 1
y 0 1 0 1 0 0
h 0 0 0 1 0 0
SUFFIXES:
W 0 0
X 1 0
Y 0 1
Z 1 1
```

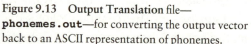

Figure 9.13   Output Translation file—
phonemes.out—for converting the output vector
back to an ASCII representation of phonemes.

19–20 represent the suffix. The MAPPINGS section of the file is always at the beginning of the file and the line MAPPINGS: is always the first line of the file. Subsequent lines identify groups of units and the codes that will be used to translate them. Hence, the line '1–6 from PHONEMES' indicates that the first 6 output units will be translated in accordance with the codes in the PHONEMES section of the file. You may only use codenames that are defined in subsequent sections of the file.

<CODENAME>: Subsequent sections of the file define the binary codes for the ASCII characters. Output Translation... will decipher the network's ASCII output by referring to these codes. You can define as many sections as you wish but the binary

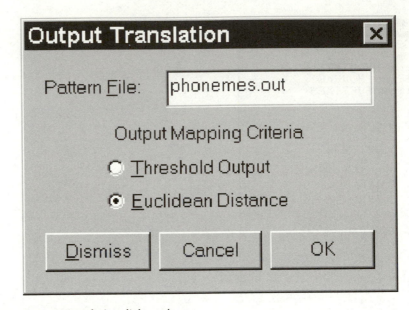

Figure 9.14   **Output Translation** dialogue box

vectors within a section must all be of the same length. In figure 9.13 it is important not to mix up the PHONEMES definitions with SUFFIXES definitions. Make sure that the number of elements in the binary vector agrees with the number of output units you have assigned to this CODENAME in the MAPPINGS section. The CODENAME must be in uppercase letters (numbers are not permitted) and end with a colon.

When you have created and saved the reference file, choose Output Translation... from the Special menu. The dialogue box shown in figure 9.14 will appear. Click on the Pattern file: box and select the **phonemes.out** reference file. Check the Euclidean Distance box and then OK the translation. Finally, check the Use Output Translation box in the Testing Options dialogue box. Now when you attempt to Verify the network has learned, the Output display will include an ASCII represent-ation of the output units together with the target output. The output display will continue to include this ASCII output until you uncheck the Use Output Translation box in the Testing Options dialogue box. Use the Output Translation technique to assess the performance of the network on the training items. Can you classify the type of errors that the network makes?

How does the network generalise?

When children and adults are presented with novel verb forms, they are able to generalise their knowledge from other verbs to produce sensible responses. For example, Berko (1958) elicited past tenses of novel verbs like *rick* from children.

They often responded with answers like *ricked*. Does your past tense network generalise to novel verbs in a similar fashion? Attempt to determine what generalisation your network has discovered about the training set by testing it on verb stems that it has never seen before. In the **Chapter Nine** folder you will find a file called **phone.test** that contains a list of verb stems that the network has not been trained on. Use this list (or part of it) to evaluate how the network generalises to novel forms. Does the network generalise equally well to all the verb stems in your test set?

10   *Connectionism and cognitive development*

Many studies of the acquisition of cognitive skills by children have found that learning appears to advance in stages. A common assumption is that the changes in behaviour which identify these stages are a consequence of the acquisition of new information processing mechanisms by the child. Learning in a connectionist model usually involves gradual changes to the strengths of the connections in a processing structure with a constant architecture. A challenge for connectionism is to show how gradual change can produce behaviour which progresses in stages. This chapter will examine the acquisition of two cognitive skills in which children's performance appears to advance in stages. In each case we will see that a connectionist model demonstrates similar behaviour to children although the underlying information processing structure and the learning rule which determines how it develops remain constant. Continuous small changes in an information processing structure can produce sudden changes in behaviour.

Stages in development—a challenge for connectionism?

A major difference between connectionist and traditional approaches to cognition is that the former models learning as well as performance. Connectionist modelling of a cognitive skill offers an explanation not just of how the system performs a task once it can do it but also of how the skill was acquired. So a natural area to test the connectionist approach to the understanding of human cognition is developmental cognitive psychology, the study of how children come to acquire cognitive skills.

The developing performance of a connectionist network learning a cognitive task appears similar to that of a child acquiring a skill. If the weights are initialised at zero the net will make no organised response to the first stimuli it experiences. Gradually, under the influence of weight changes produced by a learning rule, a processing structure develops within the net. This will start to generate coherent responses to the same stimuli which originally produced nothing. With increasing experience these responses will become more and more accurate. Eventually, if the network architecture and the learning rule are appropriate to the task, the network will not only respond correctly to the stimuli it has been taught but will be able to generate a plausible response to any novel stimulus presented to it. At this point the skill has been acquired. At the level of overall performance the parallels between the changing performance of a network and of a child as they acquire the experience necessary to master a new skill are obvious.

Since the pioneering work of Piaget, one of the ideas which has dominated experiment and theorising in developmental cognitive psychology is that cognition develops in *stages*. The claim is that as a child matures it acquires qualitatively different processing mechanisms. Thus the sort of problem it can master will depend on its current stage of development. For example, Piaget believed that an infant's cognitive processes are initially non-symbolic. In consequence its mental operations are restricted to processing the stimuli currently impinging on its sensory surfaces. So, in a famous example which will be discussed in detail in the next section, a child at this first stage of development would, according to Piaget, be unable to perform a task which required a representation of an object to be maintained after it had disappeared from view. The next stage of development sees the emerging ability to use symbols. The child can now represent stimuli which are no longer present and so can perform tasks, such as responding to an invisible object, which were impossible at the previous stage.

Many approaches to cognitive development assume that the new abilities associated with stage changes reflect the emergence of new cognitive mechanisms. A qualitative change in behaviour (such as demonstrating knowledge that an object continues to exist even though it is out of sight) is assumed to reflect a qualitative change in the underlying representation of the object (in this case, according to Piaget, the development of symbolic representation). Piaget called the process whereby these qualitative changes took place *accommodation*. Connectionist models of cognitive development do not involve changes of architecture, only changes of connection strength within a fixed information processing structure.[1] So the assumption that stages in behaviour reflect changes in mechanism offers a direct challenge to the connectionist approach.

In this chapter we will examine connectionist models of two tasks which were originally used by Piaget to illustrate his general theory that cognitive development takes place in stages. In both cases the model's performance undergoes stage-like change, like the child's. However, the basic architecture of the model remains constant over the course of training and the same learning rule is used. An information

---

[1]One exception is cascade correlation networks. In these a network without hidden units tries to solve a problem. If it fails it recruits hidden units and goes on doing so until it solves the problem. These have been applied to conservation problems such as the balance beam and seriation (Schultz *et al.* 1996). Another exception is genetic models where architecture and learning rules can evolve under a process of natural selection. These are discussed in chapter 14.

processing system can produce categorical changes in behaviour despite the fact that changes in the underlying processing mechanism are gradual and continuous.

The development of object permanence

Shortly after birth, infants can track a moving object but they do not appear to be aware that the object continues to exist once it has passed from view. 'Object permanence' is the name given to the understanding which the child eventually acquires that an object may continue to exist even when it is no longer visible. Piaget's views on the development of object permanence came from the study of infants reaching for hidden objects. Initially an infant will reach for a desirable object when it is visible but stop reaching if an occluding screen is lowered in front of the object. By around nine months of age an infant will continue to reach for an object after it has disappeared from view. He concluded that it was not until this age that internal representations of objects were of a form which could be maintained in the absence of an external stimulus.

Piaget's findings have been frequently replicated in experiments where children reach for objects. But a different experimental paradigm suggests that younger infants already have some form of object permanence. Studies which use the expression of surprise rather than active reaching as a measure of knowledge show that infants at around four months understand that an object continues to exist when it disappears from sight (Baillargeon 1993). A typical example of such an experiment is shown in figure 10.1. An infant looks at a ramp and track with a screen blocking part of the track. The screen is raised and lowered and then the infant watches a truck run down the ramp, behind the screen and reappear on the other side. Eventually it habituates and loses interest. Then the screen is lifted to reveal an object. This change attracts the infant's attention to the object. On an 'impossible' trial the object behind the screen blocks the track; on a 'possible' trial it does not. The infant watches the truck running down the ramp, along the track and behind the screen again. On 'impossible' trials infants show surprise if the truck reappears beyond the screen; on 'possible' trials they show surprise if it fails to reappear. The implication is that representations of an object's properties which could determine its capacity to block the movement of other objects are already in place by four months of age, and that such representations continue in the absence of direct visual input.

Modelling the development of representations which could produce object permanence

Why should an infant cease to *reach* for a concealed object, as Piaget found, if it has sufficient knowledge of hidden objects to show surprise if their properties are

(a) Habituating display

(b) Possible event

(c) Impossible event

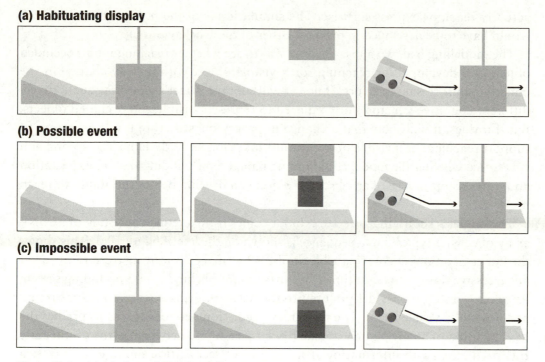

Figure 10.1 A typical set of trials in Baillargeon's experiments. The infant habituates to the first display and then sees an example of a possible or an impossible event. (Based on Baillargeon 1993.)

violated, as Baillargeon found? A possible resolution comes from considering differences in the nature of the tasks that infants are required to perform in these two experiments. In Baillargeon's experiment the infant is a passive observer, tracking a moving object. The response of surprise indicates that its expectation that the truck would reappear at a particular time and place has been violated. In Piaget's task the infant is required to make an active response to produce the reappearance of the occluded object. Reaching for an unseen object requires coordination of representations both of where the object is and of its identity (since the infant will only reach for an object she wants). Baillargeon's task, in contrast, only requires the detection that an expectation had not been fulfilled.

Mareschal *et al.* (1995) constructed a connectionist model to study the development of the representations of object identity and position which would be necessary to perform analogues of Piaget and Baillargeon's tasks. The model processes the image of a variety of objects as they move across a plane. An object may disappear behind an occluding screen but will eventually reappear on the other side. The model learns to build representations of the objects and their motion which would guide reaching for them (as in Piaget's task) or express surprise if they failed to reappear from behind an occluding screen (as in Baillargeon's task). (The network does not actually reach or express surprise. The simulation is of the representations which would have to be developed to produce either of these behaviours.)

The modelling had two aims. The first was to see whether reaching for an occluded object will develop after reaching for a visible object without any change in the underlying processing structure. If not, it will support Piaget's view that qualitatively different cognitive structures are required to represent visible and occluded objects. But if it does, it will show that a change in processing structure is not *necessary* to support reaching for invisible objects, it just takes longer to develop. The second aim was to see whether the model could mimic Baillargeon's finding that an expectation about the reappearance of an obscured object can develop before the ability to reach for it.

The model is shown in figure 10.2. Input comes from a retina consisting of a 25×4 array of cells. A typical input sequence is shown on the left of figure 10.3. This shows the image of an object covering a block of 2×2 retinal cells moving from right to left at successive times t_0 to t_5. At time t_1 it starts to move behind a 4×3 occluding screen. At times t_2 and t_3 it provides no input to the network. At t_4 it starts to reappear and at t_5 it is fully visible again. The trajectory prediction network learns to predict the next position of a moving object. The reaching response network learns to integrate this prediction with information from an object recognition module to initiate a reaching response to objects with desirable properties.

The output from the retina is processed by two separate pathways labelled 'what' and 'where' in figure 10.2. Neurological evidence shows that in the primate visual pathway, information which is used to establish an object's identity is processed predominantly along a route from primary visual cortex to the temporal lobe; information about an object's position and movement is processed predominantly by a route which goes from primary visual cortex to the parietal lobe. The model imitates the separate development of representations for object identity and motion.

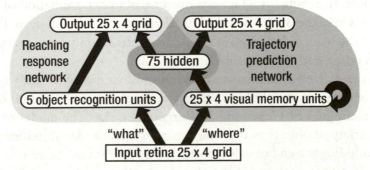

Figure 10.2 The network used by Mareschal *et al.* to simulate the development of the representations necessary to allow trajectory prediction and reaching responses (to simulate Baillargeon's and Piaget's experiments respectively).

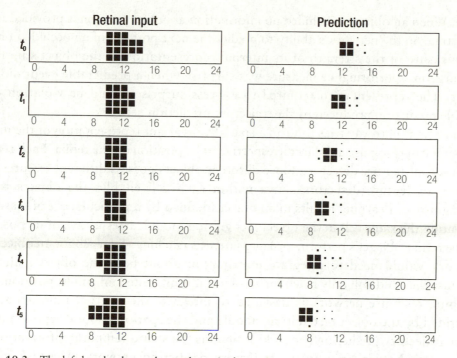

Figure 10.3 The left hand column shows the retinal image at 6 consecutive time intervals t_0 to t_5. An object moving from right to left and a stationary screen which partially or wholly occludes the object between t_1 and t_4 are projected onto the retina. The right hand column shows the network's prediction of the next position of the object on the retina.

The trajectory prediction module (the 'where' pathway) tries to predict the next position of the object. It uses a partially recurrent feedforward network trained with the backpropagation learning algorithm. Output from the retinal grid cells is mapped onto a 25×4 array of 'visual memory' units. All units in this array have a self-recurrent connection which enables them to generate a representation of the object's spatio-temporal history (see chapter 7). The response of the module is the activity of units in the 25×4 array labelled 'output'. If the prediction is correct this will match the next input to the retina.

An example of predictive tracking of an occluded object is shown in figure 10.3. The left-hand column shows the input to the retina. The right-hand column shows the output of the trajectory prediction network. In preceding time steps the 2×2 object has been moving at constant velocity from right to left across the screen. At t_0 it is about to disappear behind the occluding screen. At each subsequent time step the network correctly predicts that the object will move left by one position. Note that the prediction at t_3 (that the object will move to columns 9 and 10) differs from that at t_2 (that the object will move to columns 10 and 11) although the direct perceptual information available to the network (shown in the left-hand column) is exactly the same. When an object is occluded no information about its position is provided from the retina. So the network's ability to predict the next position of an occluded object is a measure of the strength of its internal representation of the object's motion. Baillargeon's performance measure was surprise when a predictable event did not occur. The representation required to express surprise would be violation of a reliable prediction produced by the trajectory prediction network.

The 'what' pathway tries to form a spatially invariant representation of the image so that it can recognise an object irrespective of its position on the retina. Each retinal cell has four feature detectors. Since different objects possess different features, the pattern of feature detectors active within each cell enables the objects to be distinguished. Learning results in an object (defined by a particular set of features) activating the same cell in the object recognition module irrespective of its position on the retina.[2] Piaget's performance measure was reaching. To reach for an object the network would need to integrate information about both the object's identity (because the child will only reach for an object it is interested in) and its position. The reaching response network is designed to integrate the internal representations generated by the object recognition module and the spatio-temporal representation in the trajectory prediction network. It obtains the spatio-temporal information by sharing the hidden units in the trajectory prediction network. The task of the reaching network is to output the next position for two of the objects (the desirable ones) and to output nothing for the other two (the undesirable objects). The same format is used for the output of the reaching response and tracking networks—prediction of the next stimulus position on a 25×4 array. This ensures that any difference in output from the two networks (which would be interpreted in terms of a developmental lag for the task which was slower to make correct predictions) is not an artefact of differences in the output representations.

Figure 10.4 shows the results of the simulation, plotting network performance against training trials. (An epoch is 1000 training trials). The performance index on the vertical axis is a measure of the accuracy of the network's prediction about the next position of an object. It is not possible to relate this measure directly to the behaviour of an organism using the network because the additional processes required to produce a response have not been modelled. But presumably overt behaviour will not come under the control of this network until its predictions are very reliable. To draw some conclusions about the behaviour which might emerge from this network let us assume that at least 95% reliability is required. This level is shown by the dashed line.

[2]This module makes use of an unsupervised learning algorithm developed by Foldiak (1991). The algorithm exploits the fact that two successive images which are in similar positions will probably be derived from the same object. The problems of forming a position invariant representation and the way that the Foldiak algorithm overcomes these problems are discussed in detail in chapter 13.

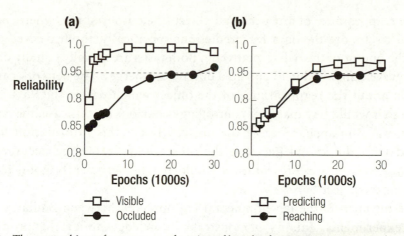

Figure 10.4 The network's performance as a function of length of training: (a) contrasts the accuracy of reaching for a visible object and reaching for an occluded object; (b) contrasts the accuracy of a prediction about the reappearance of an occluded object with the accuracy of reaching for it.

Figure 10.4(a) shows the development of the ability to predict the next position of a desired object, the prediction which would be required to control reaching. The open squares show that when the object is visible the task is learnt rapidly. Within 2 training epochs the network exceeds the 95% accuracy criterion, correctly predicting the position of desired objects and producing no output for undesired ones. The filled circles show that the model finds the task harder when the object is occluded. However, it is not impossible. With increased training the network gradually learns to make accurate predictions about the position of desired objects even when they are occluded. After 30 epochs it reaches the accuracy criterion for controlling behaviour.

This pattern mirrors Piaget's findings with infants. At the age of four months they will reach for a visible object but they stop reaching if it becomes occluded. It is not until around nine months that they continue to reach for an object after it has been occluded. Piaget proposed that this lag reflected the time taken for development of a qualitative change in object representation from one which relied on sensory input to one which was symbolic and could thus continue to control behaviour after the removal of the stimulus. This simulation shows that the change does not have to be qualitative. The representations of the object in the network remain the same in kind, as experience is acquired, but change in strength. Early in training they are not strong enough to maintain the output of the network once the retinal input ceases, but later they are.

The second result, shown in figure 10.4(b), contrasts the model's ability to make predictions about any occluded object with its ability to make the prediction only about a desired one. The open squares show the development of correct prediction about the reappearance of any occluded object (the output of the 'where' pathway). The filled circles are the data for predictions specifically about desired occluded objects (the output of the 'what' pathway). Both tasks are initially equally difficult to learn. However, after about 15 epochs a difference emerges. The network can make a prediction about the reappearance of the object which passes the 95% accuracy criterion, so it would be capable of controlling behaviour (in this case, the expression of surprise at non-appearance of the object). But if this information has to be combined with the knowledge that the object is desirable the accuracy of the prediction drops. The representation would not be sufficiently good to control reaching for the object.

This result mirrors the developmental lag observed between Baillargeon's and Piaget's experiments. Infants demonstrate knowledge about the properties of occluded objects at a time when they are unable to act towards them. The simulation suggests that the problem is not acquiring the knowledge itself, but the combining of knowledge from two different sources. The network can reach towards a desired object (when it is visible) and has knowledge about the reappearance of occluded objects. What it has difficulty in doing is combining the two sources of information.

Evaluating the model

This model provides a working implementation of a theory about how infants learn to track and reach for visible and hidden objects. The theory identifies a set of tasks that the model must perform and the information processing capacities required to perform those tasks. The model is able to make correct predictions about the order of mastery of the different tasks. The fact that the model predicts the order of emergence of various visual motor skills in children offers support for the initial insight that different aspects of children's object representations develop independently and that this independent development shapes infant performance.

The model can do more than merely mimic previously known facts. It is able to generate new experimental hypotheses which can be tested. The model processes spatio-temporal information independently of feature information: trajectory prediction is done by the 'where' channel; object identification by the 'what' channel. The model therefore makes the surprising prediction that in tracking mode there should be no surprise if an object changes its features when it reappears from behind the screen. It should only show surprise if the object reappears at the wrong time. Recent results from Baillargeon and from Xu and Carey (1996) have shown that infants even as old 12 months show no surprise at changes in the object when it reappears, provided something appears at the right time.

The critical characteristic of the approach taken by Mareschal *et al.* was the postulation of different mechanisms tuned to different aspects of the environment.

The model assumes the existence of a mechanism designed to compute object identity and a mechanism designed to track object position. Each network learns independently from the same experience. The asymmetry in performance of the reaching task and the predictive visual tracking task is a direct consequence of the requirement that computations delivered by both mechanisms need to be integrated for the former task but not for the latter. The implications of this conclusion extend beyond the domains of visual tracking and reaching. Any task that requires the integration of the computations from distinct networks is likely to be developmentally delayed compared to tasks that require the computations to be delivered from one network on its own. Given the extent to which the cognitive system appears to have developed along modular lines (see Shallice 1988), many tasks are likely to require integration of information from different sources. This may offer an explanation for developmental lags in other areas of cognitive development.

The separation of the 'what' and 'where' channels in this model is based on knowledge of the primate visual system. But one can reasonably ask how the networks got to be that way. One answer has been to propose that organisms come equipped with a range of expert networks that possess specialised computational capacities. Tasks are coopted by the specialist networks depending on the suitability of their computational properties for the task at hand. Jacobs *et al.* (1991) have shown how mixtures of expert networks exposed to a 'what/where' problem of the type described here will always assign the 'where' task to the expert network which possesses a linear activation function. The implication is that networks do not necessarily need to be designed to carry out particular tasks. Rather, the task will select the network which has the appropriate (i.e. innate) computational properties.

The balance beam problem

A second task used by Piaget to support the claim that cognitive processes develop in stages was the balance beam problem (Inhelder and Piaget 1958; see also Siegler 1981). Children are shown a balance beam with varying weights at varying distances from the fulcrum (see figure 10.5). They are asked to judge whether it will tilt when the beam is released and if so, which side will go down.

Possible types of problem are shown in the first column of table 10.1. In problems classified as 'Weight' the two Weights are at equal Distances from the fulcrum so the correct answer is determined by which Weight is larger.[3] Similarily, in the problems labelled 'Distance' the larger Distance determines the result as the Weights are equal. In problems labelled 'Conflict' the larger Weight is at a smaller Distance from the fulcrum. So the child must attend to both dimensions to get the right answer.

---

[3] In an attempt to reduce confusion we will refer to the weights on the balance beam as Weights, and the weights of the connections in the model as weights.

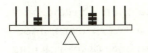

Figure 10.5 The balance beam task. The child must predict which side will go down when the beam is released.

Table 10.1 Siegler's categorisation of problems in the balance beam task. The percentage of correct responses to each problem type to be expected if the child were following one of the rules described in the text is shown.

Problem type	Level of performance		
	Rule 1	Rule 2	Rule 3
Balance	100%	100%	100%
Weight	100%	100%	100%
Distance	0%	100%	100%
Conflict – Weight	100%	100%	33%
Conflict – Distance	0%	0%	33%
Conflict – Balance	0%	0%	33%

'Conflict–Weight' indicates that the Weight difference is larger than the Distance difference so the beam will tilt to the side with the larger Weight, and so on.

Children pass through a series of stages in their responses to the balance beam problem. Their proportion of correct responses to the different types of problem is shown by the filled circles in figure 10.6. In the first stage (a) they get most Balance, Weight and Conflict–Weight problems correct and most Distance, Conflict–Distance and Conflict–Balance problems wrong. At the next stage (b) they get most Distance problems correct but still fail on Conflict–Distance and Conflict– Balance problems. At the third stage (c) they start to get some of all categories of Conflict problems

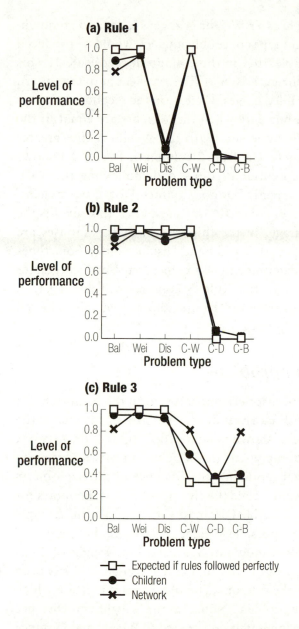

Figure 10.6 Performance on the various problem types shown in table 10.1 at different stages in development. The vertical axis shows the proportion correct; the horizontal axis refers to the problem types described in table 10.1. Bal = Balance; Wei = Weight; Dis = Distance; C–W = Conflict–Weight; C–D = Conflict–Distance; C–B = Conflict–Balance.

correct, although paradoxically they now do worse on Conflict–Weight problems than they did at the previous stage. Siegler showed that about 90% of children's responses fell into one or other of the patterns illustrated in figure 10.6, hence the claim that they constitute stages in the understanding of the problem.

Siegler showed that these response patterns would result if children were following a sequence of rules reflecting a changing significance to them of the dimensions of Weight and Distance. At the first stage the child focuses exclusively on Weight in making a decision—the side with the heavier Weight is always judged to go down. The pattern of responses to the different types of problem which would be produced by following this rule is shown in table 10.1 in the column headed Rule 1. This pattern is shown by the open squares in figure 10.6(a). The excellent fit to the pattern of children's responses (shown by the filled circles) is clear. In the second stage, they incorporate the Distance dimension, but only when the Weights are equal. If the Weights are equal, children judge that the side with the Weight at the greater Distance from the fulcrum will go down. The Rule 2 column in Table 10.1 shows what pattern of responses would be expected from a child following this rule. Distance problems would be solved correctly but not Conflict–Distance problems. Comparison of the squares and circles in figure 10.6(b) shows that this rule fits the children's responses at the second stage. In the third stage, their responses are confused under those conditions where both Weight and Distance differ. Sometimes they say that the greater Weight will determine the outcome, sometimes the greater Distance. A possible result is shown in the Rule 3 column in Table 10.1. A comparison of the squares and circles in figure 10.6(c) shows that this also is a reasonable description of the responses at stage 3.

Modelling the balance beam problem

McClelland (1989) trained a connectionist network to perform the balance beam task. (The model can be explored with **tlearn** in the exercises at the end of the chapter.) The architecture of the model is shown in figure 10.7. Input to the network is divided into two channels—one that represents the Weights of the two objects on either side of the fulcrum and one that represents the Distance of the two objects from the fulcrum. The first ten input units code the five possible Weight values for left and right and the next ten the five possible Distances for left and right. A single input unit is activated to represent each possible Weight or Distance. In figure 10.7 the network has been given the problem shown in figure 10.5. A Weight of 2 has been placed at a Distance 3 to the left of the fulcrum and a Weight of 3 has been placed at a Distance 2 to the right of the fulcrum. The filled circles indicate which input units have been activated by the problem. Note that the Weight and Distance units are themselves unstructured. The input units are related to Weight and Distance in an orderly way to make it easy for the user to see what problem the network is working on. But as far as the network is concerned the mapping of Weight and Distance values to input units is arbitrary. The network is not told explicitly which units correspond to large Weights or Distances nor which units represent the Weight or Distance of the object to the left or the right of the fulcrum. The network must discover these facts for itself.

Each bank of input units projects to separate pairs of hidden units, with each input

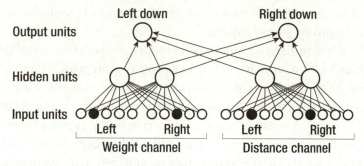

Figure 10.7 The network used by McClelland (1989) to simulate learning of the balance beam problem. (Based on McClelland 1989.)

unit projecting to both hidden units. The four hidden units project to two output units. If the activity of one output unit exceeds the activity of the other by a given margin, then the network predicts that the side whose unit is most active will go down. Otherwise it predicts that the beam will balance. Maintaining initially separate channels for Weight and Distance implements the assumption that children would see these as independent dimensions. Since the child must come to a single decision about which way the beam will tilt, the two channels must be integrated to produce a response.

The network is trained on a sample of the 625 possible combinations of Weights and Distances. The target activity is 1.0 for the output unit corresponding to the side that should go down and 0.0 for the output unit on the side that should go up. For a problem where the beam will balance, the target for both output units is 0.5. The discrepancy between the actual output and the correct output is the error signal which is used to adjust the connection strengths with the backpropagation learning algorithm.

At the beginning of training, the weights of the connections in the network are set randomly. There are no systematic differences observed in the activity of the two output units so the network responds 'balance' to all problems. Once training commences, the network's connections quickly move away from their initial random state and systematic response patterns appear. Throughout training the network is tested on novel patterns, all of which can be classified according to Siegler's taxonomy shown in table 10.1 (that is, they are examples of Balance, Weight, Distance or Conflict). McClelland found that the network's pattern of responses can be classified at different points in training by the same rules which Siegler found characterised children's responses. Furthermore, the network passes through the same sequence of stages as children. Early judgements are dominated by Weight while later in training the network learns to take Distance into account. The pattern of correct and incorrect responses as training progresses is shown by the crosses in figure 10.6. The model's performance develops in a way which closely matches that of children. The transition between consecutive stages is sudden, mimicking the stage-like transitions of young children.

As with the development of object permanence, stage-like changes in behaviour can be produced by an information processing system which changes gradually. Siegler's account of children's performance suggested that the stages in their responses corresponded to the acquisition of specific rules about the relative effects of Weight and Distance. A network cannot use a rule in the explicit form described by Siegler, so how does it come to produce rule-like behaviour? To understand why the network produces a particular response to a specific problem we need to look at the pattern of weights in the network. And to see why the response changes over time, such as the production of correct answers to Distance problems which characterises the shift from Rule 1 to Rule 2, we need to see how the weights change as the network is exposed to more problems. The exposition which follows, showing how the network produces a particular response, may seem a little long-winded, but a careful analysis of exactly why the network responds as it does this will illustrate some important general points about how networks operate.

Running the model

The weight matrix in the network after 20 training epochs is shown in the Hinton diagram in figure 10.8. Each connection in the network shown in figure 10.7 carries

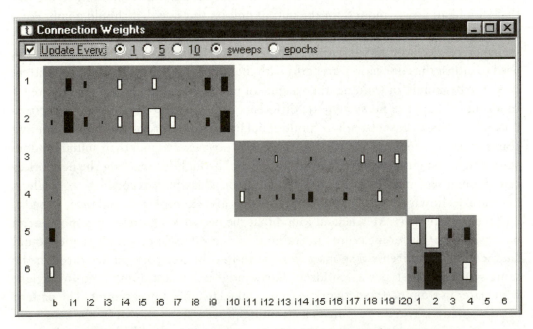

Figure 10.8   A Hinton diagram of the weight matrix after 20 training epochs.

activity from one unit (the source) to another (the target). The columns represent source units and the rows represent target units. Each rectangle at the intersection of a column and a row represents the weight of one connection in the model. White rectangles represent positive weights and black rectangles negative weights. The size of the weight is proportional to the size of the rectangle.

The ten input units representing Weight and the ten representing Distance in figure 10.7, the source of input to the four hidden units, are represented in the columns labelled i1–i20. The four hidden units, targets for activity from the input units, are represented in rows 1–4. (The column labelled b shows the biases to the four hidden units and the two output units.) So, for example, the strength of the connection between the fifth Weight input unit and the second hidden unit is shown at the intersection of column i5 and row 2. It is medium strength and positive. There are no connections between input units 1–10 and hidden units 3–4, so the area bounded by columns i1–i10 and rows 3–4 is blank.

The four hidden units are the source of input to the two output units. In this role the hidden units are represented in the columns labelled 1–4. The output units are targets for input from the hidden units and are represented in rows 5–6. So the rectangle at the intersection of the column labelled 2 and row 6 represents the strength of the connection from the second hidden unit to the right-hand output unit. This connection is large and negative. There are no connections from input units directly to output units so the area bounded by the columns labelled i1–i20 and rows 5–6 is blank.

Figure 10.8 shows the weights which have developed after 20 training epochs. At this stage the model behaves like a child at stage 1. It predicts that the beam will go down on whichever side has the larger Weight, ignoring information about Distance. The reason why the net is more influenced by Weight information than by Distance information at this stage of learning is clear. The connections between the input units representing Distance and the two right-hand hidden units (columns i11–i20 and rows 3–4), and between these hidden units and the output units (columns 3–4 and rows 5–6) are all still close to zero. Since the values are all similar, little information about the relative Distance on the two sides of the fulcrum can be represented. In contrast, the weights of connections between the input units representing Weight and hidden unit 2, and between hidden unit 2 and the output units, cover a wide range of values. So differences in Weight input on the two sides of the fulcrum will effect the response of the network. The difference between the development of the Weight and Distance channels is a consequence of a deliberate manipulation of the training regime. There is more variation in Weight across trials than in Distance. The reason why this leads to slow development in the Distance channel is discussed further in the next subsection, 'Evaluating the model'.

How does the network reach a decision about the relative size of the Weights on either side of the fulcrum? It might be natural to assume that the network would come to represent the magnitude of the Weight input directly, as one might expect a child to do. That is, input units representing Weight to the left of the fulcrum would develop positive connections to the left hand output unit in proportion to the size of the input they were coding, with similar connections developing from the input units representing the Weight on the right of the fulcrum to the right hand output unit. However, figure 10.8 shows that nothing like this happens. First, the weights of the connections between input units and hidden units (columns i1–i10, rows 1–2) seem to have little direct relation to the size of the Weight they are representing. Second, and somewhat mysteriously, the two hidden units activated by Weight information develop positive connections to the left hand output unit (columns 1–2, row 5) and negative connections to the right hand unit (columns 1–2, row 6). It might seem that the consequence of this would be that the input of a large Weight to *either* side of the fulcrum would lead to the response 'left down'. But this cannot be the case because figure 10.6(a) shows that the network gets all Weight problems correct.

The first point to note in understanding the network's solution is that the weights from inputs i1–i10 (the Weight information) show a similar pattern to both hidden units on the Weight side of the model. The only difference is that the weights are smaller on the connections to unit 1. (See rows 1 and 2 in figure 10.8.) Similarly, the weights from the two hidden units in the Weight channel to the output units show the same pattern. The connection is positive to the left hand output unit (row 5, columns 1 and 2) and negative to the right hand unit (row 6, columns 1 and 2), and in both cases the connections are smaller from unit 1. So, to simplify things, we can ignore the information which is processed via hidden unit 1 and concentrate on hidden unit 2.

All Weight input units have connections to hidden unit 2. So its activity represents the *sum* of Weight inputs from both left and right of the fulcrum. This may seem rather odd as the same sum would be reached if the Weights on left and right were equal (2,2), or if the Weight on the right was the larger (1,3), or if the Weight on the left was the larger (3,1)! Yet the network appears to have found some way of deciding which side has the heavier Weight. The weights of the connections carrying information about the Weight on the left of the fulcrum (input units 1–5) to hidden unit 2 are shown in columns i1–i5, row 2. These have relative values of approximately $-4, -1, 0, 1$ and 4. The weights of the connections carrying information about Weight on the right of the fulcrum (input units 6–10) have values of approximately $4, 1, 0, -1, -4$ (columns i6–i10, row 2). The input from input unit j to hidden unit i will, in the usual way, be $a_j w_{ij}$. Since the level of activity of an input unit does not reflect the *size* of the Weight which it represents, for ease of calculation in the following examples we can set the activity of any active input unit, a_j, to 1.0. Then the input to the hidden unit from any active input unit will be equal to the value of

Table 10.2 Net input to hidden unit 2. The rows show input units 1–5, active when Weights of 1–5 are on the left of the fulcrum. Each row is headed by the weight of the connections between that input unit and hidden unit 2. The columns are headed by the weights of the connections between input units 6–10 (which represent Weights of 1–5 on the right of the fulcrum) and the hidden unit. The matrix shows the net input to the hidden unit resulting from simultaneous input of any pair of Weights.

input unit	weight	6	7	8	9	10	input unit
		4	1	0	−1	−4	weight
1	−4	0	−3	−4	−5	−8	
2	−1	3	0	−1	−2	−5	
3	0	4	1	0	−1	−4	
4	1	5	2	1	0	−3	
5	4	8	5	4	3	0	
input unit	weight						

the weight of the connection. Thus if the Weight input to the left of the fulcrum is 1, the input to hidden unit 2 will be −4; if the Weight is 2, the input will be −1 and so on. Hidden unit 2 sums the inputs generated by the Weight inputs on the right and the left of the fulcrum. Table 10.2 shows the netinput to hidden unit 2 for all possible combinations of Weight on the left of the fulcrum (the rows, representing input units 1–5 in the model in figure 10.7) and the right of the fulcrum (the columns, representing input units 6–10 in the model). For example, if there is a Weight of 2 on the left and 4 on the right, units 2 and 9 will be active and the net input to the hidden unit will be −2.

When the Weights to the right and left of the fulcrum are the same, the inputs they produce cancel out because the weights on the corresponding input lines are equal in magnitude and opposite in sign. So the entries on the diagonal which represents equal Weights on either side (1,6 represents a Weight of 1 on both sides; 2,7 a Weight of 2 on both sides etc.) are all 0. For all combinations where the left hand Weight is larger than the right hand (entries below the zero diagonal) the netinput is positive. For all input combinations where the Weight on the right is larger than that on the left (entries above the zero diagonal) the hidden unit receives a negative input. It should now be clear what the pattern of weights from input units to hidden units has achieved. The connection strengths do not represent the magnitude of individual Weights directly. Rather, they ensure that hidden unit 2 represents the *difference*

Table 10.3 The activity level of hidden unit 2 arising from the activity of any pair of input units.

	6	7	8	9	10	input unit
1	0.5	0.2	0.1	0.05	0.01	
2	0.8	0.5	0.4	0.3	0.05	
3	0.9	0.6	0.5	0.4	0.1	
4	0.95	0.7	0.6	0.5	0.2	
5	0.99	0.95	0.9	0.8	0.5	
input unit						

between the two Weights. If the left Weight is greater, the input is positive; if the right Weight is greater, the input is negative.

To see what activity of the hidden unit is produced by this netinput we must pass it through the activation function. McClelland used a logistic activation function of the sort shown in figure 1.4(c) of chapter 1 and described in chapter 5. The logistic activation function restricts the activity of the hidden unit to the range 0–1, with a sigmoidal relationship between netinput and activity. A netinput of 0 produces an activity of 0.5. Increasingly positive input takes the activity towards 1; increasingly negative input takes the activity towards zero. Table 10.3 shows the approximate activity of hidden unit 2 which results from the netinputs shown in table 10.2. For example, if there is a Weight of 2 on the left and 4 on the right, input units 2 and 9 will be active so the activity of hidden unit 2 will be about 0.3.

The hidden unit has a positive connection to the left hand output unit (see column 2, row 5 in figure 10.8) and a negative connection to the right hand output unit (see column 2, row 6). So, applying the input $= a_j w_{ij}$ rule, we can see that when the hidden unit is active it will send positive input to the left hand output unit and negative input to the right hand output unit. An example of this network at work is shown in figure 10.9. This is an *activity* diagram rather than a weight diagram. The squares correspond to the units in the model shown in figure 10.7 with the activity level of each unit shown by the lightness of the corresponding square. A white square represents a fully active unit; a uniform grey square represents a unit with zero activity.

The lowest row shows the activity of the 20 input units. Starting from the left, the first five code the size of the Weight on the left of the fulcrum, the next five the size of the Weight on the right of the fulcrum and the next ten the corresponding Distance information. The network has been given the problem of a Weight of 3 on the first

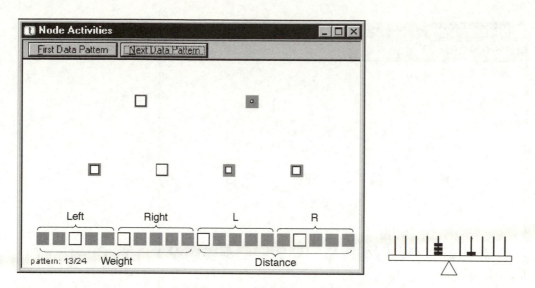

Figure 10.9   An activity diagram for the network with a Conflict–Weight problem after 20 training epochs.

peg to the left of the fulcrum and a Weight of 1 on the second peg to the right of the fulcrum. The input units which represent this information are active. The middle row shows the activity of the four hidden units. As we would expect from table 10.3, the result of a larger Weight on the left than the right at input is that the second hidden unit in the Weight channel becomes active. This in turn ensures that the left hand output unit becomes active and the right hand output unit is switched off. Thus the model predicts, correctly, that the beam will go down to the left. Given the previous analysis we would expect the network to give the correct solution to this problem. The question is what happens when the larger Weight at input is on the right? How does the network manage to turn the right hand output unit on when the connections from the Weight channel to the right hand output unit are negative?

The network's solution is demonstrated in figure 10.10. The activity of the input units shows that there is now a Weight of 1 on the peg two to the left of the fulcrum and a Weight of 3 on the first peg to the right of the fulcrum, the reverse of the first problem. Table 10.2 shows that the result of a larger Weight on the right is to produce a negative netinput to hidden unit 2. Table 10.3 shows that this will result in a relatively low activity level for the hidden units in the Weight channel. The Distance input produces little input to the Distance hidden units because the weights of the connections in this channel are low. But the result of a near zero *input* to a unit with a logistic activation function is a moderate level of *activity* of the unit. Thus the hidden units in the Distance channel are actually more active than those in the Weight channel even though they are not representing any Distance *information*. The result of this level of activity and the small positive weight from hidden unit 4 to the

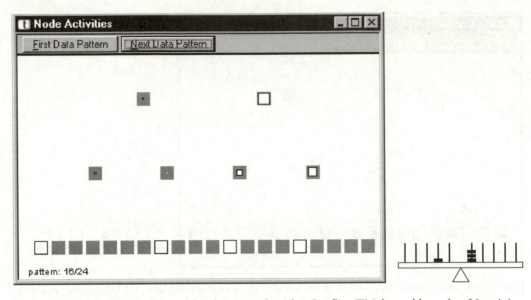

Figure 10.10 An activity diagram for the network with a Conflict–Weight problem after 20 training epochs.

right hand output unit is to produce some activity of the right hand output unit.[4] This is greater than that produced at the left hand unit by the low level of activity of the Weight hidden unit, so the network makes the correct prediction that the balance goes down to the right.

The network produces the correct response, then, but by an apparently bizarre route. The fact that the network has learnt little about Distance means that the weights in this channel are close to zero. Zero weights mean zero input to the hidden units, which means an activity level in the middle of the possible range. This is sent to the right hand output unit so it always has some positive input. The computation performed by the network can be summed up as: Set a bias to respond 'right hand down'; if the left hand Weight input is larger than the right hand Weight input, this bias will be overcome and the response will be 'left hand down'. In other words it responds right hand down by default if the left hand Weight is smaller than the right.

Is this a simulation of the development of children's thought about such problems? It seems somewhat implausible! It seems obvious from an adult perspective (although this may be misleading) that a child who can predict that the side with the heavier Weight will go down must have developed some concept of the results that Weight can achieve. This would include the fact that Weight has magnitude and that a pair of Weights can have relative magnitude. Thus, if the heavier Weight is on the right, the beam goes down to the right; if it is on the left, the beam goes down on the left.

[4]As column b in figure 10.8 shows, there is also a positive bias contributing to the activity of the right hand output unit.

The network gets the right answer to relative Weight problems in the specific context of the balance beam, but does not seem to have developed a representation which corresponds to the abstract concept of Weight. The network only has a representation corresponding to our understanding of 'Weight' if the Weight is larger to the left of the fulcrum!

Perhaps it is naïve to think that a model with 26 nodes and 48 connections could represent a complex skill which children take years to develop. However, it does demonstrate that a skill which appears to advance in discrete steps in children can be achieved by a model in which the architecture remains constant and which has a continuous learning mechanism. We will demonstrate this by looking at the network's response to the same problems after 100 epochs of training. Figure 10.11 shows how the weights in the network have developed over the extra trials. The most obvious difference is that the weights in the Distance channel have begun to develop. They have the same sort of pattern as appeared in the Weight channel although with reversed polarity. Thus the network will represent the Distance *difference*, with a large positive input to the hidden units when Distance is larger on the right and a negative input when Distance is larger on the left.

The result of showing the same two problems as before is shown in figure 10.12. The network gets both problems right but, despite the extra practice, produces a less confident response. (Compare the difference between the output units in figure 10.12 and those in figures 10.9 and 10.10.) Analysis of a complete range of problems shows that the network is now in stage 3. It does better on Distance and Conflict problems in general, although it is now worse on Conflict–Weight problems than it was in stage 1. In fact, it gets some Conflict–Weight problems wrong which earlier it got right.

Evaluating the model

The network must discover a matrix of connections which allows each channel to operate in an internally consistent fashion and the two channels to work together so that the dimensions of Weight and Distance are integrated appropriately. The stage-like behaviour of the model is directly attributable to the network discovering solutions to each of these problems at different points in its training. Why does the network initially respond more to the Weight dimension than the Distance dimension?

The training set contains more frequent variation of Weight values than Distance values. The greater variation in Weight offers the network more opportunities to extract predictive correlations between Weight and balance beam solutions. In other words, the network is more likely to reduce the error on the output units for a greater number of input patterns if it pays particular attention to the Weight channel. The

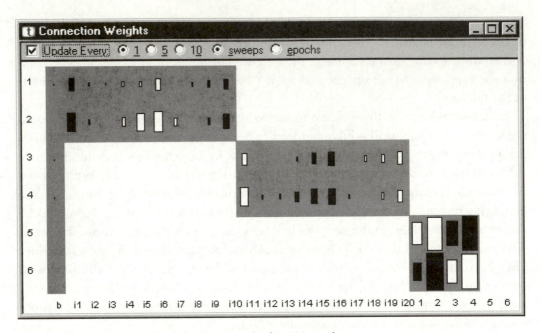

Figure 10.11   A Hinton diagram for the network after 100 epochs.

network achieves this focus by strengthening the connections, both inhibitory and excitatory, between the input units, hidden units and output units in the Weight channel. Changes are also made to the connections on the Distance side of the network. However, these changes are less frequent since the Distance dimension varies less frequently and so is less valuable to the network in predicting the correct output.

The stage-like behaviour of McClelland's model can thus be seen to arise from two assumptions. First, the network's architecture is pre-structured to process the dimensions of Weight and Distance separately before integrating them at the output level. Second, input to the network is systematically manipulated to simulate attentional differences between the two dimensions. The interaction between the structural assumptions and input assumptions results in the network first discovering the role of the Weight dimension. The connections in the Weight channel are preferentially strengthened. Next, the network discovers the role of the Distance dimension as it strengthens the connections in the Distance channel. Finally, the two dimensions are integrated through the fine tuning of the connections between the hidden and the output units. Each of these changes corresponds to individual stages in the development of the model even though the changes in the connection strengths within the network are continuous. The structural and input assumptions remain constant throughout training.

The contrasting aspects of children's information processing which Piaget referred

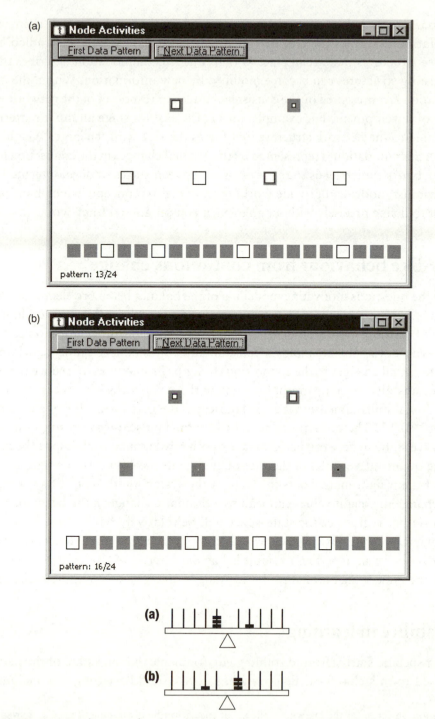

Figure 10.12 Activity diagrams for the network facing two Conflict–Weight problems after 100 training epochs.

to as *assimilation* and *accommodation* can be seen at work in the balance beam model. Assimilation describes the fact that incoming information will be handled by the cognitive structures that are in place at that time. Accommodation describes the fact that existing structures can become modified by new information. Within the model, assimilation is represented by the consistent pattern of responses of the network within a stage of development. For example, during the earliest stage all input patterns are assimilated to the network structure that forces the side with the larger Weight to go down. Accommodation is represented by the gradual changes in the connection matrix of the network which leads to the transition between stages of development. Thus a connectionist model can provide working examples of concepts which have proved difficult to define precisely without an explicit computational framework.

Stage-like behaviour from continuous change

One of the questions motivating modelling of the balance beam problem was whether stage-like behaviour can emerge from a mechanism which does not undergo any change of learning algorithm or representational mechanism. Connectionist models of cognitive development employ a constant and continuous learning algorithm that computes small changes to the connection strengths in a network to reduce the output error for any given input pattern. Learning in these networks is a process of gradient descent on a multi-dimensional error landscape like that shown for two dimensions in figure 10.13. The uneven surface of the error landscape can result in dramatic qualitative shifts in network performance over a few learning trial despite the absence of large quantitative shifts in the rate of change in the connection strengths. If the value of the weight matrix puts the state of the system on the edge of a precipice, a small change in weight values can lead to a dramatic change in the behaviour of the system. Other regions of the state-space will be relatively flat and the behavioural consequences of weight changes will be comparatively minor. Hence, learning in networks can result in periods of stable behaviour interrupted by sudden change, even though the underlying mechanism for learning is one of small continuous change.[5]

Variability in learning

Given a specific start state and training environment, the final state of the networks discussed in this chapter is determined. But it would be wrong to conclude that

---

[5]A common objection to the Darwinian theory of speciation by evolution is that a system in which change is gradual and continuous would not produce sudden jumps in outcome. The demonstration of stage-like jumps in network behaviour under a continuous learning rule shows that despite the intuitive appeal of this objection it is, perhaps, not as powerful as it seems.

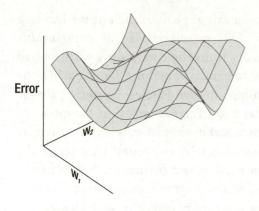

Figure 10.13 A surface showing how system error varies as two weights are varied. Learning involves choosing new weight values which will achieve gradient descent on this surface.

connectionist models necessarily predict a consistent and universal developmental trajectory. In this section we will consider how connectionist models can provide an explanation of variation in development. We will not review models of developmental variation in detail but rather point to the sources of individual variation present in connectionist networks. We will demonstrate that:

- large individual differences in network learning can result from subtle changes in the training environment and parameters of the learning mechanism;
- critical periods in development can emerge as an inherent property of the learning process itself rather than from the onset or offset of some factor that influences learning.

Individual differences

The learning algorithms used in connectionist models include a learning rate parameter. This determines how big the weight changes will be on any learning trial. Usually, the learning rate is set to a constant value for the duration of a simulation. However, it is possible to vary the learning rate both within and across simulations. Varying the learning rate within a simulation (say, reducing the learning rate as training progresses) approximates the assumption that individual learning experiences are less salient during later learning than early learning. As we shall see shortly, there are other aspects of network dynamics which can magnify or minimise the effects of a given learning experience at different points in learning. Varying the learning rate across simulations (holding other factors like training environment and start state constant) can lead to surprising and significant differences in the learning profile and final state of the network. For example, large learning rates do not always result in overall faster learning. Interference between patterns encoded in the same network can lead to a decrement in network performance. If the learning rate is large, weight adjustments made for one pattern can wipe out much of the learning for patterns processed on previous trials. This is referred to as *catastrophic interference*. For this reason, modellers usually train their networks with a small learning rate. In general, networks are prone to catastrophic interference when the tasks they are required to perform involve competing tendencies. Examples are the model of past tense learning involving regular and irregular verbs, or the model of concept formation and vocabulary growth, discussed in chapter 9, where very similar images must sometimes be associated with distinct labels. Small changes in the learning rate can also have subtle effects on network performance. For example, performance on regular verbs in the past tense model is quite sensitive to variation in the learning rate parameter while irregular verbs are more robust to such changes.

We might assume that the learning rate in the network has a psychological counterpart in the child that roughly translates into sensitivity to learning experience. Children who are oversensitive to individual experiences may find mastery of particular types of task more difficult. More generally, these models suggest that substantial individual differences in performance on a task may result from small variations in learning sensitivity. These differences go beyond merely predicting a differential speed of learning. Different components of the task (such as regular versus irregular verbs) may be differentially effected by a global change in learning sensitivity.

All the networks described so far have involved static architectures. That is, the numbers of input units, hidden units and output units do not change during the course of learning. However, some types of network models allow new nodes to be recruited during the process of learning. Selective pruning of connections and nodes can also occur in response to their lack of participation in any processing or new learning (Quartz and Sejnowski 1997). Neural networks that involve node creation and selective pruning may turn out to offer powerful ways to investigate the range of variation apparent in the developmental process. It is possible to investigate the impact of variations in network architecture in the types of model discussed already. For example, it is quite common when building a connectionist model to explore the number of hidden units that are necessary to discover the solution to a particular task. It often turns out that there exists an optimum number. Below this number, performance on the training set tends to deteriorate dramatically. Above the optimum number, performance on the training set remains stable but the ability of the network to generalise appropriately to novel patterns deteriorates. This generalisation–performance trade-off could be referred to as 'The Goldilocks Principle'. That is, you've got to get it just right—not too many, not too few. We can consider the number of hidden units available to a network as a measure of its representational resources. If the network has inadequate representational resources then it fails to solve the problem. If the network is over-endowed with representational resources then it is likely to get bogged down in memorising individual instances and fail to extract the essential aspects of the problem that would enable it to generalise to novel stimuli.

We may assume that children vary in the level of resources they invest in a particular problem domain. Connectionist models predict that increased resource allocation does not necessarily lead to a general improvement of performance. For example, over-allocation of resources may assist the child in learning a task but hinder the child in generalising the knowledge obtained to new examples. We have seen an example in which starting out with a small allocation of resources can be indispensable for the long term mastery of the problem (the acquisition of syntax discussed in chapter 9). Performance variations from simulation to simulation resulting from differential resource allocation provide a powerful framework for exploring the nature of individual variation in children. For example, varying the number of hidden units in a network trained on the past tense problem can have a dramatic effect on the network's ability to generalise to novel words (see Plunkett and Marchman 1996). This problem has been observed in children with SLI (specific language impairment).

Most networks start out life with a well-specified architecture and training environment but a randomised weight matrix. The random configuration of the weight matrix reflects the fact that the network lacks any knowledge about the nature of the problem at the start of training. It is a common experience of network modellers that different randomised start states can have dramatic effects on the learning profile and the final performance of the network. It is easy to understand why this is so by looking at figure 10.13 again. Recall that any configuration of the weight matrix in a network corresponds to a position on the error landscape. Training the network corresponds to traversing the landscape, continually attempting to move downhill to reduce the error. If you are lucky, the initial configuration of the weight matrix may be close to a solution to the problem in which case only a limited amount of training is required to achieve a mature state. Alternatively, the initial network configuration may be a long way from a global minimum and extensive training is required. In other words, there can be good initial weights and bad initial weights. Similarly, two similar sets of weights might lie on either side of a ridge. Initial learning will send the weights of the two networks in opposite directions. They might end up eventually at the same global minimum by different routes. But they might end up in separate local minima in unrelated parts of weight space.

As we shall see in chapter 14, it has been shown how connectionist networks might gradually evolve initial weight matrices that are well adapted to learning certain types of task through natural selection from a pool of slightly mutated organisms. The gene pool (i.e. the inherited starting weight matrices) will have a degree of variation that will give rise to individual differences in the behaviour of those organisms. Likewise, we may think of variations in the start state of connectionist models of development as an attempt to capture the individual variation of young children in the predisposition to learn a task. Connectionist modellers often run multiple replications of a simulation to evaluate the variability of the learning profile and the end state. The variability observed can be used to generate predictions about variability in the modelled population itself.

Critical periods

A common assumption in developmental psychology is that the capacity to learn does not remain constant throughout life. The greater plasticity of the brain for new learning during early development is most apparent in studies that compare recovery from some form of deprivation, trauma or brain damage in early life with that in later life. Similar conclusions are also reached from studies that compare the level of mastery in complex skills such as language when begun early in life with the level of mastery achieved when learning begins later in life. It is often argued that the period prior to puberty constitutes a critical period for language learning, after which time any attempt at complete mastery of a language is unlikely to succeed. Critical periods are often assumed to be domain specific. For example, learning the simple association involved in imprinting may be typical of the very earliest stages of development, whereas the learning of complex cognitive functions may cover a much wider developmental span.

Many explanations of the existence of critical periods in development appeal to maturational factors that impose external restrictions on the ability of the brain to learn. For example, constraints on synaptogenesis, and crystallisation of neural structures as a result of neuronal pruning, provide accounts for the increased difficulty of learning as development proceeds. However, this type of explanation provides little help in understanding why critical periods of development may vary so widely from one domain to the next. In contrast, connectionist approaches to learning provide a framework for understanding how critical periods in development may result from the learning process itself and are thereby tightly linked to individual tasks. In connectionist models no extrinsic mechanism is necessarily required to explain why new learning may get harder as development proceeds, as we shall now demonstrate.

Connectionist learning consists in adapting the strengths of the connections in the network until a configuration of weights suited to all the training patterns is found. The activity of a unit is determined by the net input and the activation function. The weight matrix is usually randomised at the start of training—often with the weight values constrained within some relatively small range, say ± 0.5. As a result, the net input to any given unit at the start of training is likely to be close to zero. Connectionist learning models that use gradient descent learning algorithms typically use a squashing or sigmoid activation function as shown in figure 1.4(c) of chapter 1.

The activity of a unit with a possible range of $0 \rightarrow 1$, a sigmoidal activation function and zero net input is not zero, but 0.5 (see chapter 5).

The slope of the activation function plays an important role in determining the size of the weight change that takes place on any learning trial (see equation 5.10 in chapter 5). The slope of the sigmoidal activation function is steepest where the net input is closest to zero, and flattens off when the input becomes large (positive or negative). This means that weight changes are likely to be bigger for units with a net input which is close to zero than units which receive large positive or negative input. So units with a sigmoidal activation function are maximally sensitive to learning when the input is uncommitted in either the positive or negative direction. These units possess a window of sensitivity for learning. This window is initially open in a network when the weight matrix is randomised at the start of learning. The effect of learning in the network is to strengthen the connections feeding into a unit. This is particularly true for problems which involve competition between patterns in the training environment. As connections increase in strength, the chance of the net input to a unit being close to zero decreases and the unit moves outside its window of sensitivity to learning. In fact, if the net input becomes very large, then the activity will reach a point where the slope of the activation function approaches zero. Under these circumstances, even a large error signal will produce little change in the connections attached to this unit. The network has already committed itself to a particular representation of the problem and its weight matrix has become fixed in a position from which it cannot easily escape. The network has passed through its critical period of learning.

There are several characteristics of this process that are worth noting. First, it is not all-or-none. The strength of the connections associated with a unit will change gradually during the course of training, the speed of change depending on factors like the learning rate. As long as the unit remains within its dynamic range (i.e. the slope of the activation function is not close to zero), the network will remain plastic to learning. Second, for some types of problem, the network need never move out of its window of sensitivity to learning and so never exhibit any critical period effects. This will be true for problems that do not provoke large weight changes—typically, problems which do not contain contradictory examples. Face recognition might constitute an example of a consistent problem domain which remains plastic in normals throughout the life span. In contrast, languages are not consistent in the manner in which they organise the lexicon or exploit grammatical structure. It is to be expected therefore that language learning would exhibit critical period effects. Connectionist modelling offers a natural framework for investigating non-linear patterns of learning where development passes through a critical period as well as learning capacities that remain more stable over the life-span. The power of connectionist models to deepen our understanding of these aspects of the dynamics of development has yet to be fully exploited.

Further reading

The insights into cognitive development offered by connectionism are discussed in detail in Elman *et al.* (1996).

Modelling the balance beam problem with **tlearn**

Network architecture

You will train the network on all 625 weight–distance combinations. The input and output vectors for the balance beam task are already set up in your **tlearn** folder. The files are called **bb.data** and **bb.teach**. The network architecture is defined in the **bb.cf** file. You can begin the modelling project using the Open Project option in the Network menu and choose **bb. tlearn** will automatically open all the files you need to run your model.

Look at the training files and examine how the configuration file constructs the network shown in figure 10.7 (see the User Manual in Appendix 3 if you cannot understand it). Notice that both files contain more than 625 training vectors. If you look at the end of the files you will see that a number of the patterns are repeated several times. These are just those patterns in which the distance values on either side of the fulcrum are identical. In fact, the training files contain 5 repetitions of all balance beam problems in which the distance is the same on either side of the fulcrum and just one example of every other balance beam problem. This modification of the training environment is necessary to ensure that the network sees more variation in weight than in distance.

Testing data

You will evaluate the performance of the network at regular intervals by testing it on a representative subset of the patterns on which it was trained. The test data (found in **bb_test.data**) contain 24 problems subdivided into groups corresponding to the stages of development discovered by Siegler:

(1) 4 problems represent balanced beams, problems where the weights and distances on either side of the fulcrum are identical.
(2) 4 problems in which the distance from either side of the fulcrum is the same but the weight varies.
(3) 4 problems in which the weight on either side of the fulcrum is the same but the distance varies.

(4) 12 problems where the weight and/or distance are in conflict, for example, the weight may be greater on one side but the distance is greater on the other: 4 problems in which the side with the greater weight goes down—conflict–weight; 4 problems in which the side with the greater distance goes down—conflict–distance; 4 problems in which the beam balances.

Training the network

Now train the network randomly for 10 000 sweeps using a learning rate of 0.075 and a momentum of 0.9. Set the **weight_limit** parameter to 1.0 in the **bb.cf** file. Use batch learning by setting the Update weights every: training option to 100 sweeps. Dump the weights every 400 sweeps (in the Training Options dialogue box, check the Dump weights every: box and set the value of Sweeps to 400). You may find it useful to observe the change in RMS error as you train the network, so open the Error Display.

Testing the network

As a result of training the network, you will have created a series of 20 weight files which you can use to test network performance at different stages of learning. These weight files will be called **bb–401.wts**, **bb–801.wts**, **bb–1201.wts**,..., **bb–10000.wts**. Use the **bb_test** files to evaluate the network's capacity to make balance beam judgements.

In the Testing Options dialogue box, set the weights file to **bb–401.wts** and the testing set file to **bb_test.data**. You will probably want to save your output in a file so check the Append output to File: box and specify a file name. Now Verify the network has learned. **tlearn** should output 24 pairs of numbers indicating the output activities for the 24 representative balance beam problems defined by **bb_test.data**. If you have checked the Calculate error box in the Testing Options dialogue box, you can also determine the RMS error for the individual balance beam problems. The Error Display should resemble that in figure 10.14. Now examine your output data. You will probably discover that most of the output activities are in the range 0.5 ± 0.2. Almost certainly, none of the output units that should have an activity of 1.0 or 0.0 have achieved their target values.

What constitutes successful performance in this network? We know that it is unrealistic to expect output activities to reach their absolute values of 1.0 or 0.0 (see discussion on sigmoid activation functions in chapter 5 if you want to refresh your memory about this issue), so how are we to decide which side of the beam goes down in those cases when it does not balance? The solution that McClelland suggested to this problem is to look at the *difference* in the activity of the two output units. He

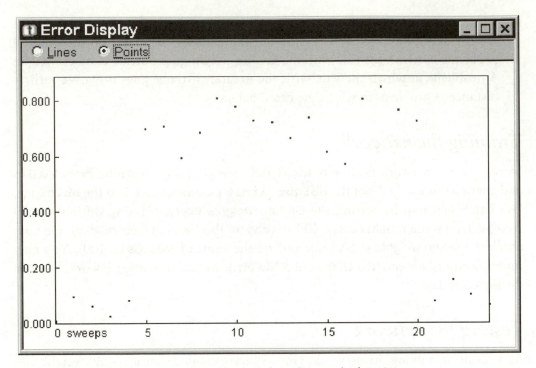

Figure 10.14 RMS error on test patterns for the balance beam task after 401 sweeps.

proposed that if one output unit exceeds the activity of the other by more than 0.33, then the side with the highest activity is judged to go down.

Exercises

1. Notice that the RMS error in figure 10.14 is lowest for the first 4 patterns and last 4 patterns in the test set. Why do you think this is the case? (If you cannot think of a reason for this, look at the listing of the test patterns in the section 'Testing data'.)

2. Do you think there is anything special about a difference of 0.33 as a criterion for deciding which side goes down?

3. Evaluate the output activities from the network after 401 sweeps of training. How many of the test problems has the network got right when judged according to the current difference criterion?

4. What stage of development do you judge the network to be in at this stage of training? Would your evaluation change if you changed the difference criterion?

5. Repeat your evaluation of network performance with the other weight files (**bb-1201.wts, bb-1601.wts**, etc.). Can you discern a sequence of stages that the network passes through in attempting to solve this problem?

11 *Connectionist neuropsychology—lesioning networks*

It is easy to simulate the effect of brain damage on a cognitive process with a connectionist network. Once it has learnt how to perform the task, a proportion of the units or connections are removed and the effect on the network's performance is determined. This chapter will examine models of damaged performance in three areas of cognition—reading, semantic memory and attention. We will see that lesioned connectionist networks can simulate patient data, both at the qualitative level, reproducing patterns of impairment, and at the quantitative level, predicting the relative magnitude of different impairments. The performance of damaged networks mimics that of brain damaged patients so successfully that this area provides some of the most persuasive evidence that the connectionist approach to understanding cognitive processes is an appropriate one.

A major contribution to the understandinging of cognitive processes has come from the study of brain damaged adults. What such patients can and cannot do after damage to a normally functioning cognitive system has provided a wealth of evidence about the system's structure. Connectionism is a natural approach to the study of damaged cognitive systems. It is easy to simulate damage; you can remove connections, alter thresholds or modulatory inputs, or add noise to connection weights, in a model of a cognitive process and see what difference it makes to the model's performance. One line of evidence in support of the connectionist approach is that, when damaged, the performance of both brains and connectionist networks degrades gracefully. That is, damage typically leads to partial loss of computational power rather than catastrophic failure. Approaches to cognition which do not use parallel distributed processing are usually unable to reproduce graceful degradation. The effect of damage leads to all-or-none functioning which is unlike the graded degradation which is often observed after minor damage to the brain. With a traditional box-and-arrow model of a cognitive process you can say that a pathway is 'damaged' but this is usually little more than hand-waving. There is no way of predicting other than in vague qualitative terms (such as the less than illuminating prediction that 'performance will get worse') what the effect of a lesion would be.

Neuropsychological study of patients has revealed a wealth of detail about patterns of cognitive impairment following brain damage. The connectionists' claim that their models have some general similarity to neural structures would be enhanced if they could go beyond the simple demonstration of graceful degradation and show that they can simulate the detail of these patterns of deficit. In this chapter we will look at three attempts to simulate the breakdown of cognitive processes in patients by lesioning models of reading, semantic memory and selective attention. We will see that these damaged models can reproduce the pattern of deficit in certain patients. In fact, they are so good at reproducing patient data that this area provides some of the most convincing evidence that the connectionist approach to cognition is an appropriate one. But they can do more than just match patient data. First, we will see that these models can offer explanations for patterns of deficit which have been difficult for non-connectionist approaches to explain. Second, connectionist models make quantitative predictions about the performance deficit to be expected after a particular lesion. So they can be used to choose between alternative models of information processing deficit, which, without connectionist implementation, would only make indistinguishable qualitative predictions of deficit. Finally, they offer an insight into the interpretation of double dissociations by showing a variety of ways in which they can arise. All in all, the connectionist approach to cognitive neuropsychology looks like a good one.

The simulation of deep dyslexia

The breakdown of reading following brain damage, acquired dyslexia, follows many different patterns. An intriguing one is the condition known as deep dyslexia. The distinguishing errors made by these patients are semantic (hence 'deep' dyslexia). When asked to read a word aloud, they might say something which is semantically related to the stimulus but has no phonological similarity to the correct response. For example, when shown NIGHT, one patient responded 'sleep'. The stimulus word must have been processed because the response was semantically related to it. But all record of its non-semantic attributes has been lost as there is no phonological relationship between stimulus and response. The traditional interpretation of this would be that there are separate semantic and non-semantic routes from orthography to phonology, and that the patient had lost the non-semantic processing route. However, deep dyslexics also make visual errors, such as responding 'sandals' to SCANDAL. In this case the patient appears to have relatively intact visual information about the stimulus but lost semantic information. So the traditional interpretation would be that the patient had lost the semantic processing route and kept the non-semantic one. To add to the confusion, deep dyslexics also produce errors such as responding 'skirt' to SHIRT. These suggest that they have kept partial information about both the appearance and the meaning of the stimulus rather than losing one and keeping the other. An intriguing error of this sort is one in which there appear to be consecutive visual and semantic errors made to the same stimulus, such as responding 'orchestra' to the word SYMPATHY. Presumably this was a visual error from SYMPATHY → symphony, followed by a semantic error from symphony → 'orchestra'.

The co-occurrence of apparently independent error types is difficult for traditional box-and-arrow models to explain. The semantic and visual errors suggest the functional separation of sub-systems involved in reading, one semantic and one non-semantic. When a single patient shows evidence of damage to independent parts of the system the modeller is forced to make the assumption that independent parts of the system have been damaged simultaneously. As the number of different error types grows and consequently the number of independent areas which appear to have been damaged, the assumption can start to strain credulity. An example of the difficulties that have faced traditional approaches to neuropsychology is shown in figure 11.1. This shows a model of the processes involved in reading. The darkened areas show which parts of the model must be damaged to explain the symptoms of deep dyslexia. In this approach the modeller has to assume that five, supposedly independent, parts of the system have all been damaged simultaneously.

We will look at a study by Hinton and Shallice (1991) which shows how a lesioned connectionist model of reading can start to offer an explanation for the pattern of errors shown in deep dyslexia. The crucial result was that a single lesion *anywhere* in

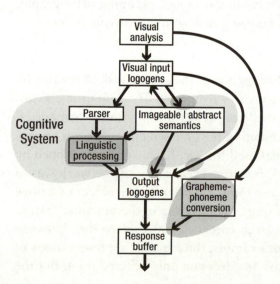

Figure 11.1 A typical box-and-arrow model of the processes involved in reading aloud. The darkened areas indicate the functions which must be damaged to produce the symptoms of deep dyslexia. (Based on Morton and Patterson 1980.)

the model would produce both visual and semantic errors, as well as mixed visual-and-semantic (SHIRT → 'skirt') and visual-then-semantic errors (SYMPATHY → 'orchestra'). This shows that different error types do not necessarily mean that different parts of the underlying system have been independently damaged. A single lesion can lead to different sorts of error.

Hinton and Shallice (1991)

Deep dyslexics cannot pronounce non-words like SLINT. In terms of the traditional '2-route' information processing approach to reading discussed in chapter 8 (and also represented by figure 11.1) these patients would be assumed to be lacking the processes which allow rule-based grapheme → phoneme conversion. Since they produce responses which bear no relation to the correct pronunciation for the word (e.g. NIGHT → 'sleep'), it is assumed that they are reading primarily by direct lexical access to semantics. This is the process that Hinton and Shallice's model simulated. Note that this is unlike the reading process which was discussed in chapter 8. Seidenberg and McClelland modelled the conversion of print directly to pronunciation (i.e. orthography to phonology). The route from print to meaning was not implemented. The computational problems involved in these two tasks are quite different. Words which are visually similar tend to have similar pronunciation. A model which maps print onto pronunciation will, in general, be required to produce similar patterns at output to words which produce similar patterns at input. But words which look similar tend to have unrelated meanings. So a model which maps print onto meaning will be required to produce dissimilar patterns at output to words which produce similar patterns at input. Since connectionist models have a natural bias to produce similar outputs from similar inputs, mapping orthography onto semantics will be more difficult than mapping orthography onto phonology.

The task

Hinton and Shallice used a greatly simplified version of the general task of reading by semantics. The stimuli were a set of 40 words, 8 from each of 5 semantic classes. These activated a set of 28 position specific letter detector input units. 'Semantics' was represented by a set of 68 units representing possible semantic features corresponding to size, texture, where found, what used for, etc. Each word was defined by a positive value on a subset of the semantic features. The task for the network was to activate the correct set of semantic features (15 on average) for the object described by each input word. Naturally there was quite high overlap in the semantic feature representation of words from within a given category and less overlap between words from different categories. Thus, for example, the semantic representations of COT and BED shared 12 common positive features and only differed on 4. But the semantic representations of COT and CAT shared a positive value for 7 features while differing on 21. This demonstrates the problem which the network will have to try and overcome during learning. The pattern set up by the input CAT will be similar to that set up by COT and quite different from that set up by BED. But the outputs (i.e. the set of semantic features turned on) in response to BED and COT must be similar, and quite different from that for CAT.

Architecture

The Hinton and Shallice model is shown in figure 11.2. Twenty-eight grapheme units, responsive to the letters in the input words, feed to 68 semantic units, via 40 hidden units. There are also recurrent connections between the semantic units and a set of 60 'clean-up' units.[1] This is the crucial feature which differentiates Hinton and Shallice's model from the Seidenberg and McClelland model. The clean-up units take input from the semantic units and pass activation back to them, activity cycling between them for a number of iterations. On each cycle the state of the semantic units changes. These connections allow the state of the output to change from that which resulted from the first pass of activity from the input units.

The recurrent connections introduce *attractor structure* into the model. An attractor is a state (i.e. a set of output unit activities) to which the system will move if the activity of its units is allowed to continue evolving in successive processing cycles after the initial state created by the input (see chapter 7). As we shall see, this has very important consequences for the network's behaviour. A feedforward network like Seidenberg and McClelland's cannot develop attractor states. There is only one computational pass through the system so there is no opportunity for the state of the output units to evolve. A recurrent network can change its state as activity cycles round the system.

The result of lesioning the network

The model was taught to produce the correct mapping of spelling pattern onto meaning by backpropagation and then lesioned by removing units or connections, or

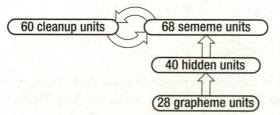

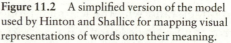

Figure 11.2   A simplified version of the model used by Hinton and Shallice for mapping visual representations of words onto their meaning.

[1]Recurrent connections permit the network to produce the correct response even if the input is a noisy version of the stimulus which it learnt. This is why Hinton and Shallice called them 'clean–up' units. In this simulation the units produce a radical change in the network's interpretation of the input rather than cleaning it up, so this name is somewhat inappropriate.

Table 11.1 The conditional probability of different error types following lesions to different parts of the model shown in figure 11.2.

Lesion position	Error rate (%)	Conditional probability of error type			
		V	V+S	S	U
Disconnect g→h	5	0.34	0.45	0.13	0.08
Disconnect h→s	3	0.11	0.30	0.56	0.04
Disconnect c→s	3	0.34	0.32	0.34	0.00

V = visual error; V+S = mixed visual and semantic error; S = semantic error; U = unrelated error. (Based on Plaut and Shallice 1993.)

by randomly changing the value of the weights. Random examples of each lesion type were performed on the network and then it was presented with the 40 words in the training set. On some trials the output pattern failed to reach the criterion required for a response to be classified as a word and the network's response was scored as an omission. But sometimes it would produce the wrong word. These errors were classified as visual (CAT → 'cot'), semantic (CAT → 'dog'), mixed (CAT → 'rat'), or unrelated (CAT → 'mug').

Naturally, the exact pattern of errors varied with the position, type and severity of the lesion. But qualitatively the results showed a similar pattern independent of the details of the lesion. Table 11.1 shows a sample of the results for lesions in different parts of the network. The first involved disconnecting grapheme to hidden unit connections (g→h) ; the second disconnecting hidden to sememe connections (h→s); the third disconnecting clean-up to sememe connections (c→s). In each case the conditional probability of the four error types is shown.

Table 11.1 shows that all lesions produced Visual, Visual+Semantic and Semantic errors, just like the deep dyslexic patients who Hinton and Shallice were trying to model. Although the exact pattern varies with lesion site, whichever part of the model is lesioned, a single lesion to the network generates the co-occurrence of unrelated error types which traditional models find difficult to explain.

Attractors

To understand why the lesioned model is capable of producing different types of error from a single lesion it is necessary to understand what an attractor does. Figure 11.3 represents the orthographic and semantic states of the network. A point in orthographic space represents the combination of input units excited by a stimulus word. A point in semantic space represents a particular combination of the 68 possible semantic features. The points corresponding to the combination of features

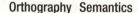

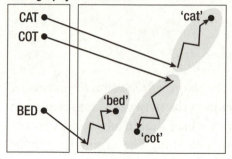

Figure 11.3 The position of CAT, COT, and BED in the orthographic and semantic space of the Hinton and Shallice model. The ovals represent attractor basins. The black dots in semantic space are the attractors. Any input falling into one of the basins will eventually reach the state represented by the attractor. (Based on Hinton and Shallice 1991.)

representing 'bed', 'cot' and 'cat' are shown as black circles. The orthographic state following the inputs CAT and COT are close together (because they are visually similar) and far from that following the input BED. The initial state of semantic space, following an input, will reflect orthography. This is shown by the arrowed lines from orthographic space to semantic space. The initial state of semantic space is similar following the inputs CAT or COT and unlike the state following the input BED. However, 'cot' and 'bed' have similar semantics which are unlike those for 'cat'. Thus the initial state following the input COT must move towards that following the input BED and away from that following CAT. This evolution of semantic state occurs as the activity cycles between semantic and clean-up units. The changes during this process are represented for each input by the jagged trajectories moving towards the states corresponding to 'bed', 'cot' and 'cat'. The trajectory for COT ends up at the semantic state representing 'cot' even though it started far away—hence the name, attractors.

Now it should be clear why recurrent connections were necessary for this model. With words, visually similarity is not related to semantic similarity. The recurrent connections allow the network to overcome the initial coding in terms of visual similarity and recode in terms of semantic similarity. In contrast, visual similarity *is* related to phonological similarity. So recurrent connections were not necessary in Seidenberg and McClelland's model, although as we saw in chapter 8 they can have useful additional properties.

Attractor basins

The network is trained on a set of 40 words. So it is necessary for it to develop a set of attractors which will take the 40 initial semantic states which are produced by the orthography of these words to the 40 semantic states representing the words. The weight changes which create the attractors turn out to have other consequences for the structure of semantic space. These are represented by the ovals around each attractor known as 'attractor basins'. Any trajectory which enters a basin will end up at the attractor which lies at its heart.

Lesioning an attractor

The result of a lesion to the model is to *change the shape of the attractor basins*. A possible new shape for the 'cot' basin after damage to the network is represented in figure 11.4. This new basin will capture trajectories which should have gone to other attractors and lose some which should have gone to 'cot'. The original attractor basin, developed during learning, represents both the spelling pattern and meaning of 'cot'. Some part of the basin will be close to that for words which are visually similar because the initial trajectory of COT will be close to those for words which are visually similar. Some part must be close to basins for words which are semantically similar, like 'bed', because the trajectory will end up close to words which are semantically similar. So the change in the shape of basins which accompanies damage to the network will lead to the capture of trajectories of words which are either visually or semantically related to the target. The lesion which produces the changes shown in figure 11.4 would produce both a visual error (CAT → 'cot') and a semantic error (BED → 'cot').

It is also clear why such a model would produce mixed errors. The basins for words which are both visually and semantically related (such as CAT and RAT) would lie closer to each other than basins for words having only one area of similarity. So lesions would be likely to produce this sort of error. The model also offers an explanation for visual-then-semantic errors. If damage to the visual end of the 'cot' basin meant that it captured the input CAT, while damage to its semantic end meant that it lost trajectories to 'bed', the consequence would be the apparently surprising one that the stimulus CAT would produce the response 'bed'.

But why does a *single* lesion cause both sorts of error? Why doesn't a lesion to the connections from the graphemic units damage the part of the attractor which is close to visually similar words, causing only visual errors, and damage to connections to

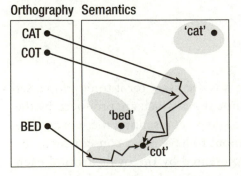

Orthography Semantics

CAT
COT

'cat'

'bed'

'cot'

BED

Figure 11.4 If the network is lesioned, the attractors change shape. Trajectories of incoming words may now fall into an adjacent attractor basin. The figure shows a visual error (CAT → 'cot') and a semantic error (BED → 'cot'). (Based on Hinton and Shallice 1991.)

the semantic units damage parts of the attractor representing semantic similarity, causing only semantic errors? The conceptualisation of visual information processing taking part in one part of the system and semantic information processing taking part in another is explicit in models like that shown in figure 11.1. The representation of the network in figure 11.2 encourages the same way of thinking—that visual and semantic processing are functionally separate in the model. But here it is misleading. During learning, error is backpropagated through the *whole* system. An error at output has a consequence right back to the earliest set of weights. So a weight change which contributes to a particular part of the attractor shape could be represented in any part of the network. It is easy to overlook this because pictures of the model which show that graphemic and semantic units are independent, suggest that graphemic and semantic processing are independent.

In fact, lesions close to orthography *are* likely to have a greater effect on visual errors, and those closer to semantics on semantic errors. This can be seen in Table 11.1. Disconnection of the g→h units causes predominantly Visual errors, and disconnection of the h→s units causes predominantly Semantic errors. But in both cases there are still a significant number of the other sort. The qualitative result, a mixture of error types, is true for all lesion sites, although the quantitative mix varies with lesion site.

Is this result dependent on fine details of the model?

Hinton and Shallice showed that the co-occurrence of visual, semantic and mixed errors, far from being mysterious, is an inevitable consequence of lesioning a connectionist network that uses attractors to map orthography to semantics. Since this same error pattern is observed in patients it encourages the view that distributed attractor networks are an appropriate model for human information processing.

One line of attack on this conclusion, as on any successful connectionist model, is that the model was very specific. Many arbitrary choices were required to make the model run. It is unclear whether the conclusion was generally true, or just reflected some lucky choices in apparently unimportant details of the model. A general problem is that the model used a particular procedure for learning, the backpropagation algorithm. This is known to be very powerful but it is not known whether it is used in the brain (see chapter 5). Was the result dependent on this? A development of the Hinton and Shallice simulation by Plaut and Shallice (1993) explored these two issues.

Network architecture
Some general decisions about network architecture are dictated by the nature of the task that Hinton and Shallice's model was trying to perform. Hidden units are required because the problem of mapping orthography to semantics is not linearly

separable (see chapter 5). Recurrent connections are required to allow attractors to develop. But within this general framework, decisions about the number of hidden units, the connection density between layers and the placing of the recurrent connection are arbitrary. Hinton and Shallice chose a low connection density. Only a random 25% of the possible connections between each layer were made. They also chose to implement recurrence with a separate set of hidden units (the 'clean-up' units) rather than, for example, connecting the semantic units back to the hidden units carrying input from orthography. Plaut and Shallice (1993) built a number of different networks, maintaining the basics of hidden units and recurrent connections, but varying the number of hidden units, the extent of connectivity between layers and the placing of the recurrent connections. This way they could see whether any of the design choices made by Hinton and Shallice were crucial to their result. Three of the networks they investigated are shown in figure 11.5. The number of hidden units are shown in each block.

(1) *Connection density.* Hinton and Shallice used sparsely connected hidden units. This provides for good discrimination among inputs but limits the complexity of the input patterns units can be responsive to. Network (a) tested the importance of low connectivity by using 100% connection density between layers. The overall number of connections is comparable to that in the Hinton and Shallice model because it has fewer hidden units.

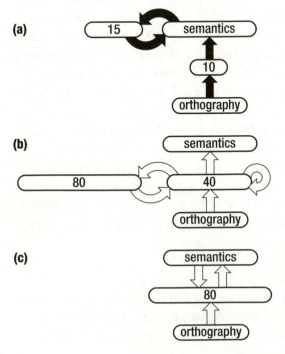

Figure 11.5 A variety of network architectures tested by Plaut and Shallice. The numbers indicate the number of hidden units. The heavy connecting lines in (a) indicate 100% connectivity. The hollow connecting lines in (b) and (c) indicate 25% connectivity. (Based on Plaut and Shallice 1993.)

(2) *Recurrence location.* Hinton and Shallice used separate clean-up units leaving the hidden units in the direct route free of the recurrence generating process. In network (b) the importance of that design choice was tested by removing the direct connections between recurrence generating units and the semantic units.

(3) *Absence of specific clean-up units.* In network (c) there were no special units involved in generating recurrence. It was achieved by the back connections from semantics to the hidden units.

All these nets were trained in the same way as the Hinton and Shallice network and then lesioned. The exact pattern of errors varied from network to network, but the crucial result was the same for all of them—all lesions produced visual, semantic and mixed errors. This suggests that it is the existence of attractors (which were formed by all networks), not the details of network architecture, which were essential to the result. Numbers of units, connection density and the placing of the recurrent units have only secondary effects on the performance of the attractors which the network generates.

Training algorithm

Hinton and Shallice used the backpropagation learning algorithm. Plaut and Shallice tested whether the use of this specific learning algorithm was crucial by teaching a network with the Contrastive Hebbian learning algorithm.

Contrastive Hebbian learning takes place in two phases:

(1) the network runs with the inputs clamped until the output units have settled on a pattern;
(2) the system is run with inputs clamped and the outputs clamped into the correct values for that input.

The first phase shows what the system does when it is trying to produce the output pattern on its own, and the second shows what it does when it is producing the right answer. Learning involves changing the weights between pairs of units in proportion to the difference in the product of their activity in phase 2 and in phase 1. (It is called Hebbian learning because weight changes are based on the product of activity of the units on either side of the connection (see chapter 3) and Contrastive because it compares the product at two times, first when running normally and secondly when it is running under the influence of the trainer.) Like backpropagation, this algorithm learns by performing steepest descent in weight space. But the mechanisms involved are rather different. The information required to modify a connection weight is available locally at that connection and it does not require the computation of error derivatives, or information to be passed backwards across a connection. However, it does require symmetric forward and backward connections and weights.

Plaut and Shallice trained the network with this algorithm and then lesioned it. At a qualitative level it produced the same mix of error types as before, and this mix was achieved wherever the lesion. Thus the basic result was not determined by the nature of the learning algorithm.

The interpretation of double dissociation

Cognitive psychologists claim to have found a *double dissociation* when they find one patient who can perform task A but not task B and a second patient can perform task B but not task A. A natural interpretation of this pattern of deficit is that the cognitive functions which perform the two tasks are independent. (The logic and limits of this inference, and examples of its use to support box-and-arrow models of cognitive function are discussed in detail in Shallice (1988).) Connectionist simulations of damaged cognitive systems allow an examination of how a particular deficit occurs. They have shown that double dissociations can arise for a variety of reasons other than the existence of independent processing structures. We will look at one demonstrated by Plaut and Shallice in this section and one shown by Farah and McClelland's model of lesioned semantic memory in the next. The inference from double dissociation to the existence of independent processing structures underlies many traditional models of cognitive function. The demonstration of double dissociation following selective lesions within a single unified processing system has led to radical rethinking in cognitive neuropsychology.

Only one semantic dimension was used in Hinton and Shallice—category membership. Other differences in the semantics of words are known to influence the reading of deep dyslexics. For example, they find abstract words (such as TACT) harder to read than visually similar concrete words (such as TACK). To see whether they could simulate this effect Plaut and Shallice taught the network pairs of visually similar abstract and concrete words. They introduced a new set of semantic features to define the abstract words and modelled the difference between concrete and abstract words by giving abstract words fewer semantic features than concrete words.

Most lesions left the system able to read concrete words better than abstract. However, lesioning one part of the system, the connections between semantic and clean-up units, produced the opposite effect—abstract words were read better than concrete. Abstract words have fewer semantic features than concrete words so they make less use of the clean-up units, relying more on the direct pathway to generate the correct semantic representation. Thus damage to the direct pathway had a proportionally greater effect on the network's ability to respond to the abstract words. But damage to the clean up units had the opposite effect, causing more damage to the network's ability to produce the correct semantics of concrete words.

This is a very significant result. Although better performance on concrete words is the norm with patients, one has been reported who shows a superiority for abstract words (patient CAV, reported by Warrington 1981). The double dissociation found between patients in the readability of abstract and concrete words has led some cognitive neuropsychologists, following the traditional interpretation of double dissociation, to claim that there are separate semantic stores for abstract and concrete words. Plaut and Shallice's result shows that a single system, representing both abstract and concrete semantics, can produce either an abstract or a concrete advantage when lesioned in different ways. The simulations allow damage to impair the direct and clean-up pathways independently, so there are independent pathways involved just as in the traditional explanation. However, in the traditional interpretation of the two pathways revealed by the double dissociation, one would process abstract semantics and the other concrete semantics. This is not the case with the network. The entire network is involved in generating the semantics of both concrete and abstract words. The two pathways revealed by the double dissociation, the direct and the clean-up pathways serve different computational roles in this process. The double dissociation comes about because those roles are differentially important for reading these two classes of words. Thus the dissociation should not be seen in terms of the surface distinction between the processes (i.e. concrete vs abstract) but rather in terms of underlying representational and computational principles (e.g. the influence of the differing numbers of semantic features in the two classes on the development of attractors).

Modelling a deficit in semantic memory

As a second example of connectionist modelling of cognitive neuropsychological data we will look at a study by Farah and McClelland (1991) who lesioned a model of semantic memory. Again we will see that a connectionist model can offer an explanation for an apparently anomalous pattern of results found with patients. We will also see an example of an important aspect of connectionist modelling in action—quantitative predictions about the effect of a specific lesion. The nature of the lesion or the fine structure of the model can be manipulated to see what will and what won't give a quantitative fit to the patient data.

Modality and category specificity in semantic memory

Separate areas in the brain analyse visual, proprioceptive and auditory input. So one might expect semantic memory to be modality specific, one part storing visual information about objects, one part storing information about actions that were appropriate with them, and so on. Support for this view comes from patients who have a deficit related to a specific input modality. For example, visual agnosics cannot recognise an object by sight but can make an action appropriate to the object if they feel it. Apraxics can recognise an object by sight but cannot perform an appropriate action with it, and so on.

However, there are patients who show a pattern of deficit which would not be expected were the semantic system modality specific. They show category specific impairments where the information lost cuts across modalities. Here are some attempts by the patient SBY, reported by Warrington and Shallice (1984), to define a variety of living or non-living things:

Wasp: 'A bird that flies'

Wheelbarrow: 'Object used by people to take material about'

Crocus: 'Rubbish material'

Submarine: 'Ship that goes underneath the sea'

Holly: 'What you drink'

Towel: 'Material used to dry people'

SBY appears to have lost information about living things without suffering any loss to her information about non-living. Her loss appears to be of a category of things rather than of a modality of information. Other patients have been reported who show the opposite pattern—a loss of knowledge about non-living things while knowledge of living things remains intact. The traditional interpretation of this double dissociation would be that there is a functional separation between knowledge about living and non-living objects in semantic memory. This would imply that semantic memory was organised by category. Organisation by modality and by category would seem to be mutually exclusive. So how can evidence from patients be found to support both modes of organisation? Farah and McClelland offered a resolution of this problem by showing that a semantic memory which is organised by modality can, nevertheless, show category specific impairment when lesioned.

The model

This has two pools of 24 input/output (I/O) units, one verbal (name units) and one visual (picture units), and 80 semantic units, some coding visual and some coding functional information (see figure 11.6). There are bidirectional connections between units both within and between pools. A semantic memory with only two types of information (visual and functional) is obviously a gross oversimplification but it serves to make the basic point that dissociations in retrievable knowledge do not necessarily reflect a corresponding dissociation in the organisation of the underlying memory.

A key component of the simulation is the representation of living and non-living items in semantic memory. To try and mimic the coding in people, and hence presumably of the patients who showed the living–non-living dissociation, they

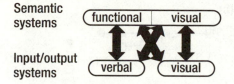

Semantic systems

Input/output systems

Figure 11.6 The architecture of the model used by Farah and McClelland. There are bidirectional connections between two pools of input/output units and a pool of semantic units. Some of the semantic units code visual attributes and some functional attributes. (Based on Farah and McClelland 1991.)

asked people to identify any visual or functional descriptors in the dictionary definitions of the living and non-living things used by Warrington and Shallice. Overall they reported about three times as many visual as functional descriptors, so Farah and McClelland divided the 80 semantic units up in the same ratio, 60 visual and 20 functional. They also marked relatively more visual than functional descriptors for both classes, 8:1 for living and 3:2 for non-living. To mimic these ratios, living things were represented by an average of 16 visual and 2 functional units; non-living by an average of 9 visual and 7 functional units.

The network was taught about the name, appearance and semantics of 10 living and 10 non-living objects. These were represented in the net as patterns of activity in each of the three pools of processing units—verbal input, visual input and semantics respectively. All 24 units in the name and picture pools were activated for each item but only a sub-set of the semantic units. The name or picture pattern was presented in training, and activation allowed to pass between units for 10 processing cycles. The Delta rule (see chapter 4) was then used to correct the other two patterns. Once the net had learnt all the patterns it was lesioned by removing a proportion of either the visual or the functional semantic units. The net was then given the task of either picture naming (present a pattern to the visual I/O units and read off the resultant pattern on the name I/O units) or generating an image to match a word (present a pattern to the name I/O units and read off the pattern on the visual I/O units).

The result is shown in figure 11.7 with the proportion of items correctly recalled plotted against the proportion of semantic units removed. The left hand figure shows the result of lesioning visual units in semantic memory and the right hand figure the result of lesioning functional units. Memory for non-living things (with data pooled across picture naming and image generation) decreases once the network is lesioned (the open squares). The deficit increases monotonically with the size of the lesion and is more or less the same whether visual or functional semantic units have been damaged. Performance never drops below about 70% correct, however large the lesion. In contrast, memory for living things (the filled circles) is strongly affected by damage to visual semantic units (performance drops close to zero with a 100% lesion) but not affected by damage to functional semantic units.

The difference between the effects in figure 11.7(a) and (b) demonstrates the double dissociation shown by patients. A lesion of the functional semantic units affects recognition of non- living things but not of living; a lesion of the visual

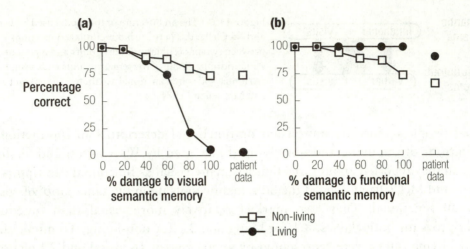

Figure 11.7   The effect of lesioning semantic units on the ability of the network to produce a name in response to a picture of an object or vice versa. The open squares show the performance when the stimuli are non-living objects and the filled circles the performance when the stimuli are living. (a) shows the effect of lesioning visual semantic units and (b) the effect of lesioning functional semantic units. In this simulation the semantic system contained 60 functional units and 20 visual units. (Based on Farah and McClelland 1991.)

semantic units produces the opposite pattern. This shows that the double dissociation observed in patients does not force one to the (somewhat implausible) interpretation of independent information storage for living and non-living things. It could arise from damage to a modality specific storage system if the coding for the two categories, living and non-living items, varied in its demands on the different modality specific components. This interpretation is similar to that of the double dissociation found by Plaut and Shallice for the retrieval of concrete and abstract words. Of course, if different information processing operations use independent processing systems then selective lesions could lead to the observation of double dissociations in patients. But different forms of coding or representation can also lead to double dissociations.

Modelling an asymmetrical double dissociation

Although the basic result was the double dissociation resulting from lesioning either the visual or the functional units in semantic memory, figure 11.7 shows that the effect is asymmetrical. Lesioning visual units had a major effect on the recall of information about living things and a minor effect on non-living; lesioning functional units also had a minor effect on the recall of information about non-living things but no effect on knowledge about living things. This is an intriguing result because an asymmetry of just this sort can be found in the patient data. The two patients

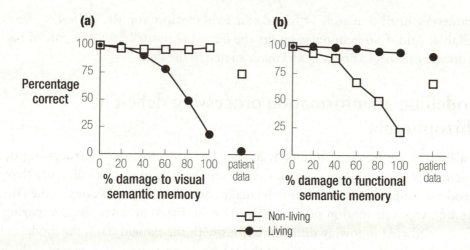

Figure 11.8 The effect of lesioning semantic units on the ability of the network to produce a name in response to a picture of an object or vice versa. The open squares show the performance when the stimuli are non-living objects and the filled circles the performance when the stimuli are living. (a) shows the effect of lesioning visual semantic units and (b) the effect of lesioning functional semantic units. In this simulation there were equal numbers of functional and visual units in semantics. (Based on Farah and McClelland 1991.)

reported by Warrington and Shallice who were impaired on living things scored an average of 3% on living and 74% on non-living. Two patients reported by Warrington and McCarthy (1983, 1987) who showed a deficit for non-living things scored 66% on non-living and 91% on living. The patient scores have been added to figure 11.7. The model's performance with 100% lesions mirrors the asymmetrical double dissociation in the patients with an implausible degree of accuracy!

It might seem likely that the asymmetry is the result of differential coding. Living things are represented largely by visual features, so their recall might be expected to be affected only by lesions to visual semantics; non-living things are represented by both visual and functional semantics so it might be expected that they would be affected by lesions to either part of semantics. A strength of connectionist models is that it is possible to test such assumptions directly. Farah and McClelland re-ran the simulation with a 2:1 ratio of visual to functional attributes for living things and a 1:2 ratio for non-living, with the result shown in figure 11.8. The basic cross-over is still found. However, the effects of lesions are now symmetrical. Damaging visual units affects living but not non-living; damaging functional affects non-living but not living. The fact that figure 11.7 is a better fit to the patient data than figure 11.8 suggests that the differential dependence on visual and functional attributes in the representation of living and non-living things, based on the results from the normal subjects, really does reflect storage in the patients. Of course, new patients may show different patterns. But the strength of a computational model is that by manipulating parameters until a match is found, an explanation for the difference may be available. And if no manipulation fits the data, the modeller will be forced back to the drawing board to find a model that can match the data.

Modelling an information processing deficit in schizophrenia

As a final example we will look at a model of an information processing deficit exhibited by schizophrenics. Again we will see that the model can do more than just reproduce the patient data. The model makes quantitative predictions of the effect of lesioning the information processing system in different ways. By comparing the deficits predicted following different lesions with the patient data, the model can be used to decide which component of the information processing system is the most likely source of the deficit in the patients.

Selective attention

Our sensory surfaces are continually bombarded by stimuli from different sources. Most of the time these are of no particular importance and our attention can safely wander from source to source. But occasionally a stimulus which carries some useful information will appear. An efficient information processing system needs to be able to lock onto a source which is providing important information and prevent distraction from rival sources which are providing uninformative stimuli. The mechanism which does this is called selective attention. It has been claimed that selective attention is one of the information processing mechanisms which is deficient in schizophrenics.

In one experimental paradigm for studying selective attention, known as Stroop, subjects are presented with words written in coloured ink. They must report the colour of the ink and try to ignore the word. The crucial observation is that people are slower to name the colour of a stimulus like RED than the colour of a stimulus like BED. (The response would be 'Green' in both cases if they were written in green ink.) The assumption is that despite the instructions to attend only to the colour of the ink, people have difficulty preventing themselves from processing the word. This has no effect when the word to be avoided is 'bed' but when the word to be ignored is 'red' confusion between the two colour names causes the response to be slowed. The extent to which subjects slow up when the to-be-ignored word is the name of a colour is a measure of the difficulty of following the instructions to concentrate on one dimension of the stimulus (the colour) and ignore the other (the word). Little interference from the confusing word implies good selective attention; a lot of interference implies poor selective attention.

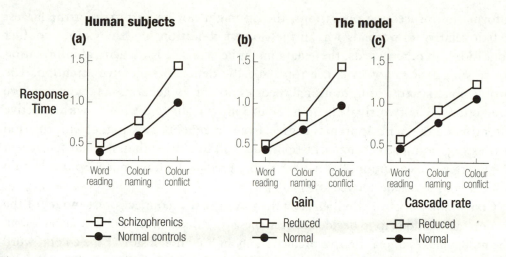

Figure 11.9 The reaction times in three conditions of a Stroop experiment. Panel (a) shows data from schizophrenics and control subjects. (The data are averaged across three experiments. For full details see Cohen and Servan-Schreiber 1992.) The filled symbols in panels (b) and (c) show a simulation of the normal data from (a) with a connectionist network. In (b) the schizophrenic data from (a) is simulated by lesioning the attention module in the network. In panel (c) the schizophrenic data in (a) is simulated by damage which affects all units in the network, not just those in the attention module. Based on Cohen and Servan-Schreiber 1992.)

One line of evidence that schizophrenics have problems with selective attention has come from experiments using the Stroop paradigm. The left hand panel of figure 11.9 shows data from three conditions of a Stroop experiment with normal subjects and schizophrenics. The first two data points in each set, labelled Word reading and Colour naming, show the reaction time in control conditions where the stimulus only has a single dimension, reading a colour word written in black ink and naming the colour of a row of letters that do not spell a word, respectively. The key condition is the third one labelled Colour conflict. This shows how long it takes to name the colour of the ink in which a conflicting colour word is written (saying 'green' in response to the word RED written in green ink). It can be seen that normal subjects are about 400 ms slower in this condition than they were at simple colour naming. But schizophrenics are particularly slow in this condition, showing about 700 ms of interference compared to the colour naming control.

A natural interpretation is that the increased interference shown by schizophrenics in panel (a) comes about because they suffer more confusing intrusion from the word when trying to name the colour of the ink than normals. Hence the inference that they have a problem with selective attention. However, the interpretation of this deficit is not straightforward. Schizophrenics are also slower in the control conditions. They are about 100 ms slower at reading words and about 200 ms slower at naming colours. If schizophrenics suffered from a general deficit which slowed all information processing operations, then it might not be surprising if the largest deficit relative to normals was in the slowest condition (i.e. the Colour conflict condition). In other words, these data might be evidence for a general information processing deficit, not evidence for a specific deficit of selective attention. The problem is that non-computational theories do not, in general, make quantitative predictions. The two rival theories 'Schizophrenics have difficulty with selective attention' and 'Schizophrenics suffer from a general slowing of information processing' both predict that schizophrenics will be slower than normal subjects in the interference condition. But neither theory predicts by how much. So the data do not allow us to decide between them.

Cohen and Servan-Schreiber (1992) showed that a connectionist model of the Stroop task could help to decide between these two alternatives. For any given lesion, the model makes a quantitative prediction about how much slower the colour–word conflict condition will be than the two control conditions. By lesioning the model in a way which corresponds to either specific damage to the attention system or to a general slowing of information processing throughout the network, it is possible to see which lesion predicts a pattern of deficit closest to that produced by the patients.

Modelling the Stroop task

Cohen and Servan-Schreiber used a connectionist model of the Stroop task developed by Cohen *et al.* (1990).[2] It is shown in figure 11.10. It operates in a somewhat circumscribed world in which the only stimuli are the words RED and GREEN each of which could be printed in either red or green ink. The network responds by naming the word or naming the colour of the ink. The colour of the stimulus excites the appropriate input unit in the Ink colour channel; the word excites the appropriate unit in the Word channel. Activation from the input units excites the hidden units in the corresponding channel and these in turn send excitation or inhibition to the response units. Because Stroop effects are reported in terms of reaction time differences between conditions, the model is designed to produce a reaction time. The output units have a threshold which must be exceeded before the network produces a response. In each processing cycle activity builds up in the output units, reflecting excitatory and inhibitory input from the word and colour channels. Reaction time is determined by the number of processing cycles required for the input to one of the response units to reach threshold. The Task demand units are the model's selective attention mechanism. These allow the network to attend to one stimulus dimension or the other. If the task is to name the colour of the ink, the Colour naming unit in the Task demand channel sends an excitatory input to the hidden units in the Ink

[2]The model was originally used to study the effects of practice on information processing by normal subjects. None of the components of the model were included to help model schizophrenic performance.

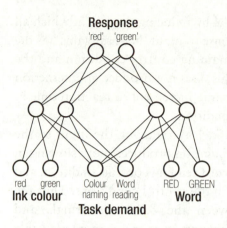

Figure 11.10 A network model which performs the Stroop task. It can read coloured words or name the colour of the ink in which they are written. ('Reading the word' is achieved if the output unit appropriate to the stimulus word is turned on; 'naming the colour' is achieved if the output unit appropriate to the colour of the stimulus is turned on.) The Task demand units are the mechanism of selective attention within the model. They bias the network to respond to one stimulus dimension or the other. (Based on Cohen, Dunbar and McClelland 1990.)

colour channel and an inhibitory input to the hidden units in the Word channel. If the task is to name the word, the Word reading unit performs the opposite function. The effect of this biasing is to make it more likely that the response units are triggered first by activation from the correct channel.

During training the model is given stimuli with only one dimension. That is, it learns to read the words RED and GREEN and name the colours red and green without competition from the other dimension. The strength of the connections builds up in the usual way using the backpropagation learning rule. The model has more training at word naming than colour naming so stronger connections develop in the word naming pathway. The model reproduces a wide range of effects shown in Stroop experiments with normal subjects (see Cohen *et al.* 1990). The filled circles in panels (b) and (c) of figure 11.9 show the performance of the model in the two control conditions and the conflict condition. It can be seen that the model can mimic both effects shown with normal subjects in panel (a): Colour naming is slower than reading, and conflicting words slow colour naming.

Lesioning the model

To mimic the performance of the schizophrenic subjects Cohen and Servan-Schreiber lesioned the model. They compared the result of lesioning it in two different ways: Reducing the rate at which all the units in the network increased their activity in response to an input, or just reducing the input from the Task demand units to the rest of the network. The first mimics a general deficit in information processing, the second a lesion to selective attention. In each case they set the level of the lesion to a point where it produced a slowing in the word reading control condition to match the slowing of the schizophrenics shown in panel (a). They then saw what the result of such a lesion was on performance in the second control condition, colour naming, and in the colour–word conflict condition.

Panel (c) shows the result of damaging the model by reducing the rate at which all units in the network increase their activity in response to input. Naturally this has the effect of increasing reaction time in the colour naming control condition and the conflict condition. However, it can be seen that this does not produce an interaction between normal and lesioned data. There is the same increment in reaction time in the other two conditions as in the word reading condition.

Panel (b) shows the result of lesioning the model by reducing the input to the network from the Task demand units. This manipulation produces more slowing in the colour naming control condition than in the word reading control condition, and even more slowing in the conflict condition than in the control conditions. Thus the model mimics the interaction observed between the data of normals and schizophrenics shown in panel (a). The simulation suggests that it is more plausible to attribute the deficit shown by schizophrenics in the Stroop task to damaged selective attention than to a general deficit in information processing.

Why does a reduction in input from the Task demand units to the hidden units cause the crucial interaction? There are two contributing factors. The first is that the weights in the colour naming channel are weaker than those in the word reading channel because the net was given less practice at the colour naming task. The result is that the input to the hidden units is lower in the colour naming channel. The second factor is the activation function of the hidden units. Cohen and Servan-Schreiber used the logistic activation function which produces a sigmoidal relation between the input to a unit and the resultant activity level. The reason why these two factors combine to produce the interaction shown in the data can be seen in figure 11.11. The input to a hidden unit is marked on the netinput axis. The solid vertical lines indicate the input in the unlesioned model. The input in the word channel is larger because the weights on the connections from the input units are larger in this channel (which is why word reading is faster than colour naming). The removal of a given amount of input from the Task demand units after they are lesioned is indicated on the netinput axis by ΔI. This produces the lower level of input marked by the dashed lines. This change in input produces the corresponding changes Δa_{wr} and Δa_{cn} in the activity of the hidden units. The change in input is the same in both channels but, because the activation function is sigmoidal, the consequence of this change on the activity of the hidden units is different. A change in an input which is on a steeper part of the curve will produce a larger change in activity, Δa. In figure 11.11 the input from the colour naming channel puts the hidden units on a steeper part of the curve than the input from the word naming channel so the loss of input from the Task demand units produces a larger drop in the activity of the colour naming hidden units. The level of activity of the hidden units determines how long the response units take to reach threshold and produce a response. Hence a reduction in input from the Task demand units produces a larger change in colour naming

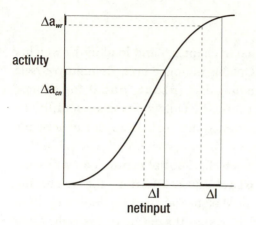

Figure 11.11 With a sigmoidal activation function the same change in netinput (ΔI) can cause a different change in activity (Δa). The change in the activity of the hidden units in the Word reading channel (Δa_{wr}) is less than that in the Colour naming channel (Δa_{cn}) because the input to the former is greater and so the units are operating at a less sensitive part of the activation function.

reaction time than in Word reading reaction time. In the Colour conflict condition the effect is exaggerated because the two channels are now in competition. Reducing the output of the Task demand units causes a reduction in the inhibition coming from the Word channel as well as a reduction in the excitation in the Colour channel. The result is the interaction shown in panel (b). Of course, the fact that it is the input to the Colour naming channel which is on the steeper part of the activation function is arbitrary. A shift in the base line would have the opposite effect with the larger change in the Word reading time. But the point is that the simulation shows how an interaction, like that found in the real data, can occur.

Further reading

The most detailed connectionist simulation of neuropsychological data to date is Plaut and Shallice (1993).

There have been connectionist models of many neuropsychological conditions other than those mentioned in this chapter. Some examples are Behrmann *et al.* (1991) and Farah *et al.* (1993).

Exercises with `tlearn`

In Chapter 8 you replicated aspects of the Plaut *et al.* model of reading aloud. In this exercise you will learn how to lesion this model and examine aspects of its behaviour when damaged. Although this modelling project does not correspond exactly to the lesioning work described in Plaut *et al.* (they lesioned an attractor network as opposed to a feedforward network), you will nevertheless be able reproduce a number of effects including the phenomenon of pronouncing irregularly spelt words as if they are regular which is observed in patients who are classified as surface dyslexic.

Lesioning the weights file

Open the **tlearn** project **plaut** that you used in chapter 8 and load in the weights file **plaut-899400.wts** using the Testing Options dialogue box. Remind yourself about the behaviour of the network on the training data (**plaut.data**) and the test data using the trained network. Remember to use the Output Translation utility to obtain interpretable output. Now lesion the trained network and test the network again.

To do this choose the Lesioning... option from the Special menu. You will see a dialogue box like that in figure 11.12. Select **plaut-899400.wts**—the weights file saved by **tlearn** at the end of training—in the Weight File: area by double-clicking on the file selection box. Then make sure that the rest of the dialogue box is the same as that shown in figure 11.12. The settings in figure 11.12 request 10% removal of the connections but no removal of nodes. This tells **tlearn** to randomly select 10% of the connections in the network and set them to zero (0.0). (Consult the User Manual in Appendix 3 for a more extensive discussion of the Lesioning utility.) Click on the Lesion button. **tlearn** will suggest a file name for the lesioned weights file, e.g. **plaut-899400-lesion.wts**. You can accept this name or suggest another one. Save the lesioned weights file. **tlearn** will also display the contents of the weights file itself. Again, if you want to learn about the format of this file, consult the User Manual.

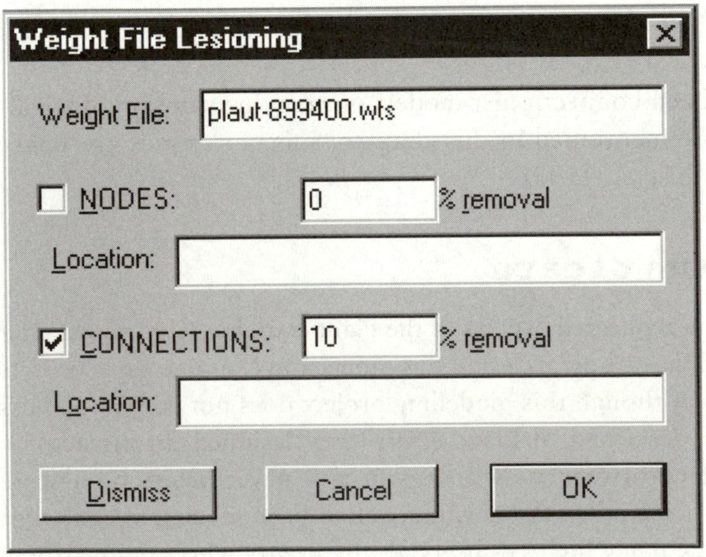

Figure 11.12. The Lesioning dialogue box.

Assessing the damage

Test the performance of the damaged network by loading in the damaged weights file—**plaut-899400-lesion.wts**—in the Testing Options dialogue box and examine the output on different sections of the training data and the test data. When we did this with the test data we found that both *have* and *mave* were now pronounced like *save*, replicating the behaviour of a surface dyslexic. Try experimenting with different levels of lesioning in the network to examine how it effects overall levels of performance. What levels of lesioning are required to bring the network to its knees and produce utter nonsense? You will discover that it is fairly robust even in the face of considerable damage.

12 *Mental representation: rules, symbols and connectionist networks*

The traditional approach to modelling cognitive processes is with rules operating on symbols. Since connectionist models have no direct representation of rules or symbols, some theorists argue that connectionist models operate, and thus offer explanations, at a level which is inappropriate for understanding cognition. Some attacks go further and suggest that there are types of rule which cannot be learnt by connectionist models and aspects of symbols which cannot be represented in them. Thus connectionism is not so much inappropriate, as fundamentally unsuitable. We will look at two examples of such problems. The first involves learning to apply a minority default to a novel stimulus. The claim is that connectionist models could never learn to do this because they are constrained to operate by analogy to previous experiences. Minority default mapping can be learnt with an appropriate training environment, but the limitations highlight networks' dependence on their training environment. The second is that many linguistic operations rely on localist representations of concepts. This is easily captured by symbolic representations but seems to be lost in the distributed representations of connectionism. However, we will suggest that symbolic attractors may perform the same functions in a connectionist network as the symbols of traditional cognitive psychology.

Learning minority default rules

When a network is tested on a pattern it has never seen before, its response reflects the similarity of the novel pattern to the patterns on which it has been previously trained. This mimics an important aspect of cognitive behaviour—the ability to generalise. If asked to read WUGGLE most people would respond with a pronunciation which reflected their knowledge of how to pronounce WAGGLE, WIGGLE and, if they had ever been a Boy Scout, WOGGLE. A connectionist net would behave the same way. The natural mechanism for generalisation offered by connectionist models is one of their attractions. But the bias which produces similar responses to similar stimuli can lead to a potentially serious problem. Cognitive mechanisms need to be flexible because domains like language are not consistent. Different responses are sometimes required to similar stimuli and, at other times, similar responses to different stimuli. The tendency of networks to produce similar responses to similar stimuli seems to deny them the required flexibility—hence this problem is known as the 'tyranny of similarity'.

In earlier chapters we have seen specific examples where networks *can* learn to overcome the similarity bias. Seidenberg and McClelland's network (chapter 8) learnt to pronounce exception words (such as HAVE) despite knowing many similar words with a different pronunciation (CAVE, RAVE, SAVE, WAVE etc). Plunkett and Marchman's network (chapter 9) which had learnt how to form the past tense of English could produce the same response (the default suffix -ed) to a range of quite different novel inputs. However, such achievements are not always easy. Extended training is often required to overcome the network's inherent bias to similarity. In contrast, a system with explicit rules has complete flexibility. If the letter string HAVE has an unusual pronunciation you just store that fact in a list of 'exception pronunciations'. If the past tense of an unknown verb is formed by adding -ed, you just store that fact as a rule and it can be applied to any novel stem.

The ease with which inflectional morphology can easily be described by a set of rules, and the difficulty which an analogy machine might have in extracting these rules from examples, have led to close scrutiny of the ability of connectionist networks to describe this area of cognition. We will examine one particular aspect of this—the minority default mapping problem. This poses no problem for a rule based system but appears to set an insoluble problem for analogy based systems like a connectionist network. The solution will clarify what a 'rule' looks like in a connectionist system. The conditions under which the problem can be solved will demonstrate limits on what a connectionist net can learn.

Default mapping

An inflection is a suffix added to a word to convey additional information such as number if it is a noun or tense if it is a verb. In English, -s indicating a plural noun and -ed indicating a past tense are examples of inflection. Adults and children respond in a predictable manner when asked to inflect a novel word. If asked to produce a plural of *wug* they are likely to say *wugs*. The traditional explanation is that this reflects the application of a default rule—that is, a rule which tells you what inflection to use with a word you have not heard before. The default represents an underlying regularity in the language—in this case, 'to form a plural add an -s'. The traditional account of inflection assumes a rule-governed process which is applied to all words, with a memory of exceptions which can override the application of the rule (see chapter 9, figure 9.1). Thus *boys* is produced by the rule, while *mans* is blocked by the existence of *men* in the memory of exceptional plural forms. The rule-governed process applies to any input so the application of the default when people are asked to inflect a novel form is to be expected.

In contrast, connectionist accounts of inflectional morphology assume a single mechanism for the processing of both regular and exception forms. Plunkett and Marchman showed that a connectionist model was capable of producing the English default past tense to novel forms—an input of *wug* produced the response *wugged*. However, in English, the past tense is relatively consistent. 86% of verbs have the regular past tense form. The network's capacity to inflect novel forms is shaped by its experience with the forms on which it has already been trained. The dominance of regular verbs in the system means that the production of the default response to a novel word is no problem for the network. A novel word is more likely to be similar to a regular word than to an irregular word. Thus the similarity bias will help the network to produce the same response to different novel inputs.

Minority defaults

This account suggests a potentially insoluble problem for a connectionist model of inflectional morphology. What would happen in a language in which the default option only applied to a *minority* of words? Now, surely, the tyranny of similarity would render the connectionist model incapable of producing the default assignment to a novel instance because a novel instance would usually be more like one of the exceptions than one of the words that took the default value.[1] Minority default assignment is, of course, no problem in a rule based system. The rule produces a response to any word which is not in the list of exceptions. It will work just the same whether 10% of the words are exceptions or 90%.

The concept of a minority default may be a difficult one to imagine for speakers of a language like English where defaults take the natural course of following the majority form, but they do exist. The 's' plural in German is the default process even though it forms a minority of the plurals in the language. That is, there are many ways of forming a plural in German, one of which is 'add an -s', but this only applies to about 5% of words. However, if you come across a word you do not know, you add an -s to form the plural.[2] Similarly the so-called 'sound' plural is the default in Arabic even though it applies to a minority of words.

---

[1]An 'exception' word is one that does not take the default value. So, in a language with a minority default, a majority of words can be exceptions.
[2]The situation in German is complex as there are sub-classes of default, such as, if it's feminine gender, add -en. However, many of the mistakes by German children learning to form plurals involve adding an inappropriate –s.

Producing a minority default appears to present an impossible challenge to connectionist models of inflectional morphology because of their similarity bias. However, Hare *et al.* (1995) have demonstrated that connectionist models *are* capable of producing a minority default response. To understand how they do this we will look at a simulation which extracts the essential components of a minority default task without including all the specific details of the language in which it occurs. Forrester and Plunkett (1994) trained a neural network to categorise input patterns into one of three classes. Imagine that the inputs are the verb stems in a language which has three ways of forming a past tense. One is, say, to lengthen the vowel, one is to make no change and one is to add -ed. The network must learn to classify each input pattern (i.e. verb stem) into its appropriate class so that the correct inflection can be applied. In this language there are only two phonological dimensions on which a word can vary. So an input pattern can be represented by a point on a two-dimensional phonological similarity plane. The distribution of the points is shown in figure 12.1. The majority of the points are clustered in two squares. The first inflectional rule applies to verbs in one square and the second to verbs in the other. In other words, verbs that sound alike tend to have the same rule for past tense formation. These two groups are the two 'exception' patterns within the language. A minority of words in the language are distributed outside these square regions. Since this is a model of minority default mapping, the inflectional rule for this third group, add -ed, constitutes the default mapping. How does a neural network trained on this distribution of points respond to novel patterns—that is, words corresponding to points in the two-dimensional plane on which it has not been trained?

The network contained two input units to specify the (x, y) coordinates of the input pattern, 20 hidden units, and three output units to classify the input patterns. The network was trained with the points shown in figure 12.1 and then tested on every point in the plane. Figure 12.2 shows the activity of the three output units for inputs in each possible position in the input space. Darker regions indicate higher

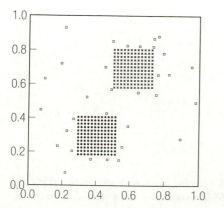

Figure 12.1 The minority default assignment problem. The axes represent phonological dimensions for the words in the training set. The position of a verb stem within this square indicates what it sounds like. The majority of verbs fall in one of the two clusters. A minority occupy random parts of the space outside these squares.

Output units

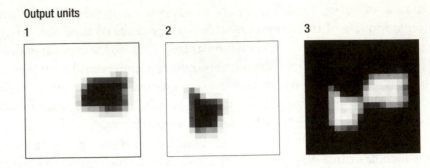

Figure 12.2   Each square shows the response of one output unit to all the points in the 2-dimensional space. Darker regions indicate higher activity. Output unit 3 represents the minority default response. The network has learnt to classify the majority of points in the plane as belonging to the minority default class.

activity. One unit identifies inputs falling in one exception region and one unit identifies input falling in the other. These would lead to the application of the appropriate exception suffixes. One unit identifies anything falling outside them and could lead to the application of the default suffix. So most of the points in the plane, which would correspond to most of the novel inputs given to the net, are treated as though they belong to the default class even though the training set contained a minority of forms in this class. The network has learnt how to apply the inflectional rules of the grammar in this language.

   This network behaves as if it had the rule: If a verb sounds like A, form a past tense by lengthening the vowel; if it sounds like B, do nothing; if it sounds like neither, add -ed. The key role is played by the hidden units. The weights to these from the input units construct an internal representation of the x and y coordinates at input. This produces a non-linear partitioning of the input space that corresponds to the partitioning required by the inflectional rules. However, there are limits to what hidden

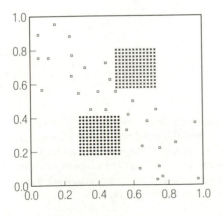

Figure 12.3   A training set where the verbs taking the default are confined to one part of the phonological space.

Output units

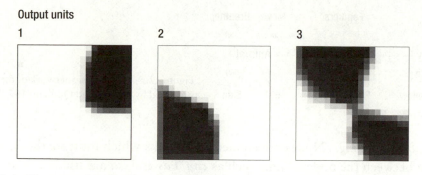

Figure 12.4 The network's classification of novel inputs when trained on the inputs shown in figure 12.3. Output unit 3 fails to capture all the points outside the domain of the two exception classes, which themselves expand to classify a greater proportion of the space.

units can do. We can illustrate this by changing the distribution of input cases to that in figure 12.3. The examples of the default mapping are confined to one diagonal region of the possible input space. Figure 12.4 shows how the network classifies the novel inputs in this case. A much greater proportion of the space is now treated as belonging to the two 'exception' classes. So a novel input in these regions would be given one of the 'exception' inflections and not the default. This demonstrates the tyranny of similarity back at work. Many points in the default space are now nearer to exemplars in one of the exception areas than to any of the default training exemplars. The network therefore allocates these areas to the corresponding exception response.

This illustrates a limitation to current connectionist networks—what they can do is determined by their training environment. A person learning the language modelled by Forrester and Plunkett could simply be told the rules that determined which inflection to apply to any verb. Connectionist networks can discover a matrix of weights from an appropriate set of learning experiences which will produce behaviour equivalent to the implementation of a rule. But at present they cannot implement the rule just by being told what it is. Since this ability is part of human cognitive skill a full description of the human cognitive system must have some way of doing this. If no way is found with connectionist nets they will remain, at best, a partial description of cognitive processes.

Symbols and distributed representations

The representations in connectionist networks are distributed. Many conventional models of cognitive processing use localist representations of concepts. The difference between these can be appreciated by considering the representation of knowledge in a semantic network. Figure 12.5 illustrates part of a typical semantic network representing knowledge about animals. Individual nodes stand for concepts such as

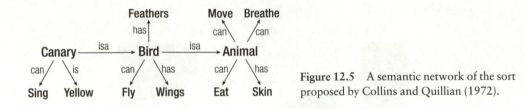

Figure 12.5   A semantic network of the sort proposed by Collins and Quillian (1972).

canary, bird or *wings*. Nodes are connected by links which indicate the conceptual relation between the nodes. Links such as *can, has* and *isa* are used to represent the knowledge that a canary is a bird or that birds have wings. In such a network the representation of knowledge is transparent. New facts can be added to the network by the addition of conceptual nodes or the creation of different types of links. Knowledge can be deleted from the network by removing links or nodes.

In contrast, in a connectionist network the representation of concepts is distributed. They are represented by patterns of activity across a collection of nodes. Individual connections do not represent conceptual relations. The connections between the nodes in a connectionist network are just excitatory or inhibitory. Change the connections and you change the knowledge. In contrast to a semantic network, it is impossible to add a new fact to the network's knowledge base by the addition of new nodes or connections. Individual facts are represented by collections of nodes and connections, often involving the entire network. New information has to be integrated with old information. Conversely, it is usually impossible to remove a single fact from the network by the deletion of a node or a connection. In contrast to the *transparency* of the semantic networks these distributed representations could be described as *opaque*—the meanings of the propositions are not readily interpretable by inspection.

Representing mental types

Fundamental to the classical view of cognition is the existence of discrete symbolic entities, like those in the network in figure 12.5, representing possible states of the world. On this view cognitive activity involves the manipulation of these symbols by rules. The interaction of symbols and rules to produce thought can be seen as similar to the interaction between words and syntax which produces language. The problem with connectionism, on this view, is that distributed representations of propositions lack the internal structure necessary to permit rule-governed transformations. Fodor and Pylyshyn (1988) argue that this counts decisively against connectionist approaches to cognition. We will look at two examples of cognitive processes which exemplify the problem. These demonstrate aspects of mental processes which Fodor and Pylyshyn referred to as their *systematicity* and *compositionality*.

Consider the compound expression <A&B>, linking the two concepts represented by the symbols <A> and <B> with the logical operation <&>. If <A&B> is true, so is <A>. It seems intuitively obvious that the human cognitive system operates in a way which preserves knowledge about components of compound expressions. If you know that Beatrice's car is fast and black, you know that it is fast, as well as fast and black. This holds however complex the knowledge. If you know that her car is fast and black and has lowered suspension and a dented front wing, you still know it's fast. The ability to draw such inferences presents no problem if the concepts are represented by localist symbols. <A> remains identifiable as <A> however many things it is linked to with <&>. But such inferences would not appear to be a natural result in a system, like a connectionist network, which represents concepts in a distributed manner. The problem is that the pattern representing the concept <A> will not, in general, be an identifiable sub-part of the pattern representing <A&B> or <A&B&C&D> or whatever. So knowing that <A&B> is not likely to provide any information directly about <A>.

A related problem appears when we consider understanding the relationship of sub-parts of different propositions. If you know that 'Beatrice's car is fast' and that 'Beatrice lost her driving licence', you have no difficulty in imagining that the pieces of knowledge may relate to the same person. This inference is easy to explain in a model which represents each concept by an identifiable localist symbol. In such a system a symbolic *type* exists for Beatrice, like the entry for <canary> in figure 12.5. Each time the *token* <Beatrice> appears in a statement it can be checked against the *type* <Beatrice>, whatever the context in which the token appeared. If the new information is consistent with information already held there the tokens can be assumed to refer to the same type, and therefore to represent information about the same thing. But consider a distributed representation of the two propositions. Something identifiable as <Beatrice> may not be an identifiable subpart of the proposition 'Beatrice's car is fast'. So it has no identifiable relation to the appearance of <Beatrice> in any other sentence. No symbol appears to exist for <Beatrice> in the connectionist network which learns that 'Beatrice's car is fast'. How then can a connectionist network capture the intuition that one and the same person is involved in each proposition if it has no symbol to represent her?

Symbolic attractors

This seems like a fairly intractable problem. However, we saw in chapter 9 that simple recurrent networks trained to predict the next word in a sentence are able to create structured representations. For example, when Elman (1990) analysed the hidden unit representations of individual words, he found that they grouped together according to their grammatical category (see figure 9.11). Furthermore, the same word in different contexts produced similar patterns of activity across the hidden units. For example, the internal representation of <John> in 'John sees Mary' was very similar to the internal representation of <John> in 'Mary sees John'. In this case, the two examples of <John> produce internal representations that are more similar to each other than they are to internal representations of other words. The differences between the patterns produced by <John> on different occasions reflected the role of the word in the sentence, subject in one case, object in another. On this account, we should expect different tokens to produce activity in the same region of mental space. So the 'symbol' of the traditional account (i.e. the type to which the tokens refer) is replaced by a 'region of mental space'. The region has an internal structure such that the precise pattern of activity following the presentation of a specific token will reflect the grammatical role of that token in the sentence.

We saw examples in chapters 7, 8 and 11 of how networks with recurrent connections can form basins of attraction so that inputs within a given range will eventually settle on an identical output. Different attractor basins capture different sets of inputs (see figure 7.10 or 11.3). To the extent that attractor basins are insensitive to small variations in input, they could be considered to have a symbolic quality. Hare *et al.* (1995) showed that an attractor network was able to exhibit default-like behaviour when the inputs to the network did not resemble exception words. The attractor basin for default inflection captured all the inputs that were not captured by exception attractor basins. Similarly, Plaut *et al.* showed how attractor basins could represent the lexical entries for words in the mental dictionary (see chapter 8). Perhaps the connectionist equivalent of a symbol is a *stable point of attraction in a recurrent network*. Rule-governed behaviour might be the trajectory through a series of attractor basins which a network passes through in performing a task such as processing a sentence (see figure 9.10).

Levels of explanation

One argument against the connectionist approach is not to deny that cognition is carried out by neural networks in the brain but to say that studying them is pointless. The networks merely implement rules and symbols in a somewhat opaque way. If one is interested in rules and symbols one should study them directly. A possible counter to this is that although one can study the rules and symbols directly one will never discover anything more than what they are. The connectionist approach may, possibly, show why they are as they are. For example, in the section 'Learning minority default rules' we discovered why a minority default rule could be learnt in a language with one distribution of words and not in a language with a different one. At the level of rules this would just be a fact; at the level of a connectionist model one can see why.

The relative merits of the traditional and connectionist approaches to cognition are affected by what different people see as a plausible scientific theory of the mind. For example, Dennett (1988) characterises the classical symbolic tradition as seeking pure, universal theories. But he suggests that evolution may not have made life quite so simple for cognitive scientists:

The mind might turn out to be more like a gadget, an object that one should not expect to be governed by deep mathematical laws but nevertheless a designed object, analysable in functional terms: ends and means, cost and benefits, elegant solutions on the one hand and on the other, shortcuts, jury rigs, and cheap ad hoc fixes (Dennett 1988, p.286).

No connectionist researcher believes that a single network architecture is adequate for modelling the variety of human cognition. Connectionists investigate the properties of different kinds of networks and the diverse potential across networks for performing different cognitive tasks. Nevertheless, the general characterisation of all connectionist networks as being statistical inference machines seems correct. So, to the extent that explanations of the human cognitive system require the postulation of innate representations that are not available from experience, connectionist models may require the addition of symbolic mechanisms.

Further reading

Two well-known attacks on the adequacy of connectionist models on the grounds that they lack rules and symbols are Fodor and Pylyshyn (1988) and Pinker and Prince (1988). An account of Fodor and Pylyshyn's arguments which may be more accessible to non-philosophers than the original is given in chapter 7 of Bechtel and Abrahamsen (1991).

The issue of how the representations within connectionist networks should be understood is explored by a variety of pro- and anti-connectionists in Smolensky (1988).

An early example of the debate about whether connectionist networks operate at an appropriate level for understanding cognitive processes can be found in the exchange between Broadbent and Rumelhart and McClelland in the *Journal of Experimental Psychology: General* (Broadbent 1985; McClelland and Rumelhart 1985; Rumelhart and McClelland 1985).

Further reading on minority defaults can be found in Clahsen *et al.* (1992), Marcus *et al.* (1995), Plunkett and Nakisa (1997), and Nakisa *et al.* (1998).

For a taxonomy of 'ways to be innate' see Elman *et al.* (1996).

13   *Network models of brain function*

The belief that models of cognitive processes should be brain-like is central to connectionism. Connectionist networks are brain-like at the level of the computational units: These are simple, there are many of them, the way in which the network operates is determined by the strength of the connections between the units, and the network learns and stores information by altering the strengths of the connections. In most connectionist models however, the overall structure has not been related to any particular brain area. Sufficient quantitative information now exists about the structure of certain brain areas, and the flow of information to and from them, to build neural network models which have structural as well as neuronal plausibility. In this chapter we will look at a model of episodic memory formation which has a structure based on the hippocampal system, and a model of visual object recognition which is based on the organisation of information processing in one of the visual pathways in the primate brain. These involve the learning mechanisms we have seen already—pattern association, autoassociation, competitive learning. But they do so in models which bear a direct relationship to known brain structures.

Memory formation in the hippocampus

The hippocampus is a structure buried deep in the medial surface of the temporal lobe in the human brain. Its position is shown in the coronal section (i.e. a cut vertically downwards) roughly in line with the ears in the upper part of figure 13.1. The lower part of figure 13.1 shows the structure of the hippocampus in more detail. It consists of two interlocking sheets of cells. One is called the cornu ammonis (CA) (because of its resemblance to a ram's horn); the other is called the dentate gyrus (DG).

   The hippocampus is involved in the learning of new information. A dramatic demonstration of this followed an operation on a patient known in the neuropsychological literature by the initials HM. To control intractable epilepsy he underwent bilateral removal of parts of the temporal lobe including the hippo-

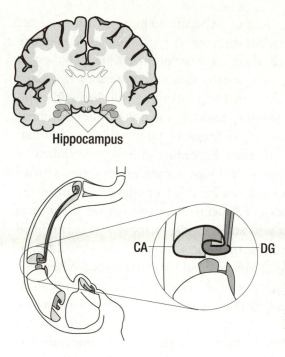

Figure 13.1 Upper: Coronal section of the human brain with the position where it cuts through the hippocampus in each hemisphere indicated. Lower: Detailed structure of the hippocampus, showing the cornu ammonis (CA) and the dentate gyrus (DG).

campus. The operation was successful in controlling the epilepsy but unfortunately led to the patient acquiring acute anterograde amnesia. After the operation he could not form consciously accessible memories of events which occurred in his everyday life. For example, he never recognised the medical staff who looked after him, even though he saw them every day. There is evidence about the function performed by the hippocampus in memory formation, about the cortical areas which project to it and about the neuronal networks within it. So it is possible to produce a theory of how some memory functions might be performed by the networks found in this brain region.

The role of the hippocampus in memory formation

There is a large literature on the memory deficits of patients who have suffered damage to the hippocampus. Although this is complex in detail, some general conclusions are possible. First, the effects of damage to the hippocampus are primarily on the ability to form new memories. Information acquired some time prior to the damage can still be used. Second, within new learning, the effects are selective. Hippocampal damage in humans leads to failure to form new episodic memories, but the formation of procedural memories continues.

Episodic memory involves recording of the events which make up day to day experience. It requires the rapid formation of associations between the elements of a particular episode. The result is the formation of a specific memory which can later be recalled by cueing with part of the original memory. A typical episodic memory might involve information about the place where an event occurred, the people who were there and what they said. Cueing someone by reminding them of the place would bring the whole episode back to mind, enabling them to recall the people and what they said. In contrast, procedural memory involves the gradual development over many related experiences of a composite memory from which individual contributing experiences cannot be easily recalled. Procedural memory is typified by skill acquisition. A tennis player gradually develops a memory for the actions required to execute an accurate serve but will not be able to remember most of the thousands of individual practice serves (i.e. specific episodes) that went into acquiring it. The contrast between procedural and episodic memory was exemplified by HM. He could do jigsaw puzzles, and if shown the same one again would do it more quickly. But each time it was shown to him he would say that he had never seen it before. He could form a procedural memory of the puzzle which could aid in its solution, but he formed no consciously accessible record of the occasions on which he had solved it.

The conclusion from the study of such patients is that the hippocampus is involved in the *formation* of certain sorts of memories rather than being the actual site of storage in the long term since access to information acquired long before the damage is preserved. The type of memory in which the hippocampus is involved would seem to be that requiring the combination of information from different sources to form consciously retrievable memories of specific events or facts. There may be temporary storage of these memories in the hippocampus, but since retrograde amnesia is temporally graded, its role as a storage location diminishes with time.

Information flow to and from the hippocampus

As the left hand side of figure 13.2 shows, the hippocampus receives input from the parahippocampal gyrus and entorhinal cortex. These areas receive input from virtually all association areas including those in the parietal, temporal and frontal lobes. So the hippocampus has available information from different sensory pathways which has already been cortically processed. There is a divergent set of backprojecting pathways from the hippocampus (via the subiculum and entorhinal cortex) to the cortical areas which provide inputs to the hippocampus. These are shown in the right hand side of figure 13.2. In addition, there are connections with sublimbic structures. These probably provide general regulation of activity in the hippocampus, making it more or less likely to operate at any particular time.

This anatomical picture is consistent with the functional role for the hippocampus

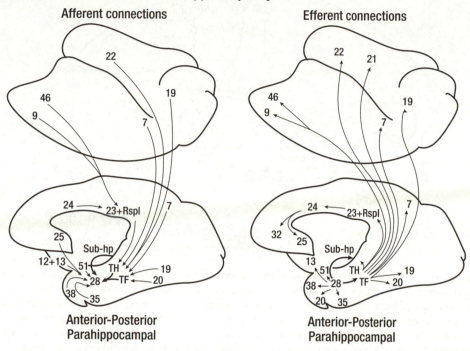

Figure 13.2 Connections between the primate hippocampus and the neocortex (from van Hoesen 1982). A medial view of the macaque brain is shown below (i.e. what would be exposed following a cut down the middle of the brain from back to front) with a lateral view (i.e. an outside surface) above (inverted). The left hand side of the figure shows that the hippocampus receives its inputs from many neocortical areas via the parahippocampal gyrus and the entorhinal cortex, area 28. The return projections to the neocortex (shown on the right) pass through the same areas. Cortical areas 19, 20 and 21 are visual association areas, 22 is auditory association cortex, 7 is parietal association cortex and 9, 46, 12 and 13 are areas of frontal association cortex.

suggested by the study of patients suffering from hippocampal damage. The hippocampus receives information from many different cortical areas. So it would be a suitable place for combining information about different aspects of an experience such as the place where it occurred (from parietal cortex), the people who were there (from temporal cortex) and what they said (from language areas). The hippocampus projects back to cortical areas, so it would not need to be the long-term depository for the memories which were formed there initially.

The internal structure of the hippocampus

The cellular structure of the hippocampus is shown in figure 13.3. This represents the exposed face of a slice through the hippocampus, like that shown in the lower part of

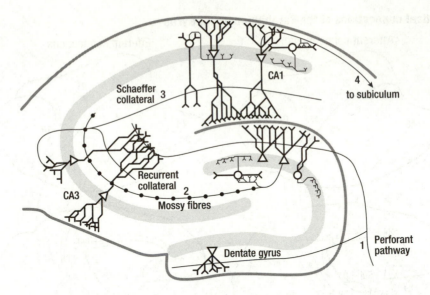

Figure 13.3 A schematic representation of connections within the hippocampus. Input comes through the perforant path (1) which synapses with the dendrites of the dentate granule cells and also with the apical dendrites of the CA3 pyramidal cells. The dentate granule cells project via the mossy fibres (2) to the CA3 pyramidal cells. The recurrent collateral system of the CA3 cells is indicated by the single axon labelled Recurrent collateral. The CA3 pyramidal cells project via the Schaeffer collateral (3) to the CA1 pyramidal cells, which in turn have connections (4) via the subiculum back to other cortical areas.

figure 13.1. The two interlocking U-shaped strings of stippled dots represent the cell bodies in the dentate gyrus and cornu ammonis. Input to the hippocampus comes on the perforant path. Information processing within the hippocampus occurs in three sequential stages—the dentate gyrus and two areas of the cornu ammonis, known as CA3 and CA1. At each stage a few representative cells and their connections are shown, greatly enlarged. To develop a computational theory of memory formation in the hippocampus it is necessary to know quantitative details of the connectivity in the dentate gyrus → CA3 → CA1 processing route. Since estimates for the rat are more detailed than those for humans we will give the numbers for the rat. These are somewhat larger in humans, especially for the number of CA1 cells.

The dentate gyrus

Input to the hippocampus from other neocortical areas comes along a group of axons known as the perforant path. This synapses with cells in the dentate gyrus. There are about 10^6 dentate granule cells. A number of the dentate gyrus cells are shown in figure 13.3, greatly enlarged, with their dendrites synapsing onto the perforant path input. An example of other cell types in the dentate gyrus is also shown. These do not synapse with incoming axons, but form inhibitory interconnections between cells in the gyrus.

The output from the dentate gyrus is carried by the mossy fibres to cells in the CA3 region. The excrescences on these fibres (which have the appearance of mosses, hence the name) are the synapses on the CA3 cells. A typical mossy fibre connects to about 15 different CA3 pyramidal cells. As there are about 300 000 CA3 pyramidal cells, each of them receives about 50 mossy fibre inputs. The probability of the output from any given dentate granule cell reaching any given CA3 cell is thus very low. There is also a direct input from the perforant path to the CA3 dendrites. There are many more (about 4000) of these inputs onto each CA3 cell, although these may be much weaker than the dentate granule cell inputs via the mossy fibres.

The CA3 region
Two of the CA3 cells have been enlarged to show the synapses onto their dendrites from the mossy fibres and the perforant path. The output from the CA3 cells branches. (Branching axons are called collaterals.) One branch forms a set of recurrent connections, synapsing back to the dendrites of other CA3 cells. The other, called the Schaeffer collateral, carries the output from the CA3 cells to CA1.

Of the roughly 16 000 synapses onto each CA3 pyramidal cell, about 12 000 are provided by the recurrent collateral axons from the CA3 cells themselves. These are so widely distributed that each CA3 cell can transmit information to most other CA3 cells within 3 synaptic steps. The CA3 system therefore is one in which intrinsic, recurrent excitatory connections are, at least numerically, the dominant source of input.

The CA1 region
There are about 400 000 CA1 cells. Each cell receives input from the Schaeffer collaterals coming from CA3. Output from the CA1 cells leaves the hippocampus and returns to the neocortical areas which provided the hippocampal perforant path inputs.

Summary
The flow of information within the hippocampal system (the entorhinal cortex, areas DG, CA3 and CA1 of the hippocampus, and the subiculum), and between the hippocampal system and the neocortex, is shown schematically on the left of figure 13.4. The solid lines show the flow of information from cortex to the hippocampal system; the dashed lines show the projections back to the cortical areas which originally supplied it with information. On the right of the figure the projections of typical cells within each area are shown.

A computational theory of hippocampal operation

The memory deficits which follow hippocampal damage imply that it is involved in the formation of episodic memories. Episodic memory involves the combination of

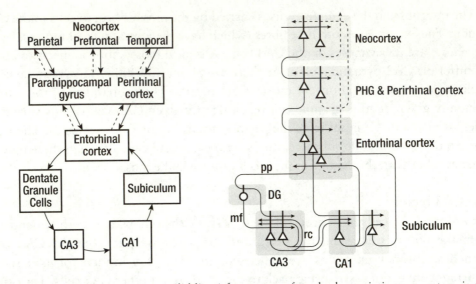

Figure 13.4 Forward connections (solid lines) from areas of cerebral association neocortex via the parahippocampal gyrus and perirhinal cortex, and the entorhinal cortex, to the hippocampus. Backprojections (dashed lines) via the parahippocampal gyrus to the neocortex. There is great convergence in the forward connections down to the single network in the CA3 pyramidal cells and great divergence again in the backprojections. Left: block diagram. Right: more detailed representation of some of the principal excitatory neurons in the pathways. Δ represents pyramidal cell bodies; ○ represents dentate granule cells. The thick lines above the cell bodies represent the dendrites; the thinner lines with arrow heads the axons. Abbreviations: DG: dentate granule cells. mf: mossy fibres. PHG: parahippocampal gyrus. pp: perforant path. rc: recurrent collateral of the CA3 hippocampal pyramidal cells.

information about different aspects of an event into a single pattern which can be recalled when cued by some component of the original input. The formation must be very quick because an event or episode might only last a few seconds. The internal structure of the DG → CA3 → CA1 processing route in the hippocampus suggests the basis for a computational theory of how episodic memory might be formed. This theory is still tentative. The aim is to illustrate how a neural network model can be based on real brain structure rather than to claim that this particular model is correct.

Sparse input from the dentate gyrus

The dentate granule cells which send an input to CA3 produce a sparse representation of the incoming signal to the hippocampus. That is, any given input pattern excites relatively few CA3 cells. In consequence different input patterns are likely to activate different sets of CA3 neurons. A sparse input enables an autoassociator to store more memories. One factor which limits the number of memories that can be stored in associative networks is the number of inputs per neuron (see Rolls and

Treves 1998). This number cannot be increased beyond about 20 000 in the brain, so the best way to maximize the capacity of the associative memory is to ensure a sparse representation at input. It appears that this strategy is used in the hippocampus.

The hypothesis is that the perforant path → dentate granule cell system acts as a competitive learning network. Competitive learning removes redundancy (see chapter 7), so the output from the DG system will be less correlated and more categorised than the inputs to it from the perforant path. Thus overlapping signals on the perforant path will be separated before they reach CA3. The role for the DG–mossy fibre system, then, would appear to be to maximise the separation of patterns reaching the CA3 autoassociation system. Recordings from CA3 cells in the primate hippocampus show that the representations of different events do tend to be uncorrelated.

Autoassociation in CA3

An episodic memory requires arbitrary sets of concurrent activities to be associated quickly and stored as one event which can be retrieved by a partial cue consisting of a sub-component of the memory. If you meet John in the street and he asks you whether you've seen Bill, you might remember the encounter even though the event only lasted a few seconds. Later, if someone asks you if you've seen John recently, you will recall where you met him and what he asked you. The ability to recall a complex memory with a cue which is a sub-component of the whole is a property of autoassociative memory (see chapter 4). The recurrent connections which are a prominent feature of the CA3 region mean that this area could act as an auto-associative memory. A new event to be memorised would be represented as a firing pattern of CA3 pyramidal cells. The pattern would be stored using associatively modifiable synapses on the recurrent connections. Subsequently retrieval of a whole representation could be initiated by the activation of some part of it.

Studies of long term potentiation (LTP) show that Hebbian synaptic modification operates over a period of about 1 s.[1] Since Hebb-like learning is known to be implemented in networks in many parts of the hippocampus, including the CA3 recurrent collateral network, the hippocampus could operate sufficiently quickly to create 'snapshots' of episodes. Within each episode there would be insufficient time to reorganise the information. Each event or episode would necessarily be stored as simple associations between the different cortical inputs which occurred during it.

The collection of events forming an episodic memory must be kept separate from other episodes, even if they are somewhat similar, so that what happened on a single occasion can later be recalled correctly. This type of memory formation may be achieved by relatively large synaptic changes which will overwrite other information.

---

[1]Learning by Hebbian association is described in chapter 3.

The ability of such a store to hold a particular piece of information will decline with time as it becomes overwritten in its turn by the large synaptic changes accompanying the storage of new episodes. Such memory for individual events may be contrasted with the type of storage which leads to the formation of procedural memories. In these many related memories are amalgamated to form a knowledge base about a particular situation. This is best performed by a succession of small adjustments to a developing semantic network so that prior knowledge stored in the network is not lost. Individual memories may be difficult to extract from such a store, but the resultant knowledge may last indefinitely.

Non-specific inputs

It seems unlikely that the hippocampus stores everything that occurs, second by second. If it did, its storage capacity would soon be exhausted, and most of the information it held would be of little interest to the organism. In an effective episodic memory, memory formation would be more likely to occur when something new happened in the environment, or when an event was accompanied by an emotional or motivational response. Events which were accompanied by pleasure, pain or novelty would be recorded, while the sensory stimulation arising from the repetitive events of daily life would not. The relatively non-specific subcortical inputs to the hippocampus may be involved in threshold setting. They would make it likely that memories would be stored when the organism was in an aroused state, but not when little of interest was occurring. Information about rewards and punishments could be incorporated into the hippocampal memory system via the inputs to the entorhinal cortex from structures such as the amygdala, which are involved in processing information about emotions.

A neural network simulation of hippocampal operation

This theory of hippocampal function in episodic memory formation was tested by simulating the real network summarised in figure 13.4 with the network model shown in figure 13.5. The aim was to see whether the network could store a large number of unrelated patterns, after only a single presentation of each one, and retrieve them from partial cues.

Figure 13.5 shows the number of units in each part of the network and the number of modifiable connections per unit from each input pathway. The entorhinal cortex is represented by 600 units. The dentate gyrus is represented by 1000 units, each with 60 modifiable connections from the entorhinal cortex. CA3 is represented by 1000 units, each with 200 recurrent modifiable connections, 120 modifiable connections from the entorhinal cortex (via the perforant path) and 4 modifiable connections from the dentate gyrus (via the mossy fibres). CA1 is represented by 1000 units each

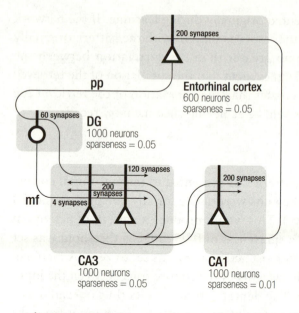

Figure 13.5 A neural network simulation of the hippocampus. The numbers of units, the numbers of modifiable connections per unit, and the sparseness for each stage of the network are shown. DG: dentate gyrus; mf: mossy fibres; pp: perforant path.

with 200 modifiable connections from CA3. The CA1 output synapses back onto the dendrites of the units in entorhinal cortex, with 200 modifiable connections per unit. These numbers reflect the relative frequency of neurons and connections per neuron in different regions of the rat hippocampus. They are scaled down to fit within a simulation of reasonable size, yet kept sufficiently large that finite size effects due to small numbers of units are not a limiting factor.

The sparseness of the representation in each area is also shown. Sparseness is a measure of the proportion of units which will be active in that area in response to an input. This was set to 0.05 for all areas except CA1 where it was set to 0.01. These figures are based on experimental work which shows that when primates or rats are involved in spatial memory tasks typically only 1–5% of cells in various parts of the hippocampus are active. The way that a given level of sparseness was achieved in practice will be described later.

The performance measure

The operation of the network was tested by giving a single presentation of a large number of random binary patterns to the entorhinal cortex. Activity passed around the network and connection strengths were changed using a Hebbian learning rule. Parts of each pattern were then presented to the entorhinal cortex as retrieval cues. The ability of the system to retrieve the whole pattern was assessed by measuring the resultant pattern of firing of the entorhinal units after the partial cue had activated the network. The performance measure used was to correlate the pattern of firing in entorhinal cortex produced by activation of the network by the retrieval cue with the pattern of firing which had been presented originally during learning. If the network had learnt nothing, the correlation of the retrieved pattern with the pattern originally presented during learning would be no greater than the correlation between the retrieval cue and the original pattern. To the extent that the correlation of the retrieved pattern with the original pattern was greater than the correlation of the retrieval cue with the original pattern, the system would be achieving cued memory recall.

Running the model

To train the model a random binary pattern was presented to the entorhinal cortex. The sparseness was such that 5% of the units were active for any one pattern (i.e. 30 of the 600 entorhinal units were active). This would produce a pattern of activity in the dentate granule units. To achieve a sparseness of 0.05 in DG a threshold was set so that the activity of all except the 5% most active units was set to zero. A Hebbian learning rule was applied to change the weights of the connections between the input and the DG units which were active. The dentate granule units thus operated as a competitive network, producing different sets of active units for each input from the entorhinal cortex. The output of the DG units activated the CA3 units, which operated as an autoassociation network because of the recurrent collaterals. A threshold was set, as before, to achieve 5% sparseness. Hebbian adjustment of synapses took place between the dendrites and the recurrent collaterals. During recall, the CA3 units changed state as the activity cycled 15 times around the recurrent connections, allowing the autoassociation effect to lead the network towards an attractor state. The output from CA3 excited the CA1 units. A threshold was set to ensure a 1% level of sparseness in the representation, and then Hebbian modification of the connections between the input from CA3 and the CA1 dendrites occurred. The output of CA1 finally provided input back to the entorhinal cortex. Here Hebbian weight adjustment took place between the output from CA1 and the original input pattern to entorhinal cortex, to implement pattern association in this pathway. The four stages of information processing, then, are competitive learning in DG, autoassociation in CA3, competitive learning in CA1 and pattern association between CA1 and entorhinal cortex.

Performance of the network

The network was given 100 random patterns to learn.[2] Recall cues were given which consisted of fragments of the original patterns. Typical performance of the network

---

[2] A crucial determinant of the number of memories an autoassociation network can hold is the number of recurrent synapses per neuron. This simulation has about 1/60th of the number of recurrent synapses per CA3 neuron that there are in a rat. So asking the model to learn 100 patterns is equivalent to asking a rat to store 6000 episodic memories.

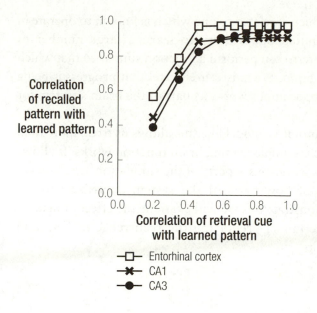

Correlation of recalled pattern with learned pattern

Correlation of retrieval cue with learned pattern

—□— Entorhinal cortex
—✗— CA1
—●— CA3

Figure 13.6 Performance of the network simulating hippocampal episodic memory retrieval. The network has been presented with 100 patterns. Performance is assessed by comparing the correlation between the recalled pattern and the pattern present during learning (vertical scale) with the correlation of the retrieval cue with the pattern present during learning (horizontal scale). The comparison is made for the complete network (pattern retrieved in entorhinal cortex) and in two earlier stages, CA3 and CA1. Successive data points moving from left to right along each curve correspond to retrieval cues which are progressively more similar to the original pattern.

is shown in figure 13.6. The horizontal axis shows the correlation between the retrieval cue and the pattern which was originally presented to be learned. Thus successive data points moving to the right show performance with cues which consist of more of the original pattern. The vertical axis shows the correlation between the retrieved pattern and the pattern which was originally presented to be learnt. The data for the pattern retrieved in the entorhinal cortex (open squares) lie above the (0,0) to (1,1) diagonal. This shows that the entorhinal firing which results from processing of the retrieval cue by the network (i.e. the recalled pattern) is closer to the originally learnt pattern than is the retrieval cue. That is, the network achieves cued recall. With a retrieval cue which correlates at about 0.4 with the original pattern, recall is perfect. The patterns of firing in the CA3 and CA1 stages during retrieval, relative to their firing to the whole input pattern, are also shown. These curves show that with partial cues, before performance asymptotes, recall gets better from CA3 to CA1 to entorhinal cortex. The reason is that after CA3 there are two sets of associative synapses, one onto CA1 and another onto entorhinal cortex, and each set can contribute to improve recall. This illustrates the value of a multistage recall process.

Figure 13.6 shows that a neural network based on the structure of the hippocampus can store a large number of unrelated patterns with a single presentation of each, and can retrieve the stored patterns from fragments of them. The immediate interest of a simulation like this is, of course, that it works. A network with the connectivity and general structure of a specific brain area, the hippocampus, presented with inputs which produce a similar sparseness of activity to that found there, using a learning algorithm which is related to one which is known to operate in this area, and given the same limited opportunity to learn a large number of memories (one presentation per pattern) can perform a function similar to that which the area appears to perform in the brain. We must, surely, feel that progress is being made in understanding how the hippocampus works as part of the brain's system for memory formation.

However, an implementable quantitative model like this allows us to do more than just show that a particular approach to implementing brain function works. It allows us to see how performance changes as various aspects of the simulation are changed. Thus we can get a clearer view of how parts of the system contribute to the performance of the whole. To demonstrate this we will examine the effect of making changes to the CA3 region in the model—removing the recurrence in CA3 and changing the nature of the CA3 units.

The role of CA3 recurrence

The role of the recurrent connections in CA3 can be examined by switching recurrence off and re-running the simulation. The result is shown in figure 13.7. If activity is not allowed to cycle round the recurrent connections in the CA3 units, the CA3 state during retrieval is close to the diagonal line running from (0, 0) to (1, 1). That is, the firing is no closer to the originally learnt pattern than it is cue. In consequence the recall at the later stages is worse than it was in figure 13.6 where recurrence was on.

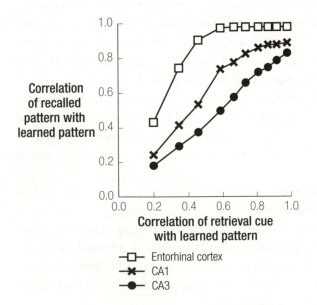

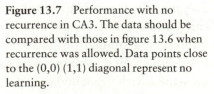

Figure 13.7 Performance with no recurrence in CA3. The data should be compared with those in figure 13.6 when recurrence was allowed. Data points close to the (0,0) (1,1) diagonal represent no learning.

Binary vs linear threshold units in CA3

The CA3 units have binary threshold activation functions.[3] That is, they do not fire if the activity level is below threshold and they fire at their maximum rate if the activity level is above threshold. It is straightforward to model the units with a different kind of activation function such as a linear threshold function. With these, provided the activation is above threshold, the firing rate rises linearly with the activation level. (A linear threshold activation function is shown in figure 1.4(b) of chapter 1.) Figure 13.8 shows the result of a simulation where the network was presented with 50 patterns.

With a binary threshold activation function, performance in entorhinal cortex is better than it was in figure 13.6 because the memory load is lighter. But the change in activation function prevents the network from performing useful retrieval. The data for the simulation where the units have a linear threshold (the filled circles) lie around the diagonal line from (0,0) to (1,1) showing that the retrieved pattern is no more similar to the pattern presented during learning than the retrieval cue. The system no longer produces recall from a partial cue. This surprising result shows the value of quantitative modelling. Without it, it is unlikely that the significance of the activation function would have been realised. With the threshold linear activation function each memory produces a graded pattern of activity in CA3. But this higher resolution for individual memories is at the expense of the number of memories which can be stored. For the hippocampus, it appears that the greatest number of memories can be stored and retrieved correctly if CA3 operates to store binary

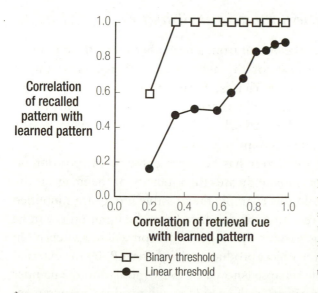

Correlation of recalled pattern with learned pattern

Correlation of retrieval cue with learned pattern

☐ Binary threshold
● Linear threshold

Figure 13.8 Recall in entorhinal cortex with a memory load of 50 patterns. The squares show performance when the CA3 units have a binary threshold activation function. The circles show performance when the CA3 units are given a linear threshold activation function.

[3]The network learns by Hebbian association, not gradient descent, so a continuous activation function is not necessary.

patterns. This theoretical analysis suggests that it would be worth examining the firing patterns of CA3 neurons to see whether they do demonstrate binary encoding. Do they tend to have either a relatively low firing rate or a relatively high rate (in practice for CA3 neurons perhaps 20 spikes/s) with little gradation in between?

Invariant visual pattern recognition in the inferior temporal cortex

We can recognise the face of someone we know, whether they are near or far away, seen full face or at an angle. The pattern of stimulation produced on the retina is quite different in each case. So the visual system must have built a representation of that face which allows recognition to occur independently of the size of the image, its position on the retina or the angle of view. We perform visual recognition so effortlessly that this may not seem to be a problem. But showing how face or object recognition could be performed independent of viewpoint has proved very difficult for cognitive science. To give some feel for the problem we will show that the response of a single neuron does not remain constant when a pattern to which it has learnt a response changes position. In consequence, single layer networks cannot perform the apparently trivial task of recognising that two images falling on different parts of the retina are the same. Similar arguments show that neurons do not generalise across scale change. So, for example, a single layer network cannot tell that the images from an object seen at different distances are of the same object.

How not to achieve position invariant object recognition

The upper part of figure 13.9 shows the output from a retina becoming the input to a one-layer pattern associator. The task for the associator is to recognise that a particular pattern has fallen on the retina. That is, it must produce the same output when the pattern falls in a different place, like that shown in the lower part of the figure. Only a single output unit of the network is shown, as the problem for the whole net is exemplified by the problem for any one unit.

In the upper part of figure 13.9 the pattern has been presented to one position on the retina. The activity of each input line indicates the intensity of the image at the corresponding point on the retina. In this example the possible inputs are simplified to 1 or 0. The pattern of activity reaching the dendrite from the input units can be represented by the vector $\mathbf{P}$. During learning the response neuron will be switched On (i.e. it will be taught to recognise the object producing the pattern $\mathbf{P}$) by the external pattern carried by the unmodifiable synapse (shown by the symbol <) in the manner described in chapter 3. Hebbian learning on the dendrite will produce an increment $\Delta \mathbf{w}$ in the set of weights activated by the input pattern on the dendrite equivalent to $\mathbf{P}$.

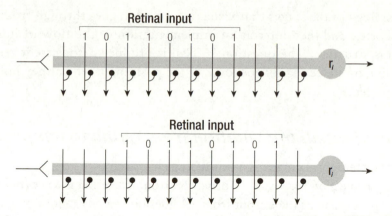

Figure 13.9   The pattern translation problem for a one-layer net.

To test whether this learning will lead to position invariant pattern recognition the same pattern is presented to a different part of the retina (as in the lower part of figure 13.9). If the pattern in the new position turns the response neuron On, position invariant pattern recognition has been achieved. The activity of the response neuron to the signal in the new position will be determined by the dot product of the vectors corresponding to the input pattern and the part of the total weight vector on the dendrite corresponding to the input lines which are active when the pattern is in this new position. Since the part of the weight vector where the learning took place is not the same as that which produces the response to the pattern in the new position, the response will not be related to the original learning. So whether the neuron is switched On or not is unpredictable. There will be no transfer of learning as the image moves from one position to another.

As we have seen in previous chapters, neural networks *can* generalise well to different but related inputs. But the type of generalisation they show is to inputs which are correlated with what they have already learnt. A change of position will destroy simple correlations between images of the same object. So will a change of size. If the object learnt in the upper part of figure 13.9 was viewed from a different distance, the image size would change and a different set of inputs would be activated. Changes brought about by changes of view pose the same problem. The image produced by the side of someone's face has little in common, point by point, with the view from the front. But if we know someone we will recognise them from most angles. The visual system must find a way of relating the different images produced by the same object so that it can produce the same response whatever the input.

There are cells in the inferior temporal visual cortex which produce the same response to a particular face irrespective of its orientation or position on the retina. So the problem of computing invariant representations has been solved by the stream of visual processing between the retina and the temporal lobe. We will summarise the neurophysiology of the stages that visual information goes through from retina to temporal cortex and then look at an implementation of the flow of information through this structure. The question is: Can it produce a consistent response to images falling on the retina independent of the position in which they fall or of the view they present?

The flow of visual information from retina to temporal lobe

V1 → inferior temporal cortex is a multi-stage hierarchy

The primary projection for visual information from the retina is to cortical area V1. Subsequent processing of the output from V1 goes on various routes, one of which is via areas V2 and V4 to the inferior temporal cortex (IT). Input to a cell in any one stage comes from spatially adjacent areas within the previous stage. Within any layer in the hierarchy there is lateral inhibition between cells.

Receptive field size

The receptive fields of neurons in the processing sequence V1 → V2 → V4 → IT become progressively larger at each stage.[4] Typical receptive fields are around 0.5–1° in V1. At a viewing distance of 1 m a receptive field of 1° covers a region about 1.75 cm in diameter. So cells in V1 are responsive only to stimuli in small regions of the visual field. Receptive field sizes increase to around 8° in V4, 20° in posterior inferior temporal cortex and 50° in the anterior inferior temporal cortex. So neurons in IT respond to the appropriate stimulus over a large area of the visual field—translation invariance has been achieved.

Speed of learning

Learning to identify new objects can occur rapidly. Just a few seconds of seeing a new face or object may enable us to recognise it later. Although verbal statements about whether an object is recognised may involve processing stages beyond IT, such as the hippocampus, new representations can be built in the inferior temporal cortex in a few seconds of visual experience. This suggests that the learning algorithm should be of the Hebbian type which allows learning to take place in a single trial.

VisNet—an approach to biologically plausible visual object identification

VisNet is a neural network model with a structure based on neurophysiological evidence about information processing in the route from V1 to inferior temporal

---

[4]The receptive field of a visual neuron is the area of the retina in which an event to which it is responsive will cause activity in the neuron.

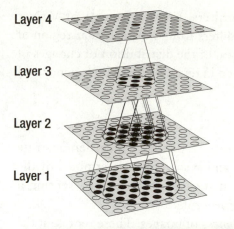

Layer 4

Layer 3

Layer 2

Layer 1

Figure 13.10   The architecture of VisNet.

cortex. The aim is to see whether such a model is capable of building representations of the stimuli presented to it which are independent of the position and angle at which they are presented.

The basic structure of VisNet is shown in figure 13.10. Successive layers of 32x32 cells correspond to successive stages in the visual system from V2 to the inferior temporal cortex. (The part of the model corresponding to V1 will be described later.) The forward connections to a cell in one layer are derived from a spatially corresponding region of the preceding layer. Each cell in the simulation receives 100 connections from the preceding layer, with a 67% probability that a connection comes from within 4 cells of the distribution centre. The result, as shown in figure 13.10, is that although any cell is only influenced by a relatively small region of the preceding layer, a cell in layer 4 could in principle be influenced by cells anywhere in layer 1. Within each layer there is lateral inhibition between cells. This enables competitive learning to operate locally within each region of a layer. Competitive networks detect correlations between the activity of the input cells, and allocate output neurons to respond to each cluster. These might be thought of as feature analysers.

Input to VisNet

The input to layer 1 of VisNet comes from a preprocessor which provides an approximation to the encoding found in visual area V1 of the primate visual system. The preprocessor consists of a series of filters. Like simple cells in V1 these each respond best to a change of stimulus intensity at a particular orientation. The spatial frequencies of the filters and their orientations are chosen to accord with the tuning profiles observed in the simple cells of V1. A filter tuned to a low spatial frequency responds best to a relatively slow change in intensity across the image. A filter tuned to a high spatial frequency will respond best to a rapid rate of change. Each small area of an image is processed by a set of these filters. Units in layer 1 of VisNet receive a random selection of the output of these filters from one particular region of the image. That is, the input to layer 1 is a function of the distribution of changes of intensity in a small region of the image, represented in terms of spatial frequency and orientation.

The trace rule

A crucial part of the network's ability to generate responses which demonstrate invariance over transformations of position, size and even view is determined by the learning rule. This is a Hebb-type rule. Since it includes a term representing a memory of previous unit activity it is called the 'trace' rule.

During training, the net is presented with *sequences* of images. These represent the same object moving across the retina (i.e. undergoing spatial transformation) or rotating (i.e. undergoing viewpoint transformation). The trace rule allows units in the network to learn correlations between successive events. Consider a single unit which is strongly activated by one stimulus. The unit's activity level will decay. But if it receives a new input before the activity has decayed to zero then the residual activity will cause the synapses activated by the new input to be strengthened in the usual Hebbian way. This will lead to the association of *successive* events. This may sound undesirable as the unit might continually be making spurious links between events which, by chance, follow each other, but are not related. But random pairings are unlikely to be repeated consistently. The events which are most likely to consistently occur successively are those following from a transformation of the same object. So these will produce the largest change in weights, and hence the greatest learning. Thus VisNet takes advantage of the statistical property of the visual world that over short time intervals it is more likely that different aspects of the same object will be being viewed, rather than different objects.

The learning rule used in VisNet is:

$$\Delta w_{ij} = \varepsilon \, a_j \, m_i^{(t)} \tag{13.1}$$

where Δw_{ij} is the change in the strength of the connection between element j of the input pattern and unit i,

ε is a learning rate constant which determines the size of weight change on any one learning trial,

a_j is the activity of the jth input to the unit,

and $m_i^{(t)}$ represents the value of the ith unit's memory trace at time t.

Thus the rule is Hebbian. Connection weights are incremented by the product of the pre-synaptic activity and the post-synaptic trace (a_j and $m_i^{(t)}$ respectively). But the usual Hebbian learning term representing the activity of the post-synaptic unit, a_i, has been replaced by $m_i^{(t)}$ (m because this term includes memory of previous activity).

The memory trace of the post-synaptic unit at time t is determined in part by the input to it at time t, and in part by a memory of its activity at time $(t - 1)$:

$$m_i^{(t)} = (1 - \eta)\, a_i^{(t)} + \eta\, m_i^{(t-1)} \tag{13.2}$$

where $a_i^{(t)}$ is the input driven activity of the ith unit at time t, computed in the usual way for a competitive network by the dot product of the external input vector and the weight vector,

$m_i^{(t-1)}$ is the memory trace of the ith unit's activity from time $(t-1)$,

and η is a constant which governs the relative influence of the new input and the previous state on the activity of unit i. If η is zero there is no memory component. The larger it gets the greater is the influence of the memory component.

Summary of VisNet

Each small region of an image presented to VisNet is processed in parallel by a set of filters tuned to a range of spatial frequencies and orientations. The output of these filters forms the input to a competitive net. The activity of these units (layer 1) will represent any correlations discovered among the output of the filters. This becomes the input to another competitive net (layer 2). This will detect correlations among the first set of correlations and, because of the convergent topography in VisNet, operate over a wider area of the original input. This is repeated over four layers. In the final layer correlations between features in any parts of the retina can be represented. Successive inputs to the net are usually transformations, either rotation or translation, of the same object. The trace learning rule allows correlations represented in the final layer to be between information in images of the same object presented to the net in different spatial positions, or between information about different views of the same object.

Testing the network

Position invariance

To see whether this net could develop representations which display position invariance, that is, could generate the same response to a stimulus independent of where it appeared on the retina, VisNet was shown the seven faces in figure 13.11. Each face was presented nine times in succession at different locations on the retina. It was then replaced by another face which was also shown at the nine places, and so on. Each face was shown for 200 such sequences.

Figure 13.12 shows the response of a unit in layer 4 to the different faces as a function of the retinal position in which they are presented to the model. The unit responds to face 1 in any location on the retina. It has no response to any other face at any location. The test for position invariance is the development of units that

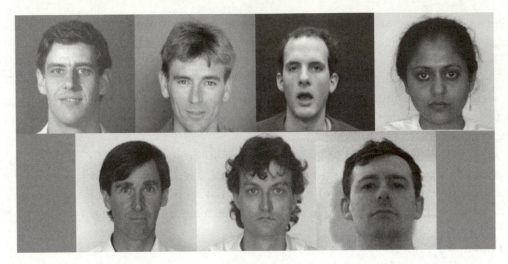

Figure 13.11   The seven faces for learning positional invariance.

respond to a particular face wherever it appears on the retina, that is, the discovery that certain combinations of features in the input (e.g. those corresponding to face 1) have been presented at many different positions. Figure 13.12 shows that some units in layer 4 *have* developed positional invariance.

To see whether the coding represented by the units in figure 13.12 was adequate for allowing each face to be recognised wherever it appeared, a fifth layer was added to the model. This consisted of seven units taking input from layer 4. It was taught using the Delta rule to turn on one unit for each face presented to the model. It was 100% accurate at identifying each face. So VisNet has succeeded in developing

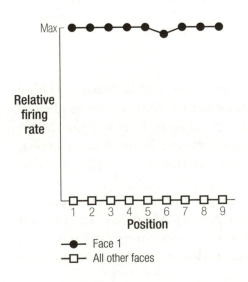

Figure 13.12   Evidence for position invariant response in a single unit in layer 4 of VisNet. The unit's response is shown as a function of the position of the face on the retina.

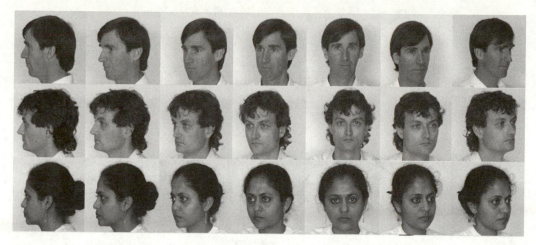

Figure 13.13   Stimuli for learning view invariance.

representations which could be used to recognise a face wherever it fell on the retina. Translation invariance has been achieved.

View invariance

To see whether the model could learn a view invariant representation, the stimuli in figure 13.13 were used. They show three different faces in seven different orientations. Different views of the same face were presented to the model in succession, then different views of the next face were shown, and so on. The sequence of seven views of each face was shown a total of 800 times.

The test for view invariance is whether units in layer 4 always respond to one particular face independent of the orientation in which it is shown to the retina. If so, then the net has built up representations which have discovered what is in common between successive images on the retina, even though the images themselves are not the same. Figure 13.14 shows the response of two of the most view invariant units in layer 4. The first unit (left) responds to any view of the first face, a little to some views of the second face and not to the third face. The second unit (right) responds to any view of the third face and little to any view of the others. View invariance has been achieved.

The importance of the trace rule for forming invariant representations

One strength of an explicit, quantitative model like VisNet is that it is possible to examine what contribution various aspects of it make to the overall performance. For example, the contribution of the memory component of the trace rule can be examined by setting η in equation 13.2 to zero. The learning rule then becomes

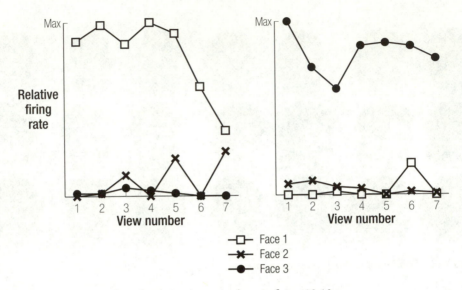

Figure 13.14 Responses of two layer 4 units to the faces in figure 13.13.

conventional Hebbian with no short term memory component. The effects of doing this in the position and view invariance experiments are shown in figure 13.15. The 'discrimination factor' is a measure of a unit's ability to generate an invariant response. In the first experiment (where the network's ability to develop position invariance is being tested) it is a measure of the unit's ability to distinguish between different faces compared to its ability to distinguish between different positions. A high discrimination factor indicates that a unit responds differently to different faces independent of their position. A unit with no position invariance would have a discrimination factor of 1. Similarly, in the second experiment, a unit without view invariance would have a discrimination factor of 1.

Figure 13.15 shows the discrimination achieved by the 30 most discriminative units trained in a simulation with the trace rule (labelled Trace) and in one where it was switched off (labelled Hebb). It is clear that the trace rule is essential. Without it no units develop position or view invariance. The failure of the net trained with the pure Hebb rule to develop position invariance is an example of the problem outlined at the beginning of this section. An image in one particular part of the retina will have more in common with another image in that place than with the same image in another place. So a simple competitive net using Hebbian learning will learn to categorise images by where they are rather than by what they are.

Brains, networks and biological plausibility

The models described in this chapter use a biologically plausible local learning rule. The signals required to alter the network equivalent of synaptic strength during

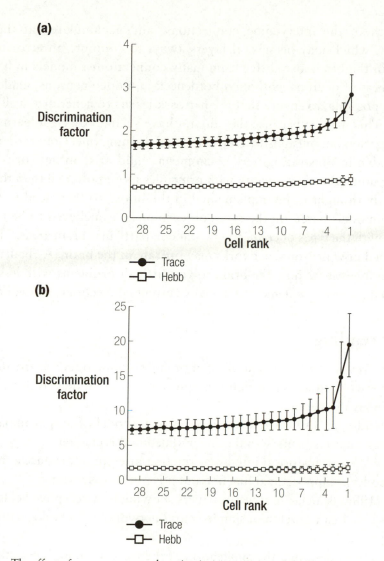

Figure 13.15 The effect of trace vs no trace learning in (a) position and (b) view invariance experiments. 'Discrimination factor' is a measure of a unit's development of position or view invariance. The discrimination factor of the 30 units with the highest discrimination developed under either trace or Hebbian learning is shown. A value of 1.0 indicates that no invariance has developed.

learning are presynaptic and post-synaptic activity. These are both available at the synapse. The systems operate by self-organising competitive learning. This is also biologically plausible as it is driven by the inputs themselves with no external teacher. Competitive learning is implemented by using lateral inhibition which is a well-known property of cortical architecture.

In contrast, many connectionist models do not use local learning rules to alter connection strengths. In backpropagation for example, information about the error in the output units of the network must be propagated backwards, proportionally to the strength of the intervening connections, and accumulated at the relevant connection, which may be several layers away, to compute an error term. Real networks in the brain also differ from many connectionist models in having very large numbers of neurons, without a bottleneck of hidden neurons, made as few in number as possible, to ensure that the network learns to generalize well to similar problems. This may be because they do not have such a powerful learning rule as backpropagation but must instead rely on a local learning rule. Connectionist models are invaluable in illustrating how phenomena could arise in networks of simple computing units. But they operate with principles more powerful than those which are currently thought to be implemented in the brain, so they need to be supplemented by models based on the types of learning rules believed to be used in the brain, and with the types of connectivity found in particular brain areas. This chapter has described how neuronal networks may operate in the brain. A challenge for the future is to investigate how the brain solves difficult problems with less powerful algorithms than those implemented in many current connectionist networks.

Further reading

Rolls and Treves (1998) is a more comprehensive introduction to biologically plausible network models of brain function where the models in this chapter are described in greater detail.

McClelland *et al.* (1995) give a computational model of hippocampal function which shares some elements with the one outlined in this chapter.

Marr (1971) is of historical interest as the first attempt to produce a quantitative network model of hippocampal function but it is not an easy read.

Linsker (1986) is a classic series of papers showing how receptive fields like those of neurons in V1 can develop in simple neural networks with biologically plausible learning.

Foldiak (1991) describes the application of the trace learning rule to the problem of translation invariance.

Rolls, E. T. and Deco, G. (2002). *Computational Neuroscience of Vision*. Oxford University Press: Oxford. This book describes biologically plausible network theories of visual object recognition, attention, short term memory and long term memory.

14   *Evolutionary connectionism*

The performance of connectionist networks can gradually evolve under Darwinian-style selection. Successive generations of a mutating network can perform a task more efficiently even though no learning algorithm changes an individual network. The weight adaptation which comes from learning during the lifetime of a network can improve performance of successive generations even though the changes are not inherited. We will look at the application of evolutionary connectionism to the real-world problem of the development of detectors for speech perception. A genetic algorithm can find a network architecture and learning rule which are capable of discriminating speech sounds after only two minutes exposure to speech. The behaviour of the network has many similarities to that of infants.

All the models described so far in this book start with a clearly defined architecture. The network develops in response to its environment by adapting its connections following a fixed learning algorithm. The final state of the network is determined by the initial decisions that the modeller made about its architecture, the learning algorithm and the environment. But these do not have to be fixed at the outset of training. An appropriate architecture and learning algorithm can emerge through a process of learning, much as the connections in a network adapt gradually in response to the training environment. In this chapter we will see how networks can evolve over successive generations to perform better than their predecessors. In the first section we will look at the evolution of a weight matrix which can produce goal directed behaviour in a network without a learning algorithm. In the second we will look at a variant in which the network has a learning algorithm, but what is learnt by each generation is not inherited. Nevertheless, successive generations learn more quickly than they do without the capability to learn. In the final section we will look at a network in which not just the weight matrix but the network architecture and learning rule evolve.

The evolutionary process operates like Darwinian natural selection. A generation of organisms with some random variation between individuals is exposed to an environment and demonstrate their relative ability at a task. The more successful organisms are allowed to reproduce. Reproduction either includes an element of random mutation to ensure variation in the next generation, or is sexual, allowing mixing of characteristics of successful parents. Successive generations are exposed to a similar environment and the networks which are chosen to produce the next generation are selected by the same criterion. As this process is similar to the phylogenesis of species, it is sometimes referred to as genetic connectionism.

The evolution of goal directed behaviour

A hallmark of intelligent behaviour is that it is directed towards a specific purpose—it is intentional. A central problem in understanding the evolution of intelligence is to show how such behaviour might emerge from simpler, non-intentional activities. Nolfi *et al.* (1994) modelled the evolution of a simple organism's ability to seek out food. Figure 14.1 shows the 'nervous system' of the organism and the 2-D grid world in which it lives. The organism receives sensory input about the distance and direction of the nearest food, and proprioceptive input about its last action. The activity of the output units (which determines the direction of the next step) is computed in the usual way by the outputs from the hidden units with the activities of these determined in turn by the output from the input units. The state of the output units allow three possible behaviours at any step—move forward, move left or move right. Food is placed at random on squares of the grid. The organism steps through the world, one square at a time. If there is food on the square, it eats it.

Although the organism has information about the position of food, it has no builtin goal of reaching food and there is no learning algorithm to teach it that goal. The pattern of behaviour, which direction it turns at any step, is determined by the weights that the organism started with. Bumping into food is a fortuitous event which will occur if the combination of input signals and weights causes a step in the

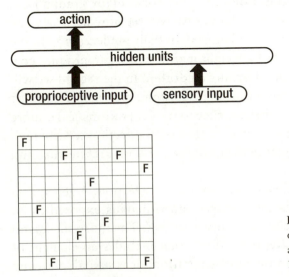

Figure 14.1 The nervous system of a simple organism which wanders over the grid, eating any food (F) it bumps into. (Based on Nolfi *et al.* 1994.)

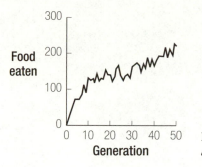

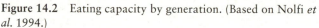

Figure 14.2 Eating capacity by generation. (Based on Nolfi *et al.* 1994.)

right direction. Those organisms which collect more food are selected to produce the next generation. There is a slight mutation of the weight matrix before reproduction. The same life cycle and selection procedure are repeated for 50 generations. Figure 14.2 shows that the amount of food eaten by successive generations increases steadily.

After several generations the descendent organisms' movements have the character of goal-oriented behaviour, directed towards food. Figure 14.3 shows typical pathways through the world for 1st and 50th generation organisms. The behaviour of the 50th generation organism appears precisely tuned towards the goal of collecting food even though it has never been explicitly instructed to seek out food.

The development of goal directed behaviour in these organisms occurs through a process of mutation and natural selection. There is no learning during the lifetime of an individual organism. However, the process of selection and weight mutation across generations achieves the same result as a learning algorithm within an individual organism. The weights that an organism is given at birth place it at some position on a weight surface like that shown in figure 14.4. (In reality it has many more dimensions but the principle of gradient descent is the same.) The valleys correspond to those weight values which would drive the organism towards food.

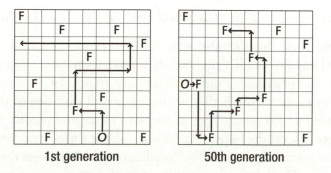

Figure 14.3 Paths taken from a randomly selected start points (O) with the same food pattern for organisms in the 1st and 50th generations. (Based on Nolfi *et al.* 1994.)

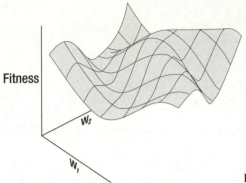

Figure 14.4   Fitness in a two-dimensional weight space.

The ridges correspond to weight values which would send the organism away from food. The selection process identifies organisms with sets of weights that convert the information on its input units about the position of food into actions which make it move towards the food. That is, it identifies those sets of weights which are lower down the slopes. The process of mutation provides an opportunity to explore the regions of weight space around these positions. The mutated organisms which get weights which correspond to positions further down the slope will be more effective at finding food than their parents. They will be selected and allowed to reproduce in their turn. The overall result across generations will be a remorseless movement towards a pattern of weights which lies in one of the valleys. This is exactly the same process which a gradient descent learning rule achieves across trials within a single organism. The simulation shows that an explicit teacher which knows the goal is not required to produce an organism which can achieve the goal. An environmental contingency, such as an increased probability of reproduction for organisms which eat more, can achieve the same result. This is Dawkins's Blind Watchmaker at work. Nobody knows what would be an effective set of weights for eating food. But the organism will discover one all the same.

The evolutionary advantage of the capacity to learn

In a second simulation the organism was given the ability to learn something during its lifetime—it learnt to predict the sensory input on the next time step. Two units were added to the organism's output layer (see figure 14.5). Their activity was treated as the organism's prediction of the angle and distance of the nearest food after it had made its next move. That is, they had to try and predict the next sensory input to the network on the basis of knowledge about the current sensory input and the current movement. (They are called 'prediction' units because they are trained to make predictions. There is nothing inherent in their structure which makes them suitable (or unsuitable) for making predictions. They are just two units added to the

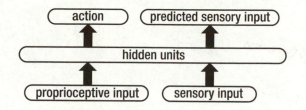

Figure 14.5 Predictive capacity added to the organism.

output layer and given an arbitrary task to learn.) On each trial the output of the prediction units is compared with the actual angle and distance information that the organism gets after it has made its move. The discrepancy between these is used as an error signal to adjust the weights using the backpropagation learning algorithm. The weights from prediction units to hidden and from hidden to input can be changed. Those connecting the hidden units to the action units cannot. Note that the changes in weights produced by the learning algorithm are not related to the organism's success in eating. The learning algorithm is concerned solely with changing weights to improve the network's ability to predict the next sensory input.

The selection procedure is the same as in the previous simulation. Organisms which collect the most food during their lifetime are permitted to reproduce. As before, the descendants inherit a mutated version of their parent's weight matrix. It is essential to note that they inherit the *initial* weight matrix of their parent, *not* the weights at the end of the exploration period (i.e. those which have been adapted by the learning algorithm). What was *learnt* is not passed on. There is no Lamarckian component to this simulation! There is no reason why the organism's capacity to learn to predict the new position of food as it moves should improve food-collecting behaviour. The prediction units do not affect the behaviour of the organism. The organism is not learning how to approach food. The training may produce weight changes that lead to the organism becoming less effective at approaching food. Figure 14.6 compares the evolution of average food collecting behaviour in organisms with or without a predictive capacity. Organisms with a predictive capacity eat more food. Thus we have the seemingly paradoxical result that the possession of a capacity which is not being selected for can lead to an evolutionary advantage for the organism which possesses it!

The reason why the capacity to learn leads to more effective eating even though the learning is not related to success at eating can be understood by referring back to figure 14.4. The weight matrix which an organism inherits places it initially at some point in weight space. The learning algorithm allows it to explore the nearby region of weight space during its lifetime to find a position which allows better prediction. If this position also, by chance, leads to more effective eating, that particular organism is likely to be one which is selected for breeding. The weights which led to effective

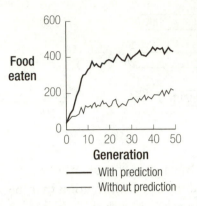

Figure 14.6   The development of food consumption across generations of organisms with predictive capacity. (Based on Nolfi *et al.* 1994.)

eating do not get passed on. But the weight changes involved in the process of learning any arbitrary task also, incidentally, identify which organisms are in a part of weight space close to a region which will produce more effective eating behaviour. The mutation before reproduction may take the organism into this region leading to more effective eating behaviour of future generations of the selected organism. Thus the *capacity* to learn—allowing an individual organism to explore its own weight space—can lead to the development of more effective behaviour across generations even though what is learnt by an individual is not passed on.

Innately guided learning in speech perception

New-born infants can recognise speech features within the first few days of life. This has been cited as evidence that the mechanisms for speech recognition must be innate as it seems impossible that learning could take place so quickly. However, there are examples of ultra-rapid learning in animals, such as imprinting and song acquisition. These are usually termed 'innately guided'. The implication is that the animal has an innate predisposition to acquire this particular pattern of behaviour. It has been proposed that the development of speech perception in infants should be viewed as an innately guided learning process. That is, the system is innately structured so that it is likely to partition continua which form the basis for classification of speech, such as voice onset time, into appropriate categories. Thus learning the sound properties of the native language can take place very quickly.

Nakisa and Plunkett (1998) developed a genetic connectionist model to see what the innately guided and the learnt components of the development of speech perception might be. The architecture and learning rules of the network were encoded in a 'genome'. New networks were generated by sexual reproduction (i.e. by random recombination of parts of two 'parental' genomes). The network took speech as its input and variants which succeeded in detecting contrastive features at output were allowed to reproduce. The genetic recombination algorithm succeeded in discovering a network which could detect speech features after only two minutes exposure to spoken English. This remarkable achievement can be viewed in two ways. Obviously it gives an insight into the performance of human infants, showing that, with the right architecture and learning rule, very rapid learning is possible. But it also demonstrates how useful genetic algorithms can be to modellers! Nakisa and Plunkett started with no clear idea of what would be required for a network to achieve ultra-rapid learning of categories suitable for partioning speech. Rather than trying endless combinations out themselves they allowed the genetic recombination algorithm to do the work for them.

The Nakisa and Plunkett model

The model uses the general architecture known as interactive activation and competition (IAC).[1] An IAC network consists of a collection of processing units divided into competitive pools. Within pools there are inhibitory connections; between pools there are excitatory connections. The network is interactive. When one pool influences another it is in turn affected by feedback from that pool. Because of these interactions the activity of units in IAC networks develops over time before settling into a steady pattern of activity. Inhibitory connections within a pool mean that one unit at a time dominates the others in a winner-takes-all fashion.

The input is a raw speech signal. A preprocessor measures the energy level in the speech signal in a set of 64 frequency bands in a range from 0 to 8 kHz.[2] These are the inputs to the 64 input units of the model. These are divided into 16 subnetworks of 4 units. Each subnetwork has its own pattern of connectivity to the output units and to itself (e.g. recurrent or not). The activity of the eight output units represents the network's interpretation of the current input. The speech signal is sampled every 10 ms. All the units in the network update their activities gradually over time. The rate of change in the activity of a unit is a weighted sum of the activity of the units which are connected to it minus a decay term. If there is no input to the unit its activity dies away exponentially at a rate determined by the time constant of the sub-network in which it is placed.

The aim of the simulation was to discover a network in which the output units manage to categorise speech input in a way which bears some relation to the phonetic features of English. That is, one in which particular output units will come on (or off) in response to the presence of features such as voiced or fricative in the phonemes in the input string. The learning rules were Hebbian in general style, strengthening connections between input and output units which were simultan-

---

[1]The Jets and Sharks model, discussed in chapter 2, is a simple example of an IAC network.
[2]This is the sort of transformation which the ear performs on auditory information. So the input to the network may be similar to that reaching the infant's auditory cortex.

eously active. These lead to a network which operates like a competitive network—it reinforces consistent patterns of activity but has no preset goal towards which it is working. There is a set of 30 learning rules in the simulation. Each sub-network selects at random from this pool, so different rules can operate in different parts of the overall network.

The architecture and learning rules for an individual network are stored in the network genome. The genome has two 'chromosomes'. One chromosome stores the attributes of each sub-network, such as the time constant and the output units to which it projects. The other chromosome stores the learning rules for the connections from each sub-network of input units to the output units. During reproduction, the two chromosomes from each parent are independently recombined. Thus new chromosomes are created with information from both parents. The use of a genetic algorithm allows the architecture, learning rules and time-constants to evolve together.

Network training and evolution

During training networks were exposed to sentences from continuous speech samples of American English dialects. At each time-step, activity was propagated through the connections from input to output. All connections were then modified according to the learning rules specified in the genome. On the next time-step a new input pattern corresponding to the next time-slice of the speech signal was presented and the process of activity propagation and weight modification repeated. This was repeated for a set of 30 different randomly selected sentences.

In the testing phase, activation was propagated through the network for a new set of sentences, with the weights fixed at the values they attained at the end of the training phase, for a new set of sentences. Network 'fitness' was calculated using a function which favoured networks that represented occurrences of the same phoneme in the test sentence in a similar way (i.e. with the same pattern of activity over the output units) and of different phonemes with a different pattern. Note that the fitness function is not looking for the development of detectors tuned to any particular speech-like features. It is just looking for the development of the ability to discriminate between phonemes. Networks which produce the highest fitness are allowed to produce the next generation.

After 100 generations of selection, networks begin to discriminate speech sounds. That is, the activity of the output units varies systematically as the speech stream varies. The same units come on (or off) when certain features such as fricatives or voicing appear in different contexts in the input stream. Figure 14.7 shows what has happened inside the network. The figure shows the response of each of the eight output units to pure tones ranging from 0 to 8 kHz. Different units become active

Output unit

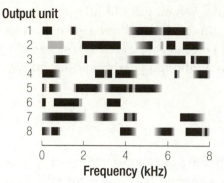

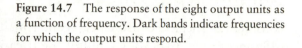

Figure 14.7 The response of the eight output units as a function of frequency. Dark bands indicate frequencies for which the output units respond.

when there is energy present in different parts of the spectrum. Since speech features are represented by the relationship between those parts of the spectrum at which energy is present or absent, this is the basis necessary for performing speech discrimination.

Since the selection algorithm selects networks which can discriminate speech sounds, perhaps it is hardly surprising that the consequence is the development of a network which can discriminate speech sounds! But there are other characteristics of the model such as the speed with which it learns, its cross-linguistic performance and its development of categorical perception which suggest that it may be an appropriate model of early speech perception.

Speed

The model discovers a set of weights which can discriminate speech features very quickly. The model shown in figure 14.7 had experienced only *2 minutes* of English speech and yet has begun to develop a structure which allows it to discriminate between phonetic features. This shows that the ability of infants to make speech discriminations in the first few days of life does not necessarily imply an innate representation of speech sounds. With the right architecture it could be learnt.

Cross-linguistic performance

The network was trained on a variety of Voice of America broadcast languages— English, Cantonese, Swahili, Farsi, Czech, Hindi, Hungarian, Korean, Polish, Russian, Slovak, Spanish, Ukrainian and Urdu. All of the languages tested were equally effective in training the network to represent English speech sounds. That is, the same initial feature detectors develop whatever language the network is first exposed to. This echoes the observation that infants are initially able to discriminate speech contrasts from any language. For example, 6–8 month old infants from an English-speaking background can distinguish the glottalised velar–uvular stop contrast /ki/–/qi/ in Nthlakapmx and the Hindi voiceless aspirated versus breathy voiced contrast /t^h/–/d^h/. But this ability is lost after about a year's exposure to any language which does not use these contrasts.

Categorical perception

Consider the fricative consonants [s] and [sh]. They are distinguished primarily by a difference in the frequency band of the frication energy. It is lower for [sh]. It is possible to create synthetic consonants in which the frequency of the energy band is gradually increased from a value which gives a pure [sh] to a value which gives a pure [s]. If people hear these they do not report a gradual transition from a pure [sh], through a mixture of the sounds, to a pure [s]. They report a relatively sharp transition from one sound to the other. The synthetic in-between sounds are classified as one sound or the other, not as a mixture. This phenomenon, which is observed in infants, is known as *categorical perception*.

A pair of real /sh/ and /s/ spectra were taken from a male speaker. Eleven speech spectra were created from these by varying the frequency of the fricative energy band to form a linear continuum from the pure /sh/ to a pure /s/. Each of the spectra was fed into a network that had been trained on 30 sentences of continuous English speech. The response of the output units to the varying spectra going from pure /sh/ to pure /s/ are shown in figure 14.8. ('Distance' is a measure of similarity, scaled such that maximum similarity was scored as 0 and minimum as 1.) Figure 14.8 shows that linear variations in the input spectrum do not result in linear changes in the activity of the output units. A categoriser using this representation would therefore shift the boundary between the two phonemes toward /sh/ and be relatively insensitive to spectral variations that occurred away from this boundary. These are the hallmarks of categorical perception.

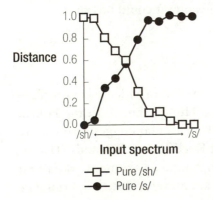

Figure 14.8   Response of the network to input on a /sh/–/s/ continuum. Circles show the distance from a pure /sh/ and squares show the distance from a pure /s/.

Nativism or constructivism?

By developing appropriate architectures, time-constants and learning rules over many generations, a system evolves in which the task of learning to represent speech sounds can be achieved after very brief exposure to speech. Evolution finds a structure which can learn quickly. However, having the correct innate architecture and learning rules is not sufficient for creating good representations. Weights cannot be inherited between generations so the network is dependent on the environment for learning a set of weights which can perform the task. If trained on acoustically filtered (i.e. unnaturally distorted) speech, the model does not form good representations. But given the sort of auditory input heard by an infant the model rapidly creates the same set of features whatever the language it hears. This demonstrates an advantage of innately guided learning over conventional self-organising networks. It is less dependent on the 'correct' environmental statistics. The model found by the evolutionary process in this simulation offers an account of how infants from different linguistic environments can come up with the same featural representation so soon after birth. In this sense innately guided learning as implemented in this model is half-way between nativism and constructivism. It shows how genes and environment *interact* to ensure the rapid development of featural representation of speech on which further linguistic development depends.

15   *A selective history of connectionism before 1986*

It might seem that connectionism burst upon the unsuspecting world of cognitive science in 1986 with the publication of Parallel Distributed Processing *by McClelland, Rumelhart and the PDP Research Group. Although this book had more impact than any other publication in the history of connectionism, it was preceded by more than 40 years of research into the computational abilities of networks of simple computing elements working in parallel. This chapter will review a number of key papers and books which are generally agreed to have influenced the direction taken by connectionist research. The aim is to give a flavour of some earlier research, not a systematic history. Detailed reviews of the period can be found in Levine (1983), Anderson and Rosenfeld (1988), Cowan and Sharp (1988) and the 1989 edition of Hinton and Anderson. Some of the papers referred to in this chapter are difficult to find in their original form. Most have been reprinted, along with historical and explanatory commentary, in a very useful collection of influential papers in connectionism edited by Anderson and Rosenfeld (1988).*

McCulloch and Pitts (1943)

Logical operations with neuron-like computational units

A key event in the history of connectionism was the publication in 1943 of a paper called 'A logical calculus of the ideas immanent in nervous activity' by McCulloch and Pitts. They demonstrated that a network of simple computing units, operating in parallel, could perform logical operations. A crucial aspect of their modelling was that the properties of the computing units were based on those of the neuron (as they were believed to be at the time the paper was written). This approach has been followed (up to a point) by contemporary connectionism. It was not followed by the mainstream of cognitive function modellers, for whom the aim was to model what the cognitive system achieved, not how it did it.

McCulloch and Pitts's 'neurons' had three properties: They were binary state devices, either On or Off; they summed input, either excitatory or inhibitory, from other neurons which were On; they had a threshold. Computation took place in a succession of time slices. In each one every neuron summed its excitatory inputs. If these exceeded its threshold, it went into the On state for the next time slice; otherwise it remained in the Off state. A single inhibitory input forced it into the Off state for the next time period.

McCulloch and Pitts showed that a network of neurons with these simple properties could compute any logical function. On the assumption that thought could be represented by logical operations on a combination of sensory input about the current state of the world and stored information about past experience, this appeared to offer a dramatic insight into how the brain might be capable of performing cognitive processes. Although McCulloch and Pitts's general proof that any logical function can be computed by such networks requires an understanding of mathematical logic, it is possible to get a feeling for their approach by considering a simple example which they describe in the paper. First they showed that patterns of inter-neuronal connections could compute the logical functions AND, OR and NOT. Then they showed how a net of neurons computing these simple functions could be put together to compute an elementary set of mental events.

Computing AND, OR and NOT

Take a network with no recurrent connections. That is, each neuron is influenced only by the state of those in the previous layer, not by feedback from subsequent layers. Given the state of the neurons in one layer at time t, what are the possible states of the neurons in the next layer at time $t + 1$? With the McCulloch and Pitts model of the neuron, there are only four possibilities. These are shown in figure 15.1. The input neurons are labelled I_1 and I_2. The response neuron is labelled R. The level of each excitatory input (marked +) is 1 and the threshold of the response neuron is 2. There could be more than two inputs, and thresholds could have any value, but more complex cases all reduce to one of the following logical operations.

(a) No information processing takes place. The input is relayed without modification.
(b) The response neuron will come on at time $t + 1$ if either input neuron is on at time t.
(c) The response neuron will only come on at time $t + 1$ if both input neurons are on at time t.
(d) The response neuron will not come on if input neuron 1 is active. (The inhibitory connection is marked −.)

The last three possibilities correspond to the response neuron performing the logical operations OR, AND and NOT respectively on the state of neurons I_1 and I_2.

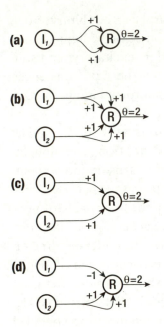

Figure 15.1 The logical operations of OR (b), AND (c) and NOT (d) performed by McCulloch and Pitts neurons. The two inputs are I_1 and I_2. The connection strengths are $+1$ and -1. The threshold (θ) of the response neuron is 2. (Based on McCulloch and Pitts 1943.)

Producing the sensations of hot and cold

To show what sort of operations a net with several layers of such computational neurons could perform, McCulloch and Pitts considered the example of the sensations produced by hot and cold objects touching the skin. There are separate sensors in the skin which respond to objects which are above and below body temperature. When they are stimulated they send signals to the brain where cells fire producing sensations of hot and cold. The natural organisation, with the sensors connected directly to the cell assemblies which produce the sensations, cannot be the whole story, because, if a cold object is briefly applied to the skin and removed, there is a transitory sensation of warmth. So there must be connections from cold sensor cells to the system involved in hot sensation. But there is no transitory sensation of warmth if the cold object is held on the skin for some time. The connections from cold sensor to hot sensation only become active if the stimulus is applied briefly.

Figure 15.2 shows McCulloch and Pitts's analysis of how such a result could be achieved with a network of neurons connected to perform the logical operations shown in figure 15.1. Each excitatory input (marked $+$) has a value of 1, and each neuron has a threshold of 2. S_h and S_c correspond to temperature sensitive sensory cells. S_h provides an input to the net when a hot stimulus is applied and S_c when a cold stimulus is applied. R_h and R_c are the response cells. R_h coming on is the system's equivalent of feeling hot; R_c coming on is the system's equivalent of feeling cold.

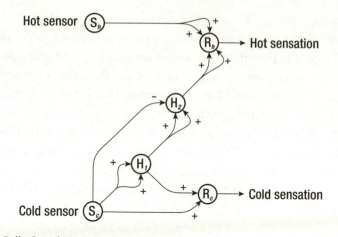

Figure 15.2 McCulloch and Pitts's network for producing the sensations of hot and cold from input to hot and cold sensors. (Based on McCulloch and Pitts 1943.)

H_1 and H_2, which lie between S_c, the cold sensor, and R_h, the hot sensation, allow for the computation which will permit the system to feel a warm sensation in response to a transitory cold input. They perform the same role as hidden units in contemporary models, allowing a reorganisation of the input. The connections from S_h and H_2 to R_h form an OR junction; if either is active, R_h will come on. The connections from S_c and H_1 to H_2 form a NOT junction; if S_c is active, H_2 will not come on.

A hot stimulus leads directly to a hot sensation (S_h to R_h). If a cold stimulus is applied to the skin at time t, and left there, H_1 will be active from time $t+1$. The inputs to R_c from S_c and H_1 will both be positive at $t+2$. Since the state of R_c is the result of an AND of these two signals it will become active and there will be a cold sensation. The inhibitory output from S_c to H_2 will mean that H_2 is never on while a cold stimulus is applied, so R_h will not come on and there will be no sensation of warmth.

If a cold stimulus is applied at time t and removed at time $t+1$ the excitatory input from S_c to H_1 will lead to H_1 being active at time $t+1$. At time $t+2$ there will be an excitatory input from H_1 to R_c, but since there will be no input from S_c to R_c (because the cold stimulus was removed at $t+1$) the threshold of R_c will not be reached and there will be no sensation of cold. At $t+2$ H_1 will be sending positive activation to H_2. Since the inhibitory connection from S_c will not be active at $t+2$, H_2 will become active at $t+3$ and produce a transitory activation of R_h at time $t+4$. QED!

It is clear why this work is seen as the forerunner of contemporary connectionism. It showed how a network of simple computing units, operating in parallel, had computational power. One difference between this and most later work is that McCulloch and Pitts modelled the computational unit as an all-or-none device. The motivation was to reflect the all-or-none nature of the pulse when a nerve fires. Later work usually allowed a continuous value for the state of each unit. This reflects the belief that nerve cells transmit a continuous range of information (for example, by firing rate), rather than just the single fact of being active or inactive. A second difference is that McCulloch and Pitts used unmodifiable connections between units. Later work was often concerned with learning, and the modification of connections was usually the way that learning was implemented. A third difference is that McCulloch and Pitts demonstrated the ability of such nets to perform logical operations. Later work has tended to concentrate on the ability of neuron-like nets to solve problems by statistical combination of evidence rather than by the application of logical relationships.

Hebb (1949)

In 1949 Donald Hebb published *The Organisation of Behavior*. The lasting importance of this book came from the proposal of a specific synaptic change which might underlie learning. This is known as the Hebb synapse. It is widely used in connectionist models today (see chapters 3 and 13). Another aspect of the book can also be seen as an influence on contemporary connectionism. Hebb put forward the case for basing models of cognitive function on what was known about the physiology of the brain.

Neuronal inspiration in psychological modelling

Hebb wrote: 'The first object of this book is to present a theory of behavior for psychologists; but another is to seek a common ground with the anatomist, physiologist, and neurologist, ... to make it possible for them to contribute to [psychological] theory.'

Hebb thought it would *help* psychological theorising if there was an input from neurophysiology. He contrasted this approach with the deliberate attempt to get neurophysiology out of psychological theories, represented in particular at that time by B.F. Skinner. For Skinner, the aim of a psychological model was to represent the rules which would allow behaviour to be predicted from knowledge of the organism's previous experience and the stimuli now facing it. The mechanism by which this behaviour was generated was, to Skinner, irrelevant. One view of those who maintained that neurophysiological plausibility was irrelevant to psychological theorising was (and still is) that the gap between our knowledge of what brain structure is and how it produces behaviour is so wide that to try and make psychological theories neuronally plausible is at best unhelpful, and at worst positively misleading. Crick has warned about the dangers of trying to model the brain while ignoring basic facts about its structure (Crick 1989; Crick and Asanuma 1986). The earliest neural network simulations provide an interesting cautionary tale, as we will see in the next section. Attempts in the mid-1950s to test Hebb's hypotheses about the formation of cell assemblies by the creation of interneuronal synaptic connections found that the more constraints based on neurophysiology that were built into their model, the better it worked.

The Hebb synapse

McCulloch and Pitts modelled the computational abilities of fixed networks. In contrast, Hebb was interested in the changes that took place in the nervous system during learning. He proposed that learning takes place by synaptic modification, that is, by modifying the strength of the connections between computing elements. This, of course, became one of the central ideas of connectionism. Hebb made a specific proposal about the form that this modification might take:

When an axon of cell A is near enough to excite a cell B and repeatedly or persistently takes part in firing it, some growth process or metabolic change takes place in one or both cells such that A's efficiency, as one of the cells firing B, is increased.

For Hebb the result of forming these connections was not simply to form direct connections between stimulus and response. It was to create interconnections between a large, diffuse set of cells, in different parts of the brain, which he called 'cell assemblies'. Hebb believed that the firing of a sequence of cell assemblies would correspond to a thought process.

It might seem intuitively obvious that forming connections between individual cells in the manner proposed by Hebb would lead to the formation of cell assemblies. But Rochester *et al.* (1956) ran a simulation and showed that, as it stood, Hebb's proposed mechanism for synaptic development did not lead to the formation of a set of independent, larger groups of cells. However, they found that cell assemblies would form provided other rules of inter-cellular interaction were added. First, with the Hebb rule working in isolation, synaptic strength just grew without bound. So they employed a normalisation rule—the total of synaptic strengths within the system was a constant. Thus any increase in strength of one connection led to a reduction in the strength of other connections. (This problem is discussed in chapter 6 in the context of training a competitive network with the Hebb rule.) Second, they added a fatigue factor: recent neuronal firing led to a reduction in the probability that the cell would fire again in the near future. Third, they introduced inhibition so that as mutual excitation between cell assemblies started to develop, it was accompanied by inhibition of other assemblies. Fourth, the model neurons' output was a continuous variable (related to frequency of firing) rather than being all-or-none. Fifth, the Hebb rule was modified so that if the input and output were uncorrelated the synaptic strength decreased. Finally, they added a 'locality' effect—units near to a neuron were more likely to be affected by it than those further away.

This set of rules goes far beyond the original Hebb proposal. But most of the additions were suggested by Hebb and his co-worker Peter Milner on the basis of known physiological facts after the failure of initial attempts to simulate the development of cell assemblies by the formation of Hebb synapses. So the spirit of neuronal inspiration in the modelling was not broken. This simulation made an instructive point about one virtue of computational models of complex systems. It is easy to think that such and such a result must follow from a particular proposal (like cell assemblies forming from synaptic growth). But until a simulation has been run you cannot be sure. As Rochester *et al.* put it: 'This kind of investigation cannot prove how the brain works. It can, however, show that some models are unworkable and provide clues as to how to revise the models to make them work.'

Rosenblatt (1958)—the perceptron

The first neural network models which are clearly recognisable as forerunners of today's are those investigated by Rosenblatt (1958, 1962). He called them *perceptrons*. This work is similar to McCulloch and Pitts's in that it explored the computational ability of networks of simple computing elements operating in parallel. But Rosenblatt thought that showing how such networks could perform complex logical operations was inappropriate for understanding information processing by the brain. His work was based on three assumptions which contrast with those of McCulloch and Pitts:

(1) Since the connections in the brain do not initially allow useful computations, order will be brought about by changes due to experience—i.e. learning.
(2) Since individual components of the system are unreliable, computation must be by probabilistic combination of evidence, rather than by precise logical operations.
(3) The task for a computational unit in the brain is to discover similarities and differences between stimuli (i.e. classification), rather than to perform logical operations.

Thus, in contrast to McCulloch and Pitts, but like Hebb, Rosenblatt's networks started with random connections and learnt how to change them to solve tasks; they involved multiple connections and distributed processing so that the loss of individual components would not affect the accuracy of the whole; and the tasks typically involved trying to learn to classify perceptual patterns.

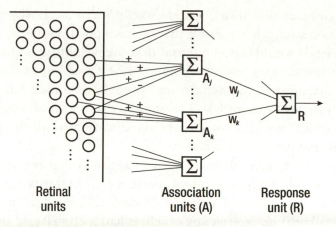

Figure 15.3 A typical Rosenblatt perceptron. (Based on Rosenblatt 1962.)

Rosenblatt investigated the computational abilities of a wide range of possible network architectures and learning rules. An example of a typical perceptron is shown in figure 15.3. The input to the system comes from a 'retina', a 10x10 mosaic of receptors which come on when light falls on them. A typical task for the perceptron would be to try to learn to distinguish vertical and horizontal bars projected onto the retina, supposedly an example of a low level perceptual skill. No one retinal receptor can decide whether a stimulus is vertical or horizontal because each receptor can be turned On by both classes of stimulus. The question is whether a suitable combination of evidence from different receptors can perform this task and whether a simple learning rule could discover the combination. The retinal units are connected to a set of 'association' units, some by excitatory connections, some by inhibitory connections. Although these connections are random they tend to come to any one association unit from a particular area of the retina. The connections from retinal to association units are fixed and unmodifiable. The association unit fires if the combination of the inputs exceeds its threshold. Thus the state of each association unit reflects the presence or absence of some randomly specified but relatively local *feature* in the stimulus falling on the retina.

The decision of the perceptron comes from the output of a response unit, R. This sums the inputs from the association units, each weighted by a modifiable A → R connection. If R comes On, in this example, the perceptron has decided that the stimulus was a vertical line; if it stays Off, it has decided that the stimulus is horizontal. During training various different horizontal and vertical lines were presented to the retina. If the R unit made the correct decision, nothing happened. But if it was wrong the training procedure altered the strengths of the connections between A units and the R unit so that, were the stimulus presented again immediately, the R unit would be more likely to make the correct response.

It was not obvious that such a system would learn to classify horizontal and vertical lines successfully. It is possible that the manipulations of the A → R weights on successive trials would cancel out and that the weights would simply oscillate without the system showing any overall improvement in ability to classify the inputs. The most important result to emerge from Rosenblatt's studies was the perceptron convergence theorem (see chapter 5). This showed that if a set of weights from A to R units existed which would allow correct classification of all the patterns in the learning set, the perceptron would find it.

The discovery of perceptron convergence suggested that perceptrons might be suitable devices for modelling visual perception. Enthusiastic simulation of perceptual processes started. Block (1962) describes the building of a real (as opposed to simulated) perceptron at Cornell. It had a 20×20 grid of photocells for the 'retina' and 512 association units. Figure 15.4 shows the performance of this machine learning to distinguish the 26 letters of the alphabet. After 15 presentations of each letter to the retina, followed by weight adjustment on trials where the perceptron made the wrong response, classification performance was perfect. Block made the point that, unlike most engineering systems, neither precision or reliability of components was important for this machine because the decisions were statistical and spread over many components. He described experiments in which components were actually removed from the machine at random without a major effect on its ability to perform previously learnt perceptual tasks. This foreshadows later citing of graceful degradation, the ability of the cognitive system to cope despite minor damage, as evidence in favour of the appropriateness of connectionist nets as models of cognitive function.

However, Rosenblatt also found that there were considerable limitations to the ability of perceptrons to perform the sort of tasks which appear to be involved in perception. For example, a perceptual device which might be thought of as a plausible mimic of human perceptual abilities should be able to learn the *concepts* of horizontal and vertical from the experience of different *examples* of horizontal and vertical lines. In fact, Rosenblatt found that although perceptrons could learn to

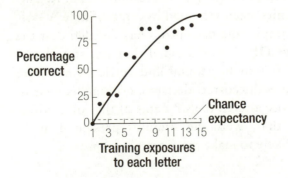

Figure 15.4 Learning of the alphabet by the Mark 1 perceptron. (Based on Block 1962.)

classify large numbers of stimuli, they were poor at extrapolating beyond the examples they had learnt during training to other members of the class which they had not seen. Learning the examples did not lead to discovery of the concept from which the examples were derived.

In summarising their abilities, he described perceptrons as showing 'striking similarities to brain-damaged patients'. They were good at learning responses to specific stimuli, but poor at performing tasks which required the discovery of some higher order abstraction based on them. An example he gives is that while perceptrons were good at learning that a response was required to a square, they were unable to discover the solution if it required the more abstract step of responding to the object to the left of the square. If humans had to discover this compound rule by trial and error, as a perceptron has to do, they would also, presumably, find it more difficult. But at least some of them would discover the answer in the end. The question was whether the sort of concept formation needed to find the answer to more abstract problems like this would require something fundamentally different from a perceptron-like network, or just a more complicated example of the same thing.

Despite the clear limitations of early perceptrons, many papers written at this time were optimistic. Block (1962) concluded: 'More advanced perceptual problems, such as figure ground determination, relations among objects in complex fields and so on, are beyond the capacity of the simple Perceptron, but it seems possible that the richer models will be able to perform these functions.' Subsequent work has justified some of this optimism. Many of the problems which could not be solved by perceptrons in the 1960s have now been solved by structures which bear a clear family resemblance to them. However, there was to be a long gap before the re-emergence in the 1980s of perceptron-like structures as plausible candidates for explaining cognitive functions. The mythology of connectionism has it that the Great Perceptron Bandwagon was stopped in its tracks by a single event—the publication in 1969 of Minsky and Papert's book *Perceptrons*.

Minsky and Papert (1969)—a critique of perceptrons

Perceptrons was a remorseless analysis of what perceptrons cannot do. The analysis was wide ranging and complex but one particular example became notorious—the inability of single layer perceptrons to solve the XOR problem.

The XOR problem and the perception of connectedness

Consider a simple McCulloch and Pitts neuron, R, receiving input from two other neurons, A and B (figure 15.5). A and B are either On (1) or Off (0). The task for R is to come On if either A or B is On, but to stay Off if both are On or if neither is On. These contingencies are shown in the following table:

Input pattern		Desired response of R
Input A	Input B	
0	0	0
0	1	1
1	0	1
1	1	0

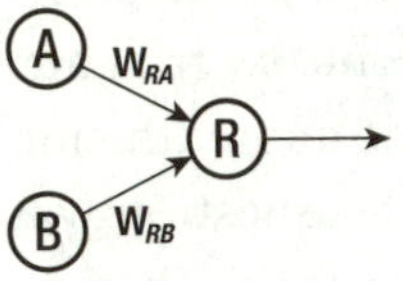

Figure 15.5 A single layer perceptron. R cannot represent the XOR of A and B.

As we saw in chapter 5, the desired response of R to the input patterns is the Exclusive OR (XOR) of the inputs. To ensure that R comes On when pattern 01 is presented, w_{RB}, the weight of the input line from B, must be positive. Similarly, to ensure that R comes On when 10 is presented, w_{RA}, the weight of the input line from A, must be positive. But these two weights guarantee that R will come On when pattern 11 is presented. So the task is impossible.

To demonstrate how this computational inability limited the role of perceptrons as fundamental building blocks of a perceptual system, Minsky and Papert considered the following problem. Take the four shapes shown in figure 15.6. They contain the same number of lines, but arranged in such a way that in (b) and (c) the lines are connected, while in (a) and (d) they form two separate figures. Imagine that they are presented to a perceptron like that in figure 15.3 which has the task of discovering which figures are connected. That is, it must try to find a set of weights from the association units to the response unit such that R is Off when (a) or (d) is presented, and On when (b) or (c) is presented.

The perceptron's retina is sampled by clusters of detectors which feed into the association units. An association unit is active if the feature detected by its retinal receptors is present in the part of the retina where they are located. The only

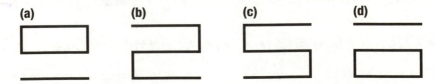

Figure 15.6 Four figures containing similar horizontal and vertical elements. Two figures are connected; two are unconnected. (Based on Minsky and Papert 1969.)

association units which are relevant to the task of distinguishing the connected and unconnected figures are those which can detect the presence of the four short vertical lines. (Let us assume that the receptive fields of these detectors are much smaller than the figure so only one vertical line will excite any one detector.) This can be represented as an XOR problem. To turn the response unit On when (b) is presented but not when (a) is presented, the weight from an association unit detecting the vertical line at the bottom left must be positive. Similarly to turn the response unit On when (c) is presented but not when (a) is presented there must be a positive weight from an association unit detecting the vertical line at the bottom right. But these two weights will ensure that the response unit comes On when figure (d) is presented. Therefore a simple perceptron, summing the weighted inputs from its association units, cannot distinguish (a) and (d) from (b) and (c). So Minsky and Papert concluded that this sort of perceptron could not compute whether all the parts of a geometric figure are connected. By showing that there were other, apparently simple, features of the visual world which such perceptrons could not compute, as well as showing that they would require implausibly large numbers of connections or amounts of time to learn some functions that they *could* compute, Minsky and Papert concluded that there was no point in pursuing perceptrons as a basis for perception. This attack was very effective at the time, and both interest and funding for network approaches to cognitive function dwindled. Artificial Intelligence, which tries to find algorithms which can solve cognitive problems without any attempt to use computational elements which are neuron-like, became more popular.

In fact, as we saw in chapter 5, computing XOR may be a problem for certain perceptrons, but it is not a problem for networks in general. As soon as hidden units are allowed between the association units and the response unit, which can perform some transformation of the information represented by the association units, it is easy for the response unit to compute the XOR of the inputs. Rosenblatt thought that multi-layer nets containing hidden units would solve problems that single layer perceptrons failed on. The problem was that no learning algorithm for training them was known. That is, with more than one layer of modifiable weights in the system no-one knew of a way to decide which weights to adjust on a given learning trial. The discovery that the backpropagation algorithm solved this problem led to the great leap forward in the problem solving power of neural nets in the mid-1980s. Minsky and Papert were aware of the greater power of multi-layer perceptrons but were pessimistic about finding an effective way to train them.

Hinton and Anderson (1981)

Despite the depressing effect of Minsky and Papert's book, work continued on neural nets in the 1970s. Unsupervised self-organizing networks operating by competition to perform feature analysis were described by von der Malsburg (1973). Formal analyses of the mathematical foundations of neural networks were being developed by Grossberg (e.g. 1976) and Arbib (e.g. Amari and Arbib 1977). The basic properties of pattern association networks were analysed in simple models (see Willshaw 1981). The number of distributed patterns that could be associated together in models with binary synapses and binary neurons was analysed. The dependence of this number on the sparseness of the distributed representation was demonstrated. Many of the properties of autoassociation networks with recurrent connections and their ability to store memories and later retrieve the whole memory from a part were described and analysed (see Kohonen 1984).

One of the first sets of papers to spell out the implications of these developments for understanding cognitive functions such as memory and perception was *Parallel Models of Associative Memory* edited by Hinton and Anderson. Pattern associators, autoassociators, competitive networks and self-organizing maps were all described in this book. It was a major step in making evident the relevance and promise of network models for understanding not only brain function, but also cognitive function.

Hopfield (1982)

Content-addressable memory in networks with attractor states

One paper which is generally agreed to have been most influential in generating interest in neural nets as models of cognitive function in the wider scientific community was Hopfield's 'Neural networks and physical systems with emergent collective computational abilities'. The 'emergent collective computational ability' demonstrated by Hopfield was content-addressable memory. He showed that a net of interconnected McCulloch–Pitts type neurons which had learnt a set of patterns could retrieve a complete pattern given a sub-part or a noisy version of it as an input. The system would retain this ability despite minor component damage. (These characteristics are highly desirable for a model of biological memory as was explained in chapters 2–4.)

Hopfield analysed a network of interconnected cells each of which can be in one of two states, firing or not firing. We will represent these states by $+1$ and -1.[1] The state of each cell, i, can be set by an external input. Alternatively it can be set by summing the influences from all the cells, j, to which it is connected, in the usual way. That is, by summing the activity of each cell it is connected to, multiplied by the

[1] It would be natural to label these states 1 and 0, but it is easier to understand the calculations which follow if they are labelled $+1$ and -1. This does not affect the predictions of the model.

strength of the connection between them ($\Sigma_j\, a_j\, w_{ij}$), and testing whether this exceeds a threshold. If it does, the cell goes into state +1; if it does not, it goes into state −1. If the cell changes state, this influences the $\Sigma_j\, a_j\, w_{ij}$ calculations of all the cells to which it is connected, possibly changing their state, and hence their influence on all the other cells to which they are connected, and so on. Hopfield showed that under certain conditions the flow of activation around the net following an input would reach a stable state. That is, no further changes of the activity of the cells would take place.

Hopfield considered a net which had acquired a set of weights by using a modified Hebbian learning rule to store a number of input patterns. To do this, an input, a particular pattern of +1s and −1s, is imposed on the net. The weight of the connections between each pair of cells is then changed according to the state of the activity of the cells on either end. If they are in the same state, the weight of the connection between them is incremented; if they are in the opposite state, the weight is decremented. This procedure is repeated for all patterns to be learnt, adding or subtracting from existing synaptic strengths. Provided the net is not presented with more patterns than it is capable of learning, the net will form a stable memory for each of these patterns.[2] That is, if the pattern is presented as an input to the net in the future the units will remain in the state imposed on them by the input pattern.

The question addressed by Hopfield was: If you take a net whose weights encode a set of memories, what will happen when a novel pattern is presented to the net, and the state of each cell is allowed to change under the influence of all the cells to which it is connected? There are two parts to Hopfield's analysis. In the first he defined the 'energy' of a net, and showed that any novel input will place the net in a state with a higher energy than that of states corresponding to its memories. Second, he showed that the flow of activation following a novel input would always move the state of the net to one of lower energy, that is, towards a state corresponding to one of its memories. This results in the system having the properties of content-addressability, fault tolerance, and noise resistance.

Input patterns and energy

Hopfield defined the energy (E)[3] of the net as:

$$E = -\tfrac{1}{2}\, \Sigma_i\, \Sigma_j\, w_{ij}\, a_j\, a_i \qquad (15.1)$$

[2]If a Hopfield net has N cells it is capable of learning about $0.14N$ random binary patterns. See Hertz *et al.* (1991).

[3]A detailed account of the rationale behind this formula can be found in Hertz *et al.* (1991), but it requires considerable mathematical sophistication to be understood. An account which is accessible to the non-mathematical can be found in Alexsander and Morton (1990), chapter 6.

To understand how the pattern of activity of the cells relates to the energy of the net, consider the three elements in the calculation of E:

(1) $w_{ij} a_j a_i$. This takes a pair of connected cells i and j, and computes the product of the activity of each and the weight of the connection between them. In the simple net which Hopfield analysed, a_i and a_j are either $+1$ or -1.

(2) $\Sigma_i \Sigma_j$ sums this quantity for every pair of connected cells in the network.

(3) The effect of the minus sign outside the $\Sigma\Sigma$ is to *reverse* the contribution of each $w_{ij} a_j a_i$ to E. If $w_{ij} a_j a_i$ is positive it reduces E; if $w_{ij} a_j a_i$ is negative it increases E. The role of the minus sign may seem so pointless that you might think that it must have some hidden significance. In fact, defining E as the negative of $\Sigma_i \Sigma_j w_{ij} a_j a_i$ does not affect the conclusions which Hopfield reached; E could equally well have been defined as a positive quantity. Rumelhart *et al.* (1986b), for example, did just that. They called the positive quantity, $\Sigma_i \Sigma_j w_{ij} a_j a_i$, Goodness, to emphasise that the larger it is, the more constraints in the network have been satisfied. Hopfield used the definition in equation 15.1 to draw attention to the parallel between the behaviour of neural nets and that of other, already well-understood, physical systems like magnetic material. In these it is conventional to define the energy of the system with a minus sign.

To compute E with equation 15.1 for a given state of the net, we must consider the activities, a_i and a_j, of each pair of connected cells, i and j, and the sign of the connection, w_{ij}, between them. If i and j are in the same state (either both $+1$ or both -1), $a_j a_i$ will be positive. So if the connection between them, w_{ij}, is positive, $w_{ij} a_j a_i$ will be positive. This connection, therefore, will reduce E (remember the minus sign in equation 15.1). But if w_{ij} is negative, $w_{ij} a_j a_i$ will be negative, and this connection will increase E. If j and i are in opposite states (one $+1$ and one -1) then the reverse will be the case—positive connections will increase E and negative connections will reduce it.

For all possible sets of states of the cells in the network the corresponding value of E can be calculated with equation 15.1. The result can be envisaged, roughly, with a diagram like that in figure 15.7. Each point on the surface corresponds to a possible

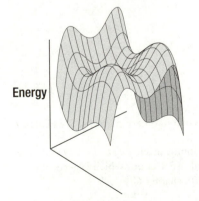

Energy

Figure 15.7   Energy vs activity state landscape.

state of the net, that is, a possible set of values of the activities of the cells. The height of the surface gives the value of E corresponding to that state. The typical result for a net with a large number of cells, which has acquired a number of memories, is a complex surface with valleys, hills, dips and ridges. It turns out that the valleys (i.e. the states of low energy) in the surface correspond to its memories. (The 'memories' are the sets of activities which the system would have in response to the inputs presented during its learning experiences.)

Novel inputs produce higher values of E than memories

The initial value of E, following presentation of a pattern which the net did not experience during the learning phase, is determined by the extent to which the input pattern is similar to one which it has learnt in the past. If the pattern is similar to a previous memory, E will be low; if not, E will be high. To understand why, it is necessary to realise that the weights in the net reflect the activity of the cells in the patterns that the net has tried to learn in the past. Positive weights form between connected cells which were in the same state (both $+1$ or both -1) during learning trials; negative weights form between cells which were in the opposite state (one $+1$, the other -1).

The contribution from each connection to the total energy of the net is determined by the sign of $w_{ij}a_j a_i$. If, following a novel input, the cells on either side of a connection are in the same state, $a_j a_i$ will be positive. If it is a connection where this has usually been true in the past there will be a positive weight, and so $w_{ij}a_j a_i$ will be positive. If the two cells are in opposite states, $a_j a_i$ will be negative. If this has usually been true in the past, there will be a negative weight, and $w_{ij}a_j a_i$ will again be positive. A connection with a positive value of $w_{ij}a_j a_i$ will lead to a reduction of E. Thus cell states which reflect patterns that the net has previously learnt lead to a low value of E. But if the state of the cells after a novel input is not the same as it has most frequently been in the past, there will be many cell pairs where the signs of $a_j a_i$ and w_{ij} will be opposite. So $w_{ij}a_j a_i$ will be negative, and E will increase. Thus activity patterns which are unlike those which the net has previously learnt lead to high values of E.

Changes in state lead to a reduction in E

Hopfield considered what happened to E when cells were allowed to change state under the influence of their neighbours after the initial imposition of a novel input pattern on the net. He found the change in E (ΔE) when a cell i changes its activation (Δa_i) by differentiating equation 15.1:

$$\Delta E = -\Delta a_i \, \Sigma_j \, w_{ij} \, a_j \qquad (15.2)$$

This equation may look intimidating but it is easy to understand in non-mathematical terms. The contribution of cell i to E (as expressed in equation 15.1) is the activity level of i, a_i, multiplied by the activity level of all the cells it is connected to and the weights of the connections between them and i. Thus the change in E (ΔE), when cell i changes activation level, will be the change in activation of i (Δa_i) multiplied by all the connections to i which contribute to E, $\Sigma_j w_{ij} a_j$.

Hopfield's crucial result comes from considering the consequences for E of changes in cell state. There are only two possibilities—a cell goes from $+1 \rightarrow -1$, or from $-1 \rightarrow +1$. If cell i goes from $+1 \rightarrow -1$, Δa_i, the change in activity, is negative. i will only go from $+1 \rightarrow -1$ if the sum of the inputs to it, $\Sigma_j w_{ij} a_j$, is negative. Since both Δa_i and $\Sigma_j w_{ij} a_j$ are negative, their product, $\Delta a_i \Sigma_j w_{ij} a_j$, will be positive. If cell i goes from $-1 \rightarrow +1$, Δa_i is positive. i will only go from $-1 \rightarrow +1$ if the overall input to it, $\Sigma_j w_{ij} a_j$, is positive. So again, $\Delta a_i \Sigma_j w_{ij} a_j$ will be positive. Since equation 15.2 shows that the change in energy, ΔE, is the negative of $\Delta a_i \Sigma_j w_{ij} a_j$, we have Hopfield's remarkable result: All changes of unit activity which occur as the state of the network evolves following an input will lead to the same result—a reduction in E.

Figure 15.7 shows why this is such a significant result. An input to the net will place it in some arbitrary position in the activity state vs energy surface. But the evolution of the state of the net across time, changes in the pattern of cells which are in $+1$ or -1 state, can only go in one direction—downhill, to a lower energy state. Changes in activity will come to an end when the system reaches a state represented by a local minimum in the surface, since any further change will lead to a state with higher energy. These low points often correspond to the states which it acquired during the learning phase—its memories. Thus, following any input, the net will evolve towards a state corresponding to one of its previous memories! It should now be clear why such a net has the properties of content-addressability, pattern completion and noise resistance. The state of the net produced by a partial or inaccurate version of a memory will have a higher energy than the state corresponding to the original memory. It corresponds to a point on one of the 'hillsides' in figure 15.7. If this is presented to the net as an input, and the state of the net is then allowed to evolve, it will move downhill to a state of lower E. Following an incomplete or noisy input, the system will evolve towards a state corresponding to one it previously learnt. That is why these stable states of the network are known as 'attractors'. Thus one of the mysterious properties of human memory, the way that partial hints or resemblances can suddenly bring back complete memories, does not require a magical, homuncular 'executive', recognising similarities and performing the memory retrieval. It can be an emergent consequence of the architecture of the system.

Appendix 1: Installation procedures for **tlearn**

This appendix describes the contents of the **tlearn** distribution disk and how to install **tlearn**. **tlearn** is a connectionist modelling simulation package that provides a graphical user interface (GUI) to back-propagation neural networks. There are versions of **tlearn** for Macintosh and Windows 95 and X Windows/Unix.

Macintosh installation

The distribution disk contains the Macintosh **tlearn** executable and associated exercise files. The **tlearn** executable file is a FAT executable which means that it can be run on both PowerPC and 680×0 Macintosh machines. The disk also provides a set of Chapter folders which contain the project files corresponding to the exercises in this book.

To install **tlearn**, copy the compressed file called **mac_tlearn** to the folder on your Macintosh where you want the application to reside. This file is a self-extracting-archive (SAE) which means that you only need to double-click on the file to begin the installation. (This Installer was created using Stuffit InstallerMaker. © 1990–96 Aladdin Systems, Inc.) You will be asked where you want to place the programme and associated exercise files. The executable is called **tlearn** and can be launched without any other changes to the machine. Note that for simulation of large networks, it may be necessary to increase the memory usage of the application through the Get Info... window available within the Finder.

Windows 95 installation

The distribution disk contains the Windows 95 **tlearn** executable and associated exercise files. To install **tlearn**, copy the compressed file call **win_tlearn(.exe)** (using Windows Explorer) to the folder on your PC where you want the application to reside. This file is a self-extracting-archive (SAE) which means that you only need to double-click on the file to begin the installation. You will be asked where you want to place the programme and associated exercise files. The executable is called **tlearn** and can be launched without any other changes to the machine. We do not recommend that you use **tlearn** running under Windows 3.x (even with Win32s extensions installed) or Windows NT/2000 Pro.

Updates and bug reports

We do not guarantee that the software provided with this book is free of bugs. In fact, we guarantee that if you try hard enough you will find some situations where **tlearn** will break! Please tell us about any software problems you experience by emailing us at

innate@crl.ucsd.edu.

We may not respond to your queries immediately but we will fix the bugs as time permits. You can obtain the latest versions of **tlearn** via anonymous ftp at crl.ucsd.edu (in the pub directory) or on the world wide web at http://crl.ucsd.edu/innate. This site is situated in San Diego. Users from the Old World may find it easier to obtain the latest versions of **tlearn** via anonymous ftp at ftp.psych.ox.ac.uk (also in the pub directory). This site is situated in Oxford, UK.

Updated versions of **tlearn** may also be downloaded from the book's web site,

http://www.oup.co.uk/isbn/0-19-852426-9

Appendix 2: An introduction to linear algebra for neural networks

This appendix describes some simple linear algebra which can help a quantitative understanding of operations in neural networks.

Vectors

A vector is an ordered set of numbers. [9 1] is a two-element vector; [4 0 3 3] is a four-element vector. Figure A2.1 shows the basic computational operation of a unit in a connectionist network—unit i sums the weighted input from a set of units indexed by j. The weight of each connection to unit i is a number, so the set of numbers corresponding to the weights w_{i1}, w_{i2} ... w_{ij} can be represented by the vector $\mathbf{w}$. Similarly, the activities, a_1, a_2 ... a_j, of the units indexed by j are a set of numbers so they can be represented by the vector $\mathbf{a}$.

The general properties of vectors have been analysed in an area of mathematics called linear algebra. Many general properties of neural networks can be understood by treating the inputs and weights as the vectors $\mathbf{a}$ and $\mathbf{w}$, and applying results from linear algebra. We will look at two results. The first shows what input patterns will produce a large net input to a unit with a given set of weights. The second shows what set of input/output transformations a network will be able to learn without interference between the patterns. A more extensive coverage of these and other

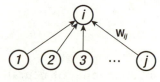

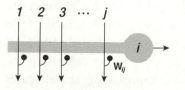

Figure A2.1   A unit i sums input from a set of units indexed by j along weighted connections, w_{ij}. In the upper figure this operation is shown in the conventional format for presenting a connectionist model. In the lower figure it is presented in a way which emphasises the relationship to neural connectivity, with the axons of the j units and the dendrite of unit i made explicit.

applications of linear algebra to neural networks (which does not require an understanding of advanced mathematics) can be found in Jordan (1986).

A geometrical interpretation of a vector

The results which follow are most easily understood in terms of a geometrical interpretation of a vector which is illustrated for a two-element vector in figure A2.2. We define two axes, x and y, at right angles to each other, and treat the first element of the vector as a distance along the x dimension and the second element as a distance along the y dimension. Any two-element vector can then be represented by a line. Figure A2.2 shows the vector [1 1] starting from the origin (0 0) and reaching the point (1 1).

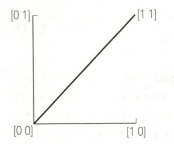

Figure A2.2. A vector in a two-dimensional space with the x axis in the [1 0] direction and the y axis in the [0 1] direction. The first element of a two element vector is the x value, and the second the y value.

In this representation a vector has *length* and *direction* and these will determine what point in vector space it will reach from a given starting point. By Pythagoras's theorem, we can calculate that the vector [1 1] has length $\sqrt{2}$, and we can see that it has a direction of 45° relative to either x or y axis. The length of the vector is determined by the magnitude of the elements; the direction by the relationship between them. Thus the vector [4 4] is longer than the vector [1 1], but points in the same direction. The vectors [3 4] and [4 3] have the same length but point in different directions. A vector with any number of elements can be represented in this way in a space with the appropriate number of dimensions. It will still have the properties of length and direction although these may not be easy to visualise.

The dot product of two vectors

An operation which is fundamental to the quantitative understanding of neural networks is the dot (or inner) product of two vectors. To obtain the dot product the corresponding terms in the two vectors are multiplied and the results summed. If the vector **a** is [1 4] and the vector **w** is [2 0] the dot product, $\mathbf{a} \cdot \mathbf{w}$, is $(1 \times 2 + 4 \times 0) = 2$.

Remember that the net input to unit i in a network is $\Sigma_j\, a_j\, w_{ij}$. So the calculation of net input is equivalent to taking the dot product of the vector representing the activities of the input units and the vector representing the weights of the connections from the input units to unit i. Calling the input activity vector $\mathbf{a}$ and the weight vector $\mathbf{w}$:

$$netinput_i = \mathbf{a} \cdot \mathbf{w} \qquad (A2.1)$$

Normalising the length of a vector

The length of a vector in the $(x\ y)$ space of figure A2.2 is $(x^2 + y^2)^{1/2}$. Since x is the first element in the vector and y the second, $(x^2 + y^2)$ is the dot product of the vector with itself. With an n-element vector we would still represent the length in n-dimensional space by taking the square root of the sum of the squares of the individual elements. So we can represent the length of a vector in terms of a dot product. The length, $|\mathbf{w}|$, of the vector $\mathbf{w}$ is:

$$|\mathbf{w}| = (\mathbf{w} \cdot \mathbf{w})^{1/2} \qquad (A2.2)$$

So, for example, if the vector $\mathbf{w}$ is [3 4]:

$$|\mathbf{w}| = (3^2 + 4^2)^{1/2}$$
$$= 25^{1/2}$$
$$= 5$$

We can scale a vector by dividing each element by the length of the vector. This process is called normalisation. All normalised vectors have a length of 1.0. In the example above, the normalised vector $\mathbf{w}$ would be [3/5 4/5] and:

$$|\mathbf{w}| = [(3/5)^2 + (4/5)^2]^{1/2}$$
$$= (9/25 + 16/25)^{1/2}$$
$$= 1$$

The angle between two vectors

The geometrical interpretation of a vector represented in figure A2.2 illustrates the idea of the direction of a vector, so it is easy to imagine the concept of the angle between two vectors. For example, the angle between the vectors [1 0] and [0 1] is $90°$, and between [1 0] and [1 1] it is $45°$. The angle, θ, between two vectors can be expressed in terms of their dot product. If the two vectors are $\mathbf{a}$ and $\mathbf{w}$, it can be shown that:

$$\cos \theta = (\mathbf{a}/|\mathbf{a}|) \cdot (\mathbf{w}/|\mathbf{w}|) \qquad (A2.3)$$

Equation A2.3 computes the normalised dot product. That is, it computes the dot product of two vectors which have been normalised to a length of 1.0. To illustrate this calculation with a simple example, let **a** be the vector [0 1] and **w** the vector [1 1]. The length of vector **a** is $(0 \times 0 + 1 \times 1)^{1/2} = 1$ and the length of vector **w** is $(1 \times 1 + 1 \times 1)^{1/2} = \sqrt{2}$. So the normalised vector **a** is [0 1] and the normalised vector **w** is $[1/\sqrt{2} \ 1/\sqrt{2}]$. By equation A2.3:

$$\cos \theta = [0 \ 1] \cdot [1/\sqrt{2} \ 1/\sqrt{2}]$$
$$= 0 + 1/\sqrt{2}$$
$$= 0.707$$

So:

$$\theta = \cos^{-1}(0.707)$$
$$= 45°$$

Once vectors have been normalised, the angle between them is a measure of their similarity. Vectors with similar values for corresponding elements point in a similar direction. Once the length of the vectors is fixed, the more similar the two vectors, the higher their dot product. The normalised dot product produces a value which varies from +1 for two vectors pointing in the same direction, through 0 for two vectors at right angles, to −1 for two vectors pointing in opposite directions.

Consider two vectors which have a dot product of zero. When $\cos \theta = 0$ the angle between the vectors is 90°. Such vectors are described as orthogonal. If the vectors **a** and **w**, representing the input activations and the weights respectively, were orthogonal, then the net input to the unit would be zero. If instead the two vectors had zero angle between them, then the normalised dot product would be 1. For intermediate similarities of the two vectors, the degree of similarity would be expressed by the relative magnitude of the normalised dot product. Thus we can think of the basic operation performed by units in connectionist models, computing the level of the net input, as measuring the similarity between their current input vector and their weight vector. This is the basis of generalisation in pattern associators (see chapter 3) and of the operation of competitive nets (see chapter 6).

Linear combinations of vectors and linear independence

Two vector operations which allow us to investigate whether there are any limitations to the set of input/output transformations which a network can learn with a given weight matrix are vector addition and vector multiplication. These can be understood with the geometrical interpretation of a vector illustrated in figure A2.2. Imagine that one were to start at the origin (0 0) and move to the point represented by the vector [1 0] and then, starting from there, move to the point represented by the vector [0 1] (i.e. moving one unit in *y* while remaining at the same position in *x*). One would arrive at the same point as one would by taking the vector

[1 1] from the starting point (0 0). That these two operations achieve the same result (i.e. arriving at the point (1 1)) is an example of the principle of vector addition. The result of combining the two vectors is equivalent to the result which would be achieved by the vector obtained by the element-by-element addition of the two vectors. In this case, [1 0] + [0 1] is equivalent to [1 1]. A similar result holds for scaling a vector by a constant. Starting at the origin, (0 0), the vector [1 1] reaches the point (1 1). Repeating the operation [1 1] from there reaches (2 2). In other words, 2[1 1] is equivalent to [2 2]. Multiplying a vector by a constant is equivalent to multiplying each of its elements by the constant. Combining the examples of addition and multiplication above gives us the result that [2 2] is equivalent to 2[1 0] + 2[0 1].

Any point in the $(x\ y)$ plane in figure A2.2 can be reached by adding (or subtracting) appropriate multiples of [1 0] and [0 1]. A vector is represented by the position in vector space of its end-point. So any two-element vector is equivalent to a suitably scaled combination of [1 0] and [0 1]. For example, [7 11]   7[1 0] + 11[0 1], [−1.5 4.2]   −1.5[1 0] + 4.2[0 1], and so on. It is easy to see this when the two vectors are [1 0] and [0 1], but the result is a general one, not dependent on having zero elements in the vectors. Any two-element vector can be made by scaling and addition of any other pair of two element vectors (provided they are not co-linear such as [1 1] and [2 2]). The same principle applies with larger vectors. In general, n-element vectors are equivalent to scaled combinations of other n-element vectors.

The consequence of this for the range of input/output transformations which a linear network can learn is very important. The output of a network is determined by the net input, and this is determined by the dot product of input vector and weight vector. The dot product is determined by the length and direction of the vectors. As we have just seen, a scaled combination of any pair of two-element vectors can reach the same point in $(x\ y)$ space, and thus have the equivalent length and direction, as any two-element input vector. So, once a network with two input units has been trained on two input vectors, its response to any new input vector is determined. It will be the combination of the response to the first two, scaled in the same way that the input vectors would be scaled to produce the new input vector. For example, take a single layer network with two input units and two output units that has been trained to produce the pattern (0.7 0.5) in response to the input [3 1] and the pattern (0.1 0.7) in response to the input [2 5]. If it is then given the input [5 6], it will produce the output (0.8 1.2) (because [5 6]   [3 1] + [2 5]). If it is given the input [6 1] it will produce the output (1.5 0.9) (because [6 1]   2.15[3 1] − 0.23[2 5]). And so on for any new input. Any attempt to teach the network a different response (by changing the weights) will lead to the loss of the ability to produce the correct response to [3 1] and [2 5]. The general conclusion is this: The response of a network to any input pattern which can be made by linear combination (addition, subtraction and multiplicative scaling) of input patterns which it has already learnt is determined. Thus a linear network can only learn arbitrary responses to sets of input patterns which cannot be achieved by combination of other input patterns. Such sets are known as *linearly independent*.

A special case of linear independence which is easy to appreciate is orthogonality. Take the set of input patterns [1 0 0], [0 1 0], and [0 0 1]. (These are orthogonal because the dot product of any two is zero.) They are linearly independent because none can be made by linear addition or multiplication of the other two. If these were the three input patterns to a network, any arbitrary set of responses could be associated with the three inputs because a different set of weights would be used to store each pattern. Imagine that the pattern [1 1 1] is now added to the set. The set is no longer linearly independent because the fourth pattern can be made by summing the other three. The same set of weights will be used to produce the response to these patterns as were used to respond to the other three. So whatever responses have been associated with the first three patterns will determine the response of the network to the fourth.

Linear and non-linear systems: a caveat

Much of the interest in the vector analysis of neural network operations comes from the fact that with this approach it is possible to analyse the theoretical abilities of networks rather than trying to generalise from the success or failure of specific simulations. For example, it can be shown that the requirement for a perceptron with a linear activation function, trained with the Hebb rule, to learn a set of arbitrary input/output transformations is that the input patterns must be orthogonal. If the Delta rule is used, the requirement is the less restrictive one that the patterns must be linearly independent. However, results such as these are only true for networks with *linear* dynamics. That is, those in which the output is a linear function of the input. The vector operations that we have considered so far have all assumed linearity. For example, in a linear system the vector [2 2] produces dot products double that of the vector [1 1], so the output in response to the input [2 2] would be double that to the input [1 1]. Similarly, the section on linear independence above required that the result of combining the inputs [3 1 2] and [4 1 5] was equivalent to the input [7 2 7].

Much of the power of networks in the brain, and connectionist models, comes from the fact that they are *non-linear*. Non-linearity is achieved by using properties such as thresholds or saturation at high levels of input. If an output unit has a threshold of 5 then the input [2 2] to a weight vector [1 1] would not have double the effect of the input [1 1]. The net inputs would be different (4 and 2) but, because of the threshold, the resulting activity of the output unit would be the same, zero. Similarily, the result of an activation function which saturated at high input levels would be that the response of an output unit to the input [10 10 10] would not necessarily be 10 times that to the input [1 1 1].

All the networks described in chapters 8 to 14 which simulate the performance of real cognitive tasks are non-linear. Limitations such as the requirement that input patterns should be orthogonal to be acquired by a Hebbian network do not apply to non-linear networks. Unfortunately it is much harder to analyse non-linear networks, so simple generalisations about what non-linear networks can or cannot do are not easy to make. But note that non-linear activation functions such as the sigmoid have a quasi-linear component for net inputs around zero. Linear algebra can be used for understanding the operation of the network in the region where its response is linear.

Appendix 3: User manual for `tlearn`

This reference manual provides documentation on **tlearn** software version 1.0.1. The first section provides a quick introduction to the software and its functionality. The second section gives complete descriptions of the application's menus and dialogue boxes. The third section offers a quick reference to command keys and other shortcuts. The final section offers some advice on troubleshooting and other error messages.

Introduction

tlearn is a neural network simulator which implements the backpropagation learning rule, including simple recurrent network learning and backpropagation through time, and provides a number of displays which show the network internals. **tlearn** includes a fully functional text editor as well as a number of data analysis utilities.

Configuration files

tlearn organises files and simulations into projects. The project file is a machine readable file which stores information about option settings for training and testing. The name of the project file specifies the name of the project and acts as the prefix for other associated files for the project. There are three necessary associated files for every project, namely the **<fileroot>.cf, <fileroot>.data** and **<fileroot>.teach** files, where **<fileroot>** is the name of the project file. A complete description of these files is given in the section *Network configuration and training files*.

Editor functions

The **tlearn** text editor includes standard text editor features (e.g., Find and Replace, Cut, Copy and Paste, Revert, Go To Line, and a current line number indicator). As well as the standard features **tlearn** provides two text utilities, namely Sort... and Translate... which are found in the Edit menu. Sort provides a mechanism for sorting of files with arrays of numeric values. Translate allows a set of find and replace actions to be carried out in an automated way. These utilities are fully described in the section *Menu and dialogue reference* where the description of their associated dialogue boxes is given. Editor shortcut keys are given in the section *Command key and shortcut reference.*

Network training and testing functions

`tlearn` provides two types of network run modes: training and testing. These functions are found in the Network menu. The Train the network action begins training from an initial set of random weights and trains the network for the specified number of sweeps. The number of training sweeps is set in the Training Options dialogue box. The Resume training action resumes training from the current set of weights for a further specified number of sweeps. Further options and settings for training are described in the *Menu and dialogue reference* section where the Training Options dialogue is described.

The Verify network has learned action presents the trained network with a testing set specified in the Testing Options dialogue box. The values of the output node/s for each data presentation are given in the Output window. The Probe selected nodes action similarly presents the specified data set to the network and in this case outputs the values of the selected nodes specified in the .cf file. All the training and testing actions can be aborted by choosing Abort from the Network menu or the `tlearn` Status display.

Network utilities

There are two Network utilities located in the Special menu. These are Output Translation... and Lesioning... The Output Translation... utility allows the translation of 0/1 vectors to text. When the network operation is verified, or the network activities display is used to display network outputs, the output translation can also be given. The Output Translation... utility is described fully in the *Menu and dialogue reference* section where the Output Translation dialogue is described.

The Lesioning... utility allows weight files for a specific network to be modified so that the effects of lesioning the network, i.e., removing some connections or nodes, can be examined. The Lesioning... utility is described fully in the *Menu and dialogue reference* section where the Lesioning dialogue is described.

Data analysis functions

There are two Data Analysis utilities located in the Special menu, namely Cluster Analysis... and Principal Component Analysis.... The Cluster Analysis... utility allows a hierarchical clustering to be performed on a set of data vectors. The Cluster Analysis... utility is described fully in the *Menu and dialogue reference* section where the Cluster Analysis dialogue is described.

The Principal Component Analysis... utility allows the principal components of a set of data vectors to be determined and the projection of such data onto its principal components to be obtained. The Principal Component Analysis... utility is described fully in the *Menu and dialogue reference* section where the Principal Component Analysis dialogue is described.

`tlearn` *displays*

`tlearn` has seven displays which illustrate different aspects of the network simulation or show the results of some of the data analysis utilities. Three of the displays can be selected only when there is a project open as they rely on the definition of the network provided by the object files. The project dependent displays are the Node Activities display, the Connection Weights diagram and the Network Architecture display. All of the displays (apart from the Status display) can be copied to the clipboard and pasted into word processors or other editors that can handle picture graphics.

The `tlearn` Status display (shown in figure A3.1) indicates the name of the open project, if there is one, and the current state of `tlearn` training. The status display also provides buttons to allow the display to be iconified; for the current network weights to be saved to a file; and for the network training to be aborted.

The Error Display (figure A3.2) gives a graph of error values for the training or testing actions carried out on the current network. Selection radio buttons at the top of the display allow the error graph to be shown as lines or as points.

The Node Activities display (figure A3.3) presents the activities of the nodes of the network as Hinton diagram displays. The orientation of the nodes on this display is

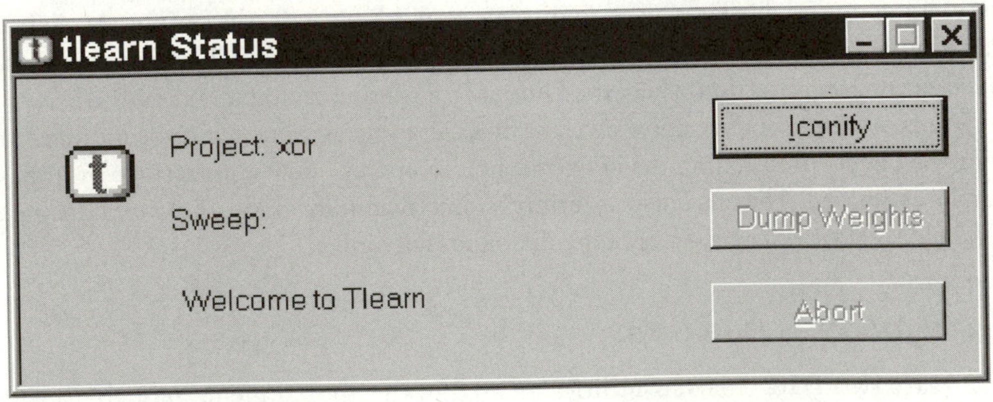

Figure A3.1 `tlearn` Status display

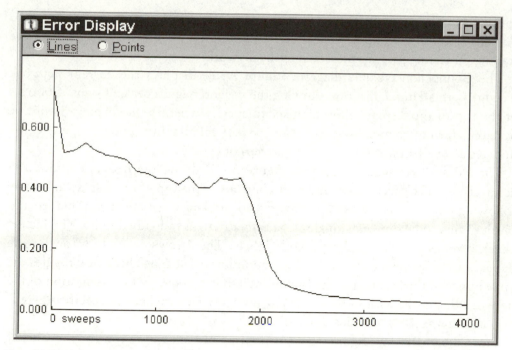

Figure A3.2   Error Display

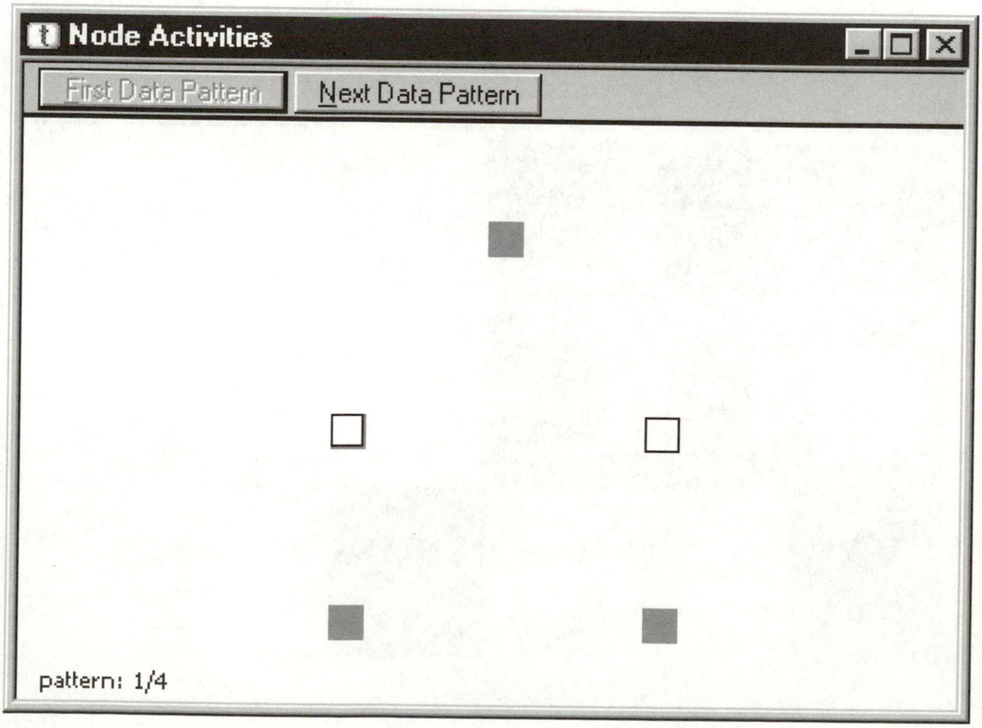

Figure A3.3   Node Activities Display

specified by the network orientation set on the Network Architecture display. Two buttons (First Data Pattern, Next Data Pattern) allow the user to step through the training or testing patterns presented to the network.

The Connection Weights diagram (figure A3.4) displays the current network weights with a Hinton diagram showing the weight magnitudes and signs. Controls at the top of the display allow the user to specify whether the display should be updated during training, and the regularity of the diagram update; specifically, updates can be set for every 1, 5, or 10 sweeps or epochs.

The Network Architecture display (figure A3.5) draws the network nodes and connections. The check boxes and radio buttons at the top of the display allow the following settings: The Slabs check box, when checked, causes the input, hidden and output units to be shown as single slabs rather than as individual units. The Labels check box toggles the display of node labels. The Arrows check box toggles the appearance of arrow heads on the connection lines. The Bias check box toggles the appearance of the bias node. The Orient: radio buttons specify the orientation of the network display as bottom-to-top or left-to-right. The orientation specified here is also used in the Node Activities display.

The Cluster Display (figure A3.6) is used to present the output of the Cluster Analysis... utility (found in the Special menu). Cluster analysis generates a cluster

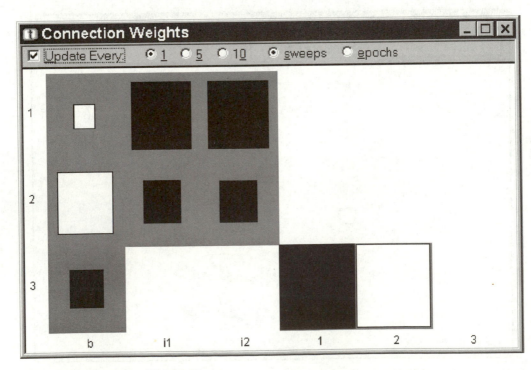

Figure A3.4   Connection Weights Diagram

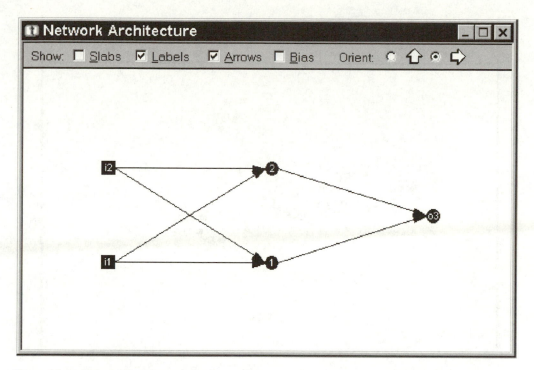

Figure A3.5   Network Architecture display

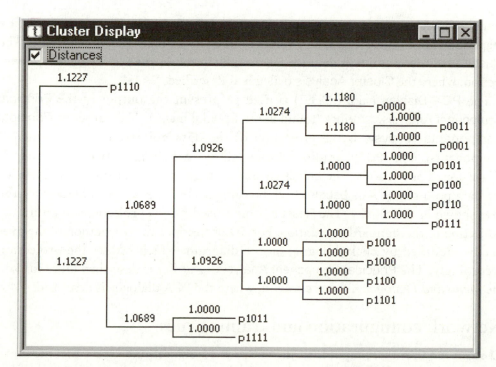

Figure A3.6   Cluster Display

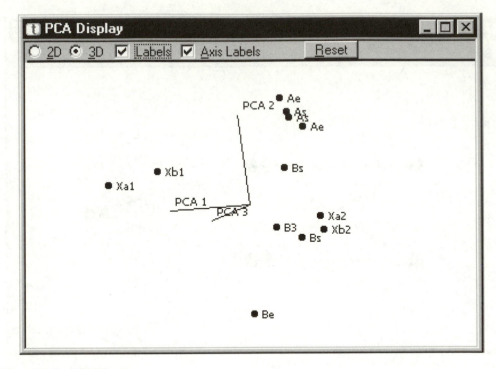

Figure A3.7   PCA Display

diagram, which is a tree illustrating the clusters of the data. The **Distances** check box toggles the appearance of distance values on the cluster diagram in the display. The **Cluster Analysis. . .** utility is described more fully in the *Menu and dialogue reference* section, where the **Cluster Analysis** dialogue is described.

The **PCA Display** (figure A3.7) is used to present the output of the **Principal Component Analysis. . .** utility (found in the **Special** menu). The output of **Principal Components Analysis** is the projection of the data points onto their principal components. The **2D/3D** radio buttons allow switching between 2- and 3-dimensioned projections. The **Labels** check box toggles the appearance of labels for the data points. The **Axis Labels** check box toggles the appearance of labels for the axes shown in the display. The **Reset** button is used for 3D projections to return the projection to the standard orientation. For 3D projections the orientation of the axes can be modified by click-dragging on the diagram, which rotates the projection accordingly. The **Principal Component Analysis. . .** utility is described more fully in the *Menu and Dialogue reference* section, where the PCA dialogue is described.

Network configuration and training files

tlearn requires three input files: the network configuration—or **c f** file, the input pattern—or **data** file, the output (teacher) pattern—or **teach** file and the project file. An additional input file may be used to specify a reset schedule for context nodes—the **reset** file. **tlearn** may also create output files for weights, error, node activations, etc. All files should begin with the same name; this is referred to as the *fileroot*. The project file is called **<fileroot>**. The project file is created automatically when the user starts a new project in **tlearn**. The different files are distinguished by having different extensions (where an extension consists of a period followed by a fixed designator). Every **tlearn** simulation will contain at least the following 4 files:

```
<fileroot>
<fileroot>.cf
<fileroot>.data
<fileroot>.teach
```

The optional reset file is called:

```
<fileroot>.reset
```

Network configuration (.cf) file

This file describes the configuration of the network. It must conform to a fairly rigid format, but in return offers considerable flexibility in architecture. There are three sections to this file. Each section begins with the keyword in upper case, flush-left. The three section keywords are **NODES:, CONNECTIONS:** and **SPECIAL:**. Note the colon. Sections must be described in the above order.

NODES:

This is the first line in the file. The second line specifies the total number of nodes in the network as '**nodes = #**'. Inputs do *not* count as nodes. The total number of inputs is specified in the third line as '**inputs = #**'. The fourth line specifies the number of nodes which are designated as outputs according to '**outputs = #**'. (Note that these two lines essentially give the lengths of the **.data** and **.teach** vectors.) Lastly, the output nodes are listed specifically by number (counting the first node in the network as 1) in the order that the **.teach** information is to be matched up with them. The form of the specification is '**output nodes are <node-list>**'. (If only a single output is present one can say '**output node is #**'). If no output nodes are present, this line is omitted. Spaces are critical.

Node number can be important for networks in which there are fixed copy-back links. Copy-back links allow for saving the node activations so that they can be used on the next sweep. Because node activations are calculated in ascending order, with the order determined by the number of the node, it is important that node activations be saved *after* they are calculated. It is also important that a unit which receives input from a node which is serving as a state/context node (and is thus storing some other node's activation from the previous time cycle) calculate its activation before the state/context node gets updated on the current sweep. Both considerations lead to the following rule of thumb: Any node receiving input from a state/context node must have a *lower* node number than the state/context node. This is illustrated in the example `.cf` file at the end of this section.

CONNECTIONS:
This is the first line of the next section. The line following this must specify the number of groups, as in '**groups** =#' (All connections in a group are constrained to be of identical strength; e.g., as in the translation invariance problem in Chapter 7 of Plunkett and Elman (1997); in most cases **groups** = 0.) Following this, information about connections is given in the form:

```
<node-list> from <node-list> [= <fixed> | <group #> | <min & max>]
```

If values are specified for **<min & max>** (e.g., −5.0 & 5.0) then the weights for the relevant connections will not be allowed to exceed these minimum and maximum values. Weights specified as **fixed** will have values fixed at their initialisation values (if **<min & max>** are set to 1.0 & 1.0, then the weights are set to 1.0 and remain unchanged throughout learning; this is typically used for connections from context units).
    It is also possible to say:

```
<node-list> from <node-list> = <min> & <max> fixed one-to-one
```

This last form is used, e.g., when node 1 is fed from node 4, node 2 is fed from node 5 and node 3 is fed from node 6, as opposed to the ususal case of node 1 being fed from nodes 4–6, node 2 being fed by nodes 4–6 and node 3 being fed by nodes 4–6.
    A **<node-list>** is a comma-separated list of node numbers, with dashes indicating that intermediate node numbers are included. A **<node-list>** contains *no spaces*. Nodes are numbered counting from 1. Inputs are likewise numbered counting from 1, but are designated as 'i1', 'i2', etc. Node 0 always outputs a 1 and serves as the bias node. If biases are desired, connections *must* be specified from node 0 to specific other nodes (not all nodes need be biased). Groups must be labelled by integers ascending in sequence from 1. It is also permissible to say

```
<group #> = <min & max>
```

provided that the group has already been completely defined.

SPECIAL:

This is the first line of the third and final section. Optional lines can be used to specify whether some nodes are to be linear ('**linear = <node-list>**'), which nodes are to be bipolar ('**bipolar = <node-list>**')[1], which nodes are selected for special printout ('**selected = <node-list>**'), and the initial weight limit on the random initialization of weights ('**weight_limit = <#>**'). Again, *spaces are critical*.

Example **.cf** files are given at the end of this main section for several network architectures.

Network data (.**data**) file

This file defines the input patterns which are presented to **tlearn**. The first line must either be '**distributed**' (the normal case) or '**localist**' (when only a few of many input lines are nonzero). The next line is an integer specifying the number of input vectors to follow. The remainder of the **.data** file consists of the input. These may be input as integers or floating-point numbers.

In the (normal) '**distributed**' case, the input is a set of vectors. Each vector contains n_i floating point numbers, where n_i is the number of inputs to the network. Note that these input vectors are always used in the exact order that they appear in the **.data** file (unless the randomization option is specified).

In the '**localist**' case, the input is a set of **<node-list>**'s (defined below) listing only the numbers of those nodes whose values are to be set to one. Node lists follow the conventions described in the **.cf** file.

Examples:

```
distributed
4
0  0
1  1
0  1
1  0
localist
4
1
2,3
2
1-3,5
```

---

[1]Linear nodes simply output the inner-product of the input and weight vectors, or *net*. Logistic units are sigmoidal: The activation function for each node is $y = 1/(1 + e^{-net})$. Logistic node output is bounded by 0 and 1. Bipolar nodes have an extended range—their output ranges continuously from -1 to $+1$. The activation function for bipolar nodes is $y = (2/(1 + e^{net})) - 1$.

Network teach (`.teach`) file

This file is required whenever learning is to be performed. As with the `.data` file, the first line must be either '`distributed`' (the normal case) or '`localist`' (when only a few of many target values are nonzero). The next line is an integer specifying the number of output vectors to follow.

In the (normal) '`distributed`' case, each output vector contains n_o floating point numbers, where n_o is the number of outputs in the network. An asterisk ('*') may be used in place of a floating point number to indicate a 'don't care' output.

In the '`localist`' case, each output vector is a list of nodes designating the nodes whose target is a 1 as opposed to a 0.

Example:
```
distributed
4
0.1
0.9
*
0.
```

Network reset (`.reset`) file

This file is required whenever the context nodes need to be reset to zero. As with the `.teach` file, the first line must be an integer specifying the number of time stamps to follow. Each time stamp is an integer specifying the time step at which the network is to be completely reset. As with the `.teach` file, the time stamps must appear in ascending order.

Example:
```
2
0
3
```

Weights (`<fileroot>-<runs>.wts`) file

At the conclusion of a `tlearn` session, the results of training are saved in a 'weights file'. This file name incorporates the fileroot, the number of learning sweeps (runs) which resulted in this network, and ends with '`wts`' as the literal extension. This file contains weights and biases resulting from training. Weights are stored for every node (except the bias node, 0), from every node (including the bias node). A sample weights file for an XOR (**2**×**2**×**1**) network would be:

```
NETWORK CONFIGURED BY TLEARN
# weights after 10000 sweeps
# WEIGHTS
# TO NODE 1
-6.995693            (from bias node)
4.495790             (from input 1)
4.495399             (from input 2)
0.000000             (from node 1)
0.000000             (from node 2)
0.000000             (from node 3)
# TO NODE 2
2.291545
-5.970089
-5.969466
0.000000
0.000000
0.000000
# TO NODE 3
4.426321
0.000000
0.000000
-9.070239
-8.902939
0.000000
```

This file can also be produced by requesting periodic check-pointing (dumping of a weights file) either in order to recreate intermediate stages of learning, or to avoid having to re-run a lengthy simulation in the event of premature termination. This weights file can be loaded into **tlearn** in order to test with a trained network.

Error (.err) file

If error logging is requested, a file will be produced containing the RMS error, saved at user-specifiable intervals.

Example .cf *files*

Example 1:

This illustrates a feedforward network which implements a **2×2×1** XOR network (cf. chapter 5). Notice that in **tlearn**, the 2 inputs are *not* nodes; the network itself has only 2 hidden nodes and 1 output node. (There are still learnable connections from the 2 inputs to the 2 hidden nodes.)

```
NODES:
nodes = 3
inputs = 2
outputs = 1
output node is 3
CONNECTIONS:
groups = 0
1-3 from 0
1-2 from i1-i2
3 from 1-2
SPECIAL:
selected = 1-2
weight_limit = 1.0
```

Example 2:

This illustrates a network that receives 3 inputs, has 4 hidden nodes, 2 output nodes and 4 copy-back nodes; each copy-back node receives the activation of the corresponding hidden node at the prior cycle. Notice that the copy-back nodes are linear, receive no bias, and have fixed downward connections from the hidden nodes. In the number scheme, **i1–i3** designate the 3 inputs; nodes **1–4** are the hidden nodes; nodes **5–6** are the output nodes; and nodes **7–10** are the copy-back (state/context) nodes.

```
NODES:
nodes = 10
inputs = 3
outputs = 2
output nodes are 5-6
CONNECTIONS:
groups = 0
1-6 from 0
1-4 from i1-i3
1-4 from 7-10
```

```
5-6 from 1-4
7-10 from 1-4 = 1. & 1. fixed one-to-one
SPECIAL:
linear = 7-10
weight_limit = 1.
selected = 1-4
```

Example 3:

This illustrates a network which receives 9 inputs, has 3 hidden nodes (**1–3**) and 1 output node (**4**). The 3 hidden nodes have limited receptive fields; each one receives connections from only 3 of the inputs. In addition, the connections are grouped (i.e. trained to assume the same values), thus benefiting from the learning that occurs for other nodes in the group (e.g., even when deprived of input). The result is that each hidden node has 3 different input weights; each of the 3 weights has a corresponding weight leading into the other 2 hidden nodes. This scheme is similar to the translation invariance network in chapter 7 of Plunkett and Elman (1997). Finally, weights are confined to the range **–5/+5**.

```
NODES:
nodes = 4
inputs = 9
outputs = 1
output node is 4
CONNECTIONS:
groups = 3
1-4 from 0
1 from i1 = group 1
1 from i2 = group 2
1 from i3 = group 3
2 from i4 = group 1
2 from i5 = group 2
2 from i6 = group 3
3 from i7 = group 1
3 from i8 = group 2
3 from i9 = group 3
4 from 1-3
group 1 = -5 & 5
group 2 = -5 & 5
group 3 = -5 & 5
SPECIAL:
selected = 1-3
weight_limit = 0.1
```

Menu and dialogue reference

The **File** *menu*

Figure A3.8 shows the file menu and associated commands, which act as follows:

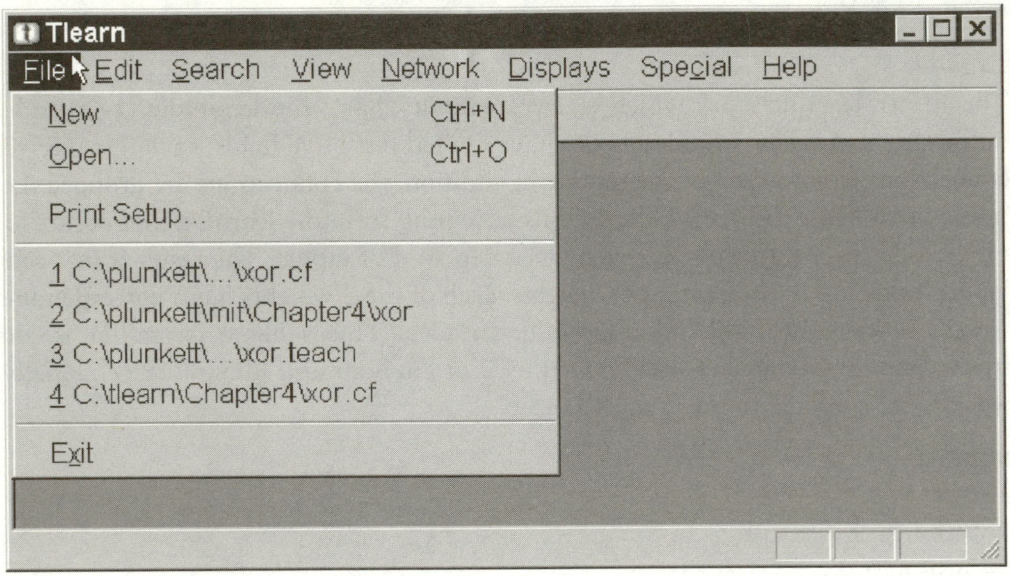

Figure A3.8 File menu

New	Creates a new text file window.
Open...	Brings up the **File Open** dialogue box to allow selection of text files for editing.
Close	Closes the current window, either a text window or a display.
Save	Saves the current text window.
Save As...	Brings up the **Save As** dialogue box where a name for saving the current text window can be selected.
Revert	Reverts to the previously saved version of the file.
Page Setup...	Brings up the **Page Setup** dialogue box.
Print...	Prints the current window. Text windows and displays (apart from the **Status** display) can be printed.
Quit	Quits tlearn.

The Edit *menu*

Figure A3.9 shows the Edit Menu. All but the last two commands (Sort... and Translate...) are standard. Note that the Copy command can also be used to copy

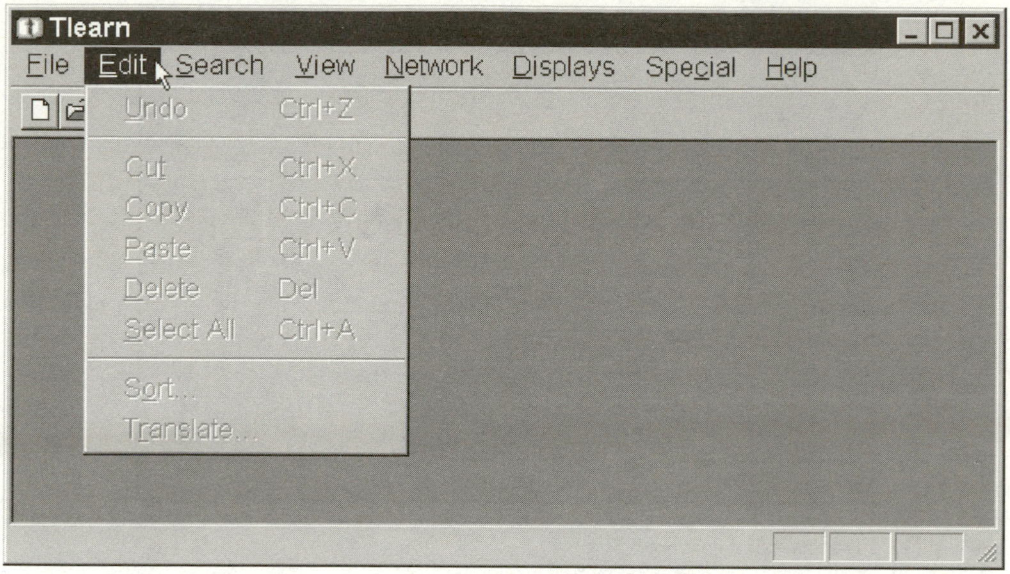

Figure A3.9 Edit menu

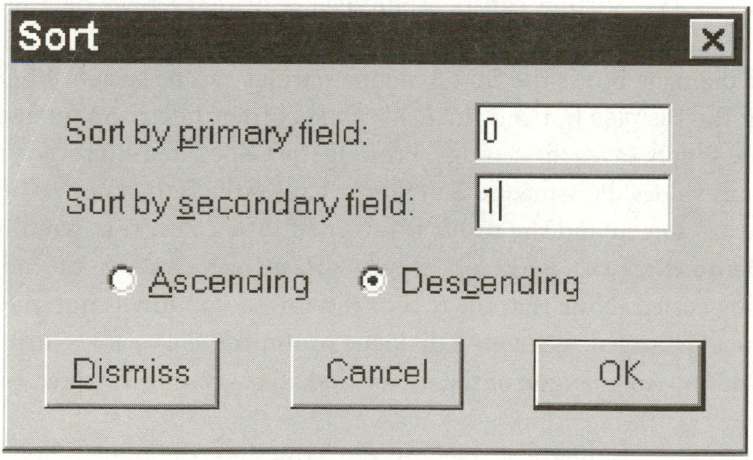

Figure A3.10 Sort dialogue box

displays to the clipboard so they can be pasted elsewhere (e.g. word processors, graphics editors). Sort... and Translate... are text utilities used for manipulating text files for use with **tlearn**.

The Sort... command brings up the Sort dialogue (shown in figure A3.10) which is used to specify settings for a Sort action to be applied to the current text window. Sorting can only be applied to text files which contain a couple array of numerical values, that is, each line of the text window must contain an equal number of

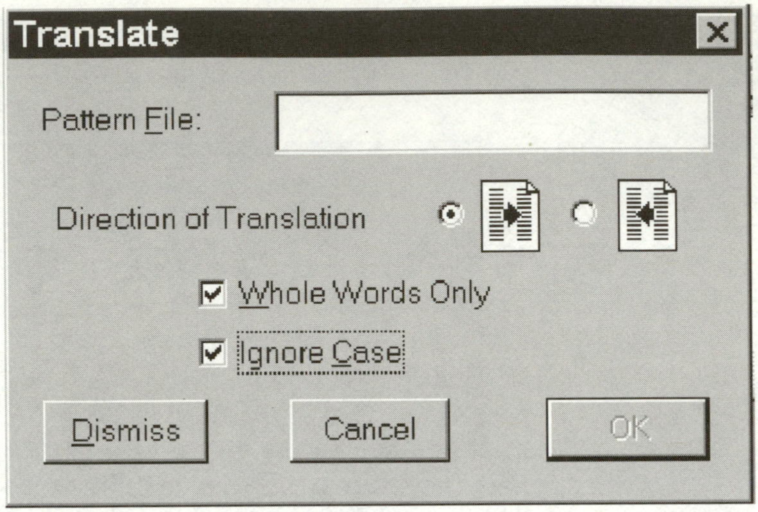

Figure A3.11   Translate dialogue box

numerical values separated by white space. The counting of fields begins at zero (0) rather than one (1). Sorting can be done over a primary field or a primary and secondary field, and the lines can be sorted in ascending or descending order. As with many of the dialogue boxes the Sort dialogue settings can be specified but dismissed (by pressing the Dismiss button). Instead of executing the action immediately, the Sort dialogue simply saves the settings. Pressing the Cancel button reverts the settings to the previous values. Pressing the Sort button causes the Sort action to be done. The lines of text are sorted and the result is returned into a new text window which is called '`<WindowName> Sorted`' where `<WindowName>` is the name of the window being sorted. Note that the text of the sorted window is not saved to a file, but when the file is saved, a Save As dialogue prompts the user for a filename for the new text window. An example of the use of Sort... is given in Chapter 5 of Plunkett and Elman 1997).

The Translate... command brings up the Translate dialogue (shown in figure A3.11) for a Translation action to be applied to the current text window. The translation requires a pattern file which contains lines which specify the translations to be performed. The format of the lines which specify the translation is as follows:

`<find_string> <replace string>`

The find string cannot contain spaces, but the replace string, which is all of the line apart from the first word or string, can contain spaces.

An example pattern file is:

```
JE Jeff Elman
KP Kim Plunkett
TL tlearn
BP Backpropagation
```

The Translation action is performed in the following manner: A new window with a copy of the text of the current window is displayed (the new window is given the name of the current window with the word 'translated' appended to it), then each line of the pattern file is used in turn and the translation is applied to the new window. If the direction of translation is from left to right then occurrences of the find string are replaced by the replace string. If the direction of translation is from right to left then occurrences of the replace string are replaced by the find string. The Whole Words Only check box when checked ensures that the string being searched for is whole words only, that is, the string has surrounding white space. The Ignore Case check box allows the searching to find strings regardless of the mixture of upper and lower case letters. An example of the use of Translate is given in chapter 8 of Plunkett and Elman (1997).

The Search *menu*

Figure A3.12 shows the Search menu. The Search menu commands act as follows:

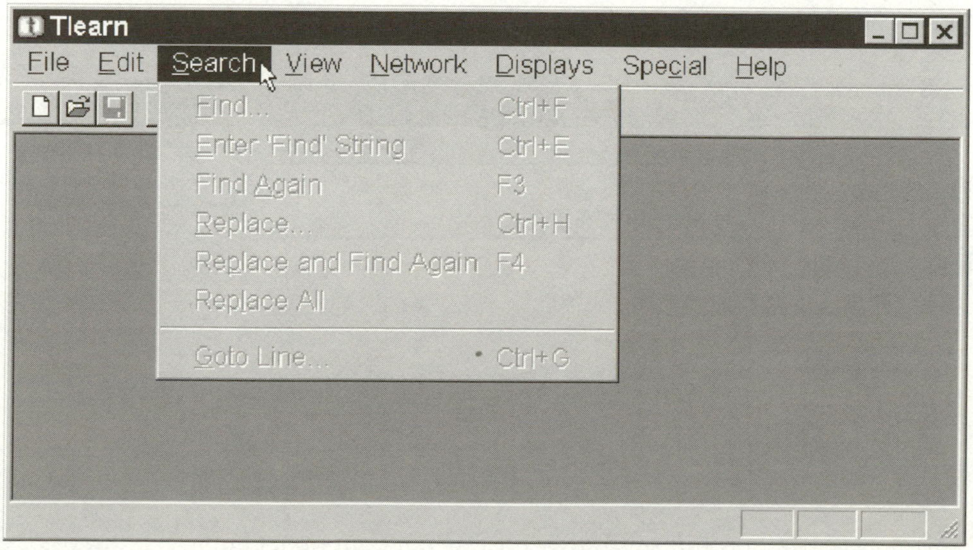

Figure A3.12 Search menu

Find…	Brings up the **Find and Replace** dialogue (shown in figure A3.13), where the **Find** string and the **Replace** string can be entered and conditions for document searching can be set.
Find Again	Repeats the previous search in the current search direction.
Replace	Replaces the currently selected **Find** string with the **Replace** string. If the current selection is empty or not equal to the **Find** string then no replacement is made. Hence, the **Replace** action is only sensibly done after a successful **Find** action.
Replace & Find Again	Replaces the selected **Find** string with the **Replace** string and searches for the next occurrence of the **Find** string.
Replace All	Replaces all occurrences of the **Find** string from the current cursor position to the end of the document. If the **Wrap Around** option is chosen then all occurrences of the **Find** string in the whole document are replaced.
Go To Line…	Brings up the **Go To Line** dialogue where the cursor is moved to the line number entered.

When a **Find** string has been entered, then the **Find** button can be pressed and a search begins for occurrences of the **Find** string in the current window starting from the current cursor position. If an occurrence of the **Find** string is found, then the search stops and the occurrence is highlighted. If no occurrence is found then the system beeps. Two of the options in the **Find and Replace** dialogue are the same as those found in the **Translate…** dialogue; namely **Whole Words Only**, which ensures that the occurrences of the **Find** string found have surrounding white space; and **Ignore Case**, which allows searching to find strings regardless of upper or lower case

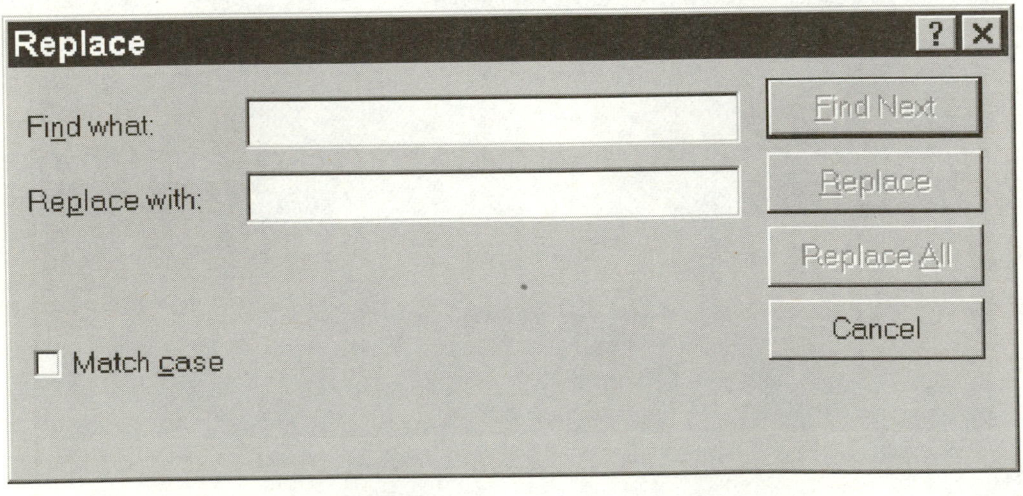

Figure A3.13   Find and Replace dialogue box

letters. The Wrap Around option causes searching which reaches the end of the current window to begin again from the start of the document. Enter 'Find' String copies the current selection into the Find string. If no text is currently selected, then this menu item is disabled.

The Network *menu*

Figure A3.14 shows the Network menu. The Network menu commands act as follows:

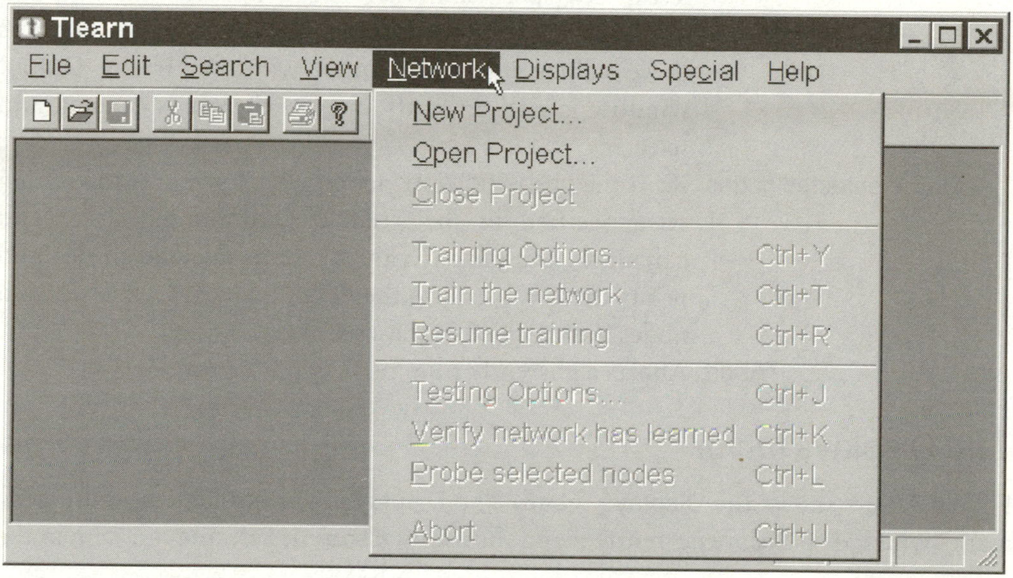

Figure A3.14   Network menu

New Project. . .   Brings up the New Project dialogue box, which allows the entry of a new project name. Once the name is chosen, **tlearn** opens three new text windows associated with the project, that is, the **<name>.cf**, **<name>.data** and **<name>.teach** files. If these files already exist in the directory in which the project was opened then the files are opened, otherwise the windows are empty.

Open Project. . .   Brings up the Open Project dialogue box, which allows the selection of **tlearn** project files. Once a project is chosen for opening, **tlearn** opens the three associated **.cf**, **.data** and **.teach** text files.

Close Project   Sets the current project to none and closes the current project's **.cf**, **.data** and **.teach** file windows, if they are currently open.

Training Options...	Brings up the Training Options dialogue box. Training Options dialogue box is described in more detail below.
Train the network	Begins training the network according to the training options set in the Training Options dialogue box.
Resume training	Resumes training from the current set of network weights.
Testing Options...	Brings up the Testing Options dialogue box. The Testing Options dialogue box is described in more detail below.
Verify network has learned	Runs the verifying network action which presents the testing set (specified in the Testing Options dialogue) and calculates the output values of the output units and prints these values into the Output window. If the Output window is not currently opened then it is opened and selected.
Probe selected nodes	Runs the probe network action which presents the testing set (specified in the Testing Options dialogue) and calculates the output values of the selected nodes and prints these values into the Output window. The selected nodes are specified in the .cf file.
Abort	Aborts a currently running network action.

The Displays *menu*

Figure A3.15 shows the Displays menu. The Displays menu indicates with check marks which displays are currently being shown by **tlearn**. Selecting an item in the

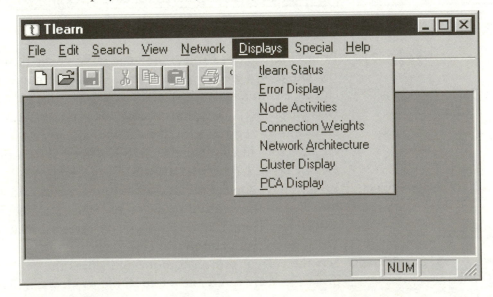

Figure A3.15   Displays menu

Displays menu either hides the display, if it is currently being shown, or shows the display if it is currently hidden. Note that a display window, if it is currently shown, can be brought to the front by selecting it from the Window menu.

The Special *menu*

Figure A3.16 shows the Special menu. The Special menu commands act as follows:

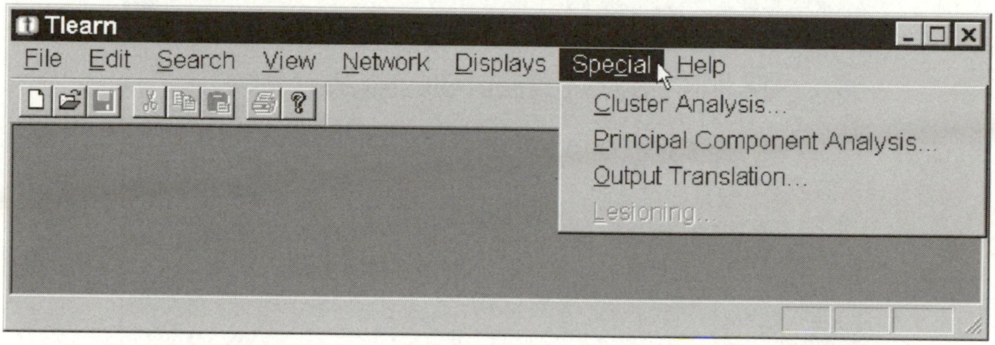

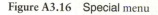

Figure A3.16   Special menu

Cluster Analysis...   Brings up the Cluster Analysis dialogue. The Cluster Analysis action allows a hierarchical clustering to be performed on a set of vectors specified in a file and for the results of the clustering to be displayed in the form of a cluster diagram which shows the tree of clusters that are identified by the clustering method. The Cluster Analysis dialogue box is described in more detail later in this section.

Principal Component Analysis...   Brings up the Principal Component Analysis dialogue. The PCA action allows the principal components of a set of vectors to be calculated and the projection of the vectors onto these principal components to be output or displayed graphically. The Principal Component Analysis dialogue box is described in more detail below.

Output Translation...   Brings up the Output Translation dialogue box. This dialogue allows the setting of the pattern file for an output translation and a setting of the Output Mapping Criteria. The Output Translation dialogue box is described below.

Lesioning...   Brings up the Lesioning dialogue box. The Lesioning action allows the lesioning of a saved weight file which can selectively remove a random proportion of a set of the network nodes or connections. The Lesioning dialogue box is described below.

The Cluster Analysis...   dialogue is shown in figure A3.17. The items in the cluster analysis dialogue are:

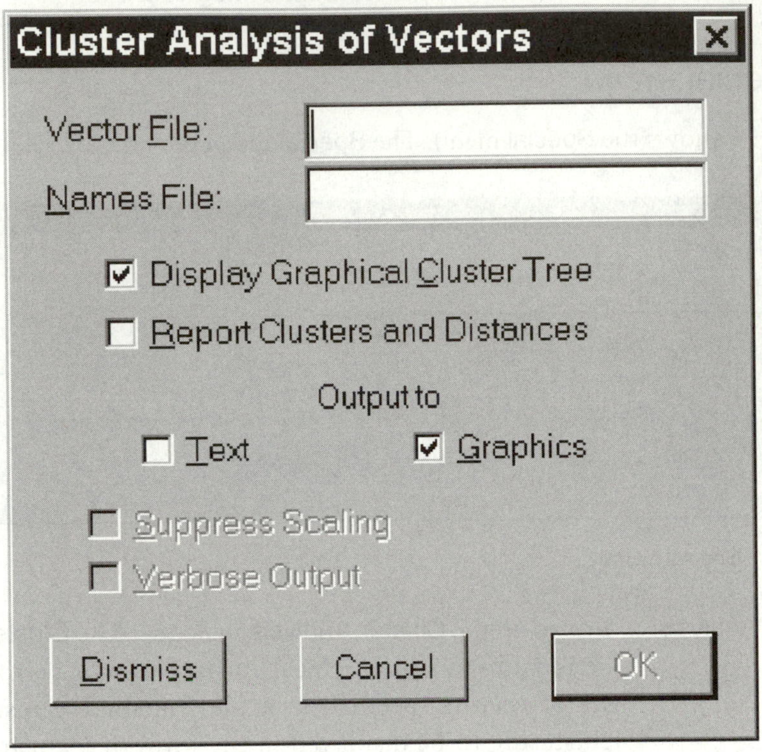

Figure A3.17   Cluster Analysis dialogue box

Vector file:	Specifies the file which contains the data vectors upon which the clustering is to be done.
Names	Specifies a file of names to be associated with the data vectors. These names are used in the cluster diagram that is displayed. The file name can be entered by typing the file name directly, or by double-clicking on the entry box and choosing the file name from a file selection box.
Display Graphical Cluster Tree	Toggles whether the cluster tree is displayed or not.
Report Clusters and Distances	Toggles whether the clusters and distances are reported in the text output and whether the distance values are reported in the graphics output.
Output to Text/Graphics	These check boxes specify whether the Cluster Analysis output is sent to the Output text window or the Cluster Display or both.

Suppress Scaling This check box suppresses scaling in the cluster analysis.
Verbose Output This check box toggles verbose output for the text output.

Once the settings for the Cluster Analysis have been set, then the cluster analysis can be performed. Either the text Output window or the Cluster Display window or both are brought to the front and the cluster diagram (and other text output, if specified) is given. An example of the use of Cluster Analysis is given in chapter 6 of Plunkett and Elman (1997).

The Principal Component Analysis... dialogue is shown in figure A3.18. The items in the PCA dialogue are:

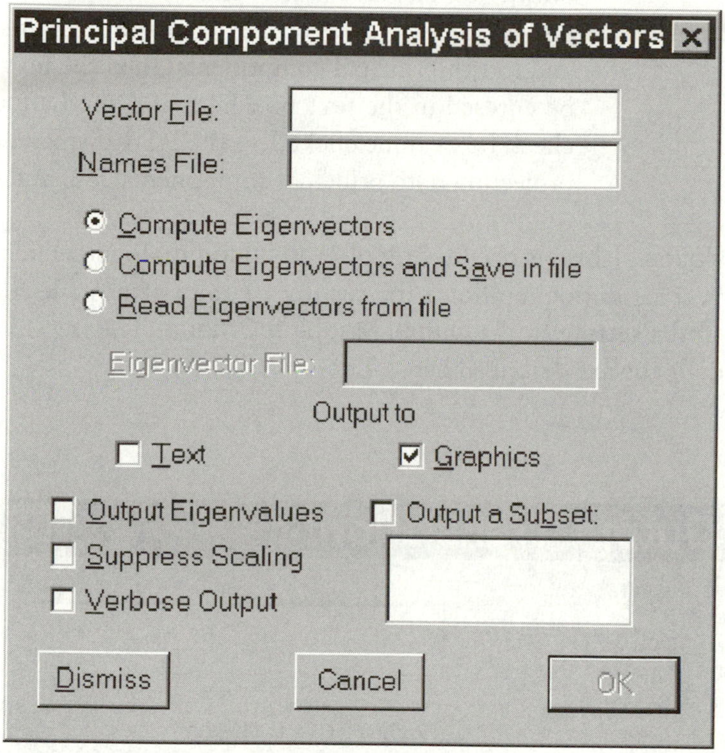

Figure A3.18 Principal Component Analysis dialogue box

Vector file: Specifies the file which contains the data vectors upon which the principal component analysis is to be done.

Names Specifies a file of names to be associated with the data vectors. These names are used in the projection of the vectors onto their principal components.

Compute Eigenvectors/ Compute Eigenvectors & Save in file/Read Eigenvectors from file These radio buttons specify whether the eigenvectors of the analysis are computed; computed and saved in a file; or not computed but read from a supplied file.

Eigenvector file	Specifies the file where the eigenvectors are saved or read.
Output to Text/Graphics	Specify whether the **Principal Component Analysis** output is sent to the **Output** text window, or the PCA Display, or both.
Output Eigenvalues	Toggles whether the eigenvalues are printed in the text output.
Suppress Scaling	Toggles whether scaling is suppressed in the principal component analysis.
Verbose Output	Toggles verbose output for the text output.
Output a subset	Toggles whether only a set of the principal components are output or displayed. For example, if the user wants to display the projection of the vectors onto their second, third and fourth principal components, then the text '2, 3, 4' can be entered in the text box here and the **Output a subset:** check box can be clicked so the PCA display will show the projection onto principal components 2, 3, and 4.

Output Translation... brings up the **Output Translation** dialogue which is shown in figure A3.19. This dialogue allows the setting of the pattern file for an **Output Translation** and a setting of the **Output Mapping Criteria**. The items in the **Output Translation** dialogue are described here.

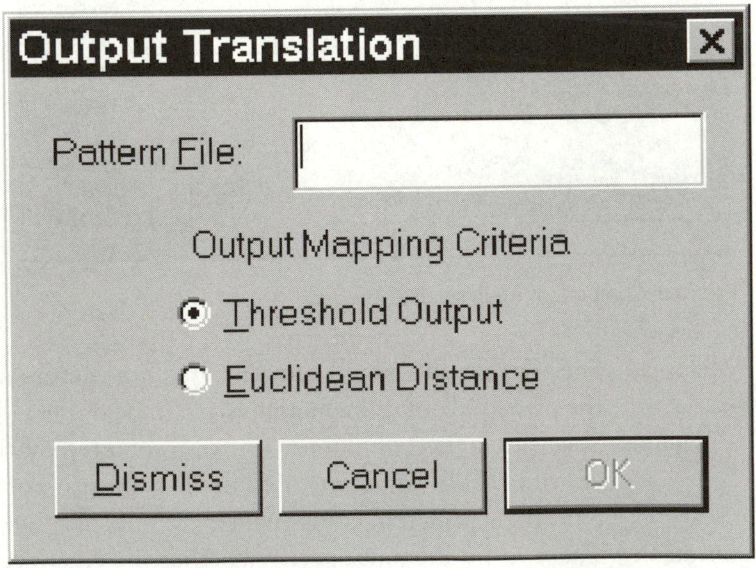

Figure A3.19   Output Translation dialogue box

Pattern file — Specifies the Output Translation definition file. The format of the Output Translation file is given below. An example Output Translation file is described in Chapter 11.

Threshold Output/ Euclidean Distance — These radio buttons specify the Output Mapping Criteria. In Threshold Output mode, when the Output Translation is applied, a threshold function is applied to the elements of the output vector converting the values to 0 and 1. If the converted output vector is not present in the Output Translation mapping then the Output Translation includes a question mark character. In Euclidean Distance mode, no function is applied to the output vector. Instead the Output Translation is determined by the closest vectors according to Euclidean distance in the Output Translation mapping.

The Output Translation utility allows the specification of arbitrary translations of 0/1 vectors to text. The Output Translation definition file allows the user to specify the splitting up of the output vector, permitting each part of the output vector to be assigned to different mappings, which are also specified in the file.

The format of the Output Translation definition file is as follows: The file begins with a **MAPPINGS:** section which specifies how the output vector is split up and by which mappings the parts of the output vector are translated. The format of lines in the **MAPPINGS:** section is as follows:

```
<node_list> from <MAPPING_NAME>
```

where **<node_list>** is a specification of a contiguous set of outputs, e.g., **1–4**; **<MAPPING NAME>** is any unique name for a mapping which will be specified in the file.

An example **MAPPINGS:** section of an Output Translation definition would be:

```
MAPPINGS:
1–6 from PHONEMES
7–12 from PHONEMES
13–18 from PHONEMES
19–20 from SUFFIXES
```

Here a mapping **PHONEMES** is to be used for nodes 1 to 6, 7 to 12 and 13 to 18 and a mapping **SUFFIXES** is to be used for nodes 19 to 20.

Following the **MAPPINGS:** section come each of the mappings for the Output Translation. Each mapping begins with a line which contains its name followed by a colon ('`:`') then any number of lines to specify the vectors to be mapped which take the following format:

`<Label> <Vector>`

An example mapping definition would be:

```
SUFFIXES:
W 0 0
X 1 0
Y 0 1
Z 1 1
```

The Lesioning… dialogue box is shown in figure A3.20. The items in the Lesioning dialogue are:

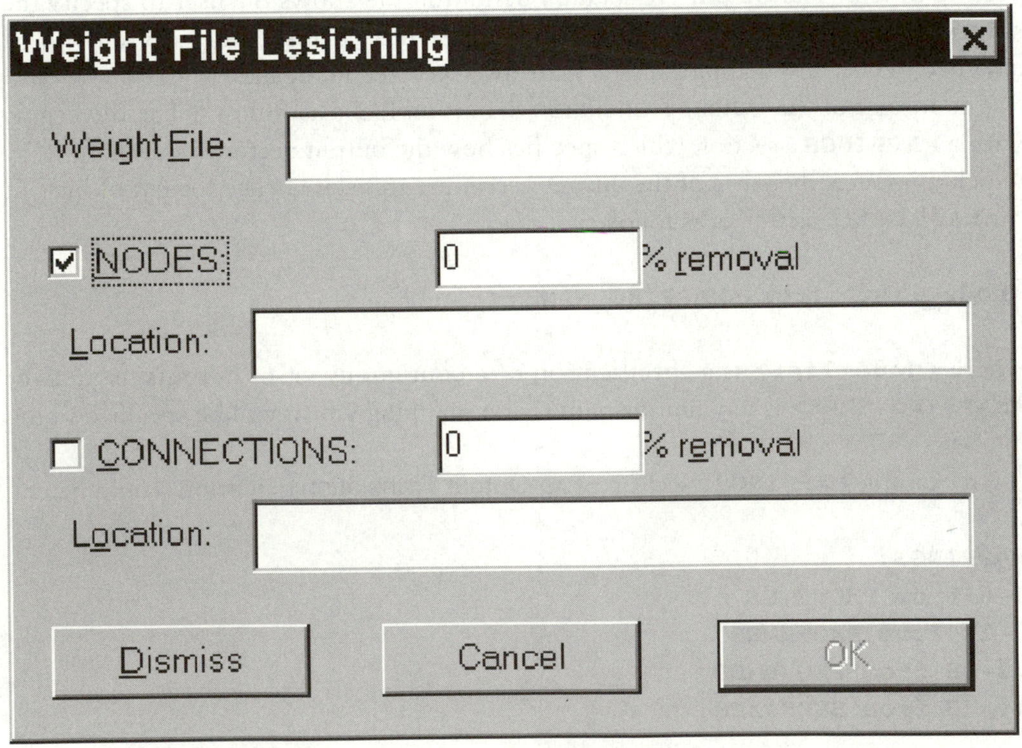

Figure A3.20   Lesioning dialogue box

Weight File   Specifies the weight file on which the lesioning is to be performed.

NODES: Specifies whether any nodes are to be lesioned. The Location: entry box is used to specify the nodes that are to be lesioned. Any list of node numbers can be entered in the format of node lists that is used in the `.cf` file. If no list of nodes is given then all the nodes are assumed to be chosen. The % removal entry box specifies the proportion of the nodes from the node list that are to be randomly chosen to be lesioned.

CONNECTIONS: Specifies whether any connections are to be lesioned. The Location: entry box is used to specify the connections that are to be lesioned. A comma-separated list of connections specifications in the format:

`<node-list> from <node-list>`

as used in the CONNECTIONS: section of a `.cf` file can be entered here. If no list of connections is given then all connections are assumed to be chosen. The % removal entry box specifies the proportion of the connections that are to be randomly chosen to be lesioned.

When the Lesioning settings have been completed and the OK button is pressed then the weights from the specified weights file are read in. If the NODES: check box was set, then the nodes to be lesioned are randomly chosen and the chosen nodes are removed from the network. This means that the nodes to be lesioned have all connections (both input and output connections) set to zero. If the CONNECTIONS: check box was set, then the connections to be lesioned are randomly chosen and the chosen connections are set to zero. The newly lesioned set of weights is displayed in a new window entitled '`<name>-lesion.wts`'. This window is an unsaved text window which can be saved and used in subsequent testing or training.

The Window *menu*

The Window menu lists the current windows that are being displayed by **tlearn** and if a window in the Window menu is chosen it is selected as the current window and brought in front of all the other windows.

Dialogue *reference*

Most of the dialogues used in **tlearn** have been discussed in the corresponding menu item that relates to their use. There remain only the Training Options and

Testing Options dialogues to be discussed in this section. Before these dialogues are discussed some general notes on the dialogues used in **tlearn** are required.

For any entry box on a dialogue that refers to a filename, the following special action is available. If the user double-clicks on the entry box associated with the filename, then a file selection box appears which allows the selection of the appropriate file, or the entry of the (possibly new) file name. This action also ensures that the file that is selected or to be saved is in the correct folder on the file system.

All dialogues have OK or action buttons and Cancel buttons. Generally the OK or action button is the default button and can be selected by pressing Return or Enter. A dialogue can be cancelled by pressing the escape key. When a dialogue is cancelled any of the changes made to the dialogue are also cancelled and the dialogue's items revert to the state they had when the dialogue was brought up. Some of the dialogues have Dismiss buttons which allow the dialogue to be dismissed, and the action associated with the dialogue not to be performed, but instead of the dialogue item values reverting to their previous state, the current state of the dialogue items is kept rather than cancelled.

The Training Options *dialogue*

There are two versions of the Training Options dialogue box: small and large. These are shown in Figure A3.21. The small Training Options dialogue is displayed by default for new projects. The small dialogue allows the modification of a subset of the training options, while the large dialogue gives the user access to all the options that are associated with training. The user can switch between the two dialogues by clicking on the more... and less... buttons at the bottom left of the dialogues.

The training options dialogue gives an interface to all of the parameters for all of the training runs performed in the current project. The parameters for different training runs are accessed via the Prev/Next buttons at the bottom of the dialogue. For a new project, these buttons are not highlighted. The number of the run and the total number of saved training parameters is given at the top of the dialogue. If the dialogue is showing a set of parameters other than that associated with the latest training run, then a Remove run button appears which allows the user to delete previous training run parameters. If the user wants to distinguish a specific training run by giving it a name, then this can be done by double-clicking the top part of the dialogue and the name of the training run can be entered (Mac only).

A description of each of the training options is given in the following.

Training Sweeps: The number of training sweeps for the training run.

Learning Rate: The value of the learning rate for backpropagation. This value is limited between 0.0 and 10.0.

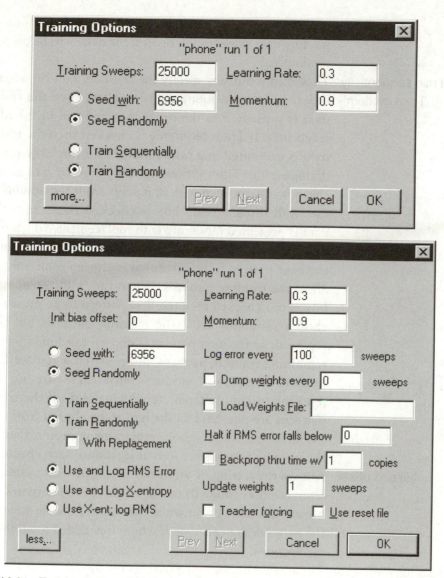

Figure A3.21   Training Options dialogue box

Momentum: The value of momentum for backpropagation. Momentum
              is limited between 0.0 and 1.0.

Seed with:/Seed   These radio buttons allow the user to specify the initial
    randomly   random seed value (Seed with:) or to allow the random
              seed itself to be chosen randomly. For training runs which
              are seeded randomly the random seed which was used
              is displayed in the text box next to Seed with:. The
              random number generator is used for generating the initial

random weights for the network and for determining the training data presentation order if the data is to be presented randomly.

Train sequentially/
Train randomly
These radio buttons specify the training data presentation order. If **Train sequentially** is checked, then the training data is presented in the order that appears in the .data/.teach files. If **Train randomly** is checked then the training data is presented in a random order. In the large training dialogue, the **Train randomly** radio button has an extra check box associated with it, namely 'with replacement.' If the 'with replacement' box is checked then the training data is presented randomly with replacement, which means that for each subsequent presentation of a training pattern, the next pattern to be presented is chosen randomly from all of the training patterns. When the 'with replacement' box is not checked then the first pattern to be presented is chosen randomly from the training patterns but is not replaced; so the next pattern is chosen randomly from the remaining training patterns and is also not replaced. This random choosing continues until there are no more patterns to choose from, at which point all the training patterns are put 'back in the hat' to be chosen from again. Training randomly without replacement ensures that all of the training patterns are seen at least once each epoch.

Init bias offset:
Allows the setting of an initial offset for the connections from the bias (node 0) to any nodes in the network. This offset only takes effect when the initial random weights of the network are calculated, where it is added to all the bias connections.

Use & log RMS error
Use & log X-entropy
Use X-ent; log RMS
These radio buttons give settings for the error function that is used by backpropagation and the error function that is displayed in the error display. Using and logging Root Mean Squared (RMS) error is the default setting. **RMS error** and **Cross entropy** (X-entropy) are often similar in their effects. Cross-entropy is explained in Chapter 9 of Plunkett and Elman (1997).

Log error every . . .
sweeps
Specifies the sweep interval at which error values are calculated and displayed on the error display.

Dump weights every
. . . sweeps
Specifies the sweep interval at which weight files can be saved.

Load weights File	Allows a saved weight file to be used instead of generating initial random weights.
Halt if RMS error falls below . . .	Specifies the error criterion for which training stops.
Back prop thru time w/ . . . copies	This option is used for training of recurrent networks using the Backpropagation through time scheme. Specifically it specifies the number of copies of the network to make for the purposes of unfolding the network's recurrent connections in time.
Update weights every . . . sweeps	Specifies the sweep interval between weight updates. Online learning occurs when weight updates occur at every sweep. Batch learning occurs when the training presentation is sequential and the update interval is equal to the number of training patterns.
Teacher forcing	Causes target feedback in recurrent networks.
Use reset file	Causes the use of a **.reset** file during training. A reset file is used for simple recurrent networks to reset the context unit activations.

The Testing Options *dialogue*

The Testing Options dialogue box is shown in figure A3.22. It is used to change options related to the testing actions (Verify the network has learned, Probe selected nodes). A description of the options on the dialogue is given in the following.

Weights file:	These radio buttons allow the selection of the Most recent: set of network weights or an Earlier one: to be used for testing. The name of the desired weight file can be typed into the text entry box next to the Earlier one: choice, or, if the user double-clicks on the text box, a file selection box can be used to select the appropriate file.
Testing set:	These radio buttons select the data (and teach) files to be used for testing. Either the Training set: or a Novel data: set can be chosen. As for the earlier weight file selection above, the name of the data set can be typed into the text entry box, or the user can double-click on the text box, and a file selection box can be used to select the **.data** file.
Test Sweeps:	The testing action can be set to run for one epoch (that is, a number of sweeps equal to the number of training patterns in the data file) or a specified number of test sweeps entered into the text entry box.

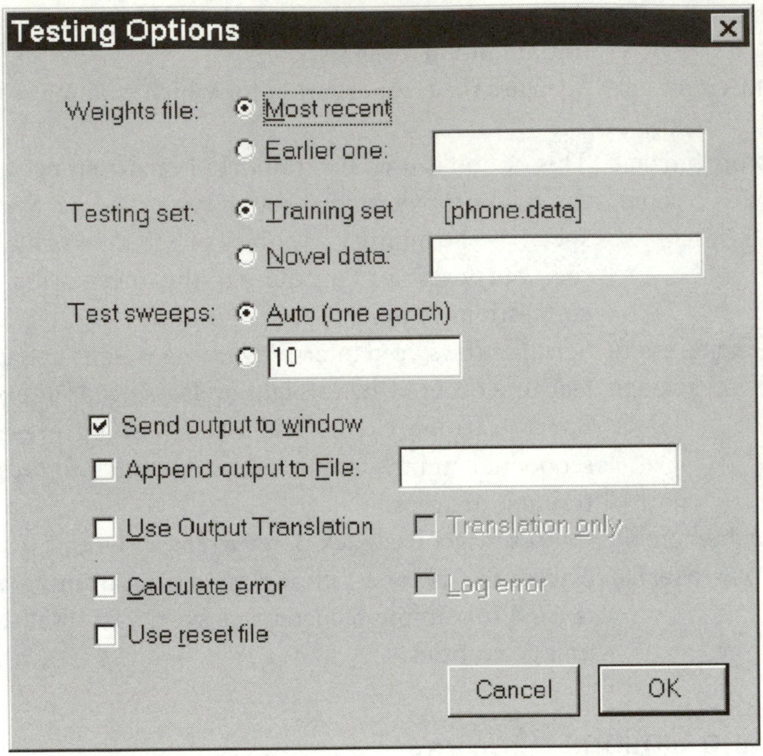

Figure A3.22   Testing Options dialogue box

Send output to window/ Append output to File:	Specify where the output of the testing actions (and also the text output of clustering and PCA actions) is sent. The output can be sent to either an output window or appended to a file, specified in the text entry box next to the **Append output to File:** check box, or both.
Use Output Translation	Causes the **Verify** action to use and print the output translation defined in the **Output Translation** dialogue. The **Translation Only** check box causes the **Verify** action to only output the translation rather than the translation and the output unit activations.
Calculate error	Causes the testing actions to produce network error calculations which appear in the error display. For the calculation of error a `.teach` file is required. For the project's normal training set defined by the `.data` file, there is already a corresponding `.teach` file, but for a novel data set, if an error calculation is required, then a novel `.teach` file must also be present for the testing actions to produce a valid error calculation.

Log error Causes the error calculation if specified by the **Calculate** error check box to be written to a file. The name of the file is **<project_name>.err**

Use reset file This check box causes the use of a **.reset** file during testing actions. A **.reset** file is mostly used for simple recurrent networks which require the activations of context units to be reset.

Command key and shortcut reference

Menu command keys

Menu keys can be seen in the appropriate menus where, if the menu item has an associated command key, it is shown at the right of the menu item.

Windows	Mac	Action
Ctrl+A	⌘ **-A**	Edit/Select All
Ctrl+C	⌘ **-C**	Edit/Copy
Ctrl+E	⌘ **-E**	Search/Enter Selection
Ctrl+F	⌘ **-F**	Search/Find...
F3	⌘ **-G**	Search/Find Again
F4	⌘ **-H**	Search/Replace & Find Again
Ctrl+J	⌘ **-J**	Network/Testing Options...
Ctrl+K	⌘ **-K**	Network/Verify the network has learned
Ctrl+L	⌘ **-L**	Network/Probe selected nodes
Ctrl+N	⌘ **-N**	File/New
Ctrl+O	⌘ **-O**	File/Open...
Ctrl+P	⌘ **-P**	File/Print...
Alt-F-x	⌘ **-Q**	File/Quit
Ctrl+R	⌘ **-R**	Network/Resume training
Ctrl+S	⌘ **-S**	File/Save
Ctrl+T	⌘ **-T**	Network/Train the network
Ctrl+U	⌘ **-U**	Network/Abort
Ctrl+V	⌘ **-V**	Edit/Paste
Alt-F-C	⌘ **-W**	File/Close
Ctrl+X	⌘ **-X**	Edit/Cut
Ctrl+Y	⌘ **-Y**	Network/Training Options...
Ctrl+Z	⌘ **-Z**	Edit/Undo
Ctrl+H	⌘ **-=**	Search/Replace
Ctrl+G	⌘ **-`**	Search/Go To Line...

Editor quick keys

Shift–arrow-keys allow the selection of text (or, if text is already selected, the extension or reduction of the text selection) to be done from the keyboard rather than with a click-drag action of the mouse.

Ctrl—left, Ctrl—right   moves the cursor to the next or previous word boundary

Crtl—up, Crtl—down   moves the cursor up/down a screenful of text

⌘—left, ⌘—right   moves the cursor to the beginning/end of a line

⌘—up, ⌘—down   moves the cursor to the beginning/end of a document

Troubleshooting

This section lists common problems and solutions.

Problem: Can't lesion weights file. **Lesion** command is disabled.

Solution: Before the lesioning action can be performed, a project must be specified. The reason for this is that the network configuration must be known for lesioning to be performed.

Problem: I have specified an **Output Translation** file in the **Special** menu, but when I probe or verify, the output translation doesn't appear.

Solution: In the **Testing Options** dialogue the **Use Output Translation** check box must be set for the **Output Translation** to be used. If you want only the **Output Translation** and not the output node activities, then the **Output Translation Only** box should be checked.

Problem: I want to display principal components other than the first two or three. How do I do this?

Solution: Specify a subset in the appropriate part of the **Principal Component Analysis** dialogue box.

Problem: Why doesn't the project change even though I close the old **.cf**, **.data**, **.teach** files and open the new files?

Solution: To use a different set of project files you need to create or open the project using the **New Project.../Open Project...** commands in the **Network** menu. The **Status display** shows the name of the current project.

Problem: The **Translate...** action translates too much and translates things I don't want translated.

Solution: The order of things in the translate file is important. Specifically, care must be taken that a later translation doesn't inadvertently retranslate a previous translation. This could occur if letters were translated to numerical vectors, and then a later translation action translated digits to letters. Unless this was a desired effect, this double translation will possibly cause havoc to the translation as intended. One piece of advice here is to ensure that no strings on the left of a translation rule appear on the right of a translation rule.

Problem: When I run **tlearn** on several projects, I'm told that there is not enough memory (for **.data** or **.teach** files, for example).

Solution: After running consecutive projects, **tlearn** may fail to release all the memory associated with the files it has used. Quitting **tlearn** and restarting should solve the problem.

Bibliography

Alexsander, I. and Morton, H. (1990). *An introduction to neural computing.* Chapman and Hall, London.

Amari, S. and Arbib, M.A. (1977). Competition and cooperation in neural nets. In *Systems neuroscience* (ed. J. Metzler). Academic Press, New York.

Anderson, J. and Rosenfeld, E. (1988). *Neurocomputing: foundations of research.* MIT Press, Cambridge, MA.

Baillargeon, R. (1993). The object concept revisited: New directions in the investigation of infant's physical knowledge. In *Visual perception and cognition in infancy* (ed. C. Granrud), pp. 265–315. LEA, London.

Barrett, M. (1995). Early lexical development. In *The Handbook of child language* (ed. P. Fletcher and B. MacWhinney), pp. 362–392. Blackwell, Oxford.

Bechtel, W. and Abrahamsen, A. (1991). *Connectionism and the mind.* Blackwell, Oxford.

Behrmann, M., Moscovitch, M. and Mozer, M. (1991). Direct attention to words and non-words in normal subjects and in a computational model: Implications for neglect dyslexia. *Cognitive Neuropsychology*, 7, 213–248.

Berko, J. (1958). The child's learning of English morphology. *Word*, **14**, 150–177.

Besner, D., Twilley, L., McCann, R. and Seergobin, K. (1990). On the association between connectionism and data: Are a few words necessary? *Psychological Review*, **97**, 432–446.

Broadbent, D. (1985). A question of levels: Comment on McClelland and Rumelhart. *Journal of Experimental Psychology: General*, **114**, 189–192.

Clahsen, H., Rothweiler, M., Woest, A. and Marcus, G. (1992). Regular and irregular inflection in the acquisition of German noun plurals. *Cognition*, **45**, 225–255.

Cohen, J. and Servan-Schreiber, D. (1992). Context, cortex, and dopamine: A connectionist approach to behavior and biology in Schizophrenia. *Psychological Review*, **99**, 45–77.

Cohen, J., Dunbar, K. and McClelland, J. (1990). On the control of automatic processes: A parallel distributed processing model of the Stroop effect. *Psychological Review*, **97**, 332–361.

Collins, A. and Quillian, M. (1972). Experiments on semantic memory and language comprehension. In *Cognition in learning and memory* (ed. L. Gregg). Wiley, New York.

Coltheart, M., Curtis, B., Atkins, P. and Haller M. (1993). Models of reading aloud: Dual-route and parallel distributed processing approaches. *Psychological Review*, **100**, 589–608.

Cowan, J. and Sharp, D. (1988). Neural nets. *Quarterly Review of Biophysics*, **21**, 365–427.

Crick, F. (1989). The recent excitement about neural networks. *Nature*, **337**, 129–132.

Crick, F. and Asanuma, C. (1986). Certain aspects of the anatomy and physiology of the cerebral cortex. In *Parallel distributed processing*, Vol.2 (ed. J. McClelland and D. Rumelhart), pp. 333–371. MIT Press, Cambridge, MA.

Dennett, D. A. (1988). When philosophers encounter artificial intelligence. *Daedalus: Journal of the American Academy of Art and Sciences*, **117**, 283–296.

Dienes, Z. (1992). Connectionist and memory array models of artificial grammar learning. *Cognitive Science*, **16**, 41–79.

Eimas, P. D., Siqueland, E. R., Jusczyk, P. and Vigorito, J. (1971). Speech perception in infants. *Science*, **171**, 303–306.

Elman, J. (1990). Finding structure in time. *Cognitive Science*, **14**, 179–212.

Elman, J. L. (1993). Learning and development in neural networks: The importance of starting small. *Cognition*, **48**, 71–99.

Elman, J. L., Bates, E., Johnson, M. S., Karmiloff-Smith, A., Parisi, D. and Plunkett, K. (1996). *Rethinking innateness: a connectionist perspective on development*. MIT Press, Cambridge, MA.

Fahlman, S. and Lebierre, C. (1990). The cascade correlation learning architecture. In *Advances in Neural Information Processing 2*, (ed. D. Touretzky), pp 524-532. Morgan Kauffman, Los Altos, CA.

Farah, M. and McClelland, J. (1991). A computational model of semantic memory impairment: modality specificity and emergent category specificity. *Journal of Experimental Psychology: General*, **120**, 339–357.

Farah, M., Reilly, R. and Vecera, S. (1993). Dissociated overt and covert recognition as an emergent property of a lesioned neural network. *Psychological Review*, **100**, 571–588.

Fenson, L., Dale, P. S., Reznick, J. S., Bates, E., and Thal, D. (1994). *Variability in early communicative development*. Monographs of the Society for Research in Child Development.

Ferguson, C. (1977). Baby talk as a simplified register. In *Talking to children* (ed. C. Ferguson and C. Snow). Cambridge University Press, Cambridge.

Fodor, J. and Pylyshyn, Z. (1988). Connectionism and cognitive architecture: A critical analysis. *Cognition*, **28**, 3–71.

Foldiak, P. (1991). Learning invariance from transformation sequences. *Neural Computation*, **3**, 193–199.

Forrester, N. and Plunkett, K. (1994). Learning the Arabic plural: The case for minority default mappings in connectionist networks. In *Proceedings of the Sixteenth Cognitive Science Society Annual Conference* (ed. A. Ram and K. Eiselt), pp. 319–323. Erlbaum, Hillsdale, NJ.

Garafolo, J. S., Lamel, L. F., Fisher, W. M., Fiscus, J. G., Pallett, D. S., and Dahlgren, N. L. (1990). *DARPA TIMIT Acoustic-Phonetic Continous Speech Corpus CD-ROM*, NIST IR 4930. National Institute of Standards and Technology, Gaithersburg, MD.

Goldfield, B. and Reznick, J. S. (1992). Rapid change in lexical development in comprehension and production. *Developmental Psychology*, **28**, 406–413.

Gopnik, A. and Meltzoff, A. (1987). The development of categorization in the second year and its relation to the other cognitive and linguistic developments. *Child Development*, **58**, 1523–1531.

Grossberg, S. (1976). Adaptive pattern classification and universal recoding: Parallel development and coding of neural feature detectors. *Biological Cybernetics*, **23**, 121–134. [Reprinted in Anderson and Rosenfeld 1988.]

Hare, M., Elman, J. L. and Daugherty, K. G. (1995). Default generalization in connectionist networks. *Language and Cognitive Processes*, **10**, 601–630.

Hebb, D. O. (1949). *The organisation of behavior*. Wiley, New York.

Hertz, J., Krogh, A. and Palmer, R. (1991). *Introduction to the theory of neural computation*. Addison-Wesley, Redwood, CA.

Hinton, G. (1986). Learning distributed representations of concepts. In *Proceedings of the 8th Annual Conference of the Cognitive Science Society*. Erlbaum, Hillsdale, NJ.

Hinton, G. (1990). Connectionist learning procedures. *Artifical Intelligence*, **40**, 185–234.

Hinton, G.E. and Anderson, J.A. (ed.) (1981). *Parallel Models of Associative Memory*. Erlbaum, Hillsdale, NJ. (2nd edition 1989.)

Hinton, G. and Sejnowski, T. (1986). Learning and relearning in Boltzmann machines. In *Parallel distributed processing*, Vol.1 (ed. D. Rumelhart and J. McClelland), pp. 282– 317. MIT Press, Cambridge, MA.

Hinton, G. and Shallice, T. (1991). Lesioning an attractor network: Investigations of acquired dyslexia. *Psychological Review*, 98, 74–95.

Hopfield, J. (1982). Neural networks and physical systems with emergent collective computational abilities. *Proceedings of the National Academy of Science*, 79, 2554–2558. [Reprinted in Anderson and Rosenfeld 1988.]

Inhelder, B. and Piaget, J. (1958). *The growth of logical thinking from childhood to adolescence*. Basic Books, New York.

Jacobs, R.A., Jordan, M.I. and Barto, A.G. (1991). Task decomposition though competition in a modular connectionist architecture: The what and where vision tasks. *Cognitive Science*, 15, 219–250.

Jordan, M. (1986). An introduction to linear algebra in parallel distributed processing. In *Parallel distributed processing*, Vol.1 (ed. D. Rumelhart and J. McClelland), pp. 365– 422. MIT Press, Cambridge, MA.

Kohonen, T. (1984). *Self-organization and associative memory*. Springer-Verlag, Berlin. (2nd edition 1988; 3rd edition 1989.)

Lashley, K. (1951). The problem of serial order in behavior. In *Cerebral mechanisms in behavior*, (ed. L. Jeffress). Wiley, New York.

Levine, D. (1983). Neuron population modelling and psychology: A review. *Mathematical Biosciences*, 66, 1–86.

Linsker, E. (1986). From basic network principles to neural architecture. *Proceedings of the National Academy of Science, USA*, 83, 7508–7512, 8390–8394, 8779–8783.

Marcus, G. (1995a). Children's overregularization of English plurals: A quantitative analysis. *Journal of Child Language*, 22, 447–459.

Marcus, G. (1995b). The acquisition of the English past tense in children and multilayered connectionist networks. *Cognition*, 56, 271–279.

Marcus, G., Ullman, M., Pinker, S., Hollander, M., Rosen, T. J. and Xu, F. (1992). *Overregularization in language acquisition*. Monographs of the Society for Research in Child Development, 57.

Marcus, G., Brinkmann, U., Clahsen, H., Wiese, R. and Pinker, S. (1995). German inflection: The exception that proves the rule. *Cognitive Psychology*, 29, 189–256.

Mareschal, D., Plunkett, K. and Harris, P. (1995). Developing object permanence: A connectionist model. In *Proceedings of the Seventeenth Annual Conference of the Cognitive Science Society* (ed. J. Moore and J. Lehman), pp. 170–175. Erlbaum, Mahwah, NJ.

Marr, D. (1971). Simple memory: A theory for archicortex. *Philosophical Transactions of the Royal Society B*, 262, 23–81.

McClelland, J. (1981). Retrieving general and specific information from stored knowledge of specifics. In *Proceedings of the Third Annual Meeting of the Cognitive Science Society*, pp. 170–172.

McClelland, J. L. (1989). Parallel distributed processing: implications for cognition and development. In *Parallel distributed processing: implications for psychology and neurobiology* (ed. R. Morris). Clarendon Press, Oxford.

McClelland, J. and Rumelhart, D. (1985). Distributed memory and the representation of general and specific information. *Journal of Experimental Psychology: General*, 114, 159–188.

McClelland, J. and Rumelhart, D. (1986). A distributed model of human learning and memory. In *Parallel distributed processing*, Vol.2 (ed. J. McClelland and D. Rumelhart), pp. 170–215. MIT Press, Cambridge, MA.

McClelland, J. and Rumelhart, D. (1988). *Explorations in parallel distributed processing*. MIT Press, Cambridge, MA.

McClelland, J., McNaughton, B. and O'Reilly, R. (1995). Why there are complementary learning systems in the hippocampus and neocortex: insights from the successes and failures of connectionist models of learning and memory. *Psychological Review*, **102**, 419–457.

McCulloch, W. and Pitts, W. (1943). A logical calculus of the ideas immanent in nervous activity. *Bulletin of Mathematical Biophysics*, **5**, 115–133. [Reprinted in Anderson and Rosenfeld 1988.]

Minsky, M. and Papert, S. (1969). *Perceptrons*. MIT Press, Cambridge, MA.

Morrell, F. (1972). Integrative properties of parastriate neurons. In *Brain and Human Behavior*, (ed. A. Karczmar and J. Eccles). Springer-Verlag, Berlin.

Morton, J. and Patterson, K. (1980). A new attempt at an interpretation, or, an attempt at a new interpretation. In *Deep Dyslexia,* (ed. M. Coltheart, K. Patterson and J. Marshall). Routledge and Kegan Paul, London.

Nakisa, R. C., and Plunkett, K. (1998). Evolution of a rapidly learned representation for speech. *Language and Cognitive Processes*. (In press.)

Nakisa, R. C., Plunkett, K. and Hahn, U. (1998). A cross-linguistic comparison of single and dual route models of inflectional morphology. In *Models of Language Acquisition: Inductive and Deductive Approaches*, (ed. P. Broeder and J. Murre). MIT Press, Cambridge, MA.

Nolfi, S., Elman, J. and Parisi, D. (1994). Learning and evolution in neural networks. *Adaptive Behavior*, **3**, 5–28.

Pinker, S. (1991). Rules of language. *Science*, **253**, 530–535.

Pinker, S. (1994). *The language instinct: how the mind creates language*. William Morrow, New York.

Pinker, S. and Prince, A. (1988). On language and connectionism: Analysis of a parallel distributed processing model of language acquisition. *Cognition*, **28**, 73–193.

Plaut, D. and Shallice, T. (1993). Deep dyslexia: A case study of connectionist neuropsychology. *Cognitive Neuropsychology*, **10**, 377–500.

Plaut, D., McClelland, J., Seidenberg, M. and Patterson, K. (1996). Understanding normal and impaired reading: Computational principles in quasi–regular domains. *Psychological Review*, **103**, 56–115.

Plunkett, K. (1993). Lexical segmentation and vocabulary growth in early language acquisition. *Journal of Child Language*, **20**, 43–60.

Plunkett, K. (1995). Connectionist approaches to language acquisition. In *Handbook of child language* (ed. P. Fletcher and B. McWhinney). Blackwell, Oxford.

Plunkett, K. and Elman J. L. (1997). *Exercises in rethinking innateness: A handbook for connectionist simulations*. MIT Press, Cambridge, MA.

Plunkett, K. and Marchman, V. A. (1993). From rote learning to system building: Acquiring verb morphology in children and connectionist nets. *Cognition*, **48**, 21–69.

Plunkett, K. and Marchman, V. (1996). Learning from a connectionist model of the acquisition of the English past tense. *Cognition*, **61**, 299–308.

Plunkett, K. and Nakisa, R. C. (1997). A connectionist model of the Arabic plural system. *Language and Cognitive Processes*. (In press.)

Plunkett, K., Sinha, C., Muller, M. F. and Strandsby, O. (1992). Symbol grounding or the emergence of symbols? Vocabulary growth in children and a connectionist net. *Connection Science*, **4**, 293–312.

Posner, M. and Keele, S. (1968). On the genesis of abstract ideas. *Journal of Experimental Psychology*, **77**, 353–363.

Quartz, S. R. and Sejnowski, T. J. (1997). The neural basis of cognitive development: A constructivist manifesto. *Behavioral and Brain Sciences*. (In press.)

Rochester, N., Holland, J., Haibt, L. and Duda, W. (1956) Tests on a cell assembly theory of the action of the brain, using a large digital computer. *IRE Transactions on Information Theory*, **IT–2**, 80–93. [Reprinted in Anderson and Rosenfeld 1988.]

Rolls, E. T. (1995). A model of the operation of the hippocampus and entorhinal cortex in memory. *International Journal of Neural Systems*, **6** (supplement), 51–70.

Rolls, E. T. and Treves, A. (1998). *Neural networks and brain function*. Oxford University Press, Oxford.

Rosch, E. (1975). Cognitive representations of semantic categories. *Journal of Experimental Psychology: General*, **104**, 192–223.

Rosenblatt, F. (1958). The perceptron: A probabilistic model for information storage and organisation in the brain. *Psychological Review*, **65**, 386–408. [Reprinted in Anderson and Rosenfeld 1988.]

Rosenblatt, F. (1962). *Principles of neurodynamics*. Spartan, New York.

Rumelhart, D. and McClelland, J. (1985). Levels indeed! A response to Broadbent. *Journal of Experimental Psychology: General*, **114**, 193–197.

Rumelhart. D. and McClelland, J. (ed.) (1986a). *Parallel distributed processing*, Vol.1. MIT Press, Cambridge, MA.

Rumelhart, D. and McClelland, J. (1986b). On learning the past tense of English verbs. In *Parallel distributed processing*, Vol.2 (ed. J. McClelland and D. Rumelhart), pp. 216–271. MIT Press, Cambridge, MA.

Rumelhart, D., Hinton, G. and Williams, R. (1986a). Learning internal representations by back– propagating errors. *Nature*, **323**, 533–536.

Rumelhart, D., Smolensky, P., McClelland, J. and Hinton, G. (1986b). Schemata and sequential thought processes in PDP models. In *Parallel distributed processing*, Vol.2 (ed. J. McClelland and D. Rumelhart), pp. 7–57. MIT Press, Cambridge, MA.

Rumelhart, D. and Zipser, D. (1985). Feature discovery by competitive learning. *Cognitive Science*, **9**, 75–112.

Schyns, P. (1991). A modular neural network model of concept acquisition. *Cognitive Science*, **15**, 461–508.

Seidenberg, M. and McClelland, J. (1989). A distributed model of word recognition and naming. *Psychological Review*, **96**, 523–568.

Sejnowski, T. and Rosenberg, C. (1986). *NETtalk: a parallel network that learns to read aloud*, The Johns Hopkins University Electrical Engineering and Computer Science Technical Report JHU/EECS–86/01. [Reprinted in Anderson and Rosenfeld 1988.]

Shallice, T. (1988). *From neuropsychology to mental structure*. Cambridge University Press, Cambridge.

Shultz, T.R., Schmidt, W.C., Buckingham, D. and Mareschal, D. (1995). Modeling cognitive development with a generative connectionist algorithm. In *Developing cognitive competence: new approaches to process modelling* (ed. G. Halford and T. Simon). Erlbaum, Hillsdale, NJ.

Siegler, R. S. (1981). *Developmental sequences within and between concepts*. Monographs of the Society for Research in Child Development, **46**.

Smolensky. P. (1988). On the proper treatment of connectionism. *Behavioral and Brain Sciences*, **11**, 1–74.

Sutton, R. and Barto, A. (1981). Towards a modern theory of adaptive networks: Expectation and prediction. *Psychological Review*, **88**, 135–170.

Treves, A. and Rolls, E. T. (1994). A computational analysis of the role of the hippocampus in memory. *Hippocampus*, **4**, 374–391.

Van Hoesen, G. (1982). The parahippocampal gyrus. New observations regarding its cortical connections in the monkey. *Trends in Neurosciences,* **5**, 345–350.

Von der Malsburg, C. (1973). Self–organisation of orientation-sensitive columns in the striate cortex. *Kybernetik*, **14**, 85–100.

Wallis, G. and Rolls, E. T. (1997). Invariant face and object recognition in the visual system. *Progress in Neurobiology*, **51**, 167–194.

Warren, R. (1970). Perceptual restoration of missing speech sounds. *Science*, **167**, 392–393.

Warrington, E. (1981). Concrete word dyslexia. *British Journal of Psychology*, **72**, 175–196.

Warrington. E. and McCarthy, R. (1983). Category specific access dysphasia. *Brain*, **106**, 859–878.

Warrington, E. and McCarthy, R. (1987). Categories of knowledge: Further fractionation and an attempted integration. *Brain*, **110**, 1273–1296.

Warrington, E. and Shallice, T. (1984). Category specific semantic impairments. *Brain*, **107**, 829–854.

Widrow, B. and Hoff, M.E. (1960). Adaptive switching circuits. In *1960 IRE WESCON Convention Record*, part 4, pp. 96–104. IRE, New York. [Reprinted in Anderson and Rosenfeld 1988.]

Wilcox, T and Baillargeon, R. (in press). Object individuation in infancy: the use of featural information in reasoning about occlusion events.

Willshaw, D. (1981). Holography, associative memory, and inductive generalization. In *Parallel models of associative memory* (ed. G.Hinton and J.Anderson), pp. 103–122 (2nd edition, 1989). Erlbaum, Hillsdale, NJ.

Xu, F. and Carey, S. (1996) Infants' metaphysics: The case of numerical identity. *Cognitive Psychology*, **30**, 111–153.

Index

tlearn commands, files, menus, dialogue boxes and displays are printed in **bold** type. References to notes are indicated by a page number followed by the letter n.

a, see activity (level)
aa project 88–95
Abort 360
accommodation 211, 234
activation 18n
  see also net input
activation function 17–18, 39
  binary threshold 17–18, 101–2, 291–2
  differentiable (continuous) 97
  linear 17, 18, 102, 129
  logistic 97, 103–5, 146, 228
  sigmoid 18, 66–8, 74, 102–5, 238–9, 264–5
  threshold linear 17, 18
activity (level) (*a*) 16, 39
  decay 41n
  diagram 228–30
address 34, 36
algebra, linear 333–9
all-or-none devices 318
AND 105–6, 315, 316
Anderson, J.A. 325–6
anticipation, *see* prediction
apraxia 256
Arabic language 182, 196
arbitrary mappings 147–8, 158
architecture, network 22
Artificial Intelligence 10, 325
assimilation 234
association units 321
associative chain 139–40
asymmetry, comprehension–production 188, 192, 193–4
attention, selective 260–5
  lesioning model 263–5
  modelling Stroop task 262–3
attractor(s) 145–8
  basins 146, 147, 169, 249–50, 276
  componential 171
  deep dyslexia simulation 247, 248–9
  historical background 326–30
  lesioning 250–1

reading aloud with 169–70
  space 146–7
  symbolic 275–6
autoassociation 72–95, 190
  in hippocampus 285–6
autoassociators
  architecture 72–4, 144
  category/prototype formation 83–8
  memory properties 75–82
  operation 74–5
  simulating hippocampal function 288
  tlearn exercises 88–95
axon 53–4

backpropagation 96–7, 112–17, 118, 301–2
  biological plausibility 116–17
  cross-entropy version 174
  deep dyslexia simulation 247–8, 251, 253–4
  informal account 114
  local minima 114–16
  reading aloud 158
Baillargeon, R. 212, 213–14, 216, 218
balance beam problem 219–34
  model evaluation 231–4
  modelling 222–4
  running the model 224–31
  tlearn simulation 240–2
basins of attraction 146, 147, 169, 249–50, 276
bb project 240–2
bias 20
  node 122, 123
  similarity 269
bipolar 349
blame, assigning 114
brain
  competitive learning 133–6, 285
  damage 243–4
  layered structure 12–13, 14

network models of function 278–302

CA1 region 282, 283
  neural network model 286–7, 288, 289
CA3 region 282, 283, 285–6
  neural network model 286–7, 289–92
Cancel button 368
cascade correlation networks 211n
catastrophic interference 236
categorical speech perception 312
category 83
  formation 83–8, 134
  specificity, semantic memory 255–8
.cf files 25, 26, 340, 346, 347–9, 352–3
chromosomes 310
clauses, embedded 198, 199
clean-up units 247, 252, 253
Close 354
Close Project 359
cl program 136n
cluster analysis 199–200
Cluster Analysis... 341–2, 361, 362–3
Cluster Display 344–6
<CODENAME>: 175, 207–8
codes file 149
competition 129
competitive clusters 134–5
competitive learning 127–38
  in brain 133–6, 285
  phases 128–32
  rule 129–30
competitive networks 82n, 127–38
  architecture and operation 128–36
  invariant object recognition 295
  pattern classification 136–8

comprehension–production asymmetry 188, 193–4
computational units, *see* units, computational
connectionism 4, 9–29
  basic operations 20–1
  basic principles 11–15
  basic **tlearn** exercises 21–9
  history before 1986 314–30
  symbols/elementary equations 15–20
connectionist models 4–8, 10–11
  arguments against 268–77
  basic assumptions 11–15
connections 11–12
  density 252
  excitatory (positive) 38, 40
  inhibitory 38–9, 40
  McCullough and Pitts model 318
  recurrent, *see* recurrent connections
  selective pruning 236
  strength 13–14
CONNECTIONS: 348, 352–3, 367
Connection weights 68–9, 71, 122–4, 344
constraint satisfaction 45–8
constructivism 313
content, memory access by 34–5, 37, 42–4, 326–7
context units 143, 197
Contrastive Hebbian learning 253–4
Copy 354–5
cornu ammonis (CA) 278, 279, 282
correlated teaching 137–8
critical periods 238–40
cross-entropy 174, 370

damage
  brain 243–4
  resistance 32–4, 62
  see also lesioning
.**data** files 25, 26, 340, 346, 349
dcb project 93–5
default
  mapping 269–70
  minority, *see* minority default
degradation, graceful, *see* graceful degradation
Delta rule 19–20, 68, 98, 257
  autoassociator learning 74–5, 77
  generalised, *see* backpropagation
dendrite 53–4
dentate granule cells 282, 284–5

dentate gyrus (DG) 278, 279, 282–3
  neural network model 286–7, 288
developmental psychology 179, 210–42
discrimination factor 300, 301
Dismiss button 368
Displays menu 360–1
distributed 349, 350
distributed representations 30–50, 273–6
  constraint satisfaction 45–8
  damage resistance/fault tolerance 32–4
  pattern associators 62–3
  problems 49–50
  processing *vs* memory 48–9
  retrieving information from 35–45
dot product 59–60, 63, 129–31, 334–5
double dissociation 180–1, 254–5
  asymmetric 258–60
  deep dyslexia 254–5
  semantic memory 256–8
dual-route model, English past tense 180–2
Dump weights 120, 370
dyslexia
  deep 244–55
    double dissociation 254–5
    Hinton and Shallice model 246–54
  phonological 157
  surface 157, 267

Edit menu 354–7
editor, text 340–1
embedded clauses 198, 199
energy (*E*) 327–30
entorhinal cortex 280, 281, 284
  neural network model 286–7, 288, 291
environment, training 273
equations, elementary 15–20
.**err** file 351
error
  backpropagation 113–14, 115
  curves 100–1, 115–16, 118–19, 144, 145
  gradient descent 97, 99–105
  landscape 102, 103, 234, 235
Error Display 118–19, 205–6, 342, 343
evolution 234n, 303–13
  goal directed behaviour 304–8
  speech perception 308–13
excitation 42, 128

experience
  past 82, 83–8
  sensitivity to 236

face recognition 6–7, 239, 292–300
family tree problem 108–12
fatigue factor 319
fault tolerance 32–4, 35
  pattern associators 61–2, 71
feedback
  internal 73–4
  loops, *see* recurrent connections
  positive 43
feedforward networks
  linear 22–6
  multi-layered 183–7
  single-layered 98, 102, 105
  two-layer 158–67
File menu 354
fileroot 347
Find... 358
Find Again 358
food seeking 304–8

gene pool 237
generalisation 268–9
  past tense learning model 208–9
  pattern associators 61, 63
  performance trade-off 236–7
  reading aloud models 167, 170, 177
generalised Delta rule, *see* backpropagation
genetic models 211n, 304–13
genome 308, 310
German language 270
goal directed behaviour 304–8
Goldilocks Principle 236–7
Go To Line... 358
graceful degradation 34, 243, 322
  pattern associators 62, 63, 71
gradient descent 97, 99–105
  with sigmoid activation function 102–5
grammar
  acquisition 194–202
  universal 195, 196
'grandmother cells' 63
groups 348

Hebb, D. 54n, 318–20
Hebbian learning 39n, 54–5, 60, 68
  Contrastive 253–4
  different associations on same matrix 56–9
  in hippocampus 285, 288

recall after 56
    trace rule and 296–7, 300, 301
Hebb rule 54, 65, 74–5, 117,
    319–20
Hebb synapse 318, 319–20
hidden units 13, 97, 108–12, 325
    backpropagation of error
        113–14
    balance beam problem 222–3,
        228–30
    biological plausibility 117
    deep dyslexia simulation 247,
        251–3
    family tree task 110–12
    language acquisition models
        190, 196–7, 198, 199–200
    optimum number 236–7
    recurrent networks 142–3
    XOR problem 107–8, 118,
        122–3, 124–6
Hinton, G. 246–8, 325–6
Hinton diagram 68–9, 122–4
hippocampus 278–92
    computational theory of
        operation 283–6
    internal structure 281–3
    neural connections 280–1
    neural network simulation
        286–92
    role in memory formation
        279–80
Hopfield, J. 326–30

iac program 35n, 48n
imprinting 238
individual differences 235–8
inferior temporal cortex (IT)
    292–300
inflectional morphology 179–87,
    202
    minority default mapping
        269–73
    see also past tense
information processing
    deficit in schizophrenia 260–5
    neurally inspired 9–11
    parallel distributed 30–50, 64
    vs memory 48–9
inhibition 42, 43, 319
    lateral 294, 295, 301
innately guided learning 308–13
inner product, see dot product
input 16, 17
    connection 11–12
    external and internal 73–4
intelligence 304
interactive activation and
    competition (IAC) network
        309–10
interference 64–5
    catastrophic 236

internal representations
    hidden units 108–12, 124–6
    object identity/position 212–18
invariant visual pattern
    recognition 292–300
    importance of trace rule
        299–300
    single layer networks 292–4
    VisNet model 294–300
irregularisations 182, 185

Jets and Sharks system 35–45, 46,
    47–8, 309n
Jordan net 144

language
    acquisition 5–6, 178–209, 238,
        239
    impairment, specific 237
    speech perception model and
        311–12
latency, word naming 160–1,
    162–3
lateral inhibition 294, 295, 301
layered structure 12–13, 14
learning
    critical periods 238–40
    individual differences 235–8
    mechanism 14–15, 319
    rate 235–6
    rules, see backpropagation;
        Delta rule; Hebb rule
    sensitivity 236, 239
    supervised 127
    unsupervised 127
    variability in 234–50
    by weight change 18–20
Learning Rate 118, 368
least-mean squares (LMS) learning
    99–100, 102
lesioning 243–67
    deep dyslexia model 244–55
    pattern associators 69–71
    semantic memory model
        257–60
    Stroop task model 263–5
    tlearn simulation 265–7
Lesioning... 69–71, 266–7, 341,
    361, 366–7
letters
    input units and 159
    pattern classification 136–8
    in a sequence, predicting next
        148–51
letters project 149–50
lexical decision 158, 166–7
lexical development, early
    187–94
    connectionist model 188–92
    model evaluation 192–4

lexicon 157
linear 349
linear algebra 333–9
linear independence 336–8
linear separability 97, 105–8
linear systems 338–9
living/non-living things 256–8
localist 349, 350
local learning rules 300–2
local minima 114–16
local representations 31, 63,
    273–4
long distance dependencies 195
long term potentiation (LTP) 285

McClelland and Rumelhart
    autoassociator 75–82,
        84–6, 87–8
McClelland's Jets and Sharks
    system 35–45, 46, 47–8,
        309n
McCulloch, W. 314–18
Macintosh installation 331
mapping(s) 157–8
    arbitrary 147–8, 158
    minority default 269–70
MAPPINGS: 175, 206–7, 365
memory
    autoassociator 75–82
    content-addressable 34–5, 37,
        42–4, 326–7
    dynamic 143
    episodic 279–80, 283–6
    hippocampal function 279–80
    procedural 280
    retrieval, see recall
    rote, irregular verbs 180
    semantic, see semantic
        memory
    vs information processing 48–9
    see also learning
mental representation 268–77
mental types, representing 274–5
minority default
    mapping 269–70
    rules 268–73
Minsky, M. 323–5
modality specificity, semantic
    memory 255–8
momentum 174
Momentum: 118, 369
mossy fibres 282, 283
multi-layer networks 96–126,
    133–5
mutation 305–6

Nakisa and Plunkett model of
    speech perception 309–12
nativism 313
natural selection 237, 303–4, 305

net input 17, 39, 73–4
netinput$_i$ 16, 17, 59–60, 61–2, 128
Netinput project 24–6
Network Architecture 26, 344, 345
Network menu 341, 359–60
neurally inspired information processing 9–11
neurons 9–10, 12, 314–15
    individual firing patterns 32–3
    integration of information 11–12
    output 12
    strength of connections 14
New 354
new information, adding 49–50, 274
New Project... 359
Node Activities 28–9, 65–6, 67, 92, 125–6, 342–4
nodes 22, 39, 40, 46
    creation 236
NODES: 347–8, 352, 353, 367
noise 43–4
    reduction 92–3
    removal 63
    resistance 81–2, 83, 147, 169–70
non-linear systems 338–9
non-words
    inappropriate lexicalisation 170
    pronunciation 164–5, 166–7, 169, 246
normalisation rule 319
Norwegian language 182, 186
NOT 315, 316
nouns 200
Novel data: 92
novel information, adding 49–50, 274
novel patterns, minority default rules 268–73

object
    identity 214–15, 216, 218, 219
    permanence 212–19
    predictive tracking of occluded 215–18, 219
    recognition, position invariant 6–7, 292–300
OK button 368
Open... 354
Open Project... 23–4, 25, 359
OR 99, 100, 105–6, 315, 316
    exclusive, see XOR
orthogonality 60, 133–4, 338
orthography 158–9, 172–3, 248–9
output connection 12

Output Translation... 175–6, 206–9, 341, 361, 364–6
overextension errors 187–8, 191, 192, 194
overregularisation errors 5–6, 178, 179–80
    connectionist model 185
    symbolic account 180

Page Setup... 354
Papert, S. 323–5
pa project 65–71
parahippocampal gyrus 280, 281, 284
parallel distributed processing 30–50, 64
pasts file 205
past tense
    learning 5–6, 178, 179–87, 236
        connectionist account 183–7
        symbolic account 180–3
        tlearn simulation 202–9
    minority default mapping 269–73
pattern
    association 51–71
    classification 136–8
    completion 80–1, 83, 87–8, 92–3
    recognition, position invariant 6–7, 292–300
pattern associators 51–60, 326
    architecture 52–4, 72–3
    competitive networks and 133–4
    operation 54–60
    position invariant object recognition 292–4
    properties 61–5
    training with tlearn 65–71
perceptron 98, 320–3
    convergence rule 97–9, 102, 322
    Minsky and Papert's critique 323–5
    multi-layered 107–8, 114–16, 117–18
perforant path 282, 285
perirhinal cortex 284
phonemes
    output units and 159
    prediction of next 144–5
    restoration 47
phonemes file 203–5, 206–8
phone project 205–6
phonological error 162
    score 160–1, 163
phonological feature 159n
phonology 159, 173
phrase structures 195

Piaget, J. 211, 212–13, 217, 218, 234
Pitts, W. 314–18
plan units 141–2
Plaut and Shallice model of deep dyslexia 251–5
Plaut et al. model of reading aloud, see reading aloud, Plaut et al. model
plaut project 174–6, 266–7
Plunkett and Marchman model of past tense learning 183–6
position invariance 297–9
positive feedback 43
prediction
    evolutionary advantage 306–8
    next element in a sequence 143, 144–51
    next word in sentence 197–202
    trajectory of occluded object 215–18, 219
predtest files 150–1
Principal Component Analysis... 341–2, 346, 361, 363–4
Print... 354
Probe selected nodes 341, 360
processing, see information processing
project files 347
prototypes 63
    early lexical development 187–8, 191–2
    extraction 83–8, 93–5
pruning, selective 236

Quit 354

random dot patterns 188–9
reaction time 147
    Stroop task 262
    word naming 160–1, 162–3
reading aloud 4–5, 155–77
    connectionist approach 12–13, 20–1, 157–8
    Delta learning rule 19
    lesioned model 245–8
    Plaut et al. model 167–71
        achievements 171–2
        componential attractors 171
        input coding 167–8
        pronunciation 168–9
        reading with attractor network 169–70
        tlearn simulations 172–7, 265–7
    Seidenberg and McClelland model 158–67, 171–2
        information learnt by 165–6
        limitations 166–7

structure and operation 159–61

vs word naming experiments 161–5

traditional 2-route model 31, 156–7, 163, 164

recall
episodic memory 280, 285, 289–90
fault tolerance 61–2
from distributed database 35–45
generalisation 61
in pattern associators 56, 59–60
speed 63–4
typicality effects 44–5

receptive field size 294

recurrent collaterals 282, 283, 288, 290

recurrent connections 73, 139–40
deep dyslexia simulation 247, 249, 252–3
hippocampus 282, 283, 290
reading aloud models 169, 170

recurrent networks 139–51
controlling sequences 140–2
simple (SRNs) 142–5, 196–202
stable point of attraction 276
tlearn exercises 148–51

redundancy removal 133–4

Replace 358

Replace All 358

Replace and Find Again 358

.reset file 347, 350–1

Resume training 341, 360

retina 292–3, 321

Revert 354

'rich get richer' effect 43

root mean square (RMS) error 124, 242, 341, 370

Rosenblatt, F. 320–3

rules 178–9
local learning 300–2
minority default 268–73
symbolic, irregular verbs 180–1
syntactical 195

Rumelhart and McClelland model of past tense learning 183

Save 354

Save As... 354

Schaeffer collaterals 282, 283

schizophrenia 260–5

Search menu 357–9

segmentation errors 144–5

Seidenberg and McClelland model of reading aloud 158–67, 171–2

selected 349

selective attention, *see* attention, selective

self-organising networks 325–6

semantic errors 244–5, 248

semantic memory 255–60
asymmetrical double dissociation 258–60
modality/category specificity 255–8
modelling deficit 256–8

semantic network 273–4

semantic space 248–9

sensitivity, learning 236, 239

sequences
controlling 139, 140–2
learning with **tlearn** 148–51
prediction 144–5

Shallice, T. 246–55

similarity
tyranny of 269, 270, 273
vector 129–32

simple recurrent networks (SRN) 142–5, 196–202

Skinner, B.F. 318

Sort... 340–1, 355–6

sparseness
competitive networks 133–4
hippocampus 284–5, 287, 288

SPECIAL: 349, 352, 353

Special menu 341, 361–7

speciation 234n, 304

speech perception 3–4, 46–8, 308–13
Nakisa and Plunkett model 309–12

speed
object recognition 294
pattern associators 63–4
speech perception 311

srn project 150–1

stages, developmental 210–12, 234

state units 141–2, 143

Status display 342

Stroop paradigm 260–2
lesioning the model 263–5
modelling 262–3

subiculum 284

symbolic attractors 275–6

symbols 15–20, 273–6

synapse 14
Hebb 318, 319–20
strength 14–15, 54

syntax acquisition 194–202

teacher signal 184

.teach files 25, 26, 340, 346–7, 350

temporal cortex, inferior (IT) 292–300

test.data file 177

Testing Options... 27, 90–1, 360, 371–3

three-route approach, Norwegian past tense 182

tlearn 11
autoassociator 88–95
balance beam problem 240–2
basic exercises 21–9
command key and shortcut reference 373–4
displays 342–6
installation 331–2
learning sequences 148–51
menu and dialogue reference 354–72
network configuration and training files 346–53
past tense learning 202–9
pattern associator 65–71
reading aloud simulation 172–7
reference manual 340–75
start up 21–2
troubleshooting 374–5
updates and bug reports 332
XOR problem 117–26

topographic maps 135–6

trace rule 296–7, 299–300, 301

training environment 273

Training Options... 65, 67, 89–90, 341, 360, 368–71

Train the network 341, 360

trajectory prediction 215–18

Translate... 149, 341, 355, 356–7

troubleshooting 374–5

typicality effects 44–5

tyranny of similarity 269, 270, 273

underextension errors 187–8, 191, 192, 194

units, computational 11–12, 314–15
bias 20
clean-up 247, 252, 253
context 143, 197
hidden, *see* hidden units
orthographical 158–9
phonological 159
plan 141–2
state 141–2, 143
symbols 15–20

U-shaped learning profile 180, 181, 183

V1 cortical area 294, 295

variability, in learning 234–50

vectors 59–60, 333–9
  addition 336–7
  angle between two 335–6
  dot product of two, *see* dot
    product
  geometrical interpretation
    334
  linear independence 336–8
  multiplication 336–7
  normalising the length 335
  similarity 129–32
verbs
  clusters 200
  irregular 5–6, 179–87, 203
  see also past tense
Verify network has learned 66,
  341, 360
view invariance 7, 299
VisNet 294–9
  input 295–6
  testing 297–9
  trace rule 295–6, 299–300
visual agnosia 256

visual errors 244–5, 248
vocabulary spurt 187, 191–2,
  193, 194, 202

w, *see* weight
weight 14, 16–17, 39
  autoassociator 77–8, 79
  change, learning by 18–20
  competitive networks 129–33
  decay 177
  pattern associator 55, 56–9
  redistribution 132–3
Weights file 27
Window menu 367–8
Windows 95 installation 331
'winner takes all' effect 43
word(s)
  abstract/concrete 254–5
  boundaries 144
  comprehension–production
    asymmetry 188, 192,
    193–4

comprehension spurt 192–3
exception 4, 162, 171, 270
frequency
  effect 4–5, 161–2
  neighbourhood size
    interaction 163–4
  regularity interaction 162–3
  monosyllabic 168, 173
  naming latency 160–1, 162–3
  production spurt 192–3
  pronunciation, *see* reading
    aloud
  recognition 3–4, 46–8
  regular 4, 162, 171
.wts extension 350–1

x-ent 174
XOR 105–8, 323–5
  tlearn exercises 117–26
xor project 118–26

Connectionist modelling of cognition is inspired by the style of information processing which occurs in the brain. This book provides the ideal introduction to this powerful approach which has become a central part of modern psychological research.

Part I introduces the basic concepts of connectionism and shows how they are related to neuronal information processing. It explains why connectionist systems show brain-like properties such as content-addressable memory and tolerance of minor damage or noisy input. The architecture and properties of common connectionist models are described, and the way that these models learn from their experiences is explained. Part II explores connectionist models of a variety of cognitive processes including the acquisition of vocabulary and syntactic rules, the production of speech, the formation of episodic memories, the construction of view-invariant visual representations, the development of cognitive processes in infancy, and the breakdown of cognitive processes in brain-damaged patients. The models described range from established classics of the connectionist literature to the frontiers of current research.

The book includes a disk with the software for running **tlearn**, a user-friendly simulator for connectionist modelling. It will run on either PCs or Macs. The software includes exercises to introduce the simulator and working copies of some of the models described in the text. A reference handbook for **tlearn** is included to enable readers to build their own models.

'McLeod, Plunkett, and Rolls provide a excellent, up-to-date introduction to pa distributed processing models, and their application to a wide range of issues in cognitive neuroscience inguistic developmental psychology The pres tion is clear and self-contained, making text an excellent choice for introducing connectionist/parallel distributed proce models to students in psychology, cogn science, and cognitive neuroscience.'
James L. McClelland, Carnegie Mellon Univers

'Connectionism has provided the study cognition with its most important new theoretical methods of the last twenty However, to most students its models just been a forbidding mass of abstract This book provides a simpl introducti the applications of connectionism to c tion. Written by leading experts in area neurobiology through cognitive psycho to developmental psychology and psych guistics, it provides a definitive view on scientific utility of the approach as wel lucid introduction to its technical aspe For the first time, connectionism shoul become generally accessible to all stude cognition.'
Tim Shallice, University College London

ISBN 0-19-852426-9

9 780198 524267

OXFORD
UNIVERSITY PRESS